Heli Paulasto, Rob Penhallurick and Benjamin A. Jones
Welsh English

Dialects of English

Editors
Joan C. Beal
Karen P. Corrigan
Bernd Kortmann

Volume 12

Heli Paulasto, Rob Penhallurick
and Benjamin A. Jones
Welsh English

DE GRUYTER
MOUTON

ISBN 978-1-5015-2106-5
e-ISBN (PDF) 978-1-61451-272-1
e-ISBN (EPUB) 978-1-5015-0035-0
ISSN 2164-7445

Library of Congress Control Number: 2020938322

Bibliographic information published by the Deutsche Nationalbibliothek
The Deutsche Nationalbibliothek lists this publication in the Deutsche Nationalbibliografie;
detailed bibliographic data are available on the Internet at http://dnb.dnb.de.

© 2022 Walter de Gruyter, Inc., Boston/Berlin
This volume is text- and page-identical with the hardback published in 2021.
Cover image: Rob Penhallurick
Typesetting: jürgen ullrich typosatz, Nördlingen
Printing and binding: CPI books GmbH, Leck

www.degruyter.com

The authors dedicate this book to David Parry, whose contribution to the study of varieties of Welsh English outshines all of us.

Contents

Preface —— XI
Acknowledgements —— XV
Maps of Wales —— XVII
List of abbreviations —— XXIII

1 **Geography, demography, cultural factors, and variation** —— 1
1.1 Introduction —— 1
1.2 Geography —— 1
1.3 Demography —— 7
1.3.1 Major cities and towns —— 7
1.3.2 Historical settlement and patterns of Anglicization —— 9
1.3.3 The Welsh and English languages today: 2011 census and new legislations —— 13
1.3.4 Migration today within the country and outside —— 16
1.3.5 Ethnic and cultural communities in Wales —— 17
1.3.6 Language and identity —— 18
1.4 Regional variation —— 20
1.5 Sociolinguistics —— 25
1.5.1 Dialect attitudes and perceptions —— 26
1.5.2 Variationist linguistics —— 30
1.5.3 The Welshness of Welsh English —— 31
1.6 Corpora and resources used in the present volume —— 35
1.6.1 Welsh English data —— 36
1.6.2 Comparison corpora —— 42

2 **Phonetics and phonology** —— 45
2.1 Introduction —— 45
2.2 The phonemic system of Welsh English —— 47
2.3 Distribution of the WelE vowel phonemes in the standard lexical sets —— 48
2.4 Vowels —— 49
2.4.1 Stressed vowels —— 50
2.4.2 Unstressed vowels —— 59
2.4.3 Pharyngalization —— 60
2.5 Consonants —— 60
2.5.1 Plosives and nasals —— 60
2.5.2 Fricatives, affricates, and semivowels —— 62
2.5.3 /l/ —— 65

2.5.4	/r/ —— 66	
2.5.5	Geminate or lengthened consonants —— 67	
2.6	Suprasegmental phonology —— 68	
2.7	Summing up —— 69	

3	**Morphosyntax —— 71**	
3.1	Introduction —— 71	
3.2	Noun phrase: Irregular use of articles —— 73	
3.3	Verb phrase —— 81	
3.3.1	Periphrastic *do* —— 82	
3.3.2	Extended uses of the progressive form —— 86	
3.3.3	The perfect aspect —— 93	
3.4	Clausal and sentential structures —— 95	
3.4.1	Embedded inversion —— 95	
3.4.2	Focusing constructions —— 98	
3.4.3	Nonstandard infinitives —— 107	
3.4.4	Exclamative *there* —— 108	
3.4.5	Prepositional constructions —— 109	
3.5	Vernacular features shared with English English —— 120	
3.5.1	Plural marking —— 120	
3.5.2	Pronouns —— 122	
3.5.3	Verb inflection —— 124	
3.5.4	Negation —— 129	
3.5.5	Adverbs —— 131	

4	**Lexis and discourse features —— 133**	
4.1	Introduction —— 133	
4.2	Welsh lexicon in Welsh English —— 135	
4.2.1	General currency items —— 136	
4.2.2	Welsh dialect words with limited use —— 141	
4.3	English dialect lexicon in Welsh English —— 144	
4.3.1	Origins and geographic patterns of English-derived dialect lexicon —— 144	
4.3.2	Lexical surveys in BBC *Voices* and in Tonypandy —— 150	
4.4	Discourse features —— 157	
4.4.1	Invariant question tags —— 158	
4.4.2	Other discourse-pragmatic markers —— 169	
4.5	Welsh English phraseology —— 174	

5	**History of Welsh English** —— **177**	
5.1	Introduction —— 177	
5.2	The Anglo-Saxon period —— 179	
5.3	The Norman Conquest and the Late Middle Ages —— 180	
5.4	Acts of Union, Elizabethan theatre, and the early industrialization —— 185	
5.5	The language shift —— 189	
5.5.1	Changes in society —— 189	
5.5.2	Writers' use of Welsh English —— 191	
5.6	From the twentieth to the twenty-first century —— 195	
5.7	Changes in progress —— 200	
6	**Survey of essential works and resources** —— **205**	
6.1	Large-scale works and resources, and national overviews —— 205	
6.2	Works on individual localities and regions, and other items of interest —— 214	
7	**Sample texts** —— **219**	
7.1	Fictional text samples —— 219	
7.2.	Spoken Welsh English in the interview corpora —— 228	

References —— **237**
Index —— **259**

Preface

The English language as it is spoken in Wales is a somewhat different entity depending on one's perspective and choice of terminology. The label (WelE), used by linguists, indicates a membership in the family of World Englishes and linguistic characteristics and geographically defined borders that differentiate the variety from the neighbouring British and Irish ones. It also implies that there is *a* Welsh English, displaying some degree of internal consistency, and furthermore that this variety has some national and cultural significance in Wales.

This book aims to show that instead of a single variety, Welsh English is a cover term for diverse accents and dialects used in Wales. The geographic borders of Welsh English are also somewhat hazier than those of Wales itself: the borders and coastal areas have been highly permeable to linguistic influence for centuries and language always travels along with its speakers. In other respects, the aspects mentioned above apply: Welsh English does belong in the family of World Englishes. It is a British variety, yet it has both first and second language speakers and contains considerable cross-linguistic influence from the Welsh language. It therefore sits rather ill at ease with broad categories such as the Inner Circle (Kachru 1992) or high-contact L1 varieties (Kortmann, Lunkenheimer & Ehret 2020). Welsh English can, however, be defined as a language-shift variety, in accordance with Mesthrie and Bhatt (2008: 6). Complementing the impact of historical language shift and present-day bilingualism is the dialect influx from England, connecting Welsh English to the British territory, culture and history. The combination of these streams of influence is what creates both the diversity and the distinctiveness.

As regards national and cultural significance, Welsh English cannot compete with the indigenous minority language of Welsh. However, as shown by numerous studies discussed in this book, the English accents and dialects of Wales are not devoid of such significance either. It is not our intent to make a case for Welsh English any more than to deflate or promote Welsh; indeed, if anything, the chapters and linguistic descriptions in the present volume testify of the interconnectedness of the two languages in the minds and communities of their speakers. The study of the dialects and sociolinguistics of Welsh has a longer history than that of Welsh English (e.g. Durham & Morris 2016), which reflects the seniority of Welsh as a local vernacular. Despite its medieval roots, Welsh English as we know it today is young, also in comparison to many other World Englishes.

The present book is intended to provide an update on the current knowledge of the variety. The previous major publications on the subject include three regional volumes of the *Survey of Anglo-Welsh Dialects* written by David Parry (1977, 1979) and Rob Penhallurick (1991), and the fourth compilation volume (Parry

1999). Apart from Penhallurick's North Welsh English volume, however, these books have enjoyed limited circulation. Another major, book-length publication on Welsh English is *English in Wales*, edited by Nikolas Coupland (1990b) in association with Alan Thomas. These publications have been instrumental in putting WelE on the map in English linguistics, offering an exhaustive account of the traditional rural dialects as well as of certain aspects of sociolinguistic variation. Recent decades have witnessed an increase of interest in the Welsh dialects of English in the form of several PhD theses (e.g. Paulasto 2006, Podhovnik 2008, Quaino 2011, Hejná 2015, Roller 2016, Jones 2018) utilizing more recent data and sociolinguistic methods of research. Our aim is to bring these data and studies together for a comprehensive description of the present-day status of Welsh English in various parts of the country.

As a result of the authors' fields of expertise, we are especially utilizing the interview corpora collected by Heli Paulasto in the Southwest, Southeast and North Wales in 1995–2000 and 2012, the Millennium Memory Bank data from 1998–1999 and BBC Voices survey from 2004–2005, which Rob Penhallurick is well acquainted with, and the survey of English in Gwent conducted by Benjamin A. Jones (2016b). Further information on the corpus data is presented in Section 1.6 and in association with the related results. The *Survey of Anglo-Welsh Dialects* recordings and publications are consulted as well, but the focus of the book is on the recent research materials.

In addition to new materials, we are taking a more variationist and quantitative approach to Welsh English than the traditional descriptions of the variety. Although we have an excellent overview of the structural and lexical characteristics of (traditional) Welsh English, few of the structural characteristics have been studied quantitatively, in order to see to what extent the features in fact emerge in regional varieties, who uses them, or how the usage patterns compare across different areas. Chapter 3 on morphosyntax, in particular, takes full advantage of Heli Paulasto's interview corpora, which involve speakers of different ages and linguistic backgrounds in different parts of the country. In this sense, the present volume wishes to exceed the expectations of a typical handbook and provide fresh research on language variation within Welsh English. The same applies to Chapter 4 on lexis and discourse features, which avails of recent lexical surveys in the southeast of Wales by Paulasto and Jones as well as corpus-based analyses of invariant tags and discourse-pragmatic markers.

To be able to contextualize Welsh English as a variety of World Englishes, we furthermore pay attention to the neighbouring British and Irish varieties as well as to the global spread of specific features. The study of English language morphosyntax on a global scale has benefited enormously from endeavours such as the *electronic World Atlas of Varieties of English* (eWAVE; Kortmann et al. 2020) and dedicated research across the English language complex. These diverse multilingual settings of present-day English form the broad framework also for the study of Welsh English.

As to the division of labour in the book, Heli Paulasto has been responsible for Chapters 3 and 4, Rob Penhallurick for Chapters 2 and 6, and Ben Jones for Chapters 5 and 4.5. Ben Jones and Heli Paulasto contributed to Chapter 7, and Chapter 1 is a joint effort.

Acknowledgements

We would like to thank all of the informants who contributed to the various surveys of Welsh English conducted by the authors. We are also in grateful debt to our several mentors, especially Markku Filppula and David Parry. For their immense patience, support and feedback, our thanks to the editorial board of the Dialects of English series, particularly Karen Corrigan, and to the production team at De Gruyter. Heli Paulasto would also like to thank the Academy of Finland for the post-doctoral research funding (project number 258999) that launched work on the present volume.

Heli Paulasto, Rob Penhallurick and Ben Jones, March 2020

Maps of Wales

Map 1: Cities, towns and other settlements

XVIII — Maps of Wales

Map 2: The historic or ancient counties of Wales

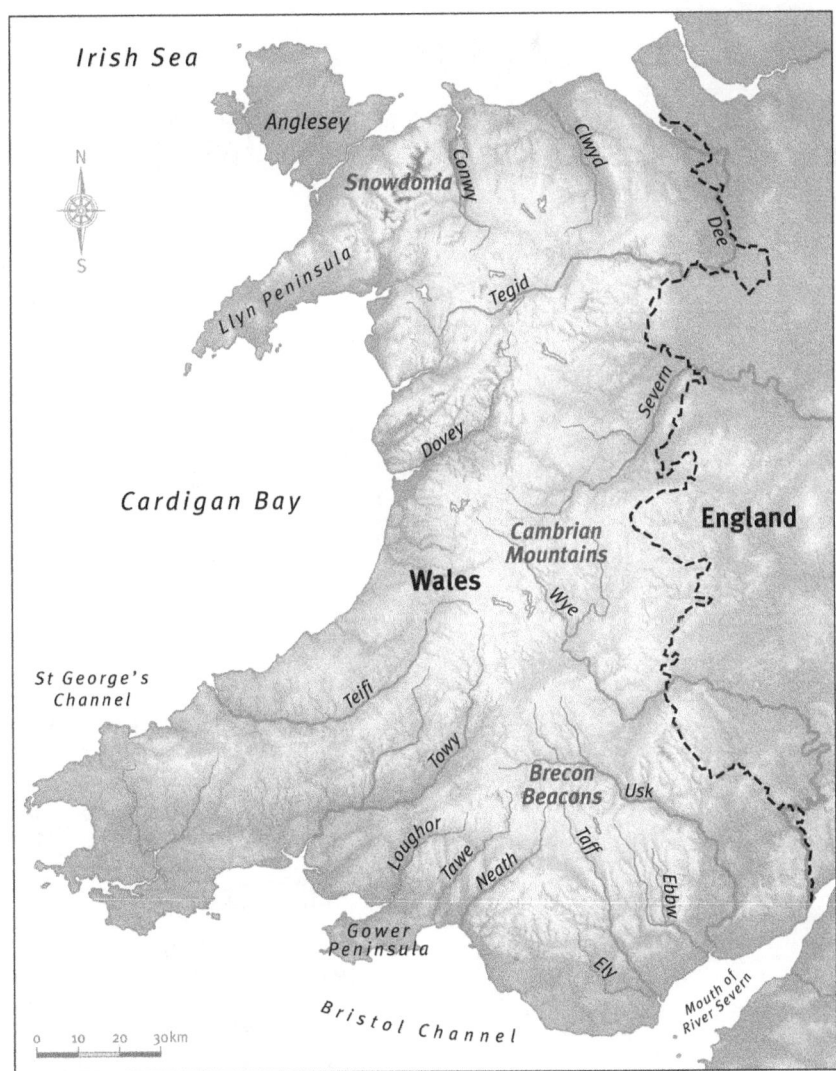

Map 3: Main topographical features of Wales

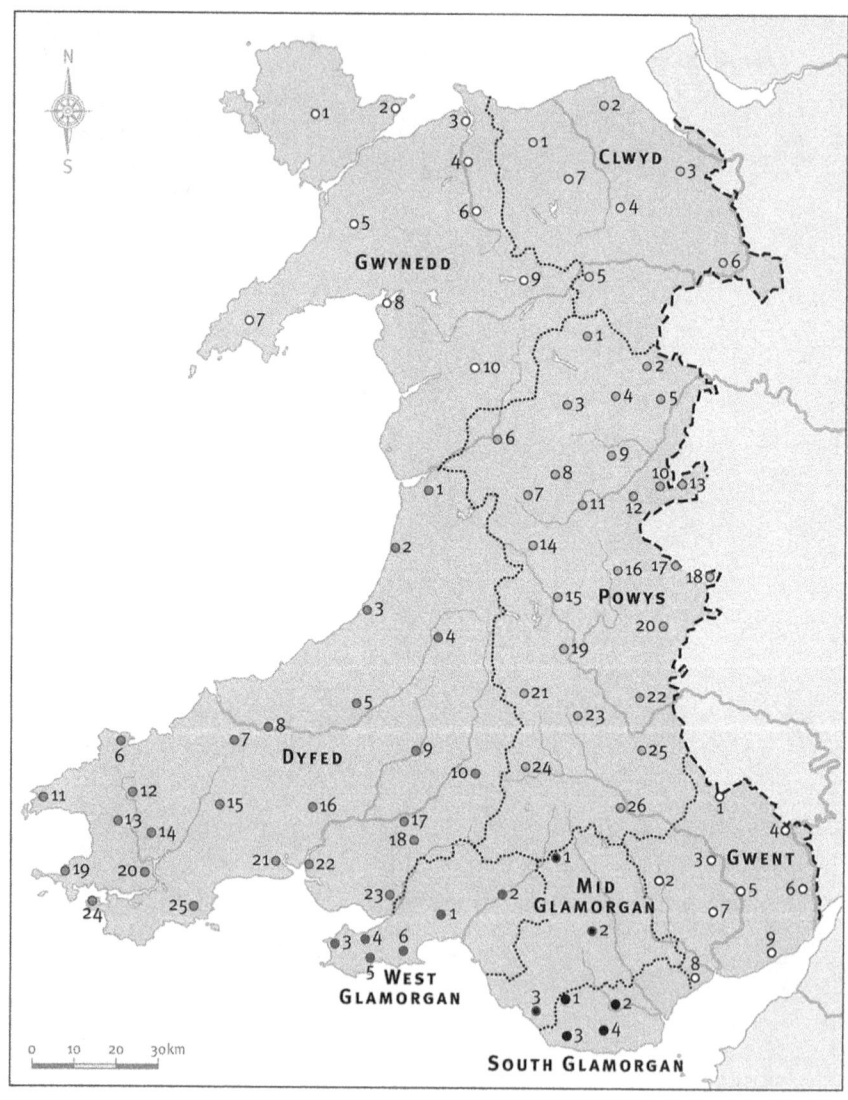

Map 4: Map of the rural locality network of the Survey of Anglo-Welsh Dialects

Gwynedd

1. Trefor
2. Llangoed
3. Gyffin
4. Dolgarrog
5. Talysarn
6. Betws-Y-Coed
7. Botwnnog
8. Ynys
9. Fron-goch
10. Rhydymain and Dolgellau

Clwyd

1. Llanfair Talhaiarn
2. Trelawnyd
3. Buckley
4. Llanfair Dyffryn Clwyd
5. Cynwyd
6. Overton and Bangor-Is-Y-Coed
7. Nantglyn

Powys

1. Llangynog
2. Llanfechain
3. Foel
4. Pont Robert
5. Guilsfield
6. Cemmaes Road
7. Staylittle
8. Carno
9. Tregynon
10. Forden
11. Llandinam
12. Kerry
13. Churchstoke
14. Llangurig
15. Rhayader
16. Llanbister
17. Knighton and Knucklas
18. Stanage Park
19. Llanafan Fawr
20. New Radnor
21. Llanwrtyd Wells
22. Painscastle
23. Upper Chapel
24. Trecastle
25. Talgarth
26. Talybont-on-Usk

Dyfed

1. Furnace
2. Rhydyfelin
3. Llanon
4. Tregaron
5. Lampeter and Drefach
6. Goodwick
7. Boncath
8. Cenarth
9. Llansawel
10. Myddfai
11. St David's
12. Wolf's Castle
13. Camrose
14. Wiston
15. Login
16. Newchurch
17. Gelli Aur
18. Llandybie
19. Marloes
20. Llangwm
21. Laugharne
22. Ferryside
23. Llangennech
24. Angle
25. St Florence

West Glamorgan

1. Glais
2. Resolven
3. Llangennith
4. Llanrhidian
5. Horton
6. Bishopston

Mid Glamorgan

1. Penderyn
2. Porth
3. St Brides Major

South Glamorgan

1. Llangan
2. Peterston-super-Ely
3. Llantwit Major
4. Llancarfan

Gwent

1. Pandy
2. Manmoel
3. Llanofer
4. Rockfield
5. Usk
6. Tintern
7. Llanddewi Fach
8. Marshfield
9. Undy

List of abbreviations

AmE	American English
ANT	Anterior marker
ASS	Assertion marker
BahE	Bahamian English
BlSAfE	Black South-African English
BrE	British English
Bre	Breconshire/Brecknockshire
Carm	Carmarthenshire
Cdg	Cardiganshire/Ceredigion
CGC	Ceri George Corpus
Cl	Clwyd
DAR	Definite article reduction
DEF	Definite article
Dy	Dyfed
EDD	*English Dialect Dictionary*
EI	Embedded inversion
EModE	Early Modern English
EngE	English English
eWAVE	electronic World Atlas of Variation of English
FF	Focus fronting
FRED	Freiburg English Dialect Corpus
FUT	Future tense
Gn	Gwynedd
GPC	*Geiriadur Prifysgol Cymru*
Gw	Gwent
HebE	Hebrides English
ICE	International Corpus of English
IM	Imperfective marker
IndE	Indian English
IrE	Irish English
KenE	Kenyan English
L1	First language
L2	Second language
LC	Llandybie Corpus
LOCNESS	Louvain Corpus of Native English Essays
MG	Mid-Glamorgan
MLE	Multicultural London English
MxE	Manx English
NP	Noun phrase
NWC	North Wales Corpus
OED	*Oxford English Dictionary*
OrShE	Orkney and Shetland English
P	Powys
P/C	Pidgin/creole

Pem	Pembrokeshire
PF	Progressive form
PL	Plural
PP	Prepositional phrase
PRES	Present tense
PRT	Preterite
pttw	Per ten thousand words
RPA	Relative particle
RVE	Rhondda Valleys English
RWC	Radio Wales Corpus
SAWD	Survey of Anglo-Welsh Dialects (survey and corpus data)
SAWD	*Survey of Anglo-Welsh Dialects* (published volumes)
SBCSAE	Santa Barbara Corpus of Spoken American English
ScE	Scottish English
SG	South Glamorgan / Singular
SED	Survey of English Dialects (survey and corpus data)
SED	*Survey of English Dialects* (published volumes)
SingE	Singapore English
StE	Standard English
TC	Tonypandy Corpus
TrC	Trinidad Creole
VN	Verbal noun
Voices	BBC *Voices* in Wales
VP	Verb phrase
WelE	Welsh English
WG	West Glamorgan
ZPM	Zero plural marking

1 Geography, demography, cultural factors, and variation

1.1 Introduction

This chapter introduces the backdrop for Welsh English (WelE). It is a variety with considerable internal variation, largely as a result of the geography of the country, which has guided the Anglicization process along specific pathways during the centuries. Between the two main forces of the indigenous Welsh language culture and the neighbouring English language one, WelE has been forged differently according to the historical phase in question, the geographic region, the demographic factors at play, and the linguistic elements that these factors have brought into the mix.

We will begin by describing the geography of Wales and its impact on patterns of demography and language shift. Section 1.3 presents demographic changes in Wales over time, particularly in terms of numbers of Welsh and English speakers, in and out-migration, and the shifting sociolinguistic roles of the two languages to their speakers. Section 1.4 focuses the discussion on the Welsh varieties of English and the linguistic result of the geographic and demographic factors, in other words, on models of regional variation within WelE based on linguistic and perceptual evidence. The section also describes the main forces in operation in the regional varieties and presents an overview of research conducted on different regional varieties. Section 1.5 contains a similar overview of the sociolinguistics of WelE and sociolinguistic research on the subject, including dialect attitudes and perceptual dialectology as well as variationist research. We will also briefly consider the role of WelE as a symbol of Welsh national and cultural identity in light of the thoughts and opinions that our informants have presented on the subject during the sociolinguistic interviews. The final section of this chapter describes the WelE corpora and surveys that have been utilized in the linguistic analysis of this book. Other corpora and resources on WelE are described in Chapter 6.

1.2 Geography

There is a conservation charity called Size of Wales whose aim is "to raise funds for forests and raise awareness of the importance of forests in tackling climate change" (Size of Wales website). The charity chose its name because the phrase "an area the size of Wales" has been frequently used to depict rates of forest destruction. In fact, the phrase has been used in various contexts since the 1840s: to help us picture the size of other (apparently less well-known) territories; to describe a huge Antarctic iceberg called A-68 (actually only a quarter the size of Wales); and to estimate the zone that an asteroid or a nuclear bomb could devastate (Frampton 2019). The subject of the present book, Welsh English, is, we can safely claim, spoken in an area larger than the size of Wales, for the reason that not all speakers of Welsh English spend all of their lives domiciled in Wales. We can also state with certainty that the *Urheimat* of Welsh English is Wales, and that Wales is an area the size of over two million hectares (or 21,000 square kilometers) located at the west of the main island of the British Isles. From north to south it measures some 320 kilometers, and from east to west about 190 kilometers at its broadest, 80 kilometers at its narrowest.

In this section, we give an overview of the geography and geology of Wales, offering also some introductory analysis of the effects on demography and language use, which leads us to propose our basic model of the regional divisions of Wales.

Wales is known as a land of mountains and hills, but there are low-lying areas too, and the lowlands are the most populated areas. The majority of Wales is over 180 meters above sea level, and this central highland mass rises to a peak of just beyond one thousand meters at Mount Snowdon in the northwest. The west and northwest are dominated by the Cambrian Mountains and the south by the Brecon Beacons. In addition, there are the Clwydian Hills in the northeast, on the east flank of the River Clwyd, and the Black Mountains at the eastern edge of the Brecon Beacons. The highlands can be divided into the mountains, above 600 meters, mostly restricted to the northwest, and the moorlands, between 180–600 meters, characterized by rounded hills, damp soils, and coarse pasture. Fringing the central highland mass on all sides are the lowlands, that is, those areas below 180 meters. These are the coastal areas to the north, south, and west, and the borderlands with England to the east.

The west coastal strip is comparatively narrow and less populated, containing a scattering of small towns, the largest being Aberystwyth, which recorded a population of just under 16,500 in the 2011 UK census. The most densely populated and urbanized areas are the southeast and northwest. The southeast contains Wales's three biggest cities: the capital, Cardiff (the city authority area has a population of nearly 350,000), Swansea (240,000), and Newport (145,000). (Precise figures are provided in Section 1.3 below.) We should mention that many would dispute our putting Swansea into the southeast, for in terms of traditional rivalries in the national sport, rugby union, Swansea belongs to the southwest, in contrast to the eastern clubs of Cardiff and Newport. To be more geographically accurate, then, Swansea and its neighbour, Llanelli, are located pretty much midway along the south coast of Wales. Wales is also home to the two smallest cities in Britain: the cathedral communities of St David's in the far southwest and St Asaph in the north. There is one more city in Wales, Bangor in the northwest corner (population 19,000, over 50 per cent of this number made up by students at the University). The fourth largest urban area in Wales is Wrexham (60,000) in the northeast, only 20 kilometers from the historical English city of Chester, and within the sphere of influence of the great northwestern English conurbations of Merseyside and Greater Manchester.

The coastline of Wales runs for 1,200 kilometers in total. The north coastal plain is narrower than that of the south, and it is only since the completion of the Chester to Holyhead railway in 1848 that it has been used for a major routeway. The lowlands of the south are broader, and are not unvaryingly flat but undulating with their own hills and valleys. The Gower Peninsula in particular is renowned for its stunning sandy beaches and limestone cliffs with their sea caves, including Paviland Cave, site of one of the first discoveries of modern archaeology, the oldest anatomically modern skeleton found in Britain, that of a young man ceremonially buried 34,000 years ago. The southern lowlands allowed the Romans and later the Normans to penetrate westwards across Wales, and provided the location in the 1850s for the railway that linked Newport in the east with Milford Haven in the west. The most extensive stretch of motorway in Wales, the M4, completed in 1993, also runs east–west through the southern lowlands. Communication routes in Wales have historically been located much more along the east–west axis afforded by the southern and northern coastal plains than on the north–south axis across the lightly populated central highland mass. This is an important factor in the development of the chief north–south dialectal divisions in both Welsh and Welsh English.

The central mass is itself not uniformly elevated. There are also many low-lying valleys following river courses radiating outwards from the highland. Along the eastern border with England, for example, three expanses of lowland issue respectively from the River Dee in the north, the River Severn in the centre, and the Rivers Wye and Usk in the south. These too have been historical routeways into Wales from the east. The boundary between Wales and England corresponds generally to the linear earthwork Offa's Dyke, constructed in the late eighth century probably by the Angles who had settled east of it, and which therefore denotes approximately the western limit of an English-speaking population at that time. The border runs north–south for over 200 kilometers. The Local Government Act of 1972 confirmed that Monmouthshire in the southeast was considered to be part of Wales, having enjoyed a rather ambiguous nationality previously.

As can be gathered from the above, Wales is surrounded on three sides by the sea: the Bristol Channel to the south, and St George's Channel and the Irish Sea to the west and north. Like the other western coastal territories of Europe, Wales enjoys (if that is the right word) a North Atlantic climate carried by prevailing westerly winds, and temperatures tend to be mild and precipitation plentiful. Maritime contact across the Bristol Channel with the southwest of England was involved in the early Anglicization of the Gower Peninsula and south Pembrokeshire. The southwest coast of England is just 50 kilometers away from Gower. In the twelfth century, following Norman intrusions, communities of English speakers were planted in the Gower Peninsula and Pembrokeshire, which to this day are known as "Little Englands beyond Wales". Further east, the Vale of Glamorgan, a low plateau generally about 60 meters high with a geology favourable to agriculture, was also subject to early Anglicization, as were the eastern border areas of Wales. While the Celts of Wales had already experienced invasion from the first to the fifth century AD by the Romans, from the seventh century onwards by the Saxons and Angles (the English), and from the ninth century by the Vikings, it was the Normans in the eleventh century who made the most telling inroads up to that point. In the late eleventh century, there were Norman assaults all along the borderlands and also deep into the northwest and southwest of Wales. Marcher Lordships (the name derives from the noun *march* 'border, boundary, frontier') were established by the Normans in the border areas and through most of the south during the twelfth century, and with the Anglo-Normans came English speakers. (See Chapter 5 of the present book for more detail on history.)

Between the southern lowlands and the borderlands are the famous South Wales valleys (such as the Tawe, the Neath, Rhondda Fach and Fawr, the Taff, and the Ebbw), known colloquially simply as "The Valleys", whose rivers cut into a coalfield which extended nearly 145 kilometers from Pembrokeshire in the west to Monmouthshire in the east at an average width of 24 kilometers. This coalfield contained several types of coal as well as iron ore, and was underlain and ringed by carboniferous limestone, and by the early nineteenth century this combination of resources had become important to the growing iron smelting industry. By the end of the nineteenth century, the Industrial Revolution had transformed South Wales, which now added steel and tin production to its coal, iron, and copper industries. Major urban ports were constructed in Llanelli, Swansea, Barry, Cardiff, and Newport.

Similar developments on a lesser scale occurred in North Wales, where a narrow outcrop of coal measures ran south–north from near Oswestry at the English border to Point of Ayr at the mouth of the Dee Estuary on the north coast. Further west in North Wales, slate mining and quarrying had become a significant industry by the 1870s, though the numbers employed were small compared with the hundreds of thousands of coal miners in Wales, reaching a peak of over 270,00 in 1920 (BBC Wales History 2008). Gold mining also featured on a small scale in the northwest and southwest, especially in the late nineteenth to early twentieth century.

As a result of the Industrial Revolution, the population of Wales grew enormously, particularly in the urbanized south. In 1851, the population of Wales was approaching 1.2 million; by 1914, it was over 2.5 million (John Davies 2007: 387). The percentage of people employed in agriculture declined markedly in proportion to the huge increase in those working in industry (although even in the early twenty-first century over 80 per cent of the land area of Wales remains in agricultural use). The rural districts experienced depopulation, while people moved in copious numbers to Glamorganshire and Monmouthshire, not only from other parts of Wales but also from England, Ireland, and Scotland, and there were immigrants from mainland Europe and other parts of the world too. Between 1901 and 1914, the population of the southeast increased by over 650,000 and at this time "only the United States excelled Wales in the ability to attract immigrants" (John Davies 2007: 475). By 1911, nearly two-thirds of the population of Wales lived in Glamorganshire and Monmouthshire, which also boasted higher numbers of non-Welsh-born residents than other parts of Wales. There was a consequent upheaval in the linguistic character of the country. Janet Davies (2000: 89) states that between 1801 and 1891 the number of English monoglots in Wales increased seven-fold, and the number of inhabitants with some knowledge of English increased seventy-fold. By the census of 1901, nearly 50 per cent of the population of Wales spoke English only, 15 per cent Welsh only, and nearly 35 per cent were bilingual in English and Welsh; in the census of 1911, these figures become 54 per cent English only, 8.5 per cent Welsh only, and no change in bilinguals (the number of "no statements" was higher in 1911; census data here obtained via *A Vision of Britain Through Time* website, 2009–2017, especially Table 127).

A regional breakdown of the 1911 census data (Local Distribution 1913) shows Wales divided down the middle into a west half of predominantly Welsh-speaking counties, with the exception of Pembrokeshire, which is an extension of the predominantly English-speaking east half of the country. (See Ellis [1882] and Southall [1892: 33] for further insight into this.) In summary, this linguistic division is causally related to two phases of population migration: the first due to the Anglo-Norman invasion from the eleventh century onwards; and the second due to the industrialization of the south and northeast in the eighteenth and nineteenth centuries. Each of these phases is associated with the geography and geology of Wales – in the routeways provided by the lowlands and the Bristol Channel, in the interest of the Normans in the more fertile agricultural land, and in the exploitation of the mineral resources of the south and northeast.

Consideration of the geography and geology in this context offers us a bedrock model of the internal demarcations of modern Wales, a basis upon which we can interpret the shifting social patterns of cultural, political, and linguistic identity. As Lewis Dartnell puts it in his *Origins: How the Earth shaped human history* (2019: 4): "Cultural, social, economic and political influences are of course important – but planetary processes often form a deeper layer of explanation." The influential "Three-Wales Model" proposed by Denis Balsom in 1985 with reference to "the interrelationship of language and chosen national identity" (Balsom 1985: 6) bears a clear correlation to this bedrock division. Balsom talks of three regional social groupings as follows: *Y Fro Gymraeg* or "The Welsh-speaking Area", running down west Wales with the exception of Pembrokeshire; Welsh Wales, a Welsh-identifying but non-Welsh-speaking set, centred in the Valleys of the south; and British Wales, a British-identifying and non-Welsh-speaking group in the areas of longer-term Anglicization in the borderlands and southern lowlands. The voting patterns in the unfortunate referendum on European Union membership of June 2016 revealed an interesting geographical and social perspective in Wales, as elsewhere in Britain, and an interesting spin on the models mentioned above. Overall in Wales, the outcome was narrowly in favour of "leave", by 52.5 to 47.5 per cent. But regionally most constituencies had either bigger "remain" or "leave" majorities: most of the west, with the exception of Pembrokeshire and Anglesey, had clear results in favour of remaining; the formerly industrialized south and northeast had clear leave majorities; as did most of the rural parts and urban areas of the borderlands and south, with the exception of the Vale of Glamorgan, very narrowly remain, and Cardiff, 60 per cent remain. (See BBC News online: EU Referendum 2016 results.) Thus it seems that *Y Fro Gymraeg* and the capital had the most pro-European outlook, while the agricultural and deprived post-industrial areas registered a protest vote. (If one wanted an even more concise summary of the geography of Wales than that delivered in the present section, one could turn to *The Cockroach*, Ian McEwan's satire on Brexit: "Wales? A small country far to the west, hilly, rain-sodden, treacherous." [2019: 14–15])

The following sections look in more detail at the demographic, cultural, and linguistic patterns introduced briefly here, which we conclude with a short summary of the principal locations of more recent immigration into Wales. From the late nineteenth into the mid twentieth century, there was significant Italian and Jewish immigration, for the most part into South Wales. In the mid-to-late twentieth century, thousands of British Commonwealth citizens (especially from the Indian subcontinent) settled in the main Welsh cities, and after Britain joined the European Union in 1973, the EU's freedom of movement policy enabled fellow European citizens to reside in Wales, again mostly in the chief urban areas. Cardiff especially became known for its multicultural population. The UK census of 2011 showed that Cardiff had 45,000 foreign-born residents (13 per cent of its total population). In the early years of the twenty-first century, Swansea has become increasingly cosmopolitan, with 150 languages represented among the city's schoolchildren (Cheesman and Çelik 2017: 11). In 2011, 5.5 per cent of the usual resident population of Wales as a whole (that is, just over 168,000 people) had been born outside the UK (Office for National Statistics, 2012: 12), a low figure compared with England.

1.3 Demography

This subsection covers a range of topics surrounding the demography of Wales with a focus on the Welsh and English languages, Anglicization, and ethnolinguistic identity of Welsh people. It begins with a discussion of the makeup of the population, then investigates the Anglicization patterns and population movement throughout the centuries. We then focus on the present-day status of Welsh and English and the distribution of bilingual Welsh and monoglot English speakers and the socio-economic significance of bilingualism in the nation. We conclude with a discussion on the current in-migration and out-migration within the country, and the ethnographic identities of majority and minority groups in Wales. Wales is a country with two core languages, as well as being home to a multitude of minority languages. This must be borne in mind also when discussing Welsh English.

1.3.1 Major cities and towns

All of the succeeding demographic data comes from the report *2011 Census: Key statistics for Wales* (Office for National Statistics 2012; hereafter ONS 2012). At the last U.K. census in 2011, the population usually resident in Wales was 3.1 million, marking a five per cent increase since 2001 (ONS 2012). Nearly a fifth of the population (563,000) were aged 65 and over, with an increase of one percentage point since 2001, whilst six per cent (178,000) were under five years of age.

Of the twenty-two unitary authorities in Wales, nine are categorised as counties (Carmarthenshire, Flintshire, Powys, Pembrokeshire, Gwynedd, Denbighshire, Monmouthshire, Ceredigion and the Isle of Anglesey), three are cities (Cardiff, Swansea, and Newport), and ten are county-boroughs (Rhondda Cynon Taf, Caerphilly, Neath Port Talbot, Bridgend, Wrexham, the Vale of Glamorgan, Conwy, Torfaen, Blaenau Gwent, and Merthyr Tydfil).

Prior to 1996 and between 1974 and 1996, Wales was divided into eight counties: Gwent, South Glamorgan, Mid Glamorgan, and West Glamorgan, Dyfed, Powys, Gwynedd, and Clwyd. These names were chosen at the time to reflect the historic regions. This was later changed in 1996 and, consequently, figures between areas are not always easily comparable.

In 2011, the three unitary authorities with the largest populations in the country were the capital city Cardiff (346,090), the second largest city and county of Swansea (239,023), and Rhondda Cynon Taf (234,410). All these principal areas were in the south of the nation. Other largely populated urban areas in the southeast were Caerphilly (178,806), Newport (145,736) and Neath Port Talbot and Bridgend (139,812 and 139,178 respectively).

By area, the largest region of Wales is the central region of Powys (5180.37 km^2), it is also the least densely populated with an average of 26 people per square kilometre. Comparatively, the smallest region is Blaenau Gwent (108.76 km^2) although it is the fifth most densely populated region. Much of the west and north of the nation is sparsely populated. In order, the least-densely populated regions are Ceredigion, Gwynedd, Pembrokeshire and Carmarthenshire, the Isle of Anglesey and Conwy, the majority of which (excluding southern Pembrokeshire) are regions of the "Welsh heartland", that is, areas with significant Welsh language populations. Areas in North Wales that are more densely populated are Denbighshire, Wrexham and Flintshire, Anglicised regions close to the English border. See Table 1.1 for a detailed breakdown of the population statistics as of the 2011 census.

Table 1.1: 2011 Census: Usual resident population by unitary authority in Wales

Unitary Authority	Persons Number	Percentage of population	Area in km^2	Persons per km^2
Total	3,063,456	100%	20,735.11	148
Cardiff *	346,090	11.3%	140.38	2465
Swansea *	239,023	7.8%	379.74	629
Rhondda Cynon Taf -	234,410	7.7%	424.13	553
Carmarthenshire †	183,777	6.0%	2370.35	78
Caerphilly -	178,806	5.8%	277.45	644
Flintshire †	152,506	5.0%	437.54	349
Newport *	145,736	4.8%	190.52	765
Neath Port Talbot -	139,812	4.6%	441.26	317
Bridgend -	139,178	4.5%	250.75	555
Wrexham -	134,844	4.4%	503.77	268

Table 1.1: (continued).

Unitary Authority	Persons Number	Percentage of population	Area in km²	Persons per km²
Powys †	132,976	4.3%	5180.37	26
The Vale of Glamorgan -	126,336	4.1%	330.95	382
Pembrokeshire †	122,439	4.0%	1618.74	76
Gwynedd †	121,874	4.0%	2534.94	48
Conwy -	115,228	3.8%	1125.83	102
Denbighshire †	93,734	3.1%	836.74	112
Monmouthshire †	91,323	3.0%	849.15	108
Torfaen -	91,075	3.0%	125.64	725
Ceredigion †	75,922	2.5%	1785.45	43
Blaenau Gwent -	69,814	2.3%	108.76	642
Isle of Anglesey †	69,751	2.3%	711.24	98
Merthyr Tydfil -	58,802	1.9%	111.39	528

Marked * are cities, marked † are counties, and marked - are county boroughs.

Source: Office for National Statistics (2012)

1.3.2 Historical settlement and patterns of Anglicization

The following is a brief overview of the historical settlement of the nation and the processes that have led to Anglicization (see Williams 1990 for detailed discussion). For more on the specific historic development, history and perceptions of the Welsh English dialect, see Chapter 5 of the current work.

Since the early medieval period, the region today known as Wales, and its Brythonic Celtic peoples speaking various forms of "Welsh" (or *Cymraeg*), have undergone continued Anglicization pressures from the east of the British Isles. Whether by annexation of lands or through partial political alliances, Wales has aptly been described as the "first colony of an expanding English state" (Williams 1990: 19). The Anglicization began with the Norman invasion of Wales, which saw the re-settlement of English peoples along the borders and along the southern coast on the Gower Peninsula and southern Pembrokeshire (Williams 1990: 21–22). Invasions and administrative reforms in later centuries, such as the Conquest of Wales in 1282 by the English king Edward I, and the eventual annexation of the Normans' Welsh Marches and Welsh principality into England proper with the Laws in Wales Act of 1536 and 1543, stripped the Welsh of many legal and political rights. These Acts of Union made English the only official legal language of use in Wales. Welsh was not proscribed by the act, but emphasis was placed on English as the "language of [a] civilised future" (Aitchison and Carter 2000: 27). Effectively, Wales was annexed into the English state. Despite such legal obstacles, the Welsh language was still the language of the majority of people. Though Catholicism (a denomination long-associated with early Wales) had waned in Wales, the part religion played in preserving the Celtic language cannot be understated. The translation of the Bible into Welsh in 1588 and the new movement of nonconformism in Wales helped create a largely literate population where ideas of "Welshness" were capable of being transmitted (Williams 1990: 22).

Anglicization data from before the first census of 1891 can be pulled from the noted language of religious sermons in Welsh parishes (e.g. the Church in Wales archive in the National Library of Wales; Aitchison and Carter 2000: 25). Pryce (1978) presents maps from 1750–1900 to illustrate the divide between parishes that were overwhelmingly monoglot Welsh, "bi-lingual" (i.e. areas where two monolingual language groups resided, not areas that spoke both languages), and dominantly English. The English zones reflected early penetration of English from the border counties, southern Gower and Pembrokeshire, the bilingual zone reflected English settlers slowly penetrating Welsh-speaking regions like coastal resort towns where there was urbanization and economic development, and the Welsh "core" in the mountainous west and north of the nation had Anglicised zones surrounding ports such as Pwllheli and Aberystwyth.

It was not until the Industrial Revolution that the rate of Anglicization increased significantly. The second half of the 1800s saw Wales undergo an industrial expansion. Thomas (1987) suggests that one way of simplifying the Industrial Revolution of Wales is through a three-act narrative. The first era of 1780–1800 saw Wales as the "vanguard of the Industrial revolution"; here ideas of religious dissent, cultural renaissance and political radicalism were sown (Thomas 1987: 425). The second era of 1800–1846 saw the beginnings of a Welsh urbanised entity. There was a huge population increase, the numbers in South Wales rising from 315,000 to 726,000, with an overwhelming allegiance to nonconformist Christianity. Also, the formation of working-class ideologies that sought political reform saw aggression against British capitalists (e.g. Merthyr and Newport risings in 1838; Thomas 1987: 426–428). The final "act" was during 1846–1900, when the combination of free trade economies and exploitation of coal transformed the Welsh coalfield. For Glamorgan, the population soared to half a million. Thomas (1987: 430) argues the growth of the Welsh-speaking population was due to both in-migration and the "bountiful number of children raised".

There is some debate regarding the effect that the Industrial Revolution had on the linguistic forces in Wales (Williams 1990: 32). One argument suggests that it had a positive impact on the Welsh language. Both Thomas (1959, 1987) and Williams (1971, cited in Williams 1990) suggest that because the Welsh, unlike the Scottish and Irish, were able to in-migrate from rural areas to the southern urbanised coalfield rather than leave their nations, this created strong Welsh-language communities and institutions. This argument is often contested on two accounts, the first being that out-migration devastated the socio-cultural dynamic of rural communities, and second, that large numbers of non-Welsh migrants from England, Scotland and Ireland moved to the coalfield, in turn creating an Industrial Culture that was "Anglo-Welsh" in composition (Williams 1990: 33–34).

Regardless of the effect of in-migration on Welsh within the coalfield, the social integration of Wales into England was a continued fixation of the British government. Evidence of this can be seen in the Report of the Commissioners of Inquiry 1847 (infamously dubbed later as the "Treachery of the Blue Books") that condemned use of Welsh for educating children (along with the moral worth of Welsh-speaking people; Aitchison and Carter 2000: 34). The controversial Education Act of 1870 later emphasized that English should be the sole language of instruction in schools (Williams 1990: 35).

Between 1914–1945, modernist attitudes, such as liberation from traditional values in the pursuit of "progress", coupled with the devastation of the World Wars, led to English being advertized as the language of rational change for Welsh people. Parents were less likely to pass the Welsh language to their children, and the rapidly advancing modernization of the communication and transport systems brought Wales and England ever closer (Williams 1990: 36).

Due to census results, we have a thorough socio-demographic profile of this change in usage of the Welsh language (see Table 1.2). At the beginning of the period (1891), 54% of usual residents were Welsh-speaking, with 30.1% being monoglot Welsh-speakers; ten years later (1901) this monolingual reserve dropped to 15.1%, though bilingualism (i.e. this time in the sense of one individual in command of two languages) was flourishing (Williams 1990: 37). By 1911, the monolingual reserve was at 8.5% and bilinguals went from a peak of 35% to 30.8% between 1911 and 1921. By 1921 there were 155,990 monoglot Welsh-speakers, 766,103 bilinguals and 1,446,211 monoglot English (Williams 1990: 38). Aitchison and Carter (2000: 38–42) add that 1911 revealed for the first time that Welsh was no longer the majority language of the Welsh people. The mid-war economic depression of the First World War continued to speed Anglicization as class wars led to unemployment and emigration of Welsh people. The bilingual character of the

Welsh was promising but short-lived – a generational rest-stop for Anglicization rather than a chance for the nation to grasp command of two languages.

The introduction and development of mass communication transmissions and resultant dissemination of mass media such as radio and television throughout the 1920s and 1930s had their own effects on the Anglicization process, as monoglot Welsh speakers were directly exposed to English for the first time (Aitchison and Carter 2000: 40). Figures from 1951 suggest that numbers of Welsh speakers had fallen by 21.4% since 1931 (and of those, monolinguals had fallen by 58%). From 1911 until 1981, there was a proportional loss of 24.6% (Williams 1990: 39). In 1981, a mere 0.8% of the population were estimated to be monolingual Welsh speakers.

There were small legal successes for the language in the twentieth century. For example, the Welsh Courts Act of 1942, the Welsh Language Act 1967 and Welsh Language Act 1993 progressively gave legislative import to the Welsh language, gradually securing equal status with English (Aitchison and Carter 2000: 46). It could be argued that the Welsh language is no longer rapidly declining. About 18% of the population had command of the language in 1991, and this rose to 20.5% in 2001 (Aitchison and Carter 2004: 89, 49). That being said, this about-turn may be due to a change in the formulation of the question. Whereas the 1991 census asked whether the respondent spoke, read, or wrote Welsh, the 2001 census reworded this as "Can you understand, speak, read, or write Welsh". Higgs, Williams and Dorling (2004: 190–191) suspect that the additional "understand" may have led to a more positive response as a result of respondents overestimating their abilities. Today all Welsh speakers (excepting some cognitively impaired users) are functionally bilingual, though census data only records potential usage, not which language a speaker predominately uses. It is worth mentioning too that children in rural West Wales taught through the medium of Welsh may have minimal English language skills until early teenage years. However, more research is required to construct a fuller picture of English L2 skills in these predominantly Welsh language communities.

Table 1.2: Proportion of population speaking Welsh, by county, 1921–2011 (All speakers)

Percentage of all persons speaking Welsh									
	1921	1931	1951	1961	1971	1981	1991	2001	2011
Wales	37.1	36.8	28.9	26.0	20.8	18.9	18.7	20.8	19.0
Counties									
Clwyd	41.7	41.3	30.2	27.3	21.4	18.7	21.2	21.2	19.5

Table 1.2: (continued).

Percentage of all persons speaking Welsh									
	1921	1931	1951	1961	1971	1981	1991	2001	2011
Dyfed	67.8	69.1	63.3	60.1	52.5	46.3	44.1	41.4	36.8
Gwent	5.0	4.7	2.8	2.9	1.9	2.5	3.0	10.2	9.6
Gwynedd	78.7	82.5	74.2	71.4	64.7	61.2	67.1	64.5	61.3
Mid-Glamorgan	38.4	37.1	22.8	18.5	10.5	8.4	8.3	11.2	10.3
Powys	35.1	34.6	29.6	27.8	23.7	20.2	20.7	21.1	18.6
South Glamorgan	6.3	6.1	4.7	5.2	5.0	5.8	6.7	11.2	11.0
West Glamorgan	41.3	40.5	31.6	27.5	20.3	16.4	15.6	15.7	13.4

Source: Data for 1921–1981 adapted from *Census 1981 Language in Wales*, Table 4, p.50 (Williams 1990: 41), with added data for 1991–2011. Note that in 1996, all preserved counties except Powys were divided further into new principal areas (e.g. Dyfed became Carmarthenshire, Ceredigion and Pembrokeshire). Slight boundary changes will mean these decades' results are not completely analogous with prior regions. The data for 1991 are from Jones (2012: 16) and the data for 2001 and 2011 from StatsWales (2012). The data have been tallied and averaged from the newly formed counties to match the prior preserved counties.

1.3.3 The Welsh and English languages today: 2011 census and new legislations

The most recent 2011 census reports indicate that 19% of usual residents (562,000) had some command of Welsh and that 30% of these were children between 3 and 15 years old. This marks a decrease of 1.8 percentage points since 2001. There was an increase in residents aged three and over who said they had no skills in Welsh (73% or 2.2 million; ONS 2012).

These regional statistics are perhaps best presented by maps. Figure 1.1 shows the Welsh language results laid over 1909 LSOAs (Lower Layer Super Output Areas), thereby being as "consistent in population size as possible" and allowing us to view the distribution of Welsh speakers for areas smaller than electoral divisions and communities (Jones 2013: 7). Here we can see that there are still 49 regions that are over 70% Welsh-speaking, with the majority in Gwynedd, Conwy and the Isle of Anglesey. Ceredigion, Carmarthenshire, Denbighshire and northern Pembrokeshire then contribute to 131 locales that are 50–70% Welsh-speaking.

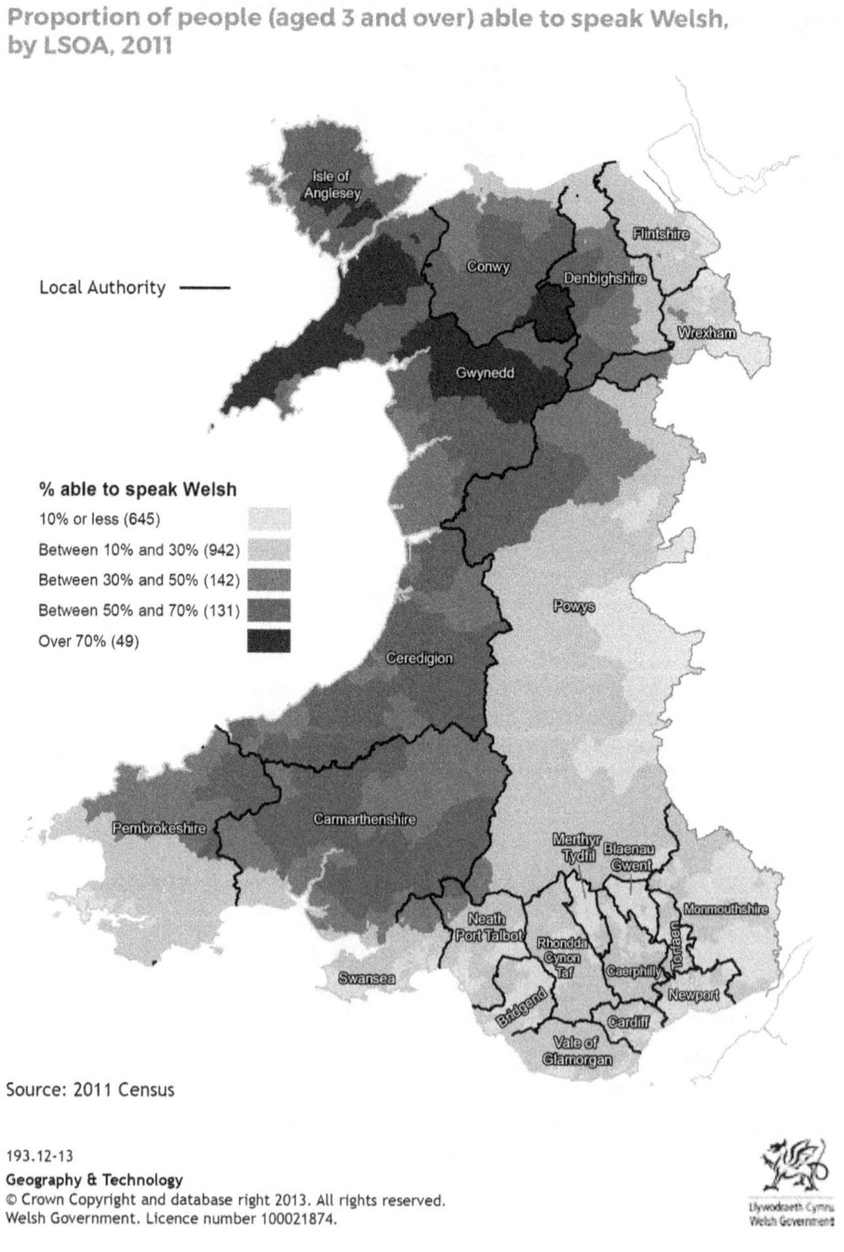

14 — 1 Geography, demography, cultural factors, and variation

Proportion of people (aged 3 and over) able to speak Welsh, by LSOA, 2011

Source: 2011 Census

193.12-13
Geography & Technology
© Crown Copyright and database right 2013. All rights reserved.
Welsh Government. Licence number 100021874.

Figure 1.1: Proportion of people (aged 3 and over) able to speak Welsh by LSOA, 2011 (Llywodraeth Cymru / Welsh Government 2017: 8).

Another way of observing the data is by the proportional difference of those able to use Welsh between 2001 and 2011 (Llywodraeth Cymru / Welsh Government 2017: 9). The results indicate that English continues to exert influence on the dominantly Welsh-speaking regions through factors such as Welsh speakers emigrating from Wales (see Section 1.3.5 below), the death of elderly speakers, and the immigration of monolingual English speakers from within or outside of Wales (Jones 2013: 9). More surprising is the increase of 2% or more in the southeast of the country. This could be explained through migratory movement from the northwest and west of the nation to these urban locales such as Cardiff (and the Vale of Glamorgan; as was reported by Aitchison and Carter 2000: 119).

Monmouthshire, though historically a well-established Anglicized zone, has made gains of over 2% in its speakers throughout the county. Williams (1990: 40) reported that the only county with proportional Welsh language growth between 1971–1981 was also Gwent / Monmouthshire. Aitchison and Carter (2000: 119) report the county being the only border county in 1991 to have more Welsh-speaking migrants outnumber resident speakers of Welsh.

Today, we cannot dismiss a new twenty-first-century sense of Welsh cultural renaissance in the county, and indeed, throughout the country. Monmouthshire's council reports that significant public interest in Welsh has led to the formation of Welsh language schools and courses throughout the county (Monmouthshire.gov 2019a, Monmouthshire.gov 2019c). Emphasis appears to be placed not just on cultural ties to the Welsh language but also on the psychological benefits of being bilingual.

This revival of Welsh language enthusiasm in predominately Anglicized areas of the southeast will be of continued interest for the English dialect research of Wales. Some early reports suggest that Welsh loanwords form a component of a "Gwent English" for young people (see Jones 2016b), and future developments will be of interest to English and Welsh language sociolinguistics going forward.

These increases in the southeast could well be preliminary outcomes of the language planning that the Welsh Government are now constructing, one of which being *Cymraeg 2050*, an initiative that wants the Welsh-using population to rise to one million speakers by 2050 (Llywodraeth Cymru / Welsh Government 2017: 2). The government wishes to "renew energy", but insists it will not force the issue, suggesting it is in the hands of Welsh citizens to take responsibility for the use of English as well as Welsh.

1.3.4 Migration today within the country and outside

This leads us into a larger discussion on the current migratory trends within Wales. Between 2001 and 2011, the population grew by 5% (153,000) and 92% of this figure (141,000) were due to immigration to Wales from other regions of the U.K. and abroad (ONS 2012). Five per cent of the people in Wales were born outside the U.K., an increase of two per cent since 2001 (ONS 2012: 3). It should be noted that less than three quarters of the population were born in Wales (73% in 2011, 75% in 2001). By far the greatest demographic of non-Welsh residents are those born in England, demonstrating the close connection the two nations have: in 2001 this was 20% and in 2011 21% (636,000; ONS 2012). In comparison, 84% of usual residents in England were born there. Understandably, this influx of migrants affects the language situation both for the Welsh language in the westerly and northwesterly regions as well as for Welsh English varieties in southern cities.

Table 1.3: Country of birth: Wales and England, 2001 and 2011, all usual residents (thousands / per cent)

Country of birth	Wales				England			
	2001		2011		2001		2011	
	Number	%	Number	%	Number	%	Number	%
Wales	2,189	75	2,226	73	610	1	507	1
England	590	20	636	21	42,969	87	44,247	83
Rest of U.K.[1]	32	1	33	1	1,010	2	922	2
Outside of U.K.	92	3	168	5	4,551	9	7,337	14

Source: *Office for National Statistics* (2012)

Notes:
1. Rest of United Kingdom includes "United Kingdom not otherwise specified".

How the resident population of Wales migrate within the country itself is also worth mentioning in regards to the language situation. Aitchison and Carter (2000: 115–122), for example, divide Wales up into five "language zones" based on the 1990s statistics: the Welsh-speaking core, the borders, the transitional zone, the old industrial regions, and conurbations (see also Section 1.2).

In the core, over 80% of in-migrants are from outside Wales and are unlikely to have any Welsh language skills. Coupled with this is the fact that out-migration is also high with 72% moving to areas outside Wales (n.b. not all Welsh speakers).

At the borders, the Welsh speakers are scarce, however, the region's similarity to the core is in in-migration. The highest figures are found in Alyn and Deeside, where 94% of in-migrants were from outside Wales. The "ill-defined" transitional zone is that between the core and the Border country. Here, figures for in-migrants from outside Wales are lower, and of all these migrants, Welsh speakers are fewer in number than the usual Welsh-speaking residents, which the authors conclude as evidence of a sort of language frontier.

The Anglicized post-industrial southern valleys have the largest percentage of Welsh-born residents (90% average), and in-migrant numbers are very low. Migration does not play a significant role in language change here. Indeed, Paulasto (2006: 30) asserts that this area could be defined as the "core" of English-speaking Wales. Of the southern conurbations, Newport has a greater number of in-migrants from outside Wales and lower proportions of Welsh-born than its environs (Borders and Valleys) and the lowest proportion of Welsh-speaking in-migrants of all districts in Wales. Swansea is similar in its demographics to the western Valleys except with a larger number of in-migrants and non-Welsh migrants. Cardiff is the outlier in that it has attracted larger percentages of Welsh-speaking in-migrants in the last decades (Aitchison and Carter 2000: 122). Although these statistics reflect late 1990s, Swansea today is a major University town in the U.K. and continues to attract migrants from around the world.

1.3.5 Ethnic and cultural communities in Wales

The usually resident population of Wales in 2011 was 96% (2.9 million) White, which was a higher percentage than in any English region (ONS 2012). Of the minority groups, Indian and "other Asian" accounted for 2.2%, Mixed or Multiple ethnicities accounted for 1.0%, African ethnicities accounted for 0.6%, and Arab and Other accounted for 0.5% (ONS 2012).

Statistics for national identity (i.e. Welsh, English, British, etc.) are also of interest. Unlike migration data, these figures cannot be used as an indication of continued Anglicization of Wales (and Welsh English) per se, but do tell us about the social complexities of cultural identity and possible language loyalties in modern Wales, especially following the 1997 public vote for the devolution of particular law-making powers in Wales and the creation of the Welsh Assembly (as of 2020, re-stylized as the Senedd Cymru / Welsh Parliament). We cannot compare this with previous census data (as identity is a new marker), but it gives us an indication of how individuals in Wales that use Welsh English may construct their own cultural identity, which may have effects on their usage of Welsh English (e.g. discussions of enregisterment).

Nearly two-thirds (65.8% or 2,017,681 million) of the residents in Wales identified as "Welsh" in 2011, and of these, 7.1% (218,000) also identified as "British". There were also 16.9% (519,165) who solely identified as "British", whilst 1.2% (38,128) responded that they also had "other" background identity (ONS 2012). Although in England more people identified as having an English national identity (up to 70%), we must bear in mind that in Wales, 21% of the population consists of English-born residents; in England only 1% the resident population is Welsh-born.

As previously noted, one distinct quality of the former "White" Welsh identity, especially in the nineteenth century, was the cultural attachment to religious nonconformism. By the twenty-first century, not only Christianity but religious identification has significantly declined and arguably no longer composes a typicality of "Welshness". Between 2001 and 2011, those identifying as Christian exhibited a 14 percentage point drop throughout Wales from 72% to 58%, a larger decrease than in any English region (ONS 2012). Now, almost a third of Welsh people identify as having no religion (32%; 983,000 people).

We can also compare national identity with ethnic identity using the census results. Harries, Byrne and Lymperopoulou (2014: 2) found that ethnic groups with immigrant backgrounds in Wales were less likely to identify Welsh as their sole national identity than respective populations in England or Scotland. Of those who did, a quarter of Black Caribbean and a fifth of Other Black groups reported only a Welsh identity, whilst Pakistani and Bangladeshi groups reported 14% and 8% respectively. All these groups only make up 0.5% of the population, but as Black minorities have been established in Wales for a century or more, this could explain their adherence to markers of Welshness. More commonly, however, these groups identified as British only (e.g. Bangladeshi 64%, Pakistani 56%, and Black Caribbean 41%), possibly reflecting a historical relationship with multiple British urban/industrial regions. All mixed ethnic groups were more likely than any other ethnic minority to identify as Welsh (47%), a higher proportion than among the equivalent populations with English and Scottish identities.

1.3.6 Language and identity

The 2011 census collected data on the main languages of Welsh citizens for the first time. Usual residents in 96.7% of households spoke either English or Welsh as a main language, with a further 1.4% of households having at least one adult who spoke English or Welsh as their main language and 0.2% of households having no adults using either language, but at least one child. 1.7% of households noted no residents using English or Welsh (ONS 2012).

There is a longstanding cultural debate about whether someone is "more Welsh" if they use the Welsh language. The latest census results shed some light on this (Harries, Byrne, & Lymperopoulou 2014: 3). Welsh speakers are more likely to report singular Welsh national identity (77%), whilst a little over a half of those who could not speak Welsh identify solely as Welsh (53%). Despite this, there is no direct association between those who claim Welshness and those who use Welsh, as for example in Merthyr, in the "Anglo-Welsh heartland", 77% of people claim a Welsh-only identity despite a low percentage of 8.9 of Welsh speakers (second to last among local authorities). These findings align well the "Three-Wales model" discussed in Section 1.2 and in the sociolinguistic studies examined in Section 1.5.

We must also consider the impact that migration from beyond the United Kingdom has on the language makeup, especially how immigrant languages might be affecting the English varieties of Wales, notably in Newport, Cardiff, and Swansea. Languages as diverse as Panjabi, Bengali, Japanese, Somali and Gujarati all have established speech communities in Wales, bringing with them new languages and new varieties of L2 English. We are starting to see some of the results of the interaction between these L2 Englishes and WelE already. For example, in a project curated by Museum Wales, *Wales' other languages* (Museum Wales 2010), volunteers were interviewed about their concept of language use in Wales. One settled L2 English speaker from Japan, for example, had acquired a marked intonational shift towards a WelE. This acquisition of a Welsh accent had been observed by other British English users, although the speaker could not discern the accent themselves. There is still much to learn about what other phonological, lexical, and morphosyntactic elements are being shared between speech communities in twenty-first-century Wales.

The idea that Wales and Welshness is malleable and an identity for all who live in the nation (i.e. civic nationalism) is an ideology that politicians and institutions surrounding the Welsh Government are keen to support. For example, the *One Wales* initiative fom 2007, a politically cross-party venture, reflected on the future of Welsh culture (One Wales 2007). It emphasized that Welsh language, arts, culture, and sport have all done much already to place Wales on the world stage and that future generations would do well to continue this. One statement read:

> We celebrate Wales as a community of diverse cultures: united for our common good, celebrating our many traditions, ensuring that Wales uses its two national languages to their full potential, and bringing people of all origins together. (One Wales 2007: 34)

The Welsh language was described as being part of the "common national heritage, identity and public good" (One Wales 2007: 34–35). Two of their proposed measures have since come to pass: further legislation on the Welsh language has secured a Welsh Language Commissioner in 2011 and a Welsh internet domain-name was created in 2014 (.wales and .cymru). Certain measures in the document, especially those that distinguish themselves from English practices, may now be identifiers of Welsh national identity and pride, one example being the idea that low income should not be a barrier to museums and galleries (all of which have free admission), whilst others are likely still a matter of debate (e.g. encouraging sports teams to be Welsh rather than British).

1.4 Regional variation

Although the English continue to see Welsh English as a fairly monolithic variety (e.g. Montgomery 2016), linguists and the Welsh themselves have long recognized different local accents and dialects within the country. The evidence is both linguistic and sociolinguistic, that is, based on structural and lexical characteristics on the one hand, and on speaker perceptions on the other. The different varieties are the outcome of multiple factors: varying histories and patterns of Anglicization, different modes of acquisition, the roles of Welsh language contact and English English (EngE) dialect contact, and the position and history of English as a community language.

Scholars identify somewhat different Welsh Englishes based on which of the above factors weigh most in their model. Before presenting our own views on the matter, let us briefly describe the shoulders we are standing on. Much of what we know about traditional dialects of WelE rests on the *Survey of Anglo-Welsh Dialects (SAWD)*, starting with David Parry's work in the 1970s (e.g. Parry 1977, 1979, Penhallurick 1991). Thomas (1984: 178–179; 1994: 112–115), using *SAWD* as his primary source, divides WelE into three main varieties – northern, southeastern and southwestern – on account of the impact of the Welsh language and EngE dialects in different areas. In his view, Englishes in the north(west) and southwest of Wales are subject to contemporary Welsh language transfer in bilingual speakers' English and thus "more dependent on the structure of Welsh" for their distinctive characteristics, whereas in the southeast (and northeast) the influence is "essentially substratal" and likely to dwindle further (Thomas 1984: 178). Conversely, the industrial southeast (and northeast) have established indigenous English dialects, which are closely related to the bordering EngE dialects.

The starting point for another trichotomy, by Gwen Awbery (1997: 86–88), is the Anglicization of Wales, leading first of all to the settlements and dialects of the longstanding English regions in south Pembrokeshire, the Gower, and the Border country. These regional varieties resemble transported dialects in the sense that they owe their distinctive characteristics solely to varieties of EngE. From the twentieth century onwards, however, the southern pockets have more or less integrated with Welsh Wales, the second region and phase in Awbery's model. This area covers all parts of Wales where Welsh either continues to be spoken as an important community language or where it held a firm position until the early twentieth century, that is, encompassing the rural southwest and north as well as the southeastern Valleys. Welsh contact influence is a common denominator in the English language spoken throughout this region, which is why Awbery (1997: 88) associates the term Welsh English primarily with Welsh Wales. Thirdly, Awbery singles out the conurbations in the Cardiff-Newport-Barry area and close to Liverpool in the northeast. The dialects of these regions are the outcome of rapid population growth and urbanization, and hence, to a great extent, independent developments similar to other urban dialects in Britain.

Perceptual dialectology is concerned with the outcomes of the above processes, in other words, the speakers' own perceptions of dialect boundaries and evaluations of the characteristics of regional dialects. These perceptions are typically multidimensional, guided by linguistic criteria but also by affective attitudes, stereotypes, and conceptions of national identity. Studies conducted in Wales show that the respondents identify several distinct dialect regions within the country, distinguished along the dimensions of linguistic form, positive or negative affective qualities, status and social norms, geo-social belonging (i.e. Welshness), and rural/urban character (Williams et al. 1996: 186; also Coupland et al. 1994, Garrett et al. 1999). The six main regions (see Figure 1.2 from Garrett et al. 1999: 325) are the Northwest (rural and North Welsh speaking); the Northeast (more urban and Anglicized); the Southwest (rural and South Welsh speaking); Mid-Wales (rural and English-speaking); the Southeast Wales Valleys (industrial, mainly non-Welsh-speaking); and the southeastern Cardiff conurbations (highly urban and Anglicized). The regions align quite well with the descriptions by Thomas and Awbery, excepting that south Pembrokeshire and the Gower are included in the Southwest (see, however, Williams et al. 1996), and Mid-Wales represents the Border country dialects. Although the respondents also mention accent characteristics (e.g. *open, rounded, full, clipped, biting, nasal*; Williams et al. 1996: 186), their descriptions overwhelmingly lean towards the above-mentioned non-linguistic dimensions (see Section 1.5).

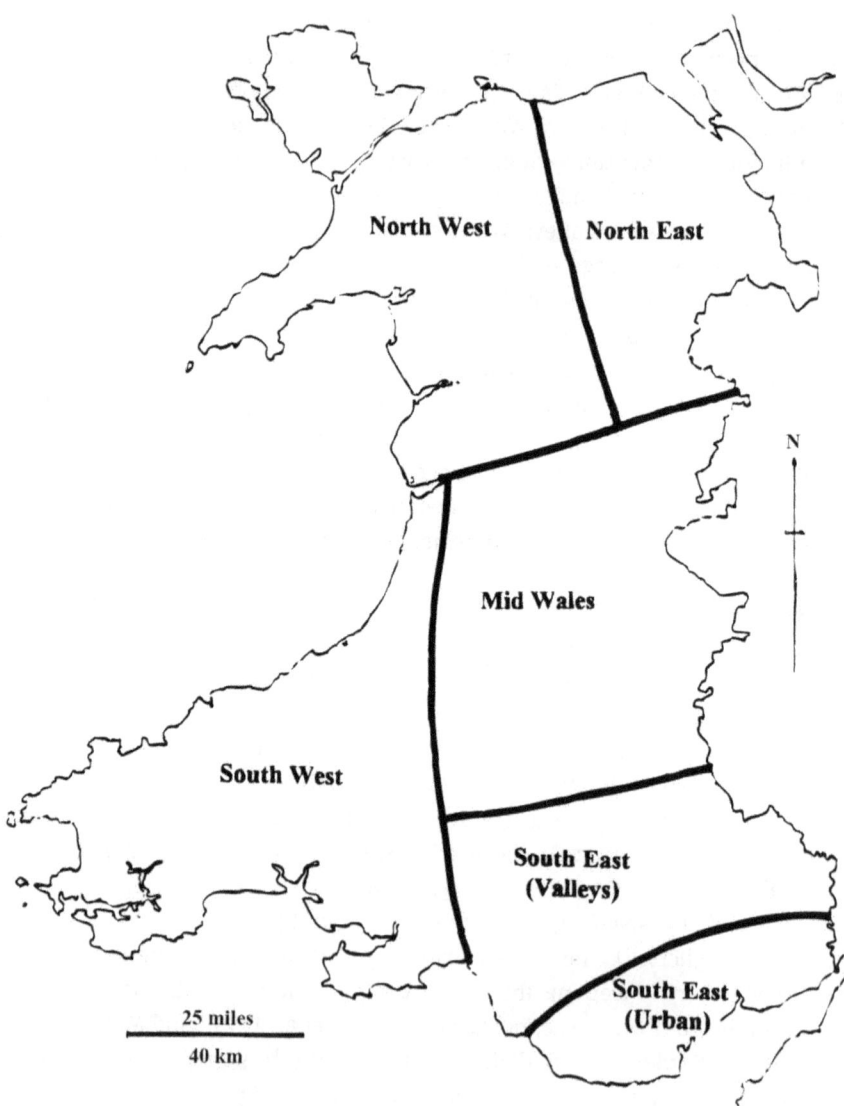

Figure 1.2: Map of Wales showing main dialect regions (Garrett et al. 1999: 325; reproduced with permission).

There is no reason to believe that the above dialect regions are the sole and final truth about the matter. The proximity effect leads speakers to be able to draw finely tuned dialect distinctions close to their home region, and, unlike the lines in the map might suggest, there are no clear and absolute differences between dialect areas; they tend to be more or less fluid instead. They are also dynamic: one of the most influential processes in present-day WelE is the levelling of highly distinctive contact-induced characteristics of grammar on the one hand and the continuing input of EngE dialects, for example, London English, on the other (see Chapter 3 and Section 4.4; Paulasto 2016). However, as the chapters in this book demonstrate, we do find structural and lexical support for the broad categories described above. Factors which operate in the context of regional variation include the following:

a) Type of language contact. Dialects spoken in the present-day Welsh-speaking areas (and to some extent in Anglicized Welsh Wales) maintain structural characteristics that arise from Welsh language contact. The main difference between the northern and southwestern varieties lies in the accents, which are influenced by the phonologies of North and South Welsh, respectively, and in the greater presence of English in the south. English has become a widely spoken community language even in those parts of the country, where the percentages of Welsh speakers are high. Hence, when talking about the morphosyntax of L1 Welsh bilinguals, it is often difficult to distinguish between individual, synchronic L1 transfer and community-based, diachronic substrate influence (cf. indigenized L2 Englishes; see, however, Mayr et al. 2017 and the discussion on lexical code-switching vs. borrowing in Section 4.2). In phonology and in the grammar of primarily English-speaking areas, the contact input is largely substratal. Studies which focus on linguistic features of the bilingual north and southwest are, for example, Parry (1979, 1990a), Penhallurick (1991, 1996), Pitkänen (2003), Paulasto (2006, 2009, 2016), Morris (2010, 2013), and Hejna (2015).

b) English as a community language and the mode of acquisition. Despite the above, the degree of Welsh contact influence in a locality does not necessarily correlate with the percentage of Welsh speakers. The depth and role of English in the community and, associated to this, the speakers' mode of English acquisition are highly significant factors as well. Paulasto (2009: 220) shows that in regional corpora from elderly informants born in the first decades of the twentieth century, the highest frequencies of Welsh-induced syntax (focus fronting and extended uses of the progressive form) can be found in Ceri George's corpus data from the southeastern Rhondda Valleys, although none of the informants are Welsh-speaking (see also Paulasto 2006: 154). L1 Welsh speakers from north(west) Wales produce a mere 11% of the Rhondda frequencies, while L1 Welsh speakers from Llandybie in the southwest display frequencies that are midway between the two end points. Paulasto argues that the main reason for the vast differences is the mode of acquisition of English, informal, interpersonal transmission having played a greater role in the south than the northwest. Paulasto (2009: 221–222) also indicates that, as regards grammatical variation in the use of the two features, it is the Llandybie informants whose English is most distinctively Welsh, with high percentages of object and adverbial fronting and habitual extension of the progressive form. In this data set, a strong position of Welsh combines with a relatively long history of using English as a community language. It should be noted that real and apparent time research shows considerable levelling in both features and both southern localities (see Chapter 3). The significance of the type of language community is examined also in Paulasto (2006).

c) Feature-based differences. Not all contact-induced features share the same geolinguistic distribution. Corpus evidence in Paulasto (2006, 2016) shows that focus fronting and invariant question tags *isn't it* and *is it* are widespread in the bilingual areas as well as in the primarily English-speaking south and east. However, habitual extension of the progressive form and extended uses of *with* are mainly found in the present-day bilingual areas. The former was previously common in the southeast Valleys, as stated above, but has since disappeared, while the latter does not emerge in Welsh-induced functions beyond the north and southwest. Roller (2016: 123-124) does not find equally clear geographic distinctions for different WelE features in the Radio Wales Corpus, but her data is somewhat limited in size for the study of regional distribution (personal communication 14 March 2018). In dialect lexicon there is obviously more variation still, examined in detail in Sections 4.2 and 4.3. In phonology, it seems that the impact of Welsh is most widespread in WelE prosody, with its characteristic lengthened consonants and intonation patterns occurring also in the southeastern Valleys area. Segmental phonology displays clearer geographic variation, Welsh-induced features being particularly common in the bilingual southwest and North Wales (see Chapter 2).

d) English English dialect contact. Dialects spoken in the southeast (the Valleys as well as the conurbations), in the Border country / Mid-Wales, and in the northeast have a higher degree of EngE dialect input than the northwestern and southwestern dialects. This applies to phonology, grammar, and lexicon. Traditional dialect lexicon, as described in *SAWD*, reveals diverse patterns of dialect contact and Anglicization in the longstanding English regions as well as along the English border and southern and northern coastlines (Section 4.3). The same areas display prominent and systematic similarities to neighbouring EngE dialects in their grammar. Although the traditional dialects are hardly spoken today and have been replaced by modern dialects (see Trudgill [1990] 1999), the same areas continue to share most of their dialectal grammar with EngE rather than with the Welsh-speaking areas (e.g. verbal inflection features, unmarked manner adverbs, certain preposition replacement features, loss or reduction of articles). Northeastern WelE belongs to an extent to the Liverpool dialect area, while southern WelE is likelier than northern WelE to adopt linguistic influence from London

English. This is especially clear in the case of the Welsh-induced invariant tag *isn't it*, which has increased in frequency in southern WelE (see Section 4.4). It appears to be reinforced by the London English tag *innit* while also going through a functional realignment with EngE usages.

Regional studies on longstanding English areas have been conducted on the Gower (Penhallurick 1994), south Pembrokeshire (Charles 1982, Parry 1990b), and Gwent (Matthews 1913, Parry 1977, Jones 2013, 2016b; see inside the publications for older sources). *The Survey of English Dialects (SED)* (Orton et al. 1962–1971) includes Monmouthshire, whose status on the border of Wales and England has varied. Most studies on the Border country, apart from Parry (1964), date even further back and hence concern the traditional dialects of the area; see Awbery (1997: 93) for a review.

e) Dialect focusing. The southeast Welsh dialects, particularly in the Valleys, are distinctive in having Welsh-induced substrate features in phonology but few Welsh-induced features of grammar. Rather, these dialects contain grammatical features not attested elsewhere in the country (e.g. periphrastic *do*, *by here/there*, *where to*, absence of -*s* with a 3sg subject). The urban dialect of the Cardiff area shares many of these features in its morphosyntax, but phonologically, it constitutes a regional accent of its own. Studies with a focus on the Valleys dialects are, for example, Windsor Lewis (1964, 1990), George (1990), Connolly (1990), Tench (1990), Walters (1999, 2001, 2003), Williams (2000, 2001, 2003), Mayr (2010) and Podhovnik (2008, 2010). Most studies on Cardiff English are sociolinguistic rather than strictly linguistic, but valuable descriptions can nevertheless be found in, for example, Coupland (1988), Mees (1983, 1990), Collins and Mees (1990), Mees and Collins (1999), and Campbell (forthc.).

1.5 Sociolinguistics

The book *Sociolinguistics in Wales*, edited by Mercedes Durham and Jonathan Morris, was published in 2016. The chapters of the book examine varying aspects of sociolinguistics in Welsh and English as well as multilingual practices, including ones that involve immigrant languages like Arabic. The balance of Welsh and English in the book is a valuable reminder that all studies and discussions on the sociolinguistics of WelE are positioned in some way in relation to the indigenous language of the country. In our previous work, Penhallurick (1993) discusses the intertwining discourses on the two languages and the consequent need to see WelE as a "national language" in the country next to Welsh. Paulasto (2006: 30–35) touches upon a number of issues which concern WelE in Welsh society, including Welsh and English language culture regions and ethnolinguistic communities, changes in the prestige of the two languages, language and dialect attitudes, and questions of national identity. Some of these will be examined in this section as well. Based on our observations and the research below, WelE in its many forms has a significant role in creating and maintaining experiences of national and cultural identity in present-day Wales, complementing rather than opposing the Welsh language.

As pointed out by Garrett et al. (2003: 20), the common denominator for research into the sociolinguistics of Wales is the Anglicization of the country, both as a language shift (i.e. the societal marginalization and consequent decline of Welsh) and a cultural process, and the ways in which it has shaped the sociolinguistic territory of the country. On the Welsh side are, for example, minority language politics, revitalization, educational policies, bilingualism, and the national significance of Welsh language culture and history. Other issues can be examined from the direction of either English or Welsh, including language attitudes, ideologies and enregisterment, folklinguistic perceptions, questions of national, social or linguistic identity, regional or sociolinguistic variation in language, or cross-linguistic influence. The breadth of research on the above subject areas is vast and extends relatively far back, as a result of the salience of this bilingual setting in Britain during the time when sociolinguistics was emerging as a major field of study. Garrett et al. (2003: 18), for example, mention that attitude studies in the context of Welsh language education were begun in the late 1940s (Jones 1949) and in the context of Welsh English accents and dialects in the 1970s (Giles 1970). This section aims to present a concise summary of perspectives and findings relevant for the sociolinguistics of Welsh English and highlight some of the more recent studies. Subsection 1.5.3 focuses on the subject of national and linguistic identity as described by the informants of the Urban Survey of Anglo-Welsh Dialects corpus (Urban SAWD) as well as the Llandybie Corpus (LC), North Wales Corpus (NWC) and Tonypandy Corpus (TC; for the corpora, see Section 1.6).

1.5.1 Dialect attitudes and perceptions

There is a sizeable body of work on WelE dialect attitudes, paving the way and contributing in significant ways to this field of sociolinguistic research in general. Much of the early research in the 1970s and 1980s was conducted using indirect methods, such as experiments and the matched-guise technique, with a focus on accent variation (for reviews, see Giles 1990, Coupland et al. 1994, Garrett et al. 2003). Several studies indicate that (South) Welsh respondents rated Welsh-accented speakers less favourably than RP Speakers in terms of qualities associated with overt prestige, that is, as less intelligent, active, happy, ambitious or self-confident. The Welsh accent was however associated with positive qualities such as honesty, trustworthiness, good-naturedness and sense of humour, which imply in-group solidarity and covert prestige (see, e.g. Giles 1971, Bourhis et al. 1975, Bourhis 1977, Bourhis & Giles 1977). Matters were made more complicated with the addition of the Welsh language as a variant. The participants' first language would affect the results in varying, sometimes contradictory ways. In Bourhis et al. (1973), bilingual as well as monoglot English-speaking respondents from Pontypridd considered the Welsh accent to be on par with Welsh in positive traits, while Price et al. (1983) found bilingual Welsh adolescents from Carmarthenshire to favour RP as well as the Welsh language over Welsh-accented English, which they associated with unintelligence and selfishness. The studies, in other words, reflect regional as well as L1-based variation on whether people consider the Welsh accent of English to suffice as a symbol of Welsh in-group identity. These two factors have been found to influence perceptions of dialect regions as well (Coupland et al. 1994). In addition to cognitive responses, Bourhis & Giles (1976) observed that the choice of accent or language affects individuals' behaviour: the audience of a Welsh language theatre performance in Cardiff were more compliant with a request voiced through the loudspeakers in Welsh than in RP or either mild or broad WelE. The audience of an English language performance, on the other hand, were persuaded best by a broad Welsh-accented request.

English participants' assessments of WelE accents in comparison to RP were generally quite negative (Giles & Marsh 1979, Giles et al. 1981, Brown et al. 1985), although in Giles's (1970) early attitude study involving several British English (BrE) accents, southwest English pupils rated it very favourably. More recent opinions have been gleaned from a BBC Voices survey, conducted in the UK in November 2004, and a YouGov survey from 2014. The BBC survey, examined by Coupland and Bishop (2007), asked respondents to rate 34 accents, including Welsh, Cardiff and Swansea. In pleasantness, the Welsh accent was rated 14th and in prestige, 18th, that is, a mid-position rating on both accounts. The urban accents received a lower rating, positioned 24th–27th in both pleasantness and prestige. The YouGov survey, then, requested simple positive or negative ratings, which were used to calculate a net score for each accent (Dahlgreen 2014). Of the twelve British and Irish accents included, the Welsh accent was rated as the third most popular. Attitudes towards the Welsh accent seem to have become more positive during the past few decades.

From the 1990s onwards, the matched-guise technique has given way to folk-linguistic and perceptual approaches, where the respondents themselves have the possibility to define language varieties and dialect areas as well as their attitudes towards them (e.g. Williams et al. 1996: 172). One of the central outcomes of these studies (e.g. Coupland et al. 1994, Williams et al. 1996, Garrett et al. 1995,

1999) is the identification of several distinct dialect regions within Wales along the dimensions of "perceived linguistic features, affective qualities, prestige, urban/rural character, and, in particular, perceives Welshness" (Garrett et al. 1999: 324). The studies indicate that the main dialect regions are (at least) six: the Northwest, the Northeast, the Southwest, Mid-Wales, the Southeast Valleys and the Urban Southeast. The linguistic characteristics of WelE dialect regions are discussed in subsection 1.4. above, but as these studies show, conceptions of a dialect region are the sum total of many aspects beyond language features. In Coupland et al. (1994: 480), schoolteachers from across the country evaluate the Northwest, Southwest and Southeast Valleys accents as Truly Welsh, while these areas receive varying scores on the attributes of Prestige, Pleasantness and Dynamism. The Southwestern accent fares best on all accounts, while the Urban Southeast and the Northeast are rated poorly across the board. Garrett et al. (1999) contrast teachers' responses with those of teenagers, showing that young people find the Northeastern and Cardiff accents most attractive in affiliative terms but agree with the teachers on the Welshness of the Southwest and Valleys accents. The authors conclude (1999: 345) that Welshness continues to be associated with the Welsh-speaking areas (and culturally significant Southeast Valleys) even in the regional dialects of English.

Montgomery (2016) carries on the map-based tradition of folklinguistics in Wales by studying the dialect perceptions of A-level students in localities along the Welsh border. The study confirms the proximity effect, that is, respondents distinguishing a greater number of dialect areas closer by than further away, and the associated significance of the border: the English respondents only identify "Welsh" and "Cardiff" accents, while the Welsh ones differentiate between North and South Wales as well as assorted other dialects, such as the southeast Welsh Valleys. The Welsh students also identify numerous EngE dialects, which is telling of the relative salience and familiarity of EngE dialect variation as opposed to that of WelE (see also Montgomery 2014). The study reveals that the South Welsh accent is viewed more positively than others and described, for example, as "Gentle" and "Friendly" as opposed to the "Harsh" and "Scouse" north(east) or "Common" and "Chavvy" Valleys accents (Montgomery 2016: 165, 170–174). The south Welsh and Valleys accents are also considered "Patriotic" or "Welshy", which Montgomery (2016: 173–174) interprets as symbolizing a strong Welsh identity.

A different kind of approach to dialect perceptions is taken by Durham (2015, 2016), who uses Twitter as her source of data to investigate salience and enregisterment of WelE dialect features on the one hand and dialect attitudes on the other. Durham (2016) finds that British tweeters' attitudes towards the Welsh accent are mostly positive, which aligns with recent survey results (see above). However, of the three dimensions of language attitudes outlined by Zahn and

Hopper (1985), the positive tweets relate almost exclusively to that of social attractiveness (with keywords such as *love, want, hot, sexy, amazing, cute, attractive, marry*) rather than superiority (e.g. education, class, intelligence) or dynamism (e.g. strength, enthusiasm, talkativeness; Durham 2016: 184, 192–198). This implies that in terms of overt prestige, attitudes towards WelE have not necessarily changed a great deal since the 1970s. The Welsh accent is, however, increasingly associated with other Celtic accents and its growing TV-visibility has raised its profile among dialects of English in general.

The concept of salience, then, is central in the studies by Durham (2015) and Roller (2016). Durham (2015) focuses on dialect performance tweets and picks out recurring dialect and accent characteristics, which can hence be considered salient to the tweeters. At the top of the list of morphosyntactic features are right dislocation (i.e. emphatic tags), verbal / extension of *-s*, and clause-final *like*, none of which are, in fact, restricted to WelE. They are, however, features used in southeast and Valleys English, and, as Durham suspects, they have risen in prominence through TV series like *The Valleys* or *Gavin and Stacey*. More characteristically Welsh features, exclamative *there*, invariant tag *isn't it* and focus fronting, make a few rare appearances. Phonological features and prosody are also commented on and mimicked through respelling, more or less on point. WelE lexis in this study is commented on in Section 4.3.2.

Roller's (2016) doctoral thesis focuses on the relationship of salience and frequency, that is, the perceptions of Welsh and English respondents of features of WelE morphosyntax and their respective frequencies in corpus data. As her corpora, she uses the Freiburg English Dialect Corpus (FRED) and the Radio Wales Corpus, which consists of fully transcribed discussions in the Millennium Memory Bank (MMB) and BBC *Voices* surveys. The six features in question are focus fronting, invariant tag *isn't it*, extended habitual progressive, embedded inversion, zero past tense of regular verbs, and *that*-clause replacing infinitival subclause (e.g. *I wanted that I should get leave*, IndE & PakE; Mesthrie 2008: 629). The first four are typical of WelE and their frequencies in Roller's study are examined against Paulasto's corpus data in Chapter 3 and Section 4.4 of this book. The final two features have been selected on the basis of their rarity across Englishes, yet attested presence in WelE according to the eWAVE (Kortmann et al. 2020). However, Roller (2016: 47, 103) does not find a single instance of a *that*-clause replacing the infinitive in her corpora, and this feature is equally non-existent in all the corpora examined for the present book, which suggests that the information in eWAVE is inaccurate. Zero past tense forms of irregular verbs are found but their frequencies are low (see Section 3.5.3).

Roller's (2016: 98–101) informants in Wales as well as in London identify focus fronting and invariant *isn't it* as the most salient WelE features. The difference from the other four is statistically significant, although the features next in line are different in the two groups: zero past tense marking in London, the habitual progressive (and embedded inversion) in Wales. The Welsh hence prove to be more perceptive of their own dialect than the Londoners. Roller finds that the levels of salience broadly correlate with the corpus-based frequencies, except in the case of invariant *isn't it*, which is not particularly frequent in either FRED or RWC (for further details and comments, see Section 4.4). The study explores other avenues as well, such as the interaction of salience and pervasiveness in eWAVE, perceived non-standardness of the WelE features, and the impact of social factors and incomers on dialect perceptions.

1.5.2 Variationist linguistics

In the study of WelE dialect variation, the central pillar is the *Survey of Anglo-Welsh Dialects* published in three regional volumes by Parry (1977, 1979) and Penhallurick (1991), and finally as a compilation volume (Parry 1999). Encompassing phonology, grammar, and lexicon, *SAWD* is referenced throughout the present book, which testifies of its continuing relevance in WelE dialectology. It follows in the footsteps of the *Survey of English Dialects* (Orton 1962, Orton et al. 1962–1971), focusing on traditional dialect speakers of English and presenting a detailed qualitative cross-section of dialect variation throughout the country. Many general descriptions of WelE, which also comment on regional distinctions, are to a great extent based on the results of *SAWD* (e.g. Thomas 1984, 1985, 1994, Penhallurick 1993). More recent descriptions avail of other work as well (e.g. Penhallurick 2008a, 2008b, 2007, 2012; Paulasto 2013c).

Studies describing the phonological, grammatical or lexical features of specific regional dialects of WelE are presented in Section 1.4 above and discussed in the relevant sections of this book. Some of them take a variationist perspective, combining regional and social variables. Mees (1977, 1983, 1987, 1990) studies the development of sociolinguistic competence in Cardiff schoolchildren's English, observing, for example, that social stratification in phonological variables can be observed at an early age, working class children using, for example, H-dropping or alveolar realization of *-ing* significantly more than middle class children. Interestingly, the glottal stop is a high prestige variant for /t/, however. Jones (1990a) examines the impact of Welsh in the English of five to seven-year-old children across Wales along the dimensions of region/type of school, gender, and the linguistic and social background of the parents. Welsh-induced features are found to occur most frequently in Welsh-speaking areas and mixed schools, while other variables are less influential. Paulasto's (2006, 2009, 2016, Pitkänen 2003) research on the morphosyntax of WelE is concerned with regional variation and (apparent-time) diachronic change in a number of contact-induced dialect features. Podhovnik (2008, 2010) examines variation based on age, gender and education in the phonology of Neath English. She finds that age is probably the most influential factor, but the direction of the shift may depend on the phoneme in question; in some cases the distinctive Welsh pronunciations are strengthened in the youngest generation's speech. Morris (2013) investigates cross-linguistic convergence in the phonology of Welsh–English bilinguals in North Wales through the variables of region (Caernarfon vs. Mold), home language (English vs. Welsh), and gender. Hejna's (2015) study on consonantal pre-aspiration in Aberystwyth English shows that this feature is not only affected by phonetic and phonological conditioning, but also by the gender and age of the speakers.

Some of Nikolas Coupland's extensive work on WelE dialect attitudes is discussed above, but another important streak in his research concerns variationist sociolinguistics in the Cardiff–southeast Valleys dialect areas. In Coupland (1988), he describes the linguistic features of Cardiff English but the real focus of his work is on the social significance of accent and dialect variation, which he argues should rather be seen as active social practice. He therefore examines how WelE speakers use stylistic shifting, stylization, and accommodation for the purpose of expressing, for example, solidarity, status, class, identity, or ethnicity. The contexts vary from local community settings, such as a Cardiff travel agency (1980, 1988, 2006), to more or less performative situations, for example, radio broadcasting (1985, 1988, 2001), political discussions (1990a), and a Christmas pantomime performed in the Valleys area (2006, 2009). The pluricentricity of post-devolution English in Wales, and the social semiotic and identity-forming resources of Valleys English, in particular, are also discussed by James (2011), who describes processes of codification (in the form of Lewis 2008) and mediatization (in the radio show by Chris Needs) as well as literary representations of the variety.

1.5.3 The Welshness of Welsh English

Coupland et al. (2006) present the results of a survey investigating the ethnolinguistic identification of the Welsh, that is, how strongly they affiliate with Wales and Welshness, with regard to their home region and self-assessed Welsh skills. The regions in this study are fourteen in total, but the authors also analyse their results with respect to previous cultural models of Wales, specifically those of Balsom (1985) and Aitchison and Carter (2004). Balsom's widely known "three-Wales model" distinguishes between Y Fro Gymraeg (the Welsh-speaking "heartlands"),

Welsh Wales (English-speaking and Welsh-identifying, the southeast Valleys and wider Swansea-Llanelli area) and British Wales (English-speaking and British-identifying, eastern Wales and south Pembrokeshire). Aitchison and Carter's two-cluster model divides the country into "inner" and "outer" Wales, in the footsteps of Bowen (1959 and 1964, cited in Pryce 1978). Coupland et al. (2006: 12–13) find, firstly, that any regional categorization of their results produces quite small differences between the respondents: they all affiliate positively with Welshness, the differences being merely a matter of "relative degrees of positivity". The authors therefore conclude that "all of Wales can plausibly be described as 'Y Fro Gymraeg', which might be to say that 'all of Wales is the real Wales'" (Coupland et al. 2006: 22). A comparison of Welshness and Welsh language competence, on the other hand, shows that there is a clear but not straightforward correlation between the two, as, for example, Carmarthenshire is both highly Welsh and highly Welsh-speaking, but Newport and Monmouthshire are highly Welsh despite being low in the informants' self-assessed Welsh competence (Coupland et al. 2006: 16–17). This variation is levelled when comparing competence groups instead of specific regions: high competence generally correlates with higher scores of ethnolinguistic identification and vice versa. The impact of region on national identification is also the subject of Evans (2007).

The perceived Welshness of regional varieties of WelE has been examined in dialect attitude surveys discussed in Section 1.5.1. above. There are few qualitative studies, however, where WelE speakers describe their affiliation towards the dialect. Paulasto (2014b) conducts a content analysis of a sample of the interviews that form the basis for the Llandybie, North Wales and Urban SAWD corpora (18 / 8 / 8 informants, respectively) with the aim to assess the impact of first language, region, and time (or age of the informants) on the emerging views. The Urban SAWD interviews, which Rob Penhallurick conducted in four Welsh cities in 1986, consist of phonological questionnaires as well as lengthy sociolinguistic interviews on the topics of local community and the Welsh and English languages. This inspired Heli Paulasto to use similar discussion topics in her own interviews in Llandybie and North Wales in 1999 and 2000. The analysis is based on a categorization used in dialect attitude research: cognitive, affective and behavioural factors (Garrett et al. 2003: 3), which in social identification research are known as knowledge, affiliation and practice (Coupland 2006: 23). Of these, we will here focus on affiliation, which emerges in the interviews under the topics of language and dialect attitudes. Here, unlike in the 2014 study, we will also be able to avail of the Tonypandy Corpus interviews.

An overarching conclusion is that the linguistic identification of both L1 Welsh and L1 English-speaking informants is in some way connected to the Welsh language. Informants in the first category identify Welsh as essential and constitutive to their linguistic identity, while their affiliation to English is instrumental: knowledge of English is appreciated and seen as useful although also as a threat to the Welsh language. If the informants do not speak Welsh, they nevertheless acknowledge its existence and hence usually explain why they do not speak it and how they feel about not speaking it. This is the case in the bilingual Llandybie and North Wales localities, at any rate. The Urban SAWD interviews from the 1980s stand out in displaying rather negative views towards the Welsh language, particularly in Grangetown, Cardiff. There are monoglot English informants in Grangetown as well as in Llandybie, who express the very same opinion: "I think every Welsh person should be able to speak their own language" (Urban SAWD, Grangetown: MR). The difference is that the middle-aged Cardiff informant is referring to English, while the young Llandybie informant recorded 13 years later is talking about Welsh. In TC (from 2012), on the other hand, Welsh has historical or school-related rather than present-day community-based relevance for the informants.

As for *Welsh English*, it is quite common that the informants do not know exactly how to interpret the term, when the interviewer introduces it into the conversation. It is not known to them, because it is barely used outside English linguistics, and so they will offer various interpretations. The Welsh accent is a familiar concept, of course, and tends to subsume grammatical and lexical features. The following extract from TC illustrates the informants' association of WelE with Welsh lexical influence, which they then proceed to discuss in more detail:

(1) [Well what about Welsh English then is there such a thing as Welsh English?]
A: I think so yeah . I think we sound differently and we got different phrases too.
B: We've got different words haven't we that originated in Welsh. (TC: 6b, 3c)

Some informants bring up the term Wenglish, describing it as a mixture of English and Welsh. Depending on the respondent, the term can refer either to English with Welsh input or, less frequently, to Welsh with English input. Whichever the case, Wenglish is mostly associated with the southeast Valleys, some people even pointing out that it originates from John Edwards's *Talk Tidy* books. In Llandybie, elderly informants describe English in Wales in terms of regional variation but also as a learner language phenomenon, which shows how unfamiliar it used to be in the community (e.g. "they were piecing together the English words" [about her mother's generation] and "...we struggled on with our broken English"; LC: 1a).

Dialect attitudes are discussed fairly little in the 1980s Urban SAWD corpus. The Grangetown informants, however, state that the Welsh accent is made fun of sometimes and that people complained about radio presenter Frank Hennessy's accent when he first started on CBC (Cardiff Broadcasting Company). Cardiff English is described as terrible at its worst, yet it is pointed out that many locals are very proud of it. The dialect is, in other words, sufficient for creating a regional identity and Welsh is not needed for this purpose. Positive attitudes towards WelE seem to increase towards the 2000s in light of these corpora as well as of the surveys mentioned above. Although London English is considered "proper" in LC, the Welsh accent is seen as having positive qualities, too. Several informants in LC, NWC and TC mention that they have been complimented for their Welsh accent or that they are quite proud of it; this includes some L1 Welsh speakers, too.

(2) I used to erm, feel like erm- nothin' serious but you know, feel like they were laughing at you an' like,
[Yeah.]
you know, you're a country bumpkin if you've got a Welsh accent, you know, [*>Mm.]
we're all<* sort of flocked together. But now I feel more proud, you know. I don' know whether it's to do with getting older or whether, you know, like I was sayin' that it's a cool thing to be, you know. (NWC: 6c)

Exceptions are, for example, an L1 English LC informant, who dislikes her south Welsh accent, and a young L1 Welsh speaker who does not think that the Welsh accent is anything to be proud of, the Welsh language is. The latter reaction reflects the young, Welsh-medium-educated speakers' pride in Welsh and their awareness of a personal responsibility for its survival (see, e.g. Coupland et al. 2005).

Perhaps it is not surprising that it is the L1 English informants from Tonypandy who make the most perceptive observations on regional, stylistic and diachronic variation in WelE. Cardiff, Newport and Swansea are all considered completely different from the Rhondda, of course, but to the informants, the local accent is also distinct from the "posh" accent just a few miles south, whereas the "top of the Rhondda is more Welshy" (TC: 6b).

(3) A: you don't hear the Rhondda until you come to Dinas
B: they live the other side of Pontypridd and
[okay]
B: and you can (em)
C: once you get on the bus in Porth
B: and they they don't sound like us

[...]
B: like there's . certain words and like you know the (em) chocolate sweets Rollos
C: (mm)
B: what do you
C: we say /roːlo/
B: /roːlo/ we say /roːlo/
A: /roːlo/
C: /roːlo/
B: but my nieces will say . *>/rəʊləʊ/
C: /rəʊləʊ/<*
[yeah . yeah]
B: /rəʊləʊ/ they sound posh don't they compared to us /roːlo/ you know /roːlo/ (TC: 3a, 6b, 3c)

Informant 6b also expresses a strong linguistic self-esteem and an awareness of regional norms and prestige despite being critical of her grammar and accent. "It's complicated, isn't it."

(4) and we do tease the headmaster you know . about it and say oh you- you know . like the the food shop the co-op and he says "co-op" and I say "no . come on now you're in Tonypandy and you've gotta call it the cop" .
[<laughter>]
you know and things . you- I say "you wish you sounded like me wish you s-" . you know . to think "well hey what's wrong then why am I trying to sound like you you try and sound like me" . so
[Right]
it's just that . it's more than language isn't it it's the . the thing we've got in the Rhondda that we think (em) oh everybody's better than us and we are down there but we're not. (TC: 6b)

1.6 Corpora and resources used in the present volume

This section focuses on the research data utilized in the present volume. Further details about some of the survey and corpus data can also be found in association with the relevant chapters. Other Welsh English corpora and resources, which have been used in previous research or which can potentially be availed of for linguistic analysis, are presented in Chapter 6.

1.6.1 Welsh English data

The linguistic description of WelE in this book is partly based on previous research, but more essentially, it is based on new research, which the authors have conducted on corpus and survey data. The variationist descriptions of WelE morphosyntax in Chapter 3 and discourse features in Section 4.4 rely primarily on corpus evidence, especially on the transcribed interview corpora complied by Heli Paulasto during 1995–2012 in different parts of Wales. These corpora are, as of yet, not publicly available. We also avail of interview data stored at the SAWD archives in the care of Rob Penhallurick at Swansea University. These have typically not been transcribed in full, or there are only manual transcriptions of the data available.

As sociolinguistic interviews, Paulasto's corpora are not suited for the study of lexicon. Chapter 4 on WelE lexis is hence largely based on the survey data in *SAWD*, the linguistic commentaries of the BBC *Voices* interviews, and lexical surveys carried out by the present authors in Gwent and the Rhondda. The chapter on phonology is based on survey data, more specifically *SAWD*, the Millennium Memory Bank (MMB), and *Voices*.

The recordings span six decades, from the 1960s to the 2010s. Our informants have kindly given their consent at the time of the recordings that the data can be used for academic research. Our aim is to ensure that the data are utilized in an ethically sound manner. The corpus data, including any personal information on the informants, are stored and protected in accordance with the General Data Protection Regulation of the European Union (2016/679) pertaining to scientific research purposes. The examples and extracts provided in this volume have been pseudonymized but, through sociolinguistic necessity, they may contain some indirect personal information, such as the locality of the speaker or their first language.

The corpora and surveys referred to in the linguistic analyses are described in detail below. Further information on the compilation of SAWD, MMB, and *Voices* is available in Chapter 6.

The Llandybie corpus (LC)

Heli Paulasto conducted sociolinguistic interviews in Llandybie, Carmarthenshire, in the years 1995, 1999 and 2000, in order to investigate grammatical features of present-day WelE and changes in apparent time. The informants are thus men and women aged 18–84 and the interviews are fairly informal in style. Despite the close proximity of Swansea and the surrounding suburban area, Llandybie (along with Carmarthenshire on the whole) is fairly Welsh-speaking (62.3%

Welsh in 2001; Aitchison and Carter 2004: 151). The majority of Paulasto's informants, too, are L1 Welsh bilinguals. The corpus represents southwestern WelE with a noticeable Welsh substrate at the community level as well as some idiolectal transfer from the speakers' L1 Welsh.

Paulasto has transcribed the corpus in full, a total of 257,500 words. In order to investigate apparent-time change, the corpus has been divided into four age groups based on the birth years of the informants:

Table 1.5: Age groups in the Llandybie Corpus.

Age group I:	11 informants, b. 1915–1928	52,000 words
Age group II:	13 informants, b. 1933–1949	85,000 words
Age group III:	12 informants, b. 1950–1965	63,100 words
Age group IV:	10 informants, b. 1971–1981	57,400 words
Total	**46 informants**	**257,500 words**

The age groups are somewhat heterogeneous. Firstly, although L1 Welsh-speakers are in the majority in all groups, the numbers of L1 English speakers vary from zero in Age group I to five in Age group III. Only three informants in the corpus are non-Welsh-speaking, that is, they assess that they have no conversational competence in the language although they may have receptive competence. Secondly, the informants' ages correlate on average with their levels of education: the older the informant, the less educated. This influences the speakers' capacity for stylistic shifting in an interview situation. For further information, see Paulasto (2006: 141–146).

The North Wales corpus (NWC)

Heli Paulasto collected the North Wales corpus in 2000 to align with LC, but instead of one locality, it encompasses interviews conducted in four North Welsh towns and villages: Pencaenewydd, Llwyngwril, Llanuwchllyn and Ruthin (see Paulasto 2006: 146–148). The localities are spread out in different parts of the north, and they vary in size and percentages of Welsh speakers (from 41% in Llwyngwril to 85% in Llanuwchllyn in 2001). The informants are 23 in total, with just 4–7 informants per locality, which means that the main purpose of NWC is to offer a broad overview of northern WelE rather than to represent the dialect of each specific village.

The informants in each locality are of varying ages, from 16 to 85 overall. The corpus comprises 120,000 words in total, about half the size of LC, which leaves some age groups rather too small for the purposes of apparent-time research. NWC can be used as a reference corpus for LC, however.

Table 1.6: Age groups in the North Wales Corpus.

Age group I:	6 informants, b. 1915–1928	31,100 words
Age group II:	5 informants, b. 1938–1945	27,900 words
Age group III:	8 informants, b. 1950–1968	44,400 words
Age group IV:	4 informants, b. 1970–1984	16,600 words
Total	23 informants	120,000 words

All informants in NWC are bilingual, and only four of them speak Welsh as their L2. In the oldest age group, all informants are L1 Welsh speakers, but they differ from the respective cohort in LC in one significant respect: four of the six informants have received a college or university education and worked in middle-class professions. The formal education is reflected in their English, which is in many ways more standard than that of either younger NWC speakers or elderly Llandybie or Tonypany informants (for the impact of the mode of acquisition, see Paulasto 2009).

The Tonypandy corpus (TC)

The Tonypandy corpus was collected by Heli Paulasto in the village of Tonypandy in the Rhondda (Rhondda Cynon Taff in southeast Wales) in 2012 and transcribed by research assistant Marja Kilpiö in 2014–2015. The corpus totals 49,800 words. Although it is comparable in style to LC and NWC, it also involves a section on dialect lexicon, which is modelled on the BBC *Voices* Language Lab and Radio Wales questionnaires and hence compatible with the British dialect data. The ten informants are men and women aged 43 to 84, that is, based on their years of birth, comparable to the LC and NWC age groups II and III. The informants assess themselves to be monoglot English speakers: although many of them have limited formally acquired Welsh skills, they do not speak Welsh in the community, nor has it been spoken in their families beyond some words and phrases. This is typically the case in the locality; Welsh speakers in Rhondda Cynon Taff amount to 12.3% in the census of 2011 (Office for National Statistics).

The Survey of Anglo-Welsh Dialects corpus (SAWD)

Some of the older research materials used in this book arise from recorded Survey of Anglo-Welsh Dialects interviews, housed at Swansea University in the care of Rob Penhallurick. SAWD was designed to complement the Survey of English Dialects (SED), directed from the University of Leeds from the 1940s onwards by Eugen Dieth and Harold Orton. Both surveys were interested in the history of the English language – in researching its most traditional features as found in older speakers in rural communities. Parry (1999) contains a detailed summary as well as a phonetic and phonemic analysis of material collected between 1968–1982 from this group in 92 localities throughout Wales. This material is set out at greater length in the original data-volumes of *SAWD*, which are Parry (1977, 1979), covering the Southeast and Southwest of Wales, respectively, and Penhallurick (1991), dealing with North Wales.

As SAWD is based on the SED method of research (Orton 1962), the informants are local to the area, elderly, rural men and women, and the interviews follow a lengthy questionnaire aimed to elicit dialect phonology and lexicon. Questions on morphosyntactic features amount to some 20% of all items in the questionnaire, but the interviews, including discussions on the questionnaire items and other incidental material, can be examined with an eye on structural characteristics. The selection of the informants roughly follows the language situation in each locality: in highly Welsh-speaking localities, the informants are L1 Welsh bilinguals, while in Anglicized regions they are L1 English speakers (Parry 1999: 1–7). SAWD is considered to represent conservative, traditional dialects of WelE. Although these dialects are disappearing today along with their speakers, they give important insights into the history and development of WelE. For more information on the compilation of the survey, see Chapter 6.

The SAWD interviews have not been transcribed in their entirety. The original SAWD data are therefore used rather restrictedly as a reference corpus, and much of the morphosyntactic research is based on a small sample of 26,500 words, transcribed by Heli Paulasto. The localities are nine: Llanfair-Talhaiarn, Trelawnyd, Botwnnog, Ynys, and Fron-Goch in North Wales, and Llanon, Tregaron, Drefach and Lampeter, and Camrose in Southwest Wales. Because of the highly structured, questionnaire-based interviews, particularly in North Wales (see Paulasto 2006: 150), the quantitative results are not always comparable with corpora with less formal methods of data collection, such as Paulasto's interview corpora, or corpora used in other studies, including the Freiburg English Dialect Corpus (FRED) or the Radio Wales Corpus (RWC, Roller 2016; see Chapter 6).

Additional references are made to Paulasto's notes of the recorded SAWD interviews, which arise from a larger set of data (estimated word count of 275,000 words), compiled for the purposes of Paulasto's post-graduate research (see Paulasto 2006: 149–151). This data set has not been transcribed in total, however.

The Urban Survey of Anglo-Welsh Dialects corpus (Urban SAWD)

The Urban SAWD corpus, also housed at Swansea University, was designed as a sequel for SAWD, but with a more sociolinguistically orientated method of approach: the focus is on four urban localities in different parts of the country (Grangetown in Cardiff, Carmarthen, Caernarfon and Wrexham) and the informants are males and females of varying ages, from 12 to 82. The interviews are much less formal in style, the informants discussing their personal histories along with the localities and their language situations. They also contain a phonological word list.

The corpus was collected by Rob Penhallurick in 1986, and in 2003 Heli Paulasto's research assistant Minna Korhonen transcribed a sample of 36,600 words (of the estimated total of 160,000 words) for Paulasto's post-graduate research, not including the word list sections (see Paulasto 2006: 151–153). The transcriptions were completed during 2014–2016 by another research assistant, Marja Kilpiö, at the University of Eastern Finland. The full Urban SAWD corpus has not been utilized in the present linguistic description, however, and thus remains a future resource.

The Ceri George corpus (CGC)

Ceri George collected her interview corpus in the Rhondda in the early 1980s for her doctoral dissertation (George 1990). Her focus was on the regional dialect and lexicon, but the interviews are much more informal in style than those in SAWD. The informants are elderly men and women from various villages in the Rhondda valleys. George's original hand-written transcriptions of the interviews are held by Rob Penhallurick at the SAWD archives at Swansea University, but they have not been digitized. A sample of c. 30,050 words is used in this book to represent an earlier variety of Rhondda English (cf. the Tonypandy corpus below). These data come from four localities: Ton Pentre, Blaenrhondda, Wattstown, and Treorchy. The word count has been extrapolated from every fifth page of the hand-written transcriptions. The archives also contain 50 separate files of George's original fieldwork recordings, but these have not been availed of in the present volume.

The BBC Voices in Wales (Voices)

This set of data consists of interviews compiled for BBC *Voices* in Wales. *Voices* was a survey carried out in 2004–2005 under academic guidance, and it included audio recordings of local speakers made by the BBC's regional radio departments throughout the UK. *Voices of the UK* (2009–2012) was a British Library project which processed, analysed, and made publicly available the audio recordings of BBC *Voices* (see Penhallurick 2013). The recordings approach casual conversations rather than interviews: the informants discuss the given topics in groups, but they are also aware of being recorded for radio, which adds to the formality of the situation to some degree. In addition to dialect attitudes and experiences, the interviews centre on a set of lexical prompts designed to elicit regionally varying responses. Recordings, lasting an hour on average, have been made in 23 (mostly urban) localities: 9 in the North, 3 in Mid-Wales, and 11 in the South (see Section 2.1 and Chapter 6 for details). The first languages of the informants vary, roughly in accordance with the language situations of the localities. The selection of the informants has not always been monitored to a tee. Thus, for example, the Holyhead group includes a Rhondda man, adding Rhondda expressions into the mix, and the Talbot Green informants are travelling show people who reside in the area but only one of whom was born there. These kinds of discrepancies have been taken into account when examining the findings.

The data that have been available for the present volume consist of transcribed linguistic commentaries from 22 of the localities, excepting Tal-y-bont. Thirteen of the commentaries account for phonology and grammar features in addition to the lexical sets. The audio files are also available for inspection at the British Library Sounds archive (British Library Sounds 2009).

Even in its non-transcribed form, the corpus is highly useful for phonological description and allows for observations on the use or non-use of morphosyntactic and lexical dialect features in different part of Wales. For further information, see Penhallurick (2013) and Chapters 2 and 6.

Millennium Memory Bank (MMB)

MMB is a massive oral history project launched by BBC Radio and the British Library and carried out in the UK in 1998–1999 (Perks 2001: 95–96; Roller 2016: 81). It consists of 640 half-hour radio documentaries, which were compiled through interviews with over 6,000 British people aged five to 107, both male (56%) and female (44%), and with diverse ethnic and socio-economic backgrounds (British Library Sounds 2009). A total of 196 interviews with 280 informants have been recorded in Wales (Roller 2016: 82). In the phonology chapter, we will avail of linguistic commentaries of the MMB audio recordings, written by

Jonnie Robinson between 2004–2007 in connection with his work on the British Library's *Sounds Familiar?* and *Sounds* web-pages.

Only five of the Welsh interviews are publicly available in the online British Library Sounds Archive, but the remainder can be accessed at the British Library on request. The online recordings are accompanied by linguistic descriptions, drawing attention to accent and dialect features, but the interviews have not been transcribed in full. For further information, see Chapters 2 and 6.

1.6.2 Comparison corpora

Quantitative results drawn from WelE corpora are on some occasions compared against EngE or BrE corpus evidence. The following two corpora are central.

The Survey of English Dialects Spoken Corpus (SED)

The SED Spoken Corpus represents the traditional rural dialects of England. The corpus (478,700 words) comprises interviews with 298 elderly rural informants from all parts of England and the Isle of Man, born 1863–1909. The recordings were collected in connection with the *Survey of English Dialects* in the 1950s and 1960s (Orton 1962, Orton et al. 1962–1971) and continued until 1974, but they are not based on a questionnaire format. Rather, they contain informal, spontaneous conversations and/or interviews on "personal reminiscences or opinions, or [...] some task connected with the speaker's occupation, e.g. ploughing, harvesting, hedging," etc. (Klemola & Jones 1999: 18). The data are therefore similar in style to LC, NWC and TC (for further information, see Klemola and Jones 1999). The orthographic transcriptions carried out by Mark Jones at the University of Leeds in 1997 remain unpublished, but they were accessed through Juhani Klemola. The audio files are available at the British Library (see BL Sounds 2009).

The SED corpus serves two important functions. Firstly, it represents the historical EngE vernacular strand, which has influenced the development of varieties of WelE, particularly in the long-standing English regions but also in the more recently Anglicized areas. Up until the mid-twentieth century, traditional dialects were slow to change (Ihalainen 1994: 205, 251). Thus, as convincingly shown by Klemola (2002: 200–203), the SED data can be said to reflect EngE dialects of a much earlier period, projecting the vernacular of the nineteenth century and the time when the English language became established in Wales (Thomas 1994: 100). Secondly, the SED corpus sets a point of comparison for the elderly WelE speakers born in the early decades of the twentieth century and reveals to what extent the regional dialect features are, indeed, distinctive of WelE.

International Corpus of English Great Britain (ICE-GB)

ICE-GB is the British component in the series of corpora aimed at illustrating standard spoken and written varieties of English around the world. Each corpus consists of c. 1,000,000 words, that is, 500 sample texts of c. 2,000 words, drawn from a variety of sub-genres (see ICE Project 2009). The studies in the present volume mainly utilise the spoken sections of ICE-GB (S1A–S2B; 528,500 words) or, more specifically, the private dialogues (S1A), which are reasonably compatible with the WelE corpora. ICE-Ireland and ICE-India are also used as comparison corpora as regards some features in Chapter 3.

2 Phonetics and phonology

2.1 Introduction

This chapter on the phonetics and phonology of WelE presents a breakdown of the phonemic system of the variety taken as a whole, followed by discussion of the more striking regional and social variants of the vowel and consonant phonemes (with an emphasis on describing the geographical distributions of the variants), and concluding with a brief overview of WelE prosody.

The chief data sources used are surveys of spoken English in Wales done on a national scale, these being:
- the Survey of Anglo-Welsh Dialects (SAWD), which was carried out between 1968–1990;
- the Millennium Memory Bank (MMB), for which material was collected in 1998–1999;
- and the BBC *Voices* survey of 2004–2005.

Selected other sources are also drawn upon, such as Collins and Mees (1990), Connolly (1990), Tench (1990), Penhallurick (1994), Mees and Collins (1999), and Stefano Quaino's doctoral dissertation (2011) on the intonation of WelE in mid-west and northwest Wales. In this context, WelE is understood as the English spoken in Wales by lifelong residents, taking the speech of the older age-group investigated by SAWD as a baseline and using the later MMB and *Voices* information in order to offer indications of continuity and change as well as to provide an updated view of current usages. The selected other sources are used for further particulars and clarification. The data gathered by the national surveys above, although extensive, does not permit statistical analysis, so the patterns deduced from it must be framed as in some measure provisional, although not without authority. This chapter does not look into how the features of WelE are developing in the newer immigrant-based communities of Wales, a subject awaiting greater attention.

The main published SAWD sources used here are Parry (1977, 1979, 1999) and Penhallurick (1991). Penhallurick (1994) was not a part of the SAWD project, but is a history of one of the oldest dialects of WelE, that is, the English of the Gower Peninsula, and we have drawn upon it occasionally here. In addition, we have used an unpublished work by David Parry, completed in 2015, which reworks and refines Parry (1999). We are grateful to David Parry for making this valuable volume available to us.

The MMB and BBC *Voices* material was provided by Jonnie Robinson and his team in the sociolinguistics section of the British Library. We have here divided

the MMB localities into three broad regional groups in order to facilitate concise statements about the geographical distributions of features exhibited in the data. The localities and groups are:
- North Wales: Bangor, Bethesda, Llanwnda, Trefor;
- Mid Wales: Aberhosan, Rhayader;
- South Wales: Aberbeeg, Aberporth, Brynamman, Cardiff, Cwmfelinfach, Gorseinon, Maerdy, Monmouth, Mumbles, Mynydd-y-Garreg, Newport (Monmouthshire), Resolven, Swansea, Tremorfa (Cardiff).

Just under half of these are urban localities: Bangor, Rhayader, Cardiff, Gorseinon, Monmouth, Newport, Swansea, and Tremorfa. The remainder qualify as villages, although Bethesda is large for a village, and Mumbles is very close to the city of Swansea.

In the present chapter, we have also used phonological descriptions completed in 2010 by the *Voices of the UK* team (Holly Gilbert, Jon Herring, and Jonnie Robinson) for 12 Welsh localities in which audio recordings were made of contemporary WelE, all age-groups, for BBC *Voices*. These localities in their regional groups are:
- North Wales: Bethesda, Flint, Holyhead, Rhos-on-Sea;
- Mid Wales: Builth Wells, Newtown, Tregaron;
- South Wales: Bonymaen (Swansea), Llanelli, Risca, Splott (Cardiff), Treorchy.

With the exception of Bethesda (arguably) and Tregaron, these are all urban localities. We are grateful to Jonnie Robinson for his help in answering our queries about the MMB and *Voices* materials.

The core material on which this chapter is based can accordingly be divided into two sets:
- data collected from the 60-plus age-group between 1968–1982;
- and data collected from 18-to-80-year-olds at the turn of the twentieth and twenty-first centuries.

While there is some continuity of approach between these two sets, some other differences (in addition to the age profiles) need to be borne in mind. The large SAWD locality network was rural and the later surveys were more urban than rural, and their localities fewer in number. SAWD fieldworkers were trained in linguistics and phonetics, whereas MMB and *Voices* fieldworkers were BBC journalists, their interviews were shorter and less formally structured, and their informants generally more familiar with the experience of being audio-recorded. The material obtained by the later surveys was consequently smaller in amount and arguably more casual in style, though the lengthy SAWD interviews often garnered much casual-style pronunciation data. Although all of the MMB and *Voices* informants were recorded in their respective localities, informant criteria such as lifelong residence and their being born in the locality were less rigorously applied compared with SAWD. This affects the informant profiles of Llanelli and Risca to the extent that information from these localities has been scrutinized with added caution in compiling the present chapter. Finally, compared with other dialect surveys generally, MMB and *Voices* did not attempt to ensure that carefully defined social groups (according to class, age, sex, or ethnicity, for example) were equally represented in the sampling. The method might be described as a rather informal judgement sample, though one in which the biographical details of the informants are usually amply noted.

What the present chapter aims to do is to provide a comprehensive overview, with plenty of detail, of late-twentieth-century to early-twenty-first-century WelE pronunciation using these and other sources. The overview is an amalgam of information, and the detail also often synthesizes a selection of source evidence.

2.2 The phonemic system of Welsh English

The inventory below lists the vowel and consonant phonemes of present-day WelE, treating the variety as a national entity. It is based on information distilled from the core and other sources used in this chapter, particularly Parry (2015, unpublished, especially pp. 6, 12–26), the MMB data, and the *Voices of the UK* data.

Short vowels:	/ɪ ɛ a ă ɒ ʊ/
Long vowels:	/iː eː ɛː œː aː ɔː oː uː/
Diphthongs:	/ɪu ai au ɔi uə iə/
Unstressed vowels:	/i ɪ ə/
Consonants:	/p b t d k g f v θ ð ɬ s z ʃ ʒ x h tʃ dʒ m n ŋ l w j r r̥/

A minimal-pair elicitation tool was not used in any of the core national surveys drawn upon in the present chapter. However, the number of phonological keywords that underpins Parry's phonemicizations (1999, 2015) is nearly 150, with over 13,000 tokens in 92 localities, and the MMB and *Voices of the UK* commentaries use Wells's lexical sets (1982) to categorize their data. So while the inventory above could be characterized as awaiting further confirmation, it is based on substantial evidence and evaluation. That said, there are points in the analysis that are to an extent open to debate.

A case could be made for replacing /eː/ and /oː/ with /ei/ and /ou/, respectively, or even for including all four, an issue which is discussed further in 2.4 below, under the keywords FACE/STAY and GOAT/SNOW. A possible alternative to /œː/

would be /ɜː/, or even /e̞ː/, for which see NURSE, below. There is a hint of a developing case for adding /ɑː/ to the list of WelE phonemes; see BATH, PALM, and START. And Parry (2015: 11) reports that /iə/ and /uə/ exist only marginally in WelE, a view for which there is a degree of support in the newer data.

The inventory given here also differs in some respects from those offered in Penhallurick (2004a, 2007, 2008a). The earlier models had /ʌ/ where the present one has /ä/. This follows Parry's (2015) decision to indicate the centralized quality of this STRUT vowel in WelE compared to the /ʌ/ of RP. Earlier /ɔ/ has been replaced by /ɒ/, in light of Parry (2015), MMB, and *Voices*, but this is more a transcription choice than anything else. Earlier /oə/ has been replaced by /uə/, because of evidence from MMB and *Voices*, though there is more to say on this choice, for which see CURE, below. The inventory of unstressed vowels follows the simple versions of Penhallurick (2004a, 2008a) rather than the more ornate version of Penhallurick (2007). There is fuller discussion of the WelE unstressed vowels below.

Among the consonants, /ɬ/ and /x/ occur in WelE only in some loanwords from the Welsh language, and in Welsh personal and place names.

The next list matches the vowel phonemes above with the lexical sets introduced by Wells (1982) and augmented in Foulkes and Docherty (1999). Following Penhallurick (2004a, 2007, 2008a), STAY and SNOW have been added for comparison with FACE and GOAT, respectively. In the list below, the vowels for STAY and SNOW are not given phonemic status, so as to remain consistent with the system above. More keywords have also been appended to the list in order to elucidate some significant aspects of WelE phonology further, especially the lexical distribution of certain phonemes and variants. These additional keywords are: ONE, BOAR, POWER, FIRE, EARS, TUESDAY, STARTED, and MORNING.

2.3 Distribution of the WelE vowel phonemes in the standard lexical sets

KIT	ɪ
DRESS	ɛ
TRAP	a
LOT	ɒ
STRUT	ä
ONE	ä ~ ɒ
FOOT	ʊ
BATH	a ~ aː
CLOTH	ɒ
NURSE	œː
FLEECE	iː

FACE	eː
STAY	ei
GOAT	oː
SNOW	ou
PALM	aː
THOUGHT	ɔː
GOOSE	uː
PRICE	ai
CHOICE	ɔi
MOUTH	au
START	aː
NORTH	ɔː
FORCE	ɔː
BOAR	ɔː
SQUARE	ɛː
CURE	ɪuwə ~ uə > ɔː
POWER	auwə ~ auə
FIRE	aijə
NEAR	iə
EARS	iə ~ œː
TUESDAY	ɪu
happY	i
lettER	ə
horsES	ɪ
commA	ə
startED	ɪ
mornING	ɪ

The detail of the lexical distribution and incidence of the WelE vowel phonemes and their variants is presented in Section 2.4 below. Discussion of the characteristic WelE variants of the consonant phonemes follows in Section 2.5.

2.4 Vowels

In this section, the WelE vowel phonemes and their variants are discussed at greater length according to the categories provided by the standard lexical sets. We show how the phonemes are distributed through the sets, we discuss the variants that realize and constitute the phonemes (including some discussion of the judgements that have been made in arriving at the phonemic inventory), and we give an overview of the regional and (to some extent) social distribution of the variants in the dialects of WelE. The aim in each part of the discussion is to present a view of contemporary usages, as far as the data allows, but real-time comparisons are sometimes made, involving the older and more recent sets of data.

2.4.1 Stressed vowels

KIT

The realization of the vowel phoneme in KIT words throughout Wales is [ɪ], with little variation apart from the very occasional lowered or centralized version.

DRESS

Similarly, the realization of DRESS is consistently [ɛ].

TRAP

Across Wales the realization of the vowel phoneme in TRAP words tends to be [a]. In the older data (SAWD), other variants are found in the longer-established Anglicized areas: a raised [æ] is recorded in rural Mid Wales where the county of Powys borders with the English counties of Shropshire and Hereford; a back [ɑ] is recorded in the Gower Peninsula, south Pembrokeshire, and a couple of other localities; and a long [aː > æː] and weak diphthong [aə] are attested sporadically along the mid-to-southern Border country and in south Pembrokeshire.

LOT, CLOTH

The chief realization in LOT and CLOTH words is [ɒ], and this is the symbol used by Parry (2015) for his phonemic designation, though [ɔ] is a transcription often favoured in the SAWD data-volumes. MMB has one southeast locality (Aberbeeg) where /ɒ/ varies with unrounded [ɑ], and SAWD records this once in the north. Some words which have the short LOT/CLOTH [ɒ] vowel in current mainstream RP but an <a> in their spelling, such as *quarry*, *wanted*, *wash*, and *wasps*, can have [a > æ], or occasionally [aː ~ ɑ ~ ɑː], in WelE. Such forms are recorded only in the north in the more recent data, but in all regions by SAWD. These could be spelling pronunciations influenced by Welsh-language conventions (orthographic <wa> is pronounced [wa] in Welsh), but [a ~ æ > aː ~ æː ~ ɑ ~ ɑː] vowels were also recorded widely by the Survey of English Dialects.

STRUT

In STRUT there is a widespread tendency in all the data to a vowel raised and centralized compared with RP /ʌ/, to the extent that [ə] is a very common variant. Similarly, in unstressed syllables in WelE there is variation that ranges between [ʌ] and [ə]. In RP, by comparison, /ʌ/ is restricted to stressed syllables and /ə/ to unstressed. Wells (1982 vol. 2: 380) speaks of the "STRUT-Schwa Merger" in WelE, that is to say, the lack of phonemic distinction between /ʌ/ and /ə/. Parry (2015) consequently opts for /ʌ̈/ as the phonemic designation for STRUT vowels. The Welsh language has no /ʌ/ phoneme, but it does have /ə/, and this might be the reason behind both the centralizing tendency in STRUT and the obscuring of the phonemic distinction between /ʌ/ and /ə/.

Also, [ʊ] can occur in STRUT words, and is recorded mostly in the northeast corner of Wales in both older and newer data, and in the southwest corner in only the older material. The northeast occurrences can be readily explained by the presence of the well-known northern English [ʊ] in STRUT in neighbouring Cheshire. The southwest occurrences, mainly in south Pembrokeshire, an area subject to Anglicizing influences since the twelfth century, are more mysterious. They could result from historical connections with southwest England, but as Parry (1999: 18) points out, there is only a small amount of evidence of [ʊ] in STRUT words in the traditional accents of Cornwall, Devon and Somerset. There are also some occurrences scattered across Wales of [ɤ] in STRUT.

ONE

Wells (1982 vol. 2: 362) notes that *one* and other words which have /ʌ/ in RP and an <o> in their spelling (for example, *none, nothing, once, wonderful*), have /ɒ/ as their stressed vowel across a wide band of the mid-north of England. Similarly, in Wales ONE words at times fall in with the LOT/CLOTH groups, though more often they belong with STRUT. ONE with [ɒ ~ ɔ > a] is found across Wales, but is more common in the north. There are two likely causes for these forms: influence from nearby accents of English English; and spelling pronunciations encouraged by Welsh-language convention for pronouncing <o>. We could reasonably assume that the former cause has more effect in the areas with a longer history of Anglicization, and that the latter plays a greater part in the traditional Welsh-speaking areas.

FOOT

By far the most common realization of FOOT words is [ʊ]. Sometimes, in the north and south, unrounded [ɤ] is recorded, and sometimes in SAWD material, in Mid Wales and the longer-Anglicized southeast and southwest, a long [uː] occurs. There are also instances of "hypercorrect" [Ä > ə] in FOOT words in the older data, particularly in the northwest, east Mid Wales, and the southwest. Such instances that occur in traditional Welsh-speaking areas, in the northwest and southwest, are all of FOOT words with orthographic <u> (*bull, butcher, put, sugar*), and these might conceivably be spelling pronunciations. The instances elsewhere (east Mid Wales, the far southwest corner) might be linked with traditional [ʌ ~ ə]-forms in west and southwest of England accents.

BATH

The BATH lexical set as defined in Wells (1982 vol. 1: 133–134) can interweave with the TRAP, PALM, and START sets. Broadly speaking, in terms of WelE phonetics, there is variation in these sets between open short and long vowels, and between open front and back vowels, with the further possibility of the raising of the front vowels. One might also anticipate some rhoticity in START. In BATH words, this variation can be summarized as [a ~ aː ~ ɑː > ɑ]. In MMB and *Voices* data, the following regional trends show up in BATH: [a] dominates in the north; [a] varies with [aː] in Mid Wales, and [ɑː] occurs also to a lesser extent; in the south, [a] is marginally more common than [aː], with [ɑː] a firmer presence than in Mid and North Wales. In SAWD data, there is competition between the short forms [a > æ > ɑ] and the long forms [aː > ɑː > æː], with [a] the most common realization, occurring in all regions. Of the long realizations, [aː] is also fairly common, while [ɑː] and [æː] are less so and tend towards the mid borders. Surprisingly, there is also some rhoticity in the SAWD data in BATH, in the form of *r*-colouring, again along the mid borders. Taking all of this information into consideration, the general picture is of a contest between short [a] (affected by regional English English and perhaps Welsh-inspired spelling pronunciations) and long [aː] (maybe indicating movement towards RP, in terms of length), with a significant minority of back [ɑː] vowels. This last form signifies influence from neighbouring English English accents in the older data, and maybe amplified RP-influence in the newer data. What is missing from the data overall is detail on whether incidence of long back [ɑː] increases in keeping with higher social class and greater formality of speech style. On the basis of the BATH set alone, we can see that any phonemic distinctions along the lines of /a/, /aː/, /ɑː/ mask an apparently fluid situation. Add in information from TRAP, and a phonemic distinction between short and long vowels in this array looks feasible, though not between the front and back vowels. This discussion is continued under PALM and START, below.

NURSE

A well-known realization of NURSE identified with the southern region of WelE is the long, rounded, centralized-front, half-open [œː]. There is no simple explanation for this realization, although it might mark an intermediate stage between WelE stressed /ə/ + /r/ and RP long /ɜː/, the NURSE group being one of several subject to rhoticity in WelE. Parry (1999: 21; 2015: 89–125) shows that this [œː] realization is not exclusive to the south, but occurs throughout Wales. This is corroborated somewhat by MMB and *Voices* data, which shows it more often in the south than elsewhere. However, its main competitor, [əː], which is also widespread, is notably absent in SAWD data from the mid-southeast (especially the Rhondda Valleys), the area most associated in the public mind with [œː], though *Voices* indicates some competition between the two variants in Treorchy and Risca. Collins and Mees (1990), for Cardiff, and Connolly (1990), for Port Talbot, prefer to designate the rounded vowel as [øː], that is, they assign it a closer articulation. There is actually variation between the MMB and *Voices* commentaries in this: [ø:] is preferred in MMB, [œ:] in *Voices*. Robert Mayr (2010) carried out a precise examination of the acoustic and articulatory characteristics of this WelE variant of NURSE, concluding that [ø: ~ œ:], "rather than being a front rounded monophthong with reduced lip rounding, is, in fact, a monophthong with the acoustic characteristics of an unrounded front vowel that is not actually altogether unrounded" (Mayr 2010: 108). His acoustic analysis also favoured a close-mid height designation. Accordingly, he recommended that it be represented by [e̞:].

Rhoticity in the forms /ər/ and *r*-colouring of [ə], that is, [ɚ], also occurs occasionally in NURSE in the older data. The latter type, [ɚ], is found in the long-Anglicized southern borders, south Pembrokeshire, and south Gower, doubtless having travelled there from western accents of English English. *Voices* also records this in Newtown, Mid Wales, not far from the border with England. Examples of the former type, /ər/, are less common, and sometimes occur in Mid Wales, outside these long-Anglicized parts, where the likely cause is influence from Welsh-language convention – orthographic <r> is always articulated in Welsh. There is more on forms of rhoticity in subsection 2.5.4, below.

FLEECE

The realization of the vowel phoneme in FLEECE words throughout Wales is [i:], though [iə] is recorded a scattered number of times in SAWD, often but not exclusively in Mid Wales.

FACE/STAY and GOAT/SNOW

The variation that occurs in the FACE and GOAT lexical sets in WelE is fairly complex. Penhallurick (1993, 2004a, 2007, 2008a) attempted to draw out the regional patterns by means of adding two more lexical sets, STAY and SNOW, for comparison with FACE and GOAT, respectively, and by constructing the table reproduced here as Table 2.1 below. Here we first summarize the patterns thus revealed in the older (that is, SAWD) data, and then we look at what the newer MMB and *Voices* materials add to the picture.

Two characteristic sounds of WelE, the long monophthongs [e:] and [o:], occur throughout most of Wales in SAWD data in words such as *bacon, break, great, make* (FACE group) and *coal, road, spoke, toe* (GOAT), respectively, which have diphthongal /eɪ/ and /əʊ ~ oʊ/ in RP. On this basis, there is a case for regarding the two monophthongs as phonemic in WelE, but overall their distribution is complicated by their occurrence also in words such as *clay, drain, weigh, whey* (STAY) and *cold, shoulder, snow* (SNOW). In STAY and SNOW, it is more difficult to argue that the monophthongs are phonemic, for in these groups the diphthongs [eɪ] and [oʊ] are more likely. In addition, diphthongal forms can occur in FACE and GOAT. Table

2.1 summarizes the situation for the whole of Wales based on SAWD data, outlining the regional distribution of monophthongs and diphthongs in FACE, STAY, GOAT, and SNOW.

Table 2.1: Regional distribution of FACE/STAY and GOAT/SNOW vowels in SAWD data (the table lists only regions where one variant dominates)

	[eː]	[ei]	[oː]	[ou]
FACE	north, south, northern peripheries	southern peripheries	–	–
STAY	north	south, southern peripheries	–	–
GOAT	–	–	north, south, northern peripheries	southern peripheries
SNOW	–	–	north	south, southern peripheries

[eː] occurs most commonly in FACE, being dominant (in these words) in the central north and south, and in the northern peripheries. [ei] in FACE is dominant only in the southern peripheries. In STAY, however, the diphthong is prevalent throughout the south, while the monophthong is dominant only in the central north area. The sequence is the same for the [oː] – [ou] pair: the monophthong is dominant in GOAT everywhere but the southern peripheries, and in SNOW the diphthong dominates throughout the south, the monophthong in the central north. Neither monophthong nor diphthong dominates in STAY and SNOW in the northern peripheries.

A number of causes underlie this pattern. First, the Welsh language has no diphthongs of the /ei/ and /ou/ types, and the Welsh monophthongs /eː/ and /oː/ have historically been used in FACE/STAY and GOAT/SNOW. Running counter to this are spelling pronunciations affecting STAY and SNOW, leading to the diphthongal forms, the general rules being: spellings with <ai>, <ay>, <ei>, <ey> encourage [ei], and spellings with <ou>, <ow> encourage [ou], with <ol> spellings falling in with SNOW rather than GOAT. Furthermore, there has been influence from neighbouring accents of English English: [eː] and [oː] have been reinforced in the north of Wales by the influence of monophthongs occurring in the northwest of England; [ei] and [ou] have been supported by the diphthongs of the west and southwest of England, as well as those of RP, of course.

Again, what is missing from the SAWD data is detail on whether incidence of the more RP-like diphthongs increases in keeping with higher social class and greater formality of speech style.

But what can the newer MMB and *Voices* data tell us? It would be satisfying were updated patterns to emerge, but one has to look quite hard for patterns, especially as the more recent data gives less information on STAY and SNOW than it does on FACE and GOAT. However, the MMB and *Voices of the UK* commentaries do give us a national total of 27 assessments of FACE, 29 of GOAT, 11 of STAY, and 7 of SNOW. These assessments tend to sum up multiple tokens in each locality. The regional distributions are in summary as follows:
- in the north, monophthongs and diphthongs occur in all four lexical sets, with monophthongs in the majority in GOAT, diphthongs in the majority in STAY, and no clear majority either way in FACE (just a slight edge towards the monophthong) and SNOW;
- in Mid Wales, diphthongs are in the majority in FACE and GOAT, there is no clear majority in STAY, and there is no information for SNOW;
- in the south, monophthongs and diphthongs occur in all four lexical sets, with monophthongs marginally in the majority in FACE, diphthongs in the majority in STAY and SNOW, and the situation pretty evenly balanced in GOAT, with slightly more monophthongs there than diphthongs.

This looks like a more jumbled picture than Table 2.1 provides for the SAWD data, but it is not necessarily out of line with the prior situation, not if one sums up by saying that the diphthongal realizations seem to be on the increase and the monophthongal realizations receding. For Cardiff English, in their project charting sociophonetic variation in schoolchildren between 1976 and 1990, Mees and Collins reported (1999: 191, 201) that FACE and GOAT had generally become "obvious diphthongal glides", and this is supported by the MMB and *Voices* information for these sets in Cardiff.

One further point: in both the older and newer data there are other monophthongal and diphthongal realizations at large, such as [ɛː, ɛɪ, ɔː, ɔu], but we have subsumed these under the main realizations in the discussion above.

PALM, START

The vowel phoneme in RP in both PALM and START is /ɑː/, but Wells (1982) uses two lexical sets because of the occurrence of rhoticity in certain accents in START, though not, one would expect, in PALM. In WelE, there is evidence of rhoticity not only in START but also, surprisingly, in PALM. In SAWD, we find *r*-coloured [aɻ] and [ɑˤː] occurring in PALM and START words in the longer-Anglicized areas. Full articulation of post-vocalic /r/ in START is less attested, and is linked to influence from Welsh-language spelling-pronunciation convention. There is more on forms of rhoticity under /r/ in subsection 2.5.4, below. As for the main vowel sounds of PALM and START, there is competition across Wales between long front open [aː] and long back open RP-style [ɑː], with the front variant in the ascendancy for the most part in both older and newer data. As in the BATH set, the short open variants [a > æ > ɑ] are also possible, clustered mainly along the mid and southern borders, and in the west and southwest. The evidence from the PALM and START sets is in keeping with that provided by TRAP and BATH, in that we can reasonably argue, on the whole, for a phonemic distinction between the short and long open vowels but not between the front and back open variants, where influences from regional accents of English English, RP, and Welsh-language conventions are all at play, producing variation with some sketchy regional patterning and probably a correlation with prestige and formality. In the phonemic inventory above, we have selected the more common pronunciation as the phonemic designation /aː/ for PALM and START, and we have indicated variation between /a ~ aː/ for BATH.

A note here on PALM and START in the urban accent of Cardiff: Collins and Mees (1990: 95–96) remark that in broad working-class Cardiff English, PALM words often have a front nasalized [æː], which is "undoubtedly considered to be the most characteristic vowel of the accent" (1990: 95). Coupland (1988: 27) says that [ɛ̃ː] realizations are heard in the broadest speech, that is, in working-class male Cardiff English. Collins and Mees do not include START in their lexical sets, but the MMB and *Voices* Cardiff localities show some evidence of [æː] in PALM and START, in variation with [aː]. Collins and Mees also comment on the "apparently confusing pattern of alternation between /a/ and /aː/" in their BATH words and tentatively suggest a phonotactic pattern, in which /a/ is favoured before a nasal plus consonant and /aː/ before a fricative. Do we see this generally in WelE? According to the SAWD data, no, but some small corroboration for it can be gleaned from the MMB and *Voices* commentaries. In addition, Coupland (1988: 27) notes the tendency for the short /a/ TRAP vowel to be lengthened in Cardiff English and "apparently subject to a similar pattern [as in PALM and START] of sociolinguistic variation".

THOUGHT, NORTH, FORCE, BOAR

Wells (1982) distinguishes the three lexical sets THOUGHT, NORTH, FORCE for a combination of reasons, namely the possibility of rhoticity in certain accents in NORTH, FORCE, and other historical distinctions between the groups. The set BOAR is our own addition, in which the vowel has a different historical derivation from other FORCE words, under which it is subsumed by Wells. The dominant vowel realization in all four of these lexical sets in WelE in both older and newer data is [ɔː], sometimes transcribed as [ɒː]. However, in BOAR in the SAWD data there are common occurrences of a raised [oː] realization across Wales (such [oː] realizations occur to a lesser extent in the other sets) and of diphthongal [ɔə ~ oə > oɛ] realizations often (though not exclusively) along the border. Rhoticity can affect all of these variants in NORTH, FORCE, and BOAR, either in the form of *r*-colouring (also in THOUGHT), which occurs mainly in the longer-Anglicized areas, or in the form of a fully articulated following /r/, which extends into the areas of continuing Welsh-language influence. The MMB data records [ɔː] alternating with [ʌː] in THOUGHT words in the Cardiff localities, a point also made by Collins and Mees (1990: 95). In addition, both Connolly (1990: 123) and Tench (1990: 137–8) observe [oː] in FORCE and BOAR but [ɔː] in THOUGHT and NORTH in Port Talbot and Abercrave, respectively, two southern localities. In fact, Connolly and Tench designate this a phonemic distinction in these sets in these localities.

GOOSE

The dominant realization in GOOSE is [uː], although short [ʊ] is also recorded in certain words, especially *tooth*, giving one of the well-known lexical pronunciations of WelE. Parry's map of *tooth* (1999: 229) shows the short form covering the majority of Wales, with the exception of most of the north and a pocket in the southwest corner. Short [ʊ] in *tooth* was also found by the SED in the west of England. Wells's (1982 vol. 1: 147–149) GOOSE set includes words which in RP have a palatal semivowel /j/ or *yod* preceding /uː/. In WelE, there is a strong tendency in such words for [ɪu] to occur instead, and this group is here treated under TUESDAY, below. This [ɪu] also features in CURE.

PRICE, CHOICE, MOUTH

What these three groups have in common in the older data is a very close final element in the diphthong: [i] in PRICE and CHOICE, [u] in MOUTH. In the newer MMB and *Voices* data, these final elements are usually noted as [ɪ] and [ʊ], respectively, but these might be transcription choices rather than signifying pronunciation changes over time. In both older and newer data, a front open first element [a] in PRICE and MOUTH is common (back open [ɑ] also occurs at times, especially in the southwest). There is, however, a major counter-tendency in PRICE and MOUTH, that is, for a central [ə] to be used as the first element. SAWD data shows a pretty clear regional distribution, with [əɪ] and [əu] mostly restricted to the main southern, especially southeastern, areas. This is corroborated in the newer materials, though sometimes the British Library team chooses [ʌ] rather than [ə] for the first element. Tench's (1990: 141) view is that this variation in PRICE and MOUTH diphthongs tells us something about the chronology of English spoken in Wales:

diphthongs with central first elements indicate areas where English was spoken relatively early, while diphthongs with front open first elements indicate the more recent arrival of English. Occasionally, and more so in the south, an [ai ~ əi ~ ʌi] diphthong spills over into the CHOICE set.

SQUARE

The realization of the vowel phoneme in SQUARE words throughout Wales is usually [ɛː], with a good number of diphthongal [ɛə > eə] realizations occurring, especially in the border areas. As with NURSE, START, NORTH, FORCE, and some other sets above, rhoticity is recorded by SAWD in SQUARE, following a familiar pattern: either *r*-colouring of the vowel, which occurs mainly in the longer-Anglicized areas; or fully articulated post-vocalic /r/, which extends into the areas of continuing Welsh-language influence. Rhoticity is noted sometimes in the newer data, but not always with reference to specific lexical sets. Rhoticity in the MMB and *Voices* data is included in the discussion under /r/ in subsection 2.5.4, below.

CURE, POWER, FIRE

Taking these three sets together, there seems to be a fairly bemusing range of vowel variation. However, the three are united by a few characteristics that they have in common. First, they are all prone to the kinds of rhoticity noted several times above, in other sets. Second, there is a tendency in each set for a disyllabic structure to occur, in which the main stressed vowel and following unstressed vowel are separated by a semivowel – /w/ separating the syllables in CURE and POWER, and /j/ separating them in FIRE. In such structures, the first syllable in CURE tends towards the /ɪu/ found in TUESDAY, below, which corresponds to Welsh-language <iw>; the first syllable in POWER exhibits the variation between [au] and [əu] found in MOUTH; and the first syllable in FIRE falls in with the division between [ai] and [əi] found in PRICE. In their final unstressed syllables, [ə] can vary with [ʌ]. Overall, these disyllabic forms are widespread, but in WelE generally they alternate with other forms too, such as: [uə ~ ʊə ~ ɔː ~ ɔə ~ uː] in CURE, each of these capable of being preceded by yod; [aʊə ~ aə > aː] in POWER; and [aɪə > aə] in FIRE.

NEAR, EARS

Parry (2015: 19) notes that diphthongal [ɪə] pronunciations are to be found in SAWD data in words that belong to the NEAR set. In MMB and *Voices*, [ɪə > iə] realizations are widely recorded. Parry believes, however, that many [ɪə] transcriptions in SAWD mask a disyllabic structure in which the first and second vowels are separated by [j]. Collins and Mees (1990), Connolly (1990), and Tench (1990) all lend support to this, reporting [iːə] as the chief realization for some NEAR words in their southern localities, although such [iːjə ~ iːə] transcriptions are absent from the MMB and *Voices* data. There is a subset of NEAR words (*ears, hear, here, year*), here grouped under EARS, in which the vowel [œː] is common, often preceded by [j], which is often the initial sound of the word. In both older and newer data, these forms are more common in the south than elsewhere. Rhoticity is also found in NEAR and EARS, either as *r*-colouring or a fully articulated following /r/.

TUESDAY

In TUESDAY words, we find a WelE phoneme which does not occur in RP: /ɪu/. Wells (1982) subsumes TUESDAY words under GOOSE, but remarks (vol. 2: 385) that, in WelE, GOOSE words spelt with <eu>, <ew>, <u>, <ue> tend to be pronounced with [ɪu]. Parry (1999: 28) records [ɪu] in TUESDAY in the overwhelming majority of SAWD localities, and in MMB/*Voices* as well as SAWD [ɪu] can permeate into (other) GOOSE words, for example, *you*. It is found also in the CURE group, above. As both Parry (1999: 28) and Walters (2003a: 76) note, it is likely that there are two separate sources for this /ɪu/: one is influence from Welsh-language /ɪu/ (represented in ordinary orthography by <iw>), which undoubtedly lies behind /ɪu/ in WelE in most regions; the other is influence from similar diphthongs occurring in west of England accents, which probably affects to some extent the forms recorded in the southeast border regions. /ɪu/ is sometimes preceded by /j/, though presence of yod is more commonly associated with a following /uː/.

2.4.2 Unstressed vowels

Our commentary on the unstressed vowels of WelE is limited to a few observations on the more conspicuous features.

Walters (2003a: 74), referring to Rhondda Valleys English (southeast Wales), reports that "the vowel in the final unstressed syllables of *butter, sofa* etc. is characteristically lengthened and with a fuller quality than normally ascribed to schwa". He adds that this and the merger of /ʌ/ and /ə/ in STRUT are "paralleled in Welsh, which has a single central vowel and in which final unstressed syllables are said never to be reduced to schwa". The data in Parry (1999: 34–35; 2015: 13–14) corroborates this to some extent: [ʌ ~ ʌ̈] occur widely in the letter group in most other parts of Wales as well as in the southeast. The chief competitors are [ə] and [ɛ], with [a] and [æ] being other notable variants. Rhoticity is often associated with each of these variants. In addition, remember [ʌ ~ ə] in the final syllables of CURE, POWER, and FIRE, mentioned above. But note also that according to Ball (1988: 51) and Glyn E. Jones (1984: 53) the single central vowel of Welsh is actually schwa, and although both STRUT and letter exhibit variation between [ʌ] and [ə] types, in STRUT the "movement" compared with RP is towards schwa while in letteʀ the movement is away from schwa. There seems to be a combination of influences at work here, that is, a centralizing tendency plus a prosodic effect giving a greater level of emphasis to "unstressed" final syllables than found in other accents. Jones (1984: 53) says that stress on the final syllable of a word is frequent in Welsh, and this habit might conceivably be influencing letteʀ realizations in SAWD. In the newer MMB and *Voices* data, [ə] is the most common realization in the letteʀ and commᴀ groups, with [a] or [ɛ] sometimes occurring in the north, and r-colouring recorded in Newtown in Mid Wales.

Perhaps a similar prosodic effect contributes to the various instances of a 'full' vowel pronunciation being retained in relatively weak syllables in WelE, a trait recorded in both the older and newer materials, as for example in *benches* [bɛntʃɛz] (MMB: Bethesda), *common* [kɒmɒn] (MMB: Bethesda), and the starteᴅ group [ɛ] (*Voices*: Bonymaen). Spelling pronunciation might be another factor in these examples. There is also a widespread tendency in the happʏ group for the final vowel to be very close and at times long, even ending with a schwa-glide, as in *lovely* [ləvliːə] (MMB: Gorseinon).

2.4.3 Pharyngalization

It is commonly observed of northern accents in both Welsh and WelE that they possess a 'throaty' quality. This 'throatiness' is actually *pharyngalization*, that is, contraction of the pharyngeal arches. It probably arises out of Welsh-language influence. Glyn E. Jones (1984: 57) notes that pharyngalization affects the articulation of the two high central vowels of northern Welsh. Penhallurick (1991) records it affecting the majority of WelE vowels (except for the most open ones) in the traditional Welsh-speaking areas of North Wales. [ɫ] tends also to be pharyngalized in northern WelE – see below.

2.5 Consonants

Next we describe the more notable realizations of the WelE consonant system.

2.5.1 Plosives and nasals

Strong aspiration of /p, t, k/
In the SAWD data, strong aspiration affects the voiceless plosives /p, t, k/, particularly in word-initial and word-final positions. This strong aspiration is excep-

tionally prominent in North Wales, where it sometimes approaches affrication, but Parry (1999: 37–38; 2015: 21) notes that throughout Wales each voiceless plosive usually has strong aspiration in initial stressed position and often finally before a pause. In the newer MMB and *Voices* data, aspiration of /p, t, k/ is noted as frequent only in some northwest localities. However, the associated phenomena of spirantization of word- and utterance-final /t/, and debuccalization of /t/, have a more widespread distribution. This spirantization is where final /t/ is realized as a weak [h], as for example in *that* [ðaʰ], and this occurs in MMB in North and South WelE. Debuccalization seems to be essentially the same characteristic (but given a different label) in the *Voices* material, though it is not limited to final /t/, and it is more frequent in the North than in Mid and South Wales. Affrication of /k/ (e.g. *like* [laɪkˣ]) is also recorded as frequent in some MMB and *Voices* localities in the north. Thus an association of the voiceless plosives with forms of conspicuous aspiration is present in both older and newer data, particularly in North WelE.

T-glottaling and glottal reinforcement of /p, t, k/
Forms of glottalization are unattested in the SAWD data, but are mentioned repeatedly in MMB and *Voices*. Glottal reinforcement of /p, t, k/ is recorded as occasional in Swansea and Llanelli, as in *poppadoms* [pɒp͡ʔədɒmz] and *daughter* [dɔːt͡ʔə] (both MMB, Swansea), and *work* [wəːʔ͡k] (*Voices*, Llanelli). Full glottalization of /t/ word-medially and word-finally is found in all three broad regions by MMB and *Voices* combined, ranging between occasional and frequent use in both the northwest and southeast, but recorded as only occurring occasionally in Mid Wales. Mees and Collins (1999) found some indication of the advent of word-final /t/-glottalization in the speech of upwardly mobile young working-class females in Cardiff, which the authors believed was due to speakers following a present-day RP/"Estuary English" model in this respect. On this evidence, glottalization appears to be on the increase in WelE.

T-voicing and T-tapping
MMB and *Voices* record occasional voicing of /t/ in North, Mid, and South WelE (with the exceptions of Llanelli and Splott, where it is noted as frequent), usually when /t/ occurs between vowels. Mees and Collins (1999: 192) note it as common in medial position in Cardiff English. T-tapping, that is, /t/ articulated as [ɾ], again intervocalically, is found in MMB and *Voices* occasionally in Bangor, Bethesda, Flint, and Rhos-on-Sea in the north, Newtown in Mid Wales, and in Cardiff, Bonymaen, Risca, and Splott in the south. Penhallurick (1991: 110–14) recorded T-voicing a number of times, though always in the cluster /st/. In his SAWD overviews (1999, 2015), Parry makes no mention of forms of T-voicing.

Devoicing and unvoicing of /b, d, g/
There is some patchy evidence of devoicing and unvoicing of /b, d, g/ in the national surveys. *Voices* notes frequent devoicing in Holyhead, and Parry (1999: 37; 2015: 21) records the very occasional use of [t] finally in *cold*, *second*, and *spade*, which he links to certain English-derived loanwords in Welsh in which final /ld/ becomes /lt/, and final /nd/ becomes /nt/ (for example, *golt* 'gold', and *diamwnt* 'diamond'). Furthermore, Glyn E. Jones (1984: 41) points out that voicing is not a constant feature of the articulation of the /b, d, g/ phoneme group in the Welsh language, and this seems likely to be a factor in this feature of WelE. There is no sign in the national surveys of the strong aspiration of voiced plosives which Alan Thomas includes as a characteristic of WelE in his 1984 summary (p. 184), where he adds that it "is the source for one of the more common ways of caricaturing the phonetic characteristics of Welsh English speech in literature, in which voiceless plosives are made to substitute for voiced ones" (comments repeated by Thomas 1994: 122–123). This unvoicing, however, as we say here, is attested occasionally in our data sets.

Dental /t, d, n/
Dental realizations of /t, d, n/ occur in the SAWD data from Mid Wales and especially the north (where they are the norm). In the Welsh language, /t, d, n/ tend to have dental realizations in northern accents (Ball 1988: 54) and presumably Welsh-derived sound-substitution lies behind dental /t, d, n/ in northern WelE. Such dental realizations are infrequent elsewhere in WelE, and are not mentioned in the MMB and *Voices* commentaries.

Non-standard -ING
NG-fronting, that is, use of alveolar [-n] rather than velar [-ŋ] in -ING, is common in all regions in both older and newer national data. The occasional [-ŋk] form is noted in MMB in the southeast, for example, *nothing* [nəθɪŋk] (Cardiff).

2.5.2 Fricatives, affricates, and semivowels

/ɬ, x, r̥/
The sound system of the Welsh language contributes three additions to the WelE fricative inventory with the phonemes /ɬ, x, r̥/, but their use is mostly restricted to Welsh place and personal names. They are represented orthographically by <ll>, <ch>, and <rh>, respectively, and they can also occur in WelE in loanwords from Welsh, such as *cawellt* 'wicker basket' and *crochon* 'bread-basket'. Perhaps one should classify these as "foreignisms" rather than as fully naturalized members of

the WelE phoneme system. There is more on /r̥/ below under 2.5.4 /r/, which provides an alternative category for discussion of [r̥]-forms.

Devoicing and unvoicing of /z, ʒ, dʒ/
In the SAWD data, we find widespread use of [s] where RP has /z/ word-medially and word-finally, as for example in *thousand*, *cheese*, and *nose*. These [s]-forms occur particularly though not exclusively in the traditional Welsh-speaking regions of North and Mid Wales. Except for loanwords, the Welsh language has no voiced /z/ in contrast with voiceless /s/, and it is likely that most of the [s] realizations of /z/ in WelE are due to the historical lack of [z]-forms in Wales. Devoiced [z̥] medially and finally is also common in SAWD. MMB and *Voices* similarly record unvoiced and devoiced realizations of /z/ word-medially and -finally in North and Mid Wales, though use is described as "occasional" in some localities. In addition, the newer data includes instances of related tendencies to devoice and unvoice /ʒ/ and /dʒ/ in the same localities. Welsh has no /ʒ/, and /dʒ/ occurs mostly in borrowings from English. What we have here then, in summary, is the structure of these parts of the Welsh phonemic system (the lack of certain voiced fricatives compared with English) finding expression in WelE, though in our analysis of the WelE system we treat these fricative unvoiced and devoiced forms as realizations of the English voiced phonemes.

Initial fricative voicing
In contrast, Parry (1999: 39; 2015: 22) records the use of initial /v/ where RP has initial /f/ in *first*, *four*, and *furrow* in southeastern Powys, Monmouthshire, south Pembrokeshire, and in south Gower; as well as just the one instance of /ð/ for /θ/ in *third* in east Powys near the border (Parry 1999: 40; 2015: 22). Such Initial Fricative Voicing (Wells 1982 vol. 2: 343) is associated with west-country accents of England, where traditionally it can affect /f, θ, s, ʃ/. Penhallurick (1994: 145–148) provides evidence of voicing of initial /f, s/ in the southern half of the Gower Peninsula from the seventeenth century to the late twentieth century, though by the 1980s it was a relic feature in Gower English, and is now a folk memory. In 1982 (vol. 2: 343), Wells commented that it was "sharply recessive" also in English English. There is no evidence of it in the MMB and *Voices* commentaries. Where it occurred in WelE, Initial Fricative Voicing was no doubt due to long-standing influence from western English English.

TH-fronting
In the *Voices* commentary for Splott (Cardiff) in South Wales, TH-fronting is noted as very frequent, occurring word-initially (for example, *think* [fɪŋk]), word-medially (*nothing* [nəfɪn], *mother* [məvə]), and word-finally (*Plymouth* [plɪməf], *with*

[wɪv]). TH-fronting is also noted in the speech of a 15-year-old male in Rhayader (MMB). It is absent in the SAWD data and not recorded in any other *Voices* or MMB localities in Wales. Neither do Collins and Mees mention it in their pieces on Cardiff English (1990, 1999). However, Rowan Campbell (personal communication 2018) observes some occurrences of TH-fronting by a couple of her younger male informants in her research on dialect levelling in Cardiff. In the Splott *Voices* recording, all of the instances of TH-fronting are made by the two youngest speakers interviewed, who were aged between 18–20 at the time (2005), one female, one male. We are reminded of Peter Trudgill's 1988 update on his Norwich research in which he describes TH-fronting as an innovation "which has come completely and dramatically out of the blue" (Trudgill 1988: 42) – there was no sign of this feature in his 1968 research on Norwich (published in 1974). Trudgill concluded that this merging of /θ/ with /f/ and /ð/ with /v/ was "spreading very rapidly indeed out from London [Cockney] in all directions" (1988: 43). The Linguistic Innovators project (2004–7), which investigated the English of adolescents in London, found that an increased amount of TH-fronting was one of the characteristics of regional dialect levelling or *supralocalization* in the southeast of England, noting also its frequency in Inner London, as well as its pervasiveness in parts of Scotland and the north of England (Kerswill, Torgersen and Fox, 2007; Cheshire, Fox, Kerswill and Torgersen, 2008). Reports in a number of the essays in Foulkes and Docherty (1999) show TH-fronting attested in younger working-class speakers, especially males, in Reading, Milton Keynes, Derby, Sandwell (West Midlands of England), Sheffield, Hull, and Newcastle, as well as Norwich and London (see also Beal 2010: 80–81). In their summary of the phonology of southeastern English English, Altendorf and Watt (2008: 209) observe that TH-fronting tends to affect "sexes and classes in the following order: working-class boys > working-class girls > middle-class boys > middle-class girls". TH-fronting is a historical feature associated with working-class London speech, and its adoption by speakers in a process of geographical and social spread might be due to a mixture of reasons, such as the comparative difficulty of pronunciation of [θ, ð], rendering [f, v] an easier alternative, and diffusion from London (see Jim Milroy, 2003: 218–219, discussing Derby). The more rapid recent spread of TH-fronting beyond London might also be connected with the feature's covert prestige. In their in-depth multivariate analysis of TH-fronting in Glasgow at the beginning of the twenty-first century, Stuart-Smith et al. (2013) found that a strong psychological engagement with broadcast media (specifically the working-class London setting of the BBC Television soap opera *EastEnders*) can be an accelerating factor aiding the dissemination of this sound change. *Voices* and MMB appear to provide the earliest testimonies of its arrival in WelE.

H-dropping

The phenomenon of initial-H-dropping, or indeed of initial-H-retention, has a rather complex history, involving among other factors a changing relationship between spelling and pronunciation in certain French (ultimately Latin) loanwords (Scragg 1974: 41; Wells 1982 vol. 1: 255), and social censure of zero-H realizations from the late eighteenth century onwards. In common with many non-standard accents, WelE exhibits occasional-to-frequent H-dropping, and this is attested widely in both older and newer national data sets.

Initial-/w/-dropping

Initial /w/ is foreign to the Welsh language as an unmutated form (several consonants in Welsh are subject to mutation rules in word-initial position), and influence from this might lie behind the dropping of initial /w/ in traditional WelE, particularly in words with a following back close rounded stressed vowel, such as *woman* and *wool*, although such forms are also recorded widely by the *Survey of English Dialects* (Orton et al.: 1962–71) for England. Parry (1999: 40–41; 2015: 26) records zero-/w/ initially in these words scattered through North, Mid and South Wales. Initial-/w/-dropping is not found in the newer data, which suggests that it is recessive and possibly obsolescent.

2.5.3 /l/

The distribution of clear [l] and dark [ɫ]

The detail of the regional distribution of the two realizations of /l/ – clear [l] and dark [ɫ] – in WelE is quite intricate and a little messy, but the data from SAWD allows the following summary:
- in Mid and South Wales, clear [l] dominates – in some localities [l] is normal in all positions of the word, while in other localities it is used more extensively than in RP but nonetheless shares /l/ articulations with dark [ɫ], though not necessarily in line with the phonotactic conventions of RP, that is, [l] before a vowel, and [ɫ] before a consonant or word-finally;
- in the north, RP conventions are again often flouted, but here, particularly in the northwest, [ɫ] is found more often than in the other regions, occasionally overshadowing clear [l] in all positions, though clear [l] nevertheless remains common;
- in the north, [ɫ] is mostly pharyngalized, which Glyn E. Jones (1984: 47–49) notes as a characteristic of dark [ɫ] in the north dialect of Welsh, describing pharyngalization as the reason why South Walians refer to northerners as having a "strangulated" manner of speaking.

Thus the phoneme /l/ provides two of the popular diagnostics of WelE: a prevailing clear [l] for the main southern variety (reflecting a similar trait of southern accents of Welsh), and a dark pharyngalized [ɫ] that is associated with the main northern variety. MMB and *Voices* data corroborates these patterns, showing a prominent dark [ɫ] in the north gradually giving way to clear /l/ prominence as we travel southwards. Pharyngalization of [ɫ] was not expressly transcribed in the newer data.

Insertion of schwa before syllabic /l/
Both the older and newer national materials show a scattering of instances of schwa insertion before syllabic /l/ across all regions in words such as *apple, kettle, little, people*, and *uncle*. This is recorded more often in SAWD, especially in Mid Wales, and is perhaps another manifestation of the tendency in WelE prosody to give an increased degree of emphasis to "unstressed" final syllables (see also 2.4.2 above and 2.6 below).

2.5.4 /r/

Realizations of /r/
The Welsh language has two /r/ phonemes: a voiced alveolar rolled or trilled /r/, which is sometimes realized as a flapped or tapped [ɾ] and sometimes, particularly in the Bala area, North Wales, as a uvular rolled [ʀ] or uvular fricative [ʁ], often popularly perceived as a speech impediment in Welsh and known as *tafod tew*, literally 'thick tongue'; and a voiceless alveolar rolled /r̥/ (<rh> in ordinary orthography). Welsh /r̥/ impacts comparatively little on WelE realizations of /r/, but rolled [r] realizations occur often in the spoken English of North, Mid, and South Wales, excepting the border areas and the Gower Peninsula and south Pembrokeshire, where approximant [ɹ] is more common. There is also a higher frequency of flapped or tapped [ɾ] in WelE compared with RP, especially in traditional Welsh-speaking areas, and this can be interpreted as further evidence of Welsh-language influence on WelE. This general description derives from both the older and newer national data sets, though the newer materials evince an apparent decline in the occurrence of rolled [r]. Uvular realizations of WelE /r/ are confined to a couple of localities in the mid and west north in SAWD, but in the newer data they turn up in one locality each from the three broad regions, that is, occasional [ʁ] in Trefor (MMB), [ʁ ~ ʀ] in Aberhosan (MMB), and [ʁ] in Aberporth (MMB).

Rhoticity

Orthographic r is always articulated in the Welsh language, in all word-positions, and this practice is carried over at times into WelE, resulting in post-vocalic /r/ word-medially before a consonant and word-finally, this rhoticity being centred in the traditional Welsh-speaking areas in the west half of Wales. Using the SAWD data as our starting point, we find that this Welsh-influenced rhoticity in NURSE, START, NORTH, FORCE, BOAR, SQUARE sometimes leads to a short vowel followed by /r/ (Parry, 1999: 14–17; 2015: 12–13), such as: /ɜ̈r/ in *first, third, work* (Parry, 1999: 16; 2015: 13) in western Mid Wales; /ar ~ ɑr/ in *arm, farmer, farthing* (Parry, 1999: 15; 2015: 12) in the west; /ɔr/ in *forks, morning* and in *boar, four* (Parry, 1999: 17) a few times in North, Mid and West Wales; and /ɛr/ in *chair, mare, pears* (Parry, 1999: 14) in pockets in the west. Occasionally the short vowel minus following /r/ is recorded. Rhotic forms with long vowels are common in NURSE, START, NORTH, FORCE, BOAR, and SQUARE, with the general pattern as follows: long vowel followed by /r/ (that is, forms influenced by the Welsh pronunciation convention of always articulating orthographic *r*), widespread in the western half of Wales; long *r*-coloured vowel without a following /r/, that is, forms influenced by west of England accents, occurring in the mid-eastern and southeastern border areas of Wales, and in south Pembrokeshire and the Gower Peninsula. Rhoticity of both the Welsh-influenced kind and west-of-England type also affects CURE, POWER, FIRE and NEAR, EARS, as well as lettER.

In the MMB and *Voices* data, rhoticity is attested less often, in fact only in two north localities (Llanwnda and Trefor) and one Mid Wales locality (Newtown). In the north localities it takes the form of a weakly articulated following /r/ (Welsh style); in Newtown the instances of rhoticity are in the west-of-England style and are produced by an informant born just over the border in Shropshire.

In contrast, Mees and Collins (1999: 193) observe that Cardiff English is "totally non-rhotic".

2.5.5 Geminate or lengthened consonants

The consonants /p, b, t, d, k, g, v, θ, s, ʃ, tʃ, m, n, ŋ, l, r/ are all recorded by Parry (1999: 37–40; 2015: 21) as being subject to lengthened duration of pronunciation in WelE when located in word-medial position. Parry records these lengthened forms in most parts of Wales. In the Welsh language, medial consonants tend to be long, especially between vowels when the preceding vowel is stressed. Stephen Jones (1926: 24) stated that Welsh /p, t, k, m, ŋ, ɬ/ "are always lengthened (or doubled) when they follow a stressed vowel and are not followed by another consonant". The most likely cause for these lengthened consonants in WelE is therefore once again influence from Welsh, in this case from Welsh prosody, though the SAWD data shows lengthening affecting medial consonants when followed by a consonant as well as when followed by a vowel (for example, [pː] in *apple*, and [ʃː] in *mushrooms*). Furthermore, many instances in SAWD occur in the more Anglicized regions of Wales. The MMB and *Voices* data shows gemination of medial consonants across Wales, usually but not always between vowels, and always following stress, for example, *effort* [ɛfːət] (MMB: Bethesda), *sitting* [sɪtːɪn] (MMB: Maerdy), and *together* [təgɛðːə] (MMB: Resolven). This vibrant feature is as much a matter of WelE prosody as it is of consonant realization, and we turn now to a summary of the indicative characteristics of WelE prosody.

2.6 Suprasegmental phonology

In 1982 (vol. 2: 392), John Wells noted: "Popular English views about Welsh accents include the claim that they have a 'sing-song' or 'lilting' intonation", a characteristic associated particularly with the valleys of southeast Wales. Wells also commented on the lack of a "proper investigation of the intonation of Welsh English" at the time. Studies have been carried out since, including at least two in-depth works, that is, Walters (1999) on Rhondda Valleys English (RVE) in southeast Wales, and Quaino (2011) on English in the counties of Ceredigion and Gwynedd in west and northwest Wales, both of these being doctoral dissertations. Both researchers worked with limited audio corpora for their suprasegmental work – Walters with extracts from his own fieldwork, and Quaino with excerpts from the digitized-recordings archive of SAWD. The focus on limited amounts of data is understandable, as each item typically consists of a few seconds of continuous speech subjected to detailed acoustic analysis. Walters found clear evidence of the influence of the Welsh language in the prosodic patterns of RVE, including the following strong tendencies: shortening of the stressed vowel of words and lengthening of the succeeding consonant; an emphatic pitch-peak following a stressed syllable; and a high pitch on unstressed syllables (Walters 2001: 297–300) – in other words, the so-called "sing-song" Welsh accent. Quaino found less indication of this in his material (which was not so conversational in character as that used by Walters), but he did notice a tendency for his speakers to avoid producing successive weakly stressed syllables and successive strongly stressed syllables, and to prefer a steady 2/4 musical rhythm of alternating weak and strong syllables (see, for example, Quaino 2011: 294). Quaino also found some similarity between his material and that of Walters, such as a slight delay in the pitch rise that characterizes a stressed syllable: "The upward movement towards the stressed syllable is usually introduced by a long level tone, which delays the actual rise." (Quaino 2011: 305)

2.7 Summing up

The present chapter has offered a detailed synopsis of the sound-system of Welsh English, providing a structural analysis that updates previous accounts, a summary of the regional distributions of the main realizations and variants, and a provisional assessment of linguistic changes that appear to have taken place over the last half-century or are ongoing. With regard to the last point, we observe the following in particular: a possible decrease in the use of long monophthongs in FACE/STAY and GOAT/SNOW; signs of the advent of TH-fronting in Welsh English, chiefly so far in Cardiff English; and possible decreases in the occurrence of rolled [r] and rhoticity.

As a kind of epilogue to this chapter, we note the comparative wealth of studies on attitudes to and perceptions of Welsh English accents, especially as part of the sustained investigation of sensitivities towards linguistic varieties carried out by scholars based at Cardiff University's Language and Communication section. For example, in the early 1970s, Howard Giles undertook several studies of evaluations of accents of British English (reviewed in Giles and Powesland 1975: 28–37, 68–73). In one study (Giles 1971), groups of listeners/respondents from Somerset and South Wales rated the matched guises of two speakers performing a passage in RP, Somerset, and southern WelE accents. While the RP speakers were perceived as more ambitious, determined, industrious, intelligent, and self-confident, the non-standard speakers were perceived to have more personal integrity and greater social attractiveness (Giles and Powesland 1975: 68). Durham (2016: 185) tentatively suggests that the body of perceptual work on Welsh English from the 1970s to the present shows a slight increase in the "attractiveness" ratings for the accent – non-Welsh respondents tend to treat WelE as a single accent. Furthermore, her research, which uses data gathered from Twitter, highlights the influence of contemporary television shows (Durham 2016: 200–202) in heightening the prominence of South Wales Valleys English in the general perception of Welsh English, that is, the former is conflated with the latter. See Section 1.5 for further details on perceptual research.

3 Morphosyntax

3.1 Introduction

The dialectal features of grammar which emerge in Welsh varieties of English originate from two main sources: Welsh language contact and EngE dialect contact. Despite the reasonably high numbers of L1 Welsh speakers, the Welsh input in present-day WelE is not as distinctive as, for example, the Irish substrate in Irish English (IrE). Many of the most frequently occurring contact-induced features are structurally similar to existing (vernacular) constructions in EngE (e.g. focus fronting, extended uses of the progressive form, invariant tag *isn't it*) or otherwise widespread in varieties of English around the world (e.g. embedded inversion, irregular use of articles). They can nevertheless be traced back to Welsh contact input, as shown below. Other reasons are both historical and contemporary. The later Anglicization of most parts of Wales, for example, led to an emphasis on formal education in the dissemination of English, which restrained the imperfect acquisition of English at the community level, instrumental in the development of IrE (see Section 1.4; Paulasto 2009). More recently, the country's geographic closeness and strong political and sociocultural ties with England have, to an extent, led to standardization and dialect contact-induced merger with EngE (see Chapters 1 and 5).

In World Englishes literature, WelE is characterized as a *shift variety*, but the term receives somewhat varying interpretations. Trudgill (2009: 304) places both WelE and IrE in this category on the basis that they have shifted from second to primarily first language varieties. Mesthrie and Bhatt (2008: 6), on the other hand, observe that IrE has evolved from a shift variety into a social dialect, while WelE, with its large L1 Welsh bilingual speaker group, is still at the shift stage, as it continues to interact with and receive input from the Welsh language. Thomas (1994: 145), then, defines WelE as "a transitional phenomenon", transitionality meaning a gradual disappearance of the most distinctive Welsh-induced features of grammar under standard BrE and vernacular EngE influence. This is not reflected in its phonology, which is more resistant to change, but it is certainly evident in its morphosyntax. As demonstrated in this chapter and in Paulasto (2006, 2016), considerable levelling of contact-induced features of syntax has taken place in WelE over the past century. Whether this trend is still in progress is a question that we will examine further with regard to specific features, and at the end of Chapter 5 (5.7 Changes in progress), as regards the variety as a whole. Some of the evidence indicates that the levelling may have come to a halt: certain dialect features of syntax, such as focus fronting or the invariant tags *is it/isn't it* (examined under

Discourse features in Section 4.4), are maintained by younger generations of speakers, albeit in forms which approach EngE usages. Paulasto (2016) argues that despite the functional shifts, they nevertheless descend from regionally salient contact-induced features and, in combination with each other, continue to characterize WelE as a distinctive variety.

Like its phonology, the morphosyntax of WelE is regionally and sociolinguistically varied. The variation is largely dependent on the same factors, that is, the history of Anglicization, the role of Welsh contact influence in the locality, the role of EngE dialect contacts and their origin, and the influence of present-day standard BrE as well as of widespread vernacular features (see below). The main dialect division is between the southeast, eastern border and other long-standing English regions on the one hand, and the traditional Welsh language counties in the north and west on the other (see Section 1.4). However, the division is a matter of frequencies and historical depth of the English language rather than clear boundaries. Broadly speaking, in the south and east, the balance of EngE dialect contact and Welsh language contact influence is tilted towards the former, while in the north and west it is towards the latter. There is one factor which affects the regional phonology of WelE but which does not induce much morphosyntactic variation: the North–South dialect division of the Welsh language. There are few features with regional differences in the grammar of WelE that can be traced back to similar regional divisions in Welsh. The regionally varied usages will be examined in detail below.

The focus in this section will be on those features that are characteristic of WelE dialects in particular. It should be borne in mind, however, that spoken WelE is for the most part very similar to British Mainstream Dialects, including both StE and modern nonstandard dialects (Trudgill [1990] 1999: 5–6). Among the widespread colloquial BrE features are the default singular *there's* and multiple negation (e.g. Cheshire et al. 1993), as well as the following instances, which are noted in the linguistic commentaries for the BBC *Voices* interviews. These tend to occur in the south and east of Wales rather the west and northwest.

- *Them* for determiner *those*, e.g. *them Irish lads'll you know they'll be on us!* (*Voices*: Flint, also Talbot Green). Some use in TC.
- Reflexive with a non-reflexive function, e.g. *uh a long long time ago my two brothers George and Ralph and myself went to the Isle of Man* (*Voices*: Flint, also Holyhead, Talbot Green).
- Emphatic adverb of degree *that*, e.g. *'cause she's starting to pick up words that much quicker* (*Voices*: Newtown, also Rhos-on-Sea, Talbot Green).
- Double comparative, e.g. *I just wanted people to think I was more superior than them* (*Voices*: Splott); *English is much more easier for me to understand reading it than Welsh* (NWC: 6d).

- Zero auxiliary *have*, e.g. *yeah we got the leisure centre and we got the community centres* (*Voices*: Bon-y-Maen, also Builth Wells, Llanelli, Splott, Treorchy); *they got a different Welsh [in North Wales]* (LC: 7a); common in TC and LC, somewhat less so in NWC.
- Zero copular *be*, e.g. *she said, "what do you mean? you off your rocker, like?"* (*Voices*: Holyhead, also Talbot Green).
- Emphatic (pronoun) tags (right dislocation), e.g. *I call it 'CJ', me, now* (*Voices*: Bethesda); *I am usually cold I am* (TC: 3b); *I like to speak Welsh, I do* (LC: 2c; for further observations on right dislocation in WelE, see Durham 2015, 2019).

The most natural points of comparison for WelE morphosyntax are Standard British English, EngE dialects, and other Celtic Englishes. Especially relevant is IrE, which shares a similar two-language contact setting and a language shift, the most intense phase of which took place in the nineteenth century, preceding Wales by some sixty years (Paulasto 2009: 213; see Chapter 5). Moreover, there is by now an extensive body of research on countless aspects of IrE. References will also be made to the eWAVE (Kortmann et al. 2020) and to other, for example, postcolonial varieties of English, where relevant. Some of the terminology used to describe the features – such as extension, addition, replacement, or omission – refer to StE as an implicit benchmark variety. We emphasize that the terms are not intended to convey any prescriptive connotations, but they are pragmatic choices, aligning with commonly used terminology in dialectology, contact linguistics and World Englishes research (see, e.g. Thomason 2001, Schneider 2007, Szmrecsanyi 2013).

Sections 3.2, 3.3 and 3.4 focus on features that occur in present-day WelE, that are characteristic of the variety, and/or that mainly (or potentially) result from Welsh contact influence. Section 3.5 examines characteristics that originate from EngE dialect contact, such as the above, although possible connections to the Welsh language are investigated here too. The data used in this chapter arise from the corpora listed in Section 1.6. as well as from earlier studies, notably *SAWD* (Parry 1977, 1979, 1999, Penhallurick 1991).

3.2 Noun phrase: Irregular use of articles

Extended definite article use
There is some variation in article use in WelE in comparison to StE. The most systematic instances concern the definite article, which WelE speakers may insert in contexts where it would not be found formal standard BrE, such as with social institutions (*go to the church/school/hospital*, etc.), quantifying expressions involving *both*, or names of languages (for the findings in SAWD, see Parry 1999:

108). Nonstandard article use has been documented in numerous varieties of English around the world. Mesthrie & Bhatt (2008: 52) suggest that there is a dichotomy of over- and underuse of articles among varieties of English, the former being more characteristic of Celtic Englishes. The data in eWAVE indeed indicate that extension of the definite article in place of zero is typically a feature of northern EngE and British high-contact varieties, including Celtic Englishes, but also of Caribbean creoles and certain contact-induced varieties in Asia and Africa (Kortmann et al. 2020).

Of the Celtic Englishes, wider use of the definite article has been studied in IrE, in particular. Filppula (1999: 56–64) finds as many as seventeen contexts in IrE where the definite article is used in place of zero. Taking these categories as the starting point for the description of WelE usage reveals that many of them – but not all – are represented in the WelE corpora. As pointed out by Kallen (2013: 123–125) for IrE, the extended use of the definite article can be associated with definite/specific reference, but there are also generic uses. The following categories coincide with IrE, but there is broad variation in their frequencies. Shorrocks (1999: 31–42), then, presents a detailed functional categorization of definite article usage in the traditional urban speech of the Bolton area, northern EngE, which displays many similarities with WelE and IrE. Of the categories below, his study includes instances of nearly each one, apart from names of languages, as well as some usages that are not found in WelE. Based on his phonetic transcriptions, however, the definite article is commonly reduced in the Bolton dialect, whereas in WelE this is not the case (for definite article reduction, see the following section).

(a) Plural count nouns with generic reference. In the present-day WelE corpora, extended definite article use is only found with the noun *people*, but the transcribed SAWD interviews include other instances too. In (5a), the shortage of young singers in male voice choirs has just been discussed, making the item hearer-old, but in (5b) *beans* are mentioned for the first time.

(5) a. ...there are very old choirs, old established choirs that they've got *the young people* but there's only a handful of them now. (LC: 4f)
 b. ...put them peas in for the cows and for the cattle and- very few put *the beans* for the animals. (SAWD, Gn 7: 3)

(b) Non-count abstract nouns and concrete mass nouns. This category is relatively productive, although the majority of instances are found in SAWD or in elderly informants' speech. The use of the definite article may be based on the contextual specificity of the item in question (i.e. 'the traffic that there is now'; 'the milk that she should be producing').

(6) a. Well, parents are working and I suppose they just say, you know, have your- go to a fish shop and have... *The life* is totally different. (LC: 1a)
  b. ...we used to have bikes, we used to er, play a lot on bicycles.
     [M-hm.]
     Yes, of course there wasn't *the traffic* then so we were allowed to go into the village (NWC, Llwyngwril: 4c)
  c. [An orphan is a lamb whose mother has...]
     Died or hasn't got *the milk* to feed. (SAWD, Gn 8: 2)

(c) Quantifying expressions involving *both* (& *most, half* and *all*; of these, *the half* occurs in northern EngE; Shorrocks 1999: 39). In the WelE data, this concerns only *both* as there are no instances of the other types. *SAWD* records *the both* in numerous localities in South Wales (Parry 1999: 108), but not in the north. Instances in this category are not found in NWC, either, and there is just one occurrence in TC.

(7) a. [Where are they from?]
     Well, originally from Llandybie.
     [Both *>of them?]
     The both<* of them. (LC: 2c)
  b. [That's your first language?]
     Yes, most- some of the time.
     [What does that mean?]
     <xxx> cause b- between *the both*, yeah, it varies between *the both*. (LC: 6d)

(d) Names of languages. These receive the definite article in WelE more frequently than items in any other category. As shown by examples (8a-b) below, the usage is not systematic. Interestingly, the informants in the youngest age group in LC extend definite article use in this context quite frequently. It is also observed in TC and NWC to an extent, but not in EngE.

(8) a. Yeah some say that it's go- *the Welsh* is going to die, to be wiped, you know- be- the language would be gone, you know, like the- in Scotland now it's *the Gaelic*, you know, well they don't speak a lot of *Gaelic* now in Scotland you see. (LC: 1d)
  b. Yes, but it- the Welsh language wouldn't take you anywhere. It's *the English*.
     [I know, mm.]
     If er- you step out of Wales, and it's got to be *an English language*, hasn't it. (LC: 1a)

(e) Names of diseases or ailments. *SAWD* has *(got) the headache* (Gw 5) and several mentions of *(got) the toothache* (Cl 2, P 5/25, Dy 18, MG: Rhydri, Gw 4–5 & Newport) in the east and south of the country (Parry 1999: 108), and *the mumps* in Cardiganshire (Parry 1979: 142). Our own searches in SAWD also produced *you got the hiccup* (SAWD, Gn 7: 1) in Botwnnog on the Lleyn peninsula. There is variation in article use within this category, however, as shown in the section below. Example (9) could be included either in this group or in (b) above:

(9) He had *the coal dust* on the lungs, you know, the- the- the disease they get through working. (LC: 1b)

(f) Names of social and domestic institutions. Along with names of languages, this is the context with the most instances of definite article use in LC, particularly with *hospital* (6; 50%) but also with *school* (5; 2%) and *church* (1; 7%). Definite article use with *hospital* is globally common, however, as observed by Filppula et al. (2009: 244). Example (10b) illustrates, besides the English definite article use, also the corresponding Welsh expression, which contains the definite article *(y)r*. Comparatively few instances are found in NWC and none in TC.

(10) a. Oh I thought you were in the sixth form or something in *the school* and then you- you'd be going into a university when you're going back. (LC: 2e)
    b. My- my grandmother now, she- she used- she said something to me erm, Tuesday she- she went to *the hospital* on Tuesday. There we are, I would say, "wyt ti mynd i'*r hospit*-" I- I would say, if I was to say, er, "are you going to *the hospital* on Tuesday",
[Mm.]
in Welsh, I would say er, "wyt ti mynd i'*r hospital* dydd Mawrth?" I would use "hospital" instead of "ysbyty". (LC: 7i)
    c. I dare say I should go to *the church* more than I do (LC: 6e)
    d. Are you living in *the town* or are you living further out in, you know, in- in the country? (i.e. 'in [a] town'; LC: 5g)

(g) Expressions involving reference to body parts. Only one such instance is found, in the transcribed SAWD materials, but there seems to be no question that the informant prefers the definite article for the possessive pronoun.

(11) [When a baby hits its head on the door, there might be a slight swelling on…]

On *the forehead.* (after a patient search for the pronoun *his/her*) (SAWD, Gn 8: 1)

(h) Terms for members of the family. The definite article replaces the possessive pronoun in several instances recorded in *SAWD* in North Wales (Penhallurick 1991: 186): *the wife* (Gn 1–2/4/6/10, Cl 2–3/5–7), *the daughter* (Gn 1), *the lad* (i.e. 'my son'; Cl 2). There are also four instances of *the wife* instead of 'my wife' in LC and one in NWC but none in TC. Judging by the numerous similar instances recorded in *SED* (see Penhallurick 1991: 186), this seems to be a feature of general vernacular currency in BrE.

(i) Terms for parts of the day, week, or year (of these, seasons and *the night* are mentioned in Shorrocks 1999: 34–35). Extended use of the definite article occurs in the corpora with respect to days of the week. Expressions such as *in the summer/winter* (instead of *in summer/winter*), however, are frequent enough in present-day English so as not to warrant a separate mention in this context. The expression *in the night* is used in the data to some extent, but no more frequently than *at night* (cf. Filppula 1999: 61, who mentions that IrE speakers clearly prefer the former). In example (12a), the speaker refers to a specific Monday ('the following Monday') and Sunday ('that Sunday'). No specific reference is involved in (12b), however.

(12) a. it was Sunday, and the- they could see by the direction of the wind and everything that there was gonna be a lot of rain and a storm on *the Monday*. But of course they could not do anything, they could not harvest this corn on *the Sunday*, they- they were so strict (LC: 4a)
b. I always go to town on *the Friday*. (SAWD, Gn 8: 1)
c. I might sometimes, after I put the fire up *in the night*, I- I'll come in here, or I might dust, you know? (LC: 1c)

The English article system is vulnerable to variation regardless of the variety (see Sand 2003: 414–416). In Wales, it may nevertheless also be affected by Welsh definite article usage, which differs in relevant respects from English. Thorne (1993: 97–100) states that the definite article is used in Welsh, for example, before the names of languages, seasons, days of the week and certain diseases, and in a number of phrases where it does not occur in English, such as *yn yr ysbyty* 'in hospital', *yn yr eglwys* 'in church', *i'r ysgol* 'to school', and *i'r dref* 'to town'. The same applies to *y ddau/y ddwy* 'both' (King 1993: 115). Thorne and King also mention a number of other contexts for the Welsh definite article, such as titles and appointments, names of festivals, means of transport or the phrases 'in work' or 'to bed'. There is no corpus evidence of the definite article being transferred to WelE in these cases, but in some varieties of IrE it also occurs in these expressions (Filppula 1999: 60–63; see Corrigan 2010: 52–53 for Northern Irish usages).

As pointed out above, the definite article is used in nearly all of the above functions also in EngE and ScE, with the exception of names of languages (e.g. Shorrocks 1999: 31–42). Parry (1999: 108) mentions that *(got) the toothache/headache* is widespread in *SED*, and *the both* is also recorded, particularly in the southwestern counties. There are, in other words, contexts where EngE dialect contact is the likeliest explanation (e.g. body parts, members of the family), and other contexts, where the effects of Welsh and EngE cannot easily be told apart (e.g. names of domestic institutions). In certain cases, the Welsh contact explanation is compelling in spite of similarities in EngE. Although Sabban (1982: 384–385, cited in Filppula 1999: 69–70) refers to northern English parallels in *SED* and the *English Dialect Dictionary (EDD)* for the Hebrides English (HebE) forms *the school* and *the church*, it is unlikely that northern EngE would have a significant effect on this feature in southwestern WelE. Names of languages also appear with the definite article in ScE as well as HebE, but not in EngE dialects (Sabban 1982: 395), which points towards a common Celtic denominator rather than EngE dialect contact.

As the above results indicate, WelE is far more constrained in this respect than IrE. Filppula et al. (2009: 243) offer quantitative evidence of this. The corpora in Table 3.1 represent elderly speakers, and the figures are based on a selection of eight items including social institutions and the quantifiers *both of*, *most of* and *half of*.

Table 3.1: Definite article usage in EngE (SED), WelE and IrE (Filppula et al. 2009: 243)

Corpus	The	Ø	Total N	% The
SED (515,000, pttw)	11 (0.21)	309 (6.00)	320 (6.21)	3.4
WelE (61,400, pttw)	9 (1.47)	124 (20.20)	133 (21.66)	6.8
IrE (158,000, pttw)	21 (1.33)	111 (7.03)	132 (8.35)	15.9

Extended definite article use is most common in IrE, followed by WelE and finally SED. The WelE instances occur with three items only: *hospital* (4; 67%), *both of* (3; 33%) and *school* (2; 3%).

Apparent-time results from Llandybie show that extended definite article use is not disappearing in the dialect quite yet, and the main reason for this is the function "Names of languages", which continues to appear in the speech of the youngest age group. Table 3.2 illustrates the normalized frequencies in the corpus per age group.

Table 3.2: Apparent-time change in extended definite article use in LC.

Item	I (52,000)	II (85,000)	III (66,300)	IV (57,400)	Total N
school	2	3	0	1	6
hospital	3	1	0	3	7
church	0	0	1	0	1
both	3	0	3	1	7
language	15	4	4	9	32
other	9	4	3	1	17
Total N	32	12	11	15	70
(pttw)	(6.2)	(1.4)	(1.7)	(2.6)	(2.7)

With a wider range of function types, the frequencies are of course higher than in Table 3.1 from Filppula et al. (2009: 243). There is a considerable slump in the middle age groups and a mild rise towards the youngest speakers, which may partly be explained by age grading, the middle-aged informants resorting to a more standard form of English in an interview situation.

NWC cannot be studied in apparent time, as there are only eight instances of the above types recorded in the entire NWC (0.7 pttw), seven of them in Gwynedd. It would therefore seem that this is a southern rather than northern WelE feature. No instances are found in the speech of the youngest informants, born in 1970 or after.

Loss or reduction of indefinite and definite articles
The second type of irregular use concerns the omission or reduction of articles, which is found to occur in WelE on occasion. It is somewhat unclear, however, whether the article is in fact completely absent or whether it is simply reduced in rapid speech so as to appear to be absent. There is no research data on carefully pronounced speech to confirm the matter in one direction or the other. In eWAVE, zero article use in place of the indefinite article has a global distribution that is very different from the above, extended definite article use: It is primarily a feature of pidgins and creoles, along with a number of contact-induced varieties. Of the Celtic Englishes, it is only attested in WelE but listed as "extremely rare" (Kortmann et al. 2020). It is, however, a feature of northern EngE (Shorrocks 1999: 47, Beal 2008: 380), and Wagner (2008: 418) comments on the phonological reduc-

tion of *an* to *a* to inaudible in southwestern EngE (see also Other types of irregular use below).

Loss (or apparent loss) of the indefinite article is found in *SAWD* mainly along the English border. Parry (1999: 107) records *Could I have apple* (Cl 3, Gw: Newport) and *(got) headache* (P 16/20–21, WG 2). He points out that the latter occurs in *SED* in the vast majority of counties. The following examples arise from the SAWD transcriptions and TC, which contains several instances.

(13) a. [You'd ask him, er...]
  If he's got Ø *toothache*. (SAWD, Dy 3: 1)
 b. I got Ø *sister*, she's having a birthday that day. (SAWD, Gn 8: 1)
 c. you know you can go to Cardiff, and they got Ø *entirely different way of-* they sound entirely different don't they (TC: 5b)

Zero or reduced indefinite article usage is rare in LC and NWC. This, together with the general distribution of the feature in the above sources, indicates that it might result from EngE dialect contact. Welsh has no indefinite articles, however, and thus a transfer effect is also a possibility in the SAWD data by L1 Welsh speakers (see ex. 13b).

Some instances where the definite article is omitted are recorded in TC as well (14a). Without a systematic investigation, it is difficult to say whether this feature is functionally related to northern English definite article reduction (DAR) or zero definite article usage (e.g. Rupp & Page-Verhoeff 2005, Tagliamonte & Roeder 2009). Parry (1999: 108) mentions instances of both types in SAWD, but the reduction only occurs before vowels and takes the form [ð] or [ðə], whereas DAR occurs before consonants as well and is typically realized as [ʔ], [t], [d] or [θ] (e.g. Tagliamonte & Roeder 2009: 438–443). Example (14b) illustrates Parry's transcriptions. This feature is common in SAWD throughout Welsh-speaking Wales as well as in the south and east, which indicates that it is a phonologically conditioned characteristic rather than the outcome of EngE dialect contact. Reduction in this context has a long history in English, however (Tagliamonte & Roeder 2009: 437) and it is widespread in *SED* (Parry 1999: 108).

(14) a. they- they cleaned Ø *majority of it* up like (TC: 5c)
 b. in *th' oven, th' eaves, the 'orse* (Parry 1999: 108)
 c. to cast Ø *calf*, to slip Ø *calf* 'to calve before time' (Dy 12-13/20, SG 3), cut it with Ø *hook* (Dy 17), he used to go down Ø *pit* (Cl 3), lay Ø *table* (WG 2; Parry 1999: 108)

The zero articles in (14c), in contrast, are all recorded either in the longstanding English areas or close by in West Glamorganshire. There is no trigger in Welsh that would support the zero variant, and hence it is not surprising that the article is maintained in the Welsh-speaking areas. Tagliamonte and Roeder (2009: 436–437) examine the history of the English zero definite article as well, pointing out that this historical variant declined during the Middle English period but was maintained in some regional varieties and is "traditionally [...] associated with Southeast Yorkshire". It is not regionally widespread today, either.

Other types of irregular use
In addition to the above, Parry (1999: 107–108) pays attention to certain other nonstandard features associated with article use in SAWD. These include alternation between *a/an* before a following vowel/consonant (e.g. *a acre, a eel, a 'oliday, a 'andful; an ewe, an holiday*). The attestations are sporadic but focused mainly in the south. Similar reduction in the form of the indefinite article is found in many dialects of EngE (Britain 2007: 103–104), including the southwest (Wagner 2008: 418–419). Parry (1999: 107) mentions that in the reverse instances, the noun following *an* retains its initial consonant. The "h-dropping" observed above is discussed further in Chapter 2, but also "w-dropping" may lead to the use of *an* instead of *a*. The SAWD transcriptions include the phrase *it was an wooden block* (SAWD, Dy 4: 1), *wooden* being pronounced without the initial semi-vowel. Thomas (1994: 107–108) points out that Welsh has "no sequences of semi-vowel followed by a homorganic or near-homorganic vowel", which might here result in the loss of initial [w] and the use of the corresponding article.

Plural nouns that are treated as singular are more widespread in the data, especially the items *a scissors* and *a tongs*, which were part of the SAWD lexical questionnaire (Parry 1999: 107–108). The incidental items include *a bellows, a hames, a shears,* and *a trouser*, where the respective Welsh words are singular in form, and a few others, for example, *a scales, a stairs, a straps*. The vast majority of these instances have been recorded in the southern parts of Wales. Windsor Lewis (1990c: 116), too, makes a note of them in Glamorgan English. Similar usages are not found in the contemporary WelE corpora.

3.3 Verb phrase

There are two dialect constructions in WelE which are used to indicate habitual events: unemphatic periphrastic *do* and the progressive form (PF). Thomas (1984, 1994) considers these the "most characteristic feature" of WelE syntax

(1994: 134). The *SAWD* data (Parry 1999: 110–112) indicate that the two constructions exist in a fairly clear complementary distribution, the former being used in the very south and east of the country, while the latter is found in the bilingual or recently Anglicized areas of the north and west:

(15) Bulls *do roar* (SAWD, West Glamorgan 4 [Parry 1999: 110])

(16) [Do you do them right there?]
Yeah, yeah- no, no, we*'re doin'* them at home an' carry them there... (LC: 2d)

The regional distribution suggests that the origin of the two constructions is different: periphrastic *do* is an EngE dialect feature from southwest England, while habitual extension of the progressive *-ing* form is home-grown and Welsh-induced. Historically, the situation is a little more complicated. The PF is also used with stative verbs somewhat more freely than in standard BrE. The origins of the two constructions are examined in detail below.

3.3.1 Periphrastic *do*

In Standard English, auxiliary *do* is introduced in affirmative sentences for emphasis (e.g. *But I do think you are a good cook* ['...even if you imagine I don't']; Quirk et al. 1985: 133, 1371; called *emphatic polarity* in Huddleston and Pullum 2002: 97–98). The WelE dialect feature termed periphrastic *do*, however, has the pronunciation [də], with vowel reduction and no stress, and it is used in habitual situations, mainly in the present tense (Parry 1979: 148, Penhallurick 1994: 169). In regional terms, this southern WelE feature links to the southwest English dialects, where the construction and its semantics have been studied quite extensively (e.g. Ihalainen 1976, Klemola 1994, 1998, 2002, Jones 2002). Its origins are in the Early Modern English (EModE) affirmative declarative *do*, described by Rissanen (1991) as functionally versatile and more typical of spoken than written language. This construction lost ground and fell out of use in StE towards the end of this period (Ellegård 1953), but maintained its popularity in some regional dialects. Jones (2002: 128–129) notes, however, that periphrastic *do* in the present tense is becoming obsolete in Somerset English, while *did* is maintained better.

In traditional southwestern English this feature behaves somewhat differently from the WelE periphrastic *do*. It is frequently used in the past tense, too, and in addition to the habitual function (specifically in the past tense, see Jones 2002: 120–121), it may be used in event past and conditional/temporal clause contexts (Klemola 1998: 43–49). Klemola (1998: 37–38) furthermore cites a study by

Weltens (1983) which showed that whereas southwest English informants found periphrastic *do* to be acceptable also in punctual events, South Welsh informants only accepted habitual usages. The systematic word order changes with adverbs like *always*, which Ihalainen (1976: 609) and Jones (2002: 124) observe in the Somerset dialect, cannot be confirmed in WelE, as there are no instances involving these adverbs in the data.

Globally speaking, *do* functions as a habitual marker in a limited set of varieties (Kortmann et al. 2020). The eWAVE lists it as "pervasive" in southern Caribbean creoles (e.g. Barbados, Guyana, Trinidad) and Gullah only, while in WelE and IrE it is used sometimes/in some contexts and in southwestern EngE it is considered "extremely rare".

In *SAWD*, periphrastic *do* appears primarily in the incidental material recorded outside the survey questionnaire. There are some items in the questionnaire which are designed to elicit constructions indicating habituality: These questions produced, for example, the response *She do wear the trousers* (SG 1, Gw 1/4/6/8) in South and West Glamorgan and Gwent (Parry 1999: 110). The incidental materials include the following examples (Parry 1999: 110; Parry 1977: 161–162; Parry 1979: 148):

(17) a. you *do have* 'em by the hundred (WG 2); lime *do freshen* it (WG 2); we *do collect* different fruits (Dy/Cdg 2); the cows *do graze* in the fields (Dy/Pem 9); they *do keep* hens (P/Bre 7, MG 10/11);
 b. a machine *does do* it (P 7, Dy 4)
 c. that *did serve* (WG 3)

The recorded instances are few and scattered, but they indicate that the auxiliary *do* is nearly always used in the present tense, it is often uninflected for 3sg, and the core area for this construction is southeast Wales, the Gower peninsula and southern Pembrokeshire (for Gowerland, see also Penhallurick 1994: 168–169). A few instances have been recorded in Mid-Wales, Cardiganshire and Powys. In these cases (see 17b), the auxiliary is inflected for 3sg.

Of the present-day WelE corpora, periphrastic *do* is recorded in Tonypandy, and of the *Voices* localities, in Talbot Green in Rhondda Cynon Taff:

(18) a. he got a <laughter> he got a fast left hand. I *do call* him the seagull (TC: 2)
 b. [How does the Cardiff accent sound to you then?]
 Well I guess they *do put* a little bit of a- a twang like innit, or they present theirselves different. (TC: 3b)
 c. it's just the way I *do speak* and that's it (*Voices*: Talbot Green)

All instances are in the present tense, and none occur with a 3sg subject, which may be a coincidence or indicative of a grammatical constraint to avoid inflection (or lack thereof). The majority of instances in TC (17/22) are from one and the same informant, but it seems clear that the feature continues to be used in this area to some extent: It is used by four of the 10 informants, and with the omission of the most productive one, the normalized frequency is 1.1/10,000 words. There is, however, no straightforward distinction between the emphatic and habitual functions, as shown below.

Table 3.3 gives the functional distribution of the *do*-auxiliary in affirmative sentences in TC. The categories are three: 1) habitual periphrastic *do*, as described above; 2) explicit emphasis, where the discourse context suggests a contrastive or confirmatory/reassertive emphatic function, and 3) implicit emphasis, where the discourse trigger for the emphasis is less clear. *Do* is unstressed in the first category and stressed, or pronounced with the strong form [duː], in the latter two, but interestingly, all of the above categories involve habitual-generic situations. Some instances have a stative verb used in a non-habitual context (e.g. *I 'do think that I improve*; TC: 6b), common also in southwest English dialects (Klemola 1998: 40–43). None of the usages occur in a punctual semantic context.

Table 3.3: Functions of the *do*-auxiliary in affirmative sentences in TC (49,800 words).

Function	N	pttw	%
Habitual periphrastic *do*	22	4.42	49
Explicit emphasis	10	2.01	22
Implicit emphasis	13	2.61	29
Total	45	9.04	100

The usages found in the corpus indicate that the regional, habitual unstressed function and the emphatic function overlap. Example (19) illustrates usages with explicit emphatic polarity and a contrastive (19a) and confirmatory (19b) discourse function, whereas the examples in (20) lack polarity, that is, an explicit trigger in the conversation. Quirk et al. (1985: 1372) note that on occasion, "*do*-support is introduced where there would otherwise be no operator to bear the emphatic stress" (e.g. *You 'do look a wreck*). This may be one of the reasons for employing *do* in cases of implicit emphasis. As pointed out above, all situations are habitual ones.

(19) a. A: or your Sunday best
B: I- I personally wouldn't but er,
[Yeah.]
B: people 'do use that expression (TC: 5b)
b. [Was that authentic, is that actually how people speak or...?]
Yes, we 'do mix the Welsh and the English. (TC: 3c)

(20) a. no I think, this is the way I sound
[Right.]
and we 'do tease the headmaster you know [for not having a Rhondda accent] (TC: 6b)
b. "whatshername now" ah, "thingy" [...] we 'do chop- we chop words down though I mean
[Yeah.]
three words into one: "whatshername" (TC: 3c)

Based on the TC evidence, it seems that habituality is the central characteristic in the use of periphrastic *do* in the dialect, so much so that it also guides the emphatic use of the *do*-auxiliary. Although most speakers use the unstressed habitual "periphrastic *do* proper" fairly little, if at all, it hovers at the background of emphatic usage as well. Conversely, habitual periphrastic *do* may be evolving in the dialect so that it requires a standard, emphatic discourse context. The instances of implicit emphasis are an indication of this kind of convergent development. Unfortunately, the data do not permit closer quantitative or sociolinguistic observations.

As stated above, the regional distribution of periphrastic *do* points to EngE dialect contact. The SED Spoken Corpus shows that the core area for this construction in EngE is the southwest, more specifically Monmouthshire (in the southeast of Wales), Gloucestershire, Somerset, Dorset, Wiltshire and Herefordshire. The normalized frequencies of use in these counties exceed those of TC markedly, from 42.7 pttw in Gloucestershire to 14.4 in Herefordshire (and 30.8 in Monmouthshire; see Paulasto 2006: 244). It therefore seems clear that the direction of influence has been from England to Wales, despite the eWAVE suggesting that this feature is less commonly used in England than in Wales (Kortmann et al. 2020). It also seems that southwestern EngE has experienced considerable standardization in this respect. This conclusion is supported by Jones's (2002) findings on the current decline of the present tense periphrastic *do* in Somerset.

Another question is the historical development of periphrastic *do* – and the *do*-auxiliary in general – in England. Recent research indicates that rather than causative *do*, which has traditionally been considered the source of the *do*-auxiliary in English (e.g. Ellegård 1953), the origin of this construction lies in Brythonic substrate which dates back to the Old and Middle English periods (e.g. Tristram 1997, van der Auwera & Genee 2002, Filppula et al. 2008, McWhorter 2009). The respective Middle Welsh auxiliary construction is functionally similar to the English one. Thus, the periphrastic *do* construction in WelE might also be considered to originate from Celtic substrate, but from an older layer than the other regionally distinctive habitual construction, extended progressive form used in the traditionally Welsh-speaking parts of the country. We will turn to this feature next.

3.3.2 Extended uses of the progressive form

In comparison to StE, the progressive or BE -*ing* form is extended in WelE to habitual and some stative situations. As observed by Thomas (1985: 215), the two habitual dialect constructions, periphrastic *do* and the progressive form (PF), are used in near-complementary distribution. While the former is found in the southern and southeastern regions which Anglicized early on, by the end of the nineteenth century at the latest, the latter occurs in most parts of the west and north of Wales where English only became a prominent community language in the twentieth century. The regional distinction is not quite clear-cut, as there is some overlapping use of both constructions in the southeast. Thomas (1985: 215) and Penhallurick (1996: 312) find that besides locality, extended PF use depends on the language skills of the individuals, as it is mainly recorded from bilingual Welsh-speaking informants. This would imply direct L1 transfer. However, the corpus collected by Ceri George shows that extended uses have been common in the Rhondda, too, in the speech of elderly non-Welsh-speakers (see below).

The progressive is a core construction in present-day English, and hence its frequencies and functions have been studied extensively across varieties and genres. The general observation is that the use of PF continues to increase in standard BrE and American English (AmE), particularly in colloquial registers and in certain semantic functions (see, e.g. Leech et al. 2009: 122–136, Smitterberg 2005, Kranich 2010). As shown by Paulasto (2014a), however, the distinctive types of extension in WelE are independent of the general development. It should also be noted that wider uses of the PF are attested in World Englishes relatively frequently: Extended stative use is found in 64% of all 77 varieties in eWAVE (Kortmann et al. 2020), making it the 22nd most widespread feature of the 235 in the atlas. It occurs in a wide range of variety types and geographic areas, from traditional L1 English in the British Isles (e.g. ScE) to indigenized L2 (e.g. IndE, KenE) and creoles (e.g. in Trinidad). Extended habitual use is less common but nevertheless attested in 49% of all varieties, this time primarily in contact-induced ones (e.g. MxE, BahE, IndE, BlSAfE, TriC). In WelE, eWAVE lists both usages as "neither pervasive nor extremely rare". *SAWD* and the present corpus data, however, indicate that habitual extension is considerably more common in WelE than stative extension.

By extended use of the PF we mean, more specifically, temporally non-delimited PF in habitual and stative situations. There are other types of extension as well, but these are of little relevance for WelE. In StE, the PF can be used with dynamic (non-telic) verbs to indicate habituality within a limited time period. Temporariness is conveyed also when the PF combines with stance and certain other stative verbs (see Quirk et al. 1985: 198–199, 206), but these instances may also carry other meanings, such as agentive activity or gradual change of state (Huddleston and Pullum 2002: 167; Leech et al. 2009: 129–130). Central for the extended uses, therefore, is the lack of a temporary interpretation: The PF is used in nondelimited situations, replacing the canonical present or past simple form or another habitual marker such as the auxiliaries *would* or *used to*.

There is plenty of evidence for both types of extension in the present corpora, particularly in the north and west of the country. The regional distribution is prominent in *SAWD*, where only a few instances arise from Powys in the east or from West and South Glamorgan in the south (Parry 1999: 110–111, Penhallurick 1991: 187–191). There are no instances from Gwent or Mid Glamorgan, that is, the very southeast or the Valleys. Most occurrences are recorded in the incidental material, where extended PF use occurs in the present and past tense alike, and it may combine with (habitual) modal auxiliaries or with the perfect construction (Penhallurick 1996: 312). LC and NWC show that the feature is productive also in present-day WelE, albeit it is not very frequent in the speech of informants who are middle-aged or younger (see Figure 3.1 below). It is also recorded in the Rhondda corpora, CGC and TC, with much lower frequencies in the latter. The *Voices* commentaries contain no observations of this feature, nor is it mentioned in sources focusing on southeastern varieties (e.g. Coupland 1988, Connolly 1990, Windsor Lewis 1990c).

The following instances illustrate habitual extension in *SAWD* (Parry 1999: 111–112, Penhallurick 1996: 334–335), LC, NWC and CGC. Using the PF with the verb *speak* to indicate ability or habitual use, as in (21b), is a characteristic of WelE which stems from Welsh contact influence. The habitual modal *would* combines with the PF, as does *used to* on occasion, whereas other modal verbs barely occur in habitual PF constructions. Example (22c) gives one of the few such instances ('schools teach', i.e. *will* is a habitual rather than future modal). Perfective PF constructions, as in (23a-b), are only found in SAWD.

(21) a. she's *wearing* the trousers (SAWD: Gn 7/9, Cl 7, P 15–16, Dy 10/15); we *are dumping* it (SAWD: Dy 2); you *were tying* up the cows (SAWD: Dy 4)
b. what's the percentage of- of natives of Finland are- *are speaking* Finnish? (LC: 2e)
c. once the kids were over, he *was going* home then for his lunch, he *was bringing* the children back with him then (LC: 1c)

(22) a. some of the ladies *would be making* little prize bags (CGC: DoJ)
b. we *used to be spending* a lot of time visiting them (LC: 3c)
c. most primary schools will- *will be teaching* through the medium of Welsh (NWC, Ruthin: 6g)

(23) a. I've never *been doing* that job (SAWD: Gn 7)
b. I've *been turning* it several times (SAWD: Gn 9)

Stative extension in WelE is interesting in the sense that it very rarely concerns stative verbs, particularly private states, where the use of the PF is highly constrained in StE. Nearly all stative instances recorded by Penhallurick (1996) in northern SAWD data involve dynamic verbs used in a stative context to describe, for example, shape, position or direction, as in (24a; 1996: 325, 337). The only stative verb that occurs in Penhallurick's data is *have*, which in turn extends semantically to generic-habitual situations (24b; 1996: 324, 326; see Biber et al. 1999: 360–364 for the semantic categorization). Stative extension occurs in LC and NWC as well (25), although with a limited set of verbs (see Table 3.4), and *would* + PF combines with stative verbs as well (26).

(24) a. they'*re holding* these hooks on (SAWD: Gn 1); the shaft tha(t)'*s goin'* up (SAWD: Gn 4)
b. she's *having* a birthday that day (SAWD: Gn 8); he's *havin'* all kind of bloody names (SAWD: Cl 1)

(25) a. I think Swansea *are having* it, little bit. (on accents; LC: 7a)
b. Saintess Tybie *was living* somewhere around the sixth century (LC: 4d)

(26) you'd have a face-slip which *would be facing* outward that way (CGC: BG)

Parry (1999: 111) presents further stative instances with *think*, *be*, and *fit*. He does not distinguish between habitual and stative usages but observes that these constructions indicate "habitual action or 'universal time'". Paulasto (2006, 2014a) finds, based on the LC, that the most common stative verb to occur with the PF in WelE is in fact *live*. As a stance verb, it employs the PF in StE quite frequently to indicate a temporary state, but in WelE the PF is also used in non-delimited situations. Table 3.4, cited from Paulasto (2014a: 263), compares the distribution of stative verbs in extended PF use in three spoken English corpora: the Indian component of International Corpus of English (ICE-India), LC, and the SED Spoken Corpus. The figures indicate that stative extension in WelE rarely concerns verbs other than *live*, and that traditional EngE dialects do not employ this feature, either. In Indian English (IndE), stative extension is used much more freely. Moreover, the lexical range is wider, but there is also a clear preference for *have*. The normalized frequency (M-coefficient) indicates instances per 100,000 words.

Table 3.4: Lexical differences in the extended stative function (Paulasto 2014a: 263).

Verb	ICE-India (189,600)		Llandybie (257,500)		SED (478,700)	
	N	M-coeff.	N	M-coeff.	N	M-coeff.
living	2	1.1	26	10.1	1	0.2
having	37	19.5	3	1.2	2	0.4
knowing	1	0.5	–	–	–	–
belonging	3	1.6	–	–	–	–
existing	3	1.6	–	–	–	–
being	3	1.6	2	0.8	1	0.2
coming*	4	2.1	1	0.4	–	–
going*	–	–	1	0.4	–	–
wanting	–	–	–	–	2	0.4
other	6	3.2	2	0.7	1	0.2
Total	**59**	**31.1**	**35**	**13.6**	**7**	**1.4**

*) Dynamic verbs used here in stative contexts; cf. example (24a).

As to the origin of extended PF use, WelE scholars (e.g. Parry 1979: 148, Thomas 1985: 215, Penhallurick 1996: 311-312, Paulasto 2006: 220) concur that it arises from Welsh contact influence, whether L1 Welsh transfer or Welsh substrate in monoglot speakers' English. The imperfective construction used in Colloquial Welsh is similar to the English PF in form, consisting of BOD 'be', imperfective marker *yn* and a verbal noun, but aspectually it is wider, having both progressive and habitual meanings. It is also obligatory with numerous stative verbs, including *byw* 'live'. Thus, habitual or stative situations of the following types are expressed using the imperfective BOD periphrasis.

(27) a. *Mae*   *ef*   *yn mynd*   i'r sinema   bob wythnos
be.PRES.3SG   he   IM go.VN   to-the cinema   every week
'He goes to the cinema every week' (Thomas 1985: 215)
b. *Y*   *mae*   *yn pwyso*   pedwar pwys a hanner
ASS   be.PRES.3SG   IM weigh.VN   four pound and half
'It weighs four pounds and a half.' (Rouveret 1996: 133)

The construction is semantically ambiguous, with the potential to denote either a habitual or progressive event (e.g. *mae hi'n darllen the Daily Telegraph* 'she reads/ is reading the DT'). Transfer occurs, when a Welsh speaker replicates the imperfective construction in English using the PF in habitual or stative situations (i.e. *he is going to the cinema; it is weighing four pounds*), but extension also occurs as a conventionalized substrate feature, independent of direct transfer.

The Welsh contact origin of extended PF use is confirmed when its frequencies and functions of use are compared against traditional EngE. Table 3.5 (see Paulasto 2006: 248–249) gives the figures for extended (habitual, stative and *would/used to* + PF constructions) and delimited/progressive PF use by elderly informants in three WelE corpora (LC, NWC & CGC) and the SED Spoken Corpus. The data sets are comparable (see Section 1.6), and yet there are vast differences in the overall normalized frequencies. The oldest informants in the LC, born in the 1910s and 1920s, produce 23.7 instances pttw, out of which 12.9 are extended, while the SED informants remain in 3.7 instances (1.2 for extended uses).

Table 3.5: PF usage by elderly informants in LC, NWC, CGC and SED.

	LC (52,000)		NWC (31,100)		CGC (30,050*)		SED (478,700)	
	N	%	N	%	N	%	N	%
Extended habitual (pttw)	47 (9.0)	38	5 (1.6)	23	19 (6.2)	20	22 (0.5)	12
Extended stative (pttw)	17 (3.3)	14	–	–	3 (1.0)	3	9 (0.2)	5
Would/used to + PF (pttw)	3 (0.6)	2	2 (0.6)	9	33 (10.8)	34	25 (0.5)	14
Delim/prog habitual (pttw)	56 (10.8)	46	15 (4.8)	68	42 (13.8)	43	121 (2.53)	68
Total (pttw)	123 (23.7)	100	22 (7.1)	100	97 (31.8)	100	177 (3.7)	100

*Estimated word count (see Paulasto 2006: 153).

The two other corpora, NWC and CGC, illustrate regional differences in Wales. Unlike what one might expect, the overall figures are low in North Wales but high in the Rhondda. These corpora are small and thus not fully representative of their respective populations, but they do reflect the differences between formally and informally acquired varieties (see also Paulasto 2009). The northern, relatively highly educated informants adhere more closely to StE norms of PF usage despite being L1 Welsh speakers, whereas the monoglot English Rhondda informants display abundant use of the PF in the above functions. For the sake of comparison, Roller's (2016: 47, 103) frequencies for extended habitual PF, 15.55 pttw in FRED and 2.64 in the Radio Wales Corpus, match the present ones quite well, although the figure for FRED is notably high. Slight differences in the semantic classification may explain the difference to an extent, along with the oral history nature of the FRED corpus.

The standard, delimited/progressive function is proportionally most common in the NWC and SED, while extended habitual and stative uses are particularly characteristic of the southwestern LC. The difference between LC and NWC is likely to result, at least partly, from the position of English. In LC, too, all elderly informants are L1 Welsh speakers, but as Llandybie is situated on the border of the Anglicized South, English has a long history as a community language in the area. These informants have thus acquired the language at school as well as in the community (see Section 1.6). We conclude that informal acquisition of the regional variety of English has led to a high degree of Welsh contact influence in the speech of the elderly generation in LC as well as in CGC.

The Rhondda informants of CGC, then, employ the StE habitual markers *would* and *used to* in combination with the PF considerably frequently. It is also worth mentioning that although the Rhondda belongs in the periphrastic *do* dialect area (see Section 3.3.1), extended PF is the more common of the two constructions in CGC: Periphrastic *do* occurs only three times (1.0 pttw), with further two potential cases of implicit emphasis (0.7 pttw). However, the more recent TC shows a preference for periphrastic *do* rather than the PF, with only eight instances of the above types of extended or habitual modal PF use (1.6 pttw). This implies that over the latter half of the twentieth century, there has been a shift from the Welsh-induced feature towards the EngE feature (which, in turn, is being affected by mainstream BrE).

Besides regional variation, there are also considerable diachronic changes in the use of this feature from the early twentieth century onwards. The first observation concerns the functional range of the PF, which is reduced in the present-day corpora in comparison to SAWD. Penhallurick (1996) and Paulasto (2006) find that SAWD informants occasionally combine the habitual PF with the perfect construction, as in example (23). In these cases, the PF does not indicate possible incompleteness, nor a temporary situation or habit leading up to the present, as in StE (Quirk et al. 1985: 210–212), but general indefinite past. Semantically, these are instances of experiential perfect, to follow Comrie's (1976: 56–60) terminology. They may also denote habituality, but in negated sentences this is of course debatable (see Paulasto 2006: 230). Such occurrences are not found in any of the other WelE corpora, which indicates that this construction type is limited to L1 Welsh speakers with a comparatively low English proficiency.

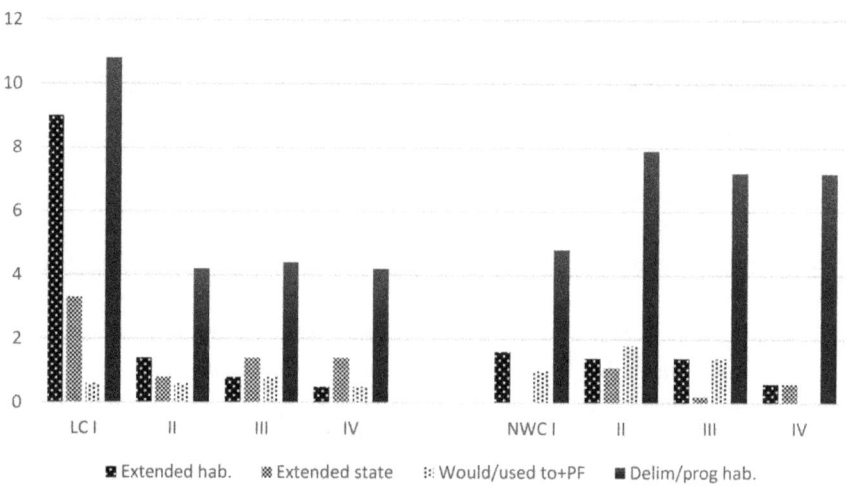

Figure 3.1: Apparent-time comparison of PF functions by four age groups of speakers (frequencies pttw).

Secondly, the apparent-time results from LC and NWC in Figure 3.1 show changes in normalized frequencies. This concerns particularly LC, where there is a considerable drop in the use of extended habitual PF from the oldest Age group I to Age group II, the decline continuing towards the youngest speakers. The changes in extended stative and habitual modal usages are less dramatic, and the standard, delimited/progressive habitual function is maintained above 4 pttw across the generations. The differences observed in LC are statistically highly significant ($p > 0.005$).

NWC presents a different picture, particularly as concerns Age group I, which gives reason to believe that the higher levels of education among the NWC I informants in comparison to LC I affect the results to some extent. The frequencies of extended use are low in all age groups, while those of progressive/delimited habitual are fairly high in groups II–IV. Both LC and NWC therefore indicate that although the extended uses have declined in the dialect, the related standard function continues to be used relatively frequently. Meriläinen, Paulasto & Rautionaho (2017) find that delimited/progressive habitual instances make up 16.5% of the total of PF use in WelE (LC & NWC), 9% in BrE (ICE-GB) and 7% in AmE (SBCSAE; based on the analysis of semantic functions in samples of 200 PF instances in spoken English). This indicates, on the one hand, that the Welsh-induced habitual extension continues to have some relevance for WelE speakers' use of the PF, and on the other, that speakers prefer to constrain the use of the habitual PF to the more widely accepted, delimited/progressive contexts.

3.3.3 The perfect aspect

WelE has very few dialect constructions in the perfect aspect in comparison to IrE, where the range of perfect constructions is much wider. The perfect progressive was brought up above (see example 23), and, as pointed out at that juncture, the regionally distinctive habitual use of this construction seems to be confined to the speech of elderly rural L1 Welsh speakers, as in the SAWD corpus. It is thus not productive in present-day WelE.

The corpora, however, contain another perfect aspect feature: the *be* perfect. This feature is rare enough that it has thus far escaped all scholarly attention in WelE literature. A handful of instances are recorded in LC (28), but there are none in TC and only one questionable case in NWC (the weak form pronunciation of *is* and *has* being similar).

(28) a. Well the boys *are grown up* with her now, you see? (LC: 1c)
 b. So that's how things *are changed*, you know (LC: 3b)
 c. And that triggered off the arthritis, which *is gone*, it- that was in nineteen-sixty-six,
 [Mm.]
 and it's progressively *gone* worse (LC: 4c)
 d. all these artists *are come* out of the Welsh language er, er, circle in you know, eisteddfodaus, things like that. (LC: 7e)

The feature follows the characteristics of the *be* perfect in IrE, occurring with intransitive verbs and being resultative in meaning, that is, the focus is on the endpoint of an activity (see Filppula 1999: 116–117). Similarly, the selection of verbs is lexically restricted: All verbs are semantically conclusive, durative and nonagentive (Quirk et al. 1985: 201), elsewhere described, more specifically, as "mutative".

As in IrE, the origin of this feature is difficult to pinpoint. The *be* perfect was still in common use in EModE (see, e.g. Kytö 1994), but there are a few sporadic instances only in the SED corpus, sprinkled from Hampshire to Cumberland, and one potential occurrence in ICE-GB. This does not lend much evidence for an EngE dialect contact hypothesis, particularly as the Anglicization of Wales is more recent than that of Ireland, and EModE features less likely to be found. The eWAVE (Kortmann et al. 2020) indicates that in the British Isles and Ireland, the *be* perfect is primarily a feature of IrE, MxE, OrShE and ScE, with some use in southwest and north EngE, while Britain (2007: 92) places it in East Midlands and western parts of East Anglia. It is safe to say, however, that this feature is not in common use in EngE, nor does it have a geographically significant distribution in the FRED corpus examined by Szmrecsanyi (2013: 51–52, 167).

Another potential source of influence is the Welsh language. However, unlike in Irish, there is no exact structural-semantic parallel in Welsh which might easily explain this feature in WelE. According to Heinecke (1999: 179–180), the perfect is "exclusively expressed periphrastically" using BOD 'be' + anterior marker *wedi* 'after' + VN, as in (29):

(29) Mae   'r   plant   wedi   canu.
 be.PRES.3SG DEF children ANT sing.VN
 'The children have sung.'

The possible Welsh contact explanation is mainly based on the use of the auxiliary verb BOD 'be' in the construction. However, there is not much evidence in support of this theory, either, as the L1 Welsh speakers, whether in SAWD or the more recent corpora, rarely employ the construction. The transcribed SAWD interviews contain a few occurrences with the verbs *go*, *come* and *die*, amounting to 1.5 pttw:

(30) a. Oat cakes, no, I don't think anybody- *is gone* out of fashion really. (SAWD: Dre6)
 b. those are- the- they*'re* all *died*. (SAWD: Fro1)

These are recorded in Drefach in north Pembrokeshire, and Fron-Goch in Gwynedd, and so the geographic distribution gives us no further clues. All informants using the *be* perfect in LC and SAWD are L1 Welsh speakers. Most of them are elderly, but two participants in their 20s and 30s use it, too.

Although it is extremely difficult to say anything definitive about the origin of this feature in WelE on the basis of these data, let us refer to Tagliamonte's (2000) finding that in Samaná English, which is an offshoot of early AAVE, the *be* perfect is likewise strongly associated with mutative verbs. Tagliamonte (2000: 348) considers this a reflection of the grammaticalization of the present perfect in English and the "principle of persistence", leaving the historical, moribund *be* perfect with traces of the original lexical meanings, which constrain its grammatical distribution. Based on its lexical characteristics, the WelE *be* perfect, too, might thus also be considered a descendant of the EModE construction.

3.4 Clausal and sentential structures

3.4.1 Embedded inversion

Inverted word order in indirect questions, also known as embedded inversion (EI), is a feature which is reported in numerous varieties of English worldwide. It is also a somewhat productive feature of WelE, especially in the bilingual regions:

(31) a. I don't know *what's the... Is this* an English or Welsh word I can't tell you. (SAWD: Gn 9: 3)
 b. Did you see what kind of coal *was it*? (SAWD: Dy 3: 1)
 c. I don't know *what's it* like with you in Finland, is it the same or... (LC: 5g)
 d. I asked them in the camp, *would they like* the plums (NWC, Criccieth: 2e)
 e. <X> asked me on Saturday night *was J.* my boyfriend (TC: 6b)

Parry (1999: 119) lists half a dozen occurrences of this type collected in the incidental material of the SAWD, primarily from Dyfed. Although Penhallurick (1991: 209–210) only records one example from North Wales, the notes taken by Paulasto from 54 hours of SAWD interviews (see Paulasto 2006: 150) contain 17 instances of EI from Dyfed and Gwynedd. Most of these occurrences are triggered by the survey questionnaire format of the interviews; the sentences in (31a), for example, arise from a discussion on the name of a specific item. Example (31b), on the other hand, illustrates EI in the SAWD incidental material. The inverted sentence structure of (31a), where the matrix clause follows the indirect question, is also relatively common in the data.

EI in other words emerges in the north as well as the south of Wales as a moderately common alternative for the canonical word order. The frequency of use is put into perspective by Meriläinen & Paulasto (2017: 684–685), who show that in WelE (LC), the total share of EI out of all indirect questions is 9.3%. In the ICE-GB spoken sections it is 1.9%, and in ICE-Ireland 13.7%, rising as high as 40.4% in Yes/No-questions in the private conversations (see below for further cross-varietal comparisons).

As suggested by Thomas (1994: 138) and Penhallurick (1991: 210), EI is most likely affected by Welsh contact influence: Welsh retains the direct question word order also in indirect questions, and the particles *a/os* similar to *whether/if* may be omitted, especially in colloquial Welsh (King 1993: 305–310, Thomas 1994: 138). King (1993: 305), in fact, points out that inserting *os* 'if' in the following type of sentence echoes English usage and "is regarded as substandard by some speakers":

(32) Dach   chi'n   gwybod   ydyn   nhw'n   dod? (King 1993: 305)
     be.2PL you-IM   know.VN   be.3PL they-IM come.VN
     'Do you know if they are coming?'

This need not be the only explanation, however. EI has been investigated in varieties of English and learner Englishes, and the conclusions are that besides substrate influence or L1 transfer, it involves ease of cognitive processing in the form of chunking, *what+is* being a typical element in the embedded clause (Hilbert 2008, 2011), and the blurring of the line between direct and indirect questions, *ask* being the typical matrix verb (Meriläinen and Paulasto 2017: 689). Cognitive factors cannot be ruled out in the case of WelE, either.

Table 3.6 shows that the frequencies of EI in WelE are in fact quite low, and the standard indirect question word order is preferred by all groups of informants. The results have been obtained by searching the corpora for six common matrix verbs: *ask, wonder, see, tell, understand*, and NEG *know* (Biber et al. 1999: 685–93). The occurrences that were not found through this search are few and involve matrix verbs and constructions such as *remember, forget, be not sure*, and *got no idea*.

Table 3.6: EI in the SAWD transcribed sample corpus and three regional corpora of WelE: percentages of use and frequencies per 10,000 words (pttw).

	WH EI %	pttw	Y/N EI %	pttw
SAWD (26,500)	15.0 (3/20)	1.1	0.0 (0/1)	–
LC (257,500)	13.4 (13/97)	0.5	4.3 (3/69)	0.1
NWC (120,000)	2.6 (1/39)	0.1	7.0 (3/43)	0.3
TC (49,800)	7.7 (2/26)	0.4	5.9 (1/17)	0.2

Generally speaking, WH-inversion is more common in WelE than Yes/No-inversion. The latter is the more common type only in NWC. The numbers in all corpora besides LC are, however, too low for a closer examination, and apart from the small SAWD corpus and LC, the percentages of use are only slightly above those obtained from standard spoken BrE (ICE-GB) and AmE student writing (Louvain

Corpus of Native English Essays; LOCNESS) by Meriläinen and Paulasto (2017: 685–687). Nevertheless, EI demonstrably occurs in the dialect. This is confirmed by our own informal observations in North and South Wales, as well as Roller (2016: 47, 103), who finds similar frequencies in her FRED (1.13 pttw) and Radio Wales corpora (0.41 pttw).

EI occurs also in the Rhondda dialect, which shows that it is not completely alien to the southeastern regional variety, either. The question of which is the primary cause, Welsh substrate or ease of cognitive processing, is of particular relevance in an area where Welsh structural impact is low at present. Moreover, the informants using EI in TC are middle-aged rather than elderly.

The Llandybie data can be examined more closely for signs of apparent-time change (Table 3.7). It is no surprise that Age group I, representing the oldest speakers of the dialect, produces the highest percentages and frequencies of use, with a drop towards the younger age groups. The instances are too few for further conclusions, however.

Table 3.7: EI in apparent time in the LC.

	WH EI %	pttw	Y/N EI %	pttw
Age I (52,000)	*27.0* (7/26)	1.3	*8.7* (2/23)	0.4
Age II (85,000)	*8.3* (1/12)	0.1	*5.9* (1/17)	0.1
Age III (66,300)	*3.2* (1/31)	0.2	*0.0* (0/19)	–
Age IV (57,400)	*11.1* (3/27)	0.5	*0.0* (0/10)	–

The four occurrences recorded from Age groups III and IV all contain the matrix construction *don't know* and the embedded clause elements *what + (i)s* (33a), while the older speakers employ EI in more varied ways (33b). The former tendency is reminiscent of the "fixed chunks" or "formulaic language", which Hilbert (2008: 275–277, 283–284) finds to be typical of EI in IndE and SingE. This suggests that the construction types for EI may have become narrowed also in WelE. Note also the absence of Yes/No-inversion (33c) in the younger speakers' English.

(33) a. I don't know if you've heard about those, you know, Welsh language- I don't know what's *mentrau*. (LC: 7e)
  b. I really don't know where *would I* have been, where *would I* have gone. (LC: 3g)
  c. And I asked the driver *would he* stop between stops for me. (LC: 2d)

The NWC findings, being so few, do not offer much in the way of apparent-time research. Differences between groups are small, Age group IV being the only one where there is not a single instance of EI.

Meriläinen and Paulasto (2017: 689) show that in favouring WH-inversion over Yes/No-inversion, WelE is similar to the majority of L1 or L2 varieties where EI is found (including English as a lingua franca; see Ranta 2013: 111, 117). They therefore consider question type to be one of the universal constraints for EI. The only exceptions to this in their data are IrE (ICE-Ireland spoken sections) and written learner English by intermediate level L1 Finnish speakers. Both data sets display a preference for Yes/No-inversion, which most likely results from both Irish and Finnish maintaining the direct question structure in indirect questions. Meriläinen and Paulasto conclude that in WelE, the Welsh contact influence may be restrained by the prominent role of formal acquisition and contacts with EngE in the history and present-day use of English in Wales.

Besides question type, another universal constraint according to Meriläinen and Paulasto (2017: 689) is the matrix verb. Across their corpus data, the percentages of EI are low with all other verbs besides *ask*, with the exception of the IrE and L1 Finnish learner corpora (see also Kolbe and Sand 2010: 36). Again, WelE follows suit: When LC, NWC and TC are considered together, EI occurs most often with the matrix verb *ask* (EI in 36.4% [4/11] of WH-questions with *ask*, and in 22.2% [6/27] of Yes/No-questions). Another fairly productive matrix verb is NEG *know* (EI in 9.2% [8/87] of WH-questions but zero [0/82] of the Yes/No type). Single instances only are recorded with other verbs. Meriläinen and Paulasto find that *ask* as the matrix verb leads particularly effectively to the blurring of the line between direct and indirect questions, which then triggers the direct question word order. This is evidenced in WelE as well.

3.4.2 Focusing constructions

Focus fronting
One of the most salient features of dialect syntax in WelE is focus fronting (FF; also termed predicate fronting, see Coupland 1988, Williams 2000). It involves a word-order change, where a focused, normally post-verbal (or verbal) item is moved initially, changing the canonical SVX word order into XSV and reversing the topic-comment information structure. The fronted item can be object (34a), adverbial (34b), subject or object predicative (34c-d), or a verb phrase (34e). The subject and verb following the focused item always contain de-focused, given information.

(34) a. Other games. *Football* we used to play like.
[Yeah.]
I used to like football. (NWC, Llanuwchllyn: 6b)
b. She's got a boyfriend,
[Mm.]
oh, go to the cinema... Er, *in Swansea* they usually go to the cinema. My youngest daughter, she goes to the cinema in Cross Hands. (LC: 5e)
c. [Penny Readings?]
Oh Penny Readings yes, that was included in the Band of Hope it was. *Penny Readings* it used to be. [...] Oh, *quite excited over that* we used to get. Very excited. *Penny Readings*, as you say, it would be like. (CGC: DoJ)
d. We've been to couple of holiday camps in recent years, just *weekend or week breaks* you might call them, you know, we don't go to the continent at all. (LC: 3c)
e. ...and the boy thought he was speaking Welsh. *Speaking English* he was. (TC: 2)

This feature of WelE is observed fairly widely in the literature, for example, by Parry (1979: 155), Thomas (1985: 215–216), Coupland (1988: 36–37), Connolly (1990: 127), and George (1990: 262–263). Williams (2000, 2003) describes the characteristics of FF in the southeastern Valleys area, while Paulasto (2006) examines regional and apparent-time variation in the use of the feature in a wide set of corpora (see also Paulasto 2009).

FF is by no means limited to WelE but occurs in vernacular EngE and AmE (see, e.g. Birner and Ward 1998) as well as in numerous contact-induced varieties of English. The eWAVE data includes the feature under the heading "Other possibilities for fronting than StE" and it is attested in 44% of the 77 varieties, mainly pidgins, creoles and indigenized L2 Englishes (Kortmann et al. 2020). Based on the examples listed on the website, this eWAVE feature encompasses not only FF but also other word order phenomena, such as topicalization, left dislocation, and cleft constructions. It is nevertheless understandable that Coupland (1988: 37) and Jones (1990a: 198) treat FF in WelE with some caution and call for empirical comparisons of WelE usages against other varieties of English.

Paulasto (2006: 165ff.) does exactly this and finds that compared to EngE usages, FF is distinctive in WelE in terms of frequency of occurrence, the type of fronted sentence element permitted and certain discourse functions. Table 3.8 gives the results from three data sets representing elderly speakers' English in WelE (LC and CGC) and in EngE (SED Spoken Corpus; Paulasto 2006: 166, 168).

Table 3.8: The use of FF in WelE (LC) and EngE (SED) corpora (fronted items and frequencies).

	O	A	SPr	OPr	VP	Total (pttw)
CGC (30,050*) %	13 17.1%	10 13.2%	32 42.1%	20 26.3%	1 1.3%	76 (25.29)
LC I (52,000) %	15 24.6%	24 41.0%	13 21.3%	8 13.1%	0 -	61 (11.73)
SED (478,700) %	43 18.9%	57 20.6%	89 32.1%	77 27.8%	11 4.0%	277 (5.79)

*) Estimated word count.

The results show that Coupland was right in his cautious approach to FF, as it occurs in traditional rural EngE quite frequently. It is, however, more than twice as frequent in the elderly WelE speakers' English in Llandybie, and more than twice that, again, in the small sample from Ceri George's transcribed interviews in the Rhondda. There is a lexical orientation in parts of CGC (absent from the SED Spoken Corpus), which raises the frequencies and the proportions of fronted predicatives: Many of these instances occur in discussions about the names of certain implements and such. These interviews are, nevertheless, comparatively conversational.

FF occurs in North Wales as well (see below and Paulasto 2006: 206–207), although the informants of comparable age in NWC use it fairly seldom (2.57 pttw). The differences in fronted elements are also noteworthy, as both SED and CGC display a preference for fronted predicatives rather than objects or adverbials, while in LC the opposite is the case. In other words, the choice of the fronted elements is less constrained in the variety with a stronger Welsh contact effect (see below). The following, rather extreme examples illustrate the communicative weight distribution in FF and the general preference for leaving the final post-verbal slot empty.

(35) a. *Quite good in Memorial hall, Llandybie,* the pictures were. (LC: 2c)
 b. *...very much involved with the WI over the years* I've been. (LC: 3g)

The comparatively high percentage of fronted VPs in SED is explained by their connection to the common use of emphatic tags in the traditional dialects of EngE (for further information, see Paulasto 2006: 169–170).

The results in Table 3.9 below, from the full-scale corpora, confirm that in the Welsh-speaking regions, objects and adverbials are fronted as readily as predicatives, if not more so (Paulasto 2006: 166). The frequencies of FF are considerably lower, however, and TC, with its large share of fronted objects, does not comply with the expectations. It should be noted that the interviews in both CGC and TC have sequences with a lexical focus, producing a certain amount of identificational FF. This affects not only predicatives, but also objects: About a half of the fronted objects in both corpora are of the type *'despicable' I would say* (CGC: DoJ); *'mitching' we always used to say* (TC: 4).

Table 3.9: The use of FF in present-day WelE corpora; fronted items and frequencies.

	Object	Adv.	S.Pred	O.Pred	VP	Total (pttw)
LC (257,500)	30	39	32	17	2	120 (4.66)
%	25.0%	32.5%	26.7%	14.2%	1.7%	
NWC (120,000)	11	11	8	8	0	38 (3.17)
%	28.9%	28.9%	21.1%	21.1%	–	
TC (49,800)	11	1	4	4	1	21 (4.22)
%	52.4%	4.8%	19.0%	19.0%	4.8%	

Roller's (2016: 47, 103) frequencies of FF in the FRED and Radio Wales corpora are 10.37 pttw and 4.58 pttw, respectively. Considering that the first corpus represents elderly rural informants, while the latter has a broad regional/age distribution, the frequencies correspond very nicely to those in Tables 3.8 and 3.9.

As the above results indicate, the forms of FF are dependent on the method of corpus collection, that is, certain types of discourse contexts trigger particular types of FF use. The same of course applies to its discourse functions. Paulasto (2006: 178ff.) divides the discourse functions of FF into six categories, illustrated below. The final, specificational category may contain brand-new information, but in all others the fronted item is always textually or situationally evoked or inferable.

(36) a. Contrastive: [The man was called a creeper?]
No, *brakesman* he was. (CGC: TS)
b. Reassertive: Er, we were doing erm, er, detonators. It was very, very dangerous. [...] Mm, *detonators* they were. (LC: 2c)
c. Confirmatory: [Do you speak Welsh here at home?]
Oh yes, *only Welsh* we speak, yes. (LC: 3d)
d. Responsive: [Do you have to travel far?]
Mm, *about seven miles* I go. (NWC: 6b)
e. Emphatic: [What about washing?]

>> Oh dear it was hard work, Ceri, *real hard work* that was. (CGC: DoJ)

f. Specificational:...it was the main part of Zante. *Lagana* it's called. (TC: 5c)

In his 2000 article, Williams finds clear functional differences between the Anglicized southeast Valleys usage ("modal", i.e. emphatic FF) and the Welsh-influenced Llandeilo dialect (information-oriented FF). However, his data for the Valleys variety consist of literary representations in Edwards (1985, 1986). When re-examining FF in Ceri George's interview corpus in 2003, Williams concludes that Edwards' description of the dialect must be considered misleading, as information-oriented FF is, in fact, the primary type in the interview data (as it is also in the St Fagan's and Miners' Library archive materials, as recognized by Williams 2003: 216). Paulasto's (2006: 189–196) quantitative examination of the full range of discourse-functional categories shows the following:

- Specificational fronting of textually inferable information (36f; also 34b and 34d above) is the primary function in all corpora, most prominently in NWC (68%) and SED (57%);
- The main difference between SED and the WelE corpora concerns the contrastive function (also 34e), which is more typical of LC, NWC and the Urban SAWD corpus (11–23%; cf. 6% in SED), being especially prominent in LC Age group I (29%);
- The responsive (see also 34a) and reassertive functions are particularly common in the WelE corpora with a questionnaire-based method of interview (SAWD & CGC);
- Emphatic fronting (see also 34c) is slightly more common in SED and LC I than in any other corpus;
- Brand-new information is fronted infrequently in all corpora.

Let us now consider these results in light of the substrate language. The canonical word order in Welsh is VSO. However, fronted constructions, including the mixed sentence and identification sentence, are employed whenever a part of the sentence is focused for contrast, emphasis or informational salience (Fife and King 1991: 145; King 1993: 143–144). Example (37) illustrates the difference in word order in a neutral context (*What happened?*) and in a focused context (*Who was it?*), where Welsh employs the unemphatic mixed sentence:

(37) a. Beth ddigwyddodd?   Torrodd   Iwan ffenest.
        what °happen.PRT.3SG   break.PRT.3SG   Iwan window
        'What happened?'   'Iwan broke a window'

b. Pwy dorrodd   y ffenest?   Iwan dorrodd   y ffenest.
   who °break.PRT.3SG the window   Iwan °break.PRT.3SG the window
   'Who broke the window?'   '(It was) Iwan (who) broke the window.'
   (King 1993: 26; Williams 2000: 215)

(38) Crys Sioned ydy   hwnna.
     shirt Sioned be.PRES.3SG that
     'That is Sioned's shirt' (King 1993: 144)

(39) Astudio   yn y llyfrgell y   bydd   hi   heno.
     study.VN   in the library RPA be.FUT.3SG she tonight
     '(It's) study in the library (that) she will tonight.' (Thorne 1993: 372)

The choice of the focused item is free: it can be the subject (37b), object, adverbial, predicative (38), or a verb phrase (39). In the identification sentence, as in (38), the predicative must precede the copular verb. In the mixed sentence, which is historically a cleft construction (Watkins 1991), fronting may be accompanied by a relative pronoun or particle (39), a relative form of the verb *be*, or only the soft mutation (37b), the final remnant of the relative clause structure. However, the fronting of the focused item is the central characteristic of the construction in present-day Welsh (e.g. Fife & King 1991: 145), and there is therefore reason to believe that this obligatory word-order change is replicated in WelE. Moreover, the functions where fronting occurs in WelE are similar to Welsh (see Watkins 1991), the contrastive and responsive functions being especially distinctive in the corpora. Paulasto (2006: 75–82) describes the relevant Welsh word order phenomena in more detail.

Birner and Ward (1998: 35, 83–88) define English FF (which they call focus preposing) as containing a fronted item, which bears the focus of the sentence, and a following open proposition, typically "given" in the discourse. The focused item stands in a textually/situationally salient "partially ordered set relation" to the preceding context (Birner & Ward 1998: 17–19). This definition includes all the above functions of FF, but it also explains why specificational fronting of inferable information is widespread throughout the data: FF does not require an explicit textual incentive from the discourse partner, nor emotive emphasis. Rather, in the typical case, the speaker him/herself uses the construction to specify a piece of information directly related to the discourse topic. This indicates that the feature is in fact cognitively motivated and as such belongs firmly in the spoken domain, which allows freer textual restructuring (see, e.g. Leech and Svartvik 1994: 200–201, Givón 2001: 250).

WelE follows Birner and Ward's description apart from the few instances (mainly by elderly speakers) where the fronted item contains brand new information. This is termed by the above authors as Yiddish-movement on account of its prominence in Yiddish-induced English (Birner & Ward 1998: 90–93). Filppula (1986: 191–204) indicates that in IrE, too, fronting brand-new information is relatively common (see Paulasto 2006: 295). Language contact has, in other words, also been found to influence the use of FF in other contact-induced varieties.

Another characteristic of FF which ties it to spoken language usage is the common emergence of mixed sentence structures, where the speaker seems to fuse two sentences together whilst saying them. These are labelled "edited" FF in Paulasto (2006: 163–65), although the frequency with which they appear in the corpora indicates that they are not random accidents of speech production but a more or less established construction type. As pointed out by Cheshire (1999: 139–142), mixed sentence structures can be highly functional. They are also common in spoken language, although they are rarely paid attention to in language or dialect descriptions. The following illustrate the edited FF construction in WelE:

(40) a. S. I went to night school, and then my employer, I was very fortunate, er, gave me *day release* it's called, one day a week off, to go to college. (NWC, Llwyngwril: 2a)
b. ...they came down *during the war* I think it was. (TC: 3b)
c. There's like different areas isn't there that they've got different, *their own sort of- kind of language* it is, isn' it. (NWC, Pencaenewydd: 8d)
d. I looove, love performing on the stage and *getting little children to perform on the stage* I enjoy. (LC: 3g)

Of these instances, the typical construction type in most WelE corpora and SED is that of (40a), where the focused item is an object predicative (Paulasto 2006: 171). The only exceptions to this are TC and NWC, where subject predicative constructions (40c) are proportionally the most frequent. The structural preferences go hand-in-hand with the key discourse function, specifying new or inferable information (Paulasto 2006: 196). Another common characteristic for edited FF is the insertion of hedges, such as *I think* in (40b) or *sort of, kind of* in (40c). Objects take the focus position in relatively few cases (40d). The data show that these mixed constructions are not constrained in spoken language usage. Rather, it is likely that the prominence of FF in WelE reinforces the sentence-final re-insertion of the subject and predicate.

Edited FF is common in all corpora discussed in this context, as shown in Table 3.10. The greatest difference is found between LC and TC. Whereas the Llandybie informants by and large employ FF as an independent construction, the Tonypandy informants are likelier to use it in mixed sentence structures.

Table 3.10: Edited FF out of the total usage.

	Edited / Total	% Edited FF
LC	26/146	17.8
NWC	14/52	26.9
CGC	23/99	23.2
TC	11/32	34.4
SED	81/358	22.6

FF, like other Welsh-induced features in WelE, is subject to diachronic change. In LC, the normalized total frequencies are considerably lower in the younger age groups than in Age group I (with a total of 11.73 pttw). On the other hand, in groups III and IV the total frequencies are roughly the same (2.38 and 2.44 pttw; Paulasto 2006: 198). Figure 3.2 shows the distributional differences of the fronted items in the four age groups, indicating that the usages have shifted from fronted adverbials and objects towards subject predicatives.

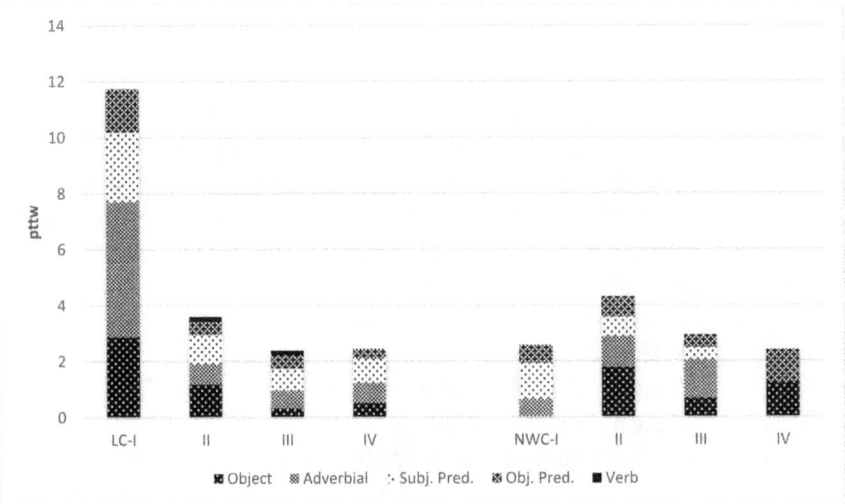

Figure 3.2: Apparent-time change in the use of FF in LC and NWC.

Similar trends are not apparent in NWC, where the instances are fewer and less conclusive: the normalized frequencies of FF are roughly equal to LC in the latter two age groups, but only two informants use the feature in the final group, and the distribution of focused items follows no clear pattern (Paulasto 2006: 200–201).

In terms of discourse functions, however, the apparent-time changes are similar in LC and NWC: The specificational function is increasingly central, rising from under 40% in Age group I to over 70% in Age group IV in both corpora. The only other function in LC with a proportional increase is the responsive one (max. 25% in Age group IV), while in NWC the contrastive function peaks in Age group III (40%) and drops to zero in the final group. All other functions are either low, on the decrease, or have disappeared amongst the youngest speaker group. Overall, the changes thus point to functional narrowing of FF in WelE (see Paulasto 2016 for further analysis).

Other recent sources, too, testify to the maintenance of FF on the one hand and low frequencies of use on the other. In the BBC *Voices* interviews, FF occurs (at least) in Bangor, Tregaron (Ceredigion), Llanelli, Bon-y-maen, Pontypridd and Treorchy (Rhondda). However, it does not occur, for example, in Bethesda, where all informants are L1 Welsh-speaking teenagers.

Cleft constructions

Cleft sentences constitute another focus construction which in IrE and HebE is found to be influenced by Gaelic contact influence (see Filppula 1999: 258–260, Shuken 1984: 155). In WelE, in contrast, cleft constructions are not particularly distinctive and follow the constraints presented by, for example, Quirk et al. (1985: 1384–1387). Hence, there is very little in the relevant literature as regards cleft constructions. The Welsh cleft sentence, that is, the mixed sentence, lost the initial copula *ys* in the late Middle Welsh period, leaving only the remnants of the relative clause construction (see Fife and King 1991, Watkins 1991). As pointed out above, the main attribute of the mixed sentence today is the word order change, placing the focused item initially. This transfers into WelE in the form of FF rather than clefting (see Thomas 1984: 216). In the present corpora, there are 51 instances of clefting in LC (against 120 of FF) and 23 in NWC (against 38 of FF), FF being the more frequent of the two in all age groups.

There are very few occurrences in the WelE corpora which stretch the general constraints on clefting. IrE takes more liberties in the use of clefting with regard to the range of focused items, as observed in southern (Filppula 1999: 250–255, Kallen 2013: 72–76) as well as northern IrE (Corrigan 2010: 76–78). WelE instances similar to IrE are given in (41a), which has an adverbial of manner in focus position, and (41b), which is an existential sentence, the cleft construction replacing existential *there*.

(41) a. ...the horse had disappeared, the tractor took over, an- and it's only- you know, *gradually* that the introduction of the modern tractor has changed farming. (LC: 4c)
b. Well, at one time, it was *only these four houses* that was here. (LC: 1c)

In Welsh, such sentence types are formed using the existential form of the verb BOD 'be', *mae*, which may or may not have an impact on the occurrence in (41b). The informant is an elderly L1 Welsh speaker whose English contains unusually large amounts of structural transfer from Welsh. This occurrence is therefore likely to be idiolectal rather than dialectal.

Relativizer omission in subject position (42a) leads to a type of mixed structure in cleft constructions. This feature is fairly common, as it is in EngE, in general (Britain 2007: 98–101). Example (42b), then, involves relativizer omission and subject-verb inversion.

(42) a. ...any sports really but it's *football* is my favourite, definitely. (NWC: 6g)
b. It's *once a week* are the bus services, which is really terrible... (LC: 7d)

EngE dialect relativizers, for example, *as, what*, are discussed further in Section 3.5 below.

3.4.3 Nonstandard infinitives

Infinitive constructions which deviate from StE are found primarily in the SAWD data. There are three types of features, and the main reason for the first two types lies in Welsh language transfer. The Welsh verbal noun operates in roles which in English are filled by either the infinitive or the present participle. This leads to the two being occasionally mixed up in elderly rural L1 Welsh speakers' English. Based on the evidence, however, this feature is highly constrained lexically. Parry (1999: 120 and 1979: 155) give examples such as (43), where *stop*, in the sense 'prevent', is followed by the infinitive rather than *from* + present participle.

(43) stop them *to go* backwards (P 4, Dy 8/10/16); stop it *to tip* over (MG 3); to stop the ashes *to come* out (SG 4)

Penhallurick (1991: 193) presents a reverse situation from North Wales, where the infinitive is replaced by the present participle. He likewise interprets this as resulting from the syntactic ambiguity of the Welsh verbal noun.

(44) you've got to put this sharp side... to cut the mouth... to make it *bleeding* (referring to the process of breaking a horse by using a special bit; *SAWD*: Cl 7)

Neither of these types is recorded in the present-day WelE corpora, which indicates that they are no longer productive.

The third type, unsplit *for to* infinitive 'to, in order to', is recorded in southeastern and southwestern localities of SAWD (Parry 1977: 178; 1979: 162). Its distribution in the longstanding English regions – Pembrokeshire, Gower and southeast Powys – points very clearly to EngE origin, particularly as this feature is well-attested in *SED*. The eWAVE (Kortmann et al. 2020) also indicates that it is particularly common in IrE and continues to be used in most EngE dialects (see Corrigan 2003 for an overview of the research and the origins of *for to* in varieties of IrE). However, Szmrecsanyi (2013: 65, 168) shows that it is one of the less frequently used dialect features in FRED and probably on the decline. Only two such instances are found in the present-day WelE corpora, one in LC and another in NWC (Pencaenewydd). The few North Welsh informants who are found to use this construction have also lived outside the area (see also Penhallurick 2008b: 366).

(45) a. I went to town *for to see* the doctor (*SAWD*: Dy 11–14/19–20/24–25, P 22/24/26, WG 6)
 b. Well there were different styles of playing it *for to get* your marble into the hole (LC: 4a)

Hence, neither the Welsh-induced nor the EngE dialectal infinitive seems to have a prominent role in WelE today.

3.4.4 Exclamative *there*

Many scholars (e.g. Parry 1979: 142; Thomas 1985: 216; Connolly 1990: 127) observe that WelE speakers may construct exclamative sentences based on the Welsh model *dyna* 'there' + adjective (see King 1993: 251). The illustration is from Parry (1999: 120):

(46) a. *There's* lovely on you! ('How lovely for you!' Dy 11)
 b. *There's* glad she was! (WG 3)

Based on the geographical distribution in Parry (1979, 1999), this seems to be mainly a feature of the bilingual or recently Anglicized south of Wales.

The present corpora contain only one occurrence (47a), which corresponds directly to the above. The phrase *there's twp* 'daft' may be something of an idiomatic collocation, as it is also listed in Parry (1999: 120). In TC, one of the informants employs a slightly different construction type, where the focal item is a noun (47b) or which is not functionally exclamative (47c).

(47) a. *There's* twp you are! ('How daft you are / Aren't you daft'; LC: 2c).
 b. A: Yeah I got to go.
   B: *There's* a pity. ('What a pity'; TC: 3a)
 c. [I was wondering who we are- who you were talking about.]
   A: Yeah that's it there.
   B: Aye *there's* a bit difficult. ('It's a bit difficult'; TC: 3a)

All of the above instances have been recorded from informants in their 80s, which indicates that this feature is receding in present-day WelE. However, Durham (2015) finds that British tweeters include exclamative *there* among morphosyntactic features which in their view represent WelE (see Section 1.5.1). It hence continues to have a part to play in the dialect.

3.4.5 Prepositional constructions

Preposition usage is known to be highly variable in New Englishes and learner English. Prepositions are added, lost, and replaced, and often this variability results from L1 transfer or substrate influence. The SAWD data presented in Parry (1999) indicate that WelE contains a wide range of distinctive prepositional features, typically originating from Welsh contact. The following discussion focuses on the semantic extension of *with*, a productive feature in some present-day varieties of WelE. Other dialectal uses of prepositions are examined further below.

Semantic extension of with

In standard British English, *with* appears in a wide range of semantic contexts (Quirk et al. 1985: 665ff), typically expressing accompaniment and instrumental, spatial, or certain other semantic relationships. In WelE, *with* has the additional function of expressing possession and associated relationships, and the primary reason usually cited to explain this extension is Welsh contact influence. Celtic languages do not have verbs corresponding to *have* but use prepositional constructions instead (e.g. Stalmaszczyk 2007). In Welsh, possession is indicated with BE + PP, more specifically BOD 'be' + object + *(gy)da* 'with' + possessor, i.e.

mae car 'da John 'John has a car' or 'There's a car with John' (see King 1993: 320). This construction underlies WelE expressions such as (48a-b) from Parry (1999: 117), although (48b) is a variation on the theme.

(48) a. There's no horns *with the sheep* about this way (*SAWD*: Dy 16)
   b. it was warm *with the cowshed* always (*SAWD*: Dy 10)

This feature is also observed by Thomas (1985: 217–218) and George (1990: 268–269), but it seems to have escaped attention in other descriptions of southern or northern WelE.

Characteristically, the notion of "possession" extends to concepts that are more loosely related to the possessor (cf. "impersonal constructions" in IrE, Moylan 2009: 59). It therefore seems that WelE speakers are exploiting the wide semantic range of *with* in English and extending its use to a number of relationships within the broader field of possession, accompaniment, and space.

The usages of *with* can be roughly divided into standard and vernacular ones. Our studies show that the vast majority of instances in WelE as well as in IrE and EngE fall under the StE categories of ACCOMPANIMENT, "HAVING", MEANS AND INSTRUMENT, COMMUNICATION AND CONDUCT, GENERAL RELATION, and other, infrequent types (for these categories, see Quirk et al. 665ff. and *Oxford English Dictionary* [*OED*] Online). The above three varieties have been studied using LC, NWC, SED Spoken Corpus West Midlands, ICE-GB, and ICE-Ireland, as shown in Table 3.11, and the results indicate that vernacular uses of *with* (see below) are more common in the WelE corpora than in BrE or IrE.

Table 3.11: Standard and vernacular functions of with in WelE, BrE and IrE corpora.

	LC	NWC	SED West	ICE-GB	ICE-IRE
Standard	852	492	373	435	453
Vernacular	120	51	15	13	11
Vernacular %	*12.3%*	*9.4%*	*3.9%*	*2.9%*	*2.4%*
Total	972	543	388	448	464

The differences across all corpora in Table 3.11 are statistically very significant (p=0.000), whereas there is no significant difference between LC and NWC (p=0.0974). TC is not included in the table, but it differs from the above two corpora in displaying very few distinctive functions of *with* (see below). The feature seems to be characteristic of the bilingual regions rather than the southeast.

Vernacular functions related to the Welsh possessive construction can be divided into POSSESSION (49) and INTEGRAL/PROXIMATE (50):

(49) a. There is a field at the top here *with us* which I own, which is called Llundain fach. (LC: 4a)
   b. [When she got older, she had problems with her hip as well ... but it was operated on.]
   Oh but it was painful *with her*. (LC: 1b; cf. *oedd poen 'da hi*, lit. 'was pain with her', i.e. 'She had pain')
   c. Well the boys are grown up *with her* now, you see? (LC: 1c)
   d. Bit expensive, it is, for travelling up that way now, the prices *with the buses* are... They're getting a bit beyond me. (LC: 2d)

(50) a. I make myself understood but well, English is- is far stronger *with me*. (NWC, Lwyngwril: 6f)
   b. ...*with us* it's- w- we notice it when it gets cold, understand, m- more than you because it's always cold *with you* I suppose isn' it? (NWC, Pencaenewydd: 6d)
   c. The mortality rate was so- so high *with young people* in those days. (LC: 4a)

It should be noted that there is no single variable context for the above types of extended *with*. The construction may replace *have*, as in (49a-b), but more commonly, it indicates a dependency relationship which in StE is indicated with the genitive (49c; 'her boys') or a compound noun (49d; 'bus prices'). Neither of the above types is found in SED West, ICE-GB or ICE-Ireland (see Figure 3.3 below). Irish differs from Welsh in that the preposition typically used in possessive constructions is *ag* 'at', and although *le* 'with' has a similar function as well (Stalmaszczyk 2007: 137–140), it seems to be less commonly transferred into IrE (Filppula 1999: 236, Kallen 2013: 175).

The POSSESSIVE type is only used by the two older age groups of LC and it is not found in NWC. The INTEGRAL/PROXIMATE type (50), which can be considered an extension of the Welsh-induced possessive construction, occurs in both corpora in nearly all age groups, including the youngest ones (see Figure 3.4 below). It is used to refer to qualities or phenomena which relate to a person, group or locality.

OED Online lists a closely related usage: "In the practice or experience of, in the life or conduct of, in (one's) case" (see also Lindstromberg 2010: 219–220):

(51) a. These fits of exaltation are not very common *with me*. (1841 E. FitzGerald Lett.)

b. These omissions would be impossible *with a copyist* who read over what he had copied. (1910 Bolland Eyre of Kent)

The difference from the INTEGRAL/PROXIMATE category is not vast, but the following instances (52) are nevertheless identified as denoting IN ONE'S CASE rather than "integral to a person" and categorized separately. Interestingly enough, these instances are also more common in the WelE corpora than the BrE or IrE corpora.

(52) a. Funny *with me* now, when I could read, I much rather er- read a- an English book than a Welsh book. (LC: 1d)
b. [...they found it more convenient to speak in English then all the time.] Yeah, yeah, I think- I think that could be true, yeah, *with a lot of youngsters*. (LC: 7c)

With has also other kinds of dialectal or vernacular meanings in WelE not found in the comparison corpora: It replaces the preposition *by* in instances loosely denoting agent (53a) or means (53b):

(53) a. I had this dreadful attack *with a dog*,
[*>Oh.]
it attacked<* me, I had ninety-four stitches in my arms. (LC: 3g)
b. the only thing I couldn't do in the farm was to kill a chicken, I couldn't do that at all. You- you just kill them *with the throat* (LC: 1d)
c. he was that much older so [...] perhaps I was led astray *with him* (LC: 7c)
d. the boys were blacklisted *with the coal board* (LC: 4f)
e. some people are quite fascinated *with the Welsh dialect* (LC: 4e)

The WelE usages originate from another Welsh preposition, *gan* (or *gyn* in speech) which is the North Welsh possessive preposition equivalent to *with*. It also has other uses both in the north and south, such as corresponding to the English *by* in passive sentences (King 1993: 277). However, most of the so-called agentive usages in the WelE corpora do not involve an actual agent in the semantic sense, a "wilful initiator of the action" (Biber et al. 1999: 123), and they combine with elements such as accompaniment (53c), institution (53d) or experience (53e). Again, the Welsh-induced construction is used in contexts where it is less likely to be constrained by StE.

Also the southern *(gy)da* 'with' has uses which can lead to preposition replacement in WelE. Parry (1999: 119) records: *They do it with hands* ('by hand'; Cl 7, Dy 16/22/23), which he ascribes to Welsh *gyda llaw*. Similar instances are found also in SAWD and LC.

Further vernacular uses of *with* in WelE that are shared by other British and Irish varieties are INSTITUTIONAL relationship (employment or other; 54), and CAUSE OR REASON (55). These two functions are attested in TC, while the previous ones are not; the Rhondda variety in other words groups with EngE and IrE in this respect.

(54) a. I'm in the Carmarthen beekeepers' association, so... Been *with them* for quite a time now. (LC: 2e)
  b. all the regulations *with the milk marketing board* an' everything was becoming quite strict. (NWC: 4d)

(55) a. he died when he was forty-six, *with cancer*. (LC: 1d)
  b. they can say that *with the way* the beams have been trimmed and you know, decoration of the wood. (NWC: 4c)
  c. A: Edinburgh is a lovely city that is.
    B: I've been to- yeah, oh I've been up there loads of times with the- *with the rugby* aye. (TC: 2)

Figure 3.3 illustrates the distribution of the different functions in the corpora. In the POSSESSIVE, INTEGRAL/PROXIMATE, and BY (AGENT/MEANS) categories WelE stands alone. Although the agentive function does not occur in the ICE-Ireland data, it has been recorded in IrE by, for example, Filppula (1999: 232–235), Moylan (2009: 58–59) and Kallen (2013: 175). ICE-Ireland is in many ways meagre in traditional vernacular uses of *with*, which indicates that this feature has become standardized to quite an extent. In the WelE corpora, too, the agentive function is mainly – but not solely – used by the older generations.

The category IN ONE'S CASE, highly common in WelE, co-occurs in both ICE corpora but not in SED. The INSTITUTIONAL function is found in all corpora, ICE-GB nearly matching LC and NWC, while CAUSE & REASON is primarily a function of SED West and ICE-Ireland. The category OTHER, consisting of various usages not listed above, nor in Quirk et al. (1985) or *OED* Online, is also fairly productive in these WelE corpora. These instances include *be with* 'live with', *bright with Welsh, call/query with someone* (LC); *not silly with it* 'about', *meet with someone, based with* 'in', *relate information with someone* (NWC).

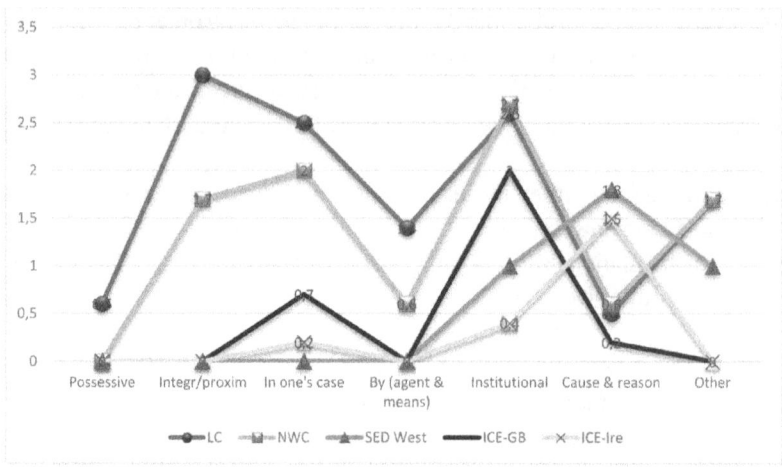

Figure 3.3: Vernacular usages in the WelE, BrE and IrE corpora (pttw).

In addition to regional variation across the British Isles and Ireland, there is also diachronic variation in WelE. The overall frequencies for vernacular functions in LC indicate a fall from 7.5 to 2.2 pttw between Age groups I and III, after which there is a rise to 4.2 pttw in Age group IV. However, in Figure 3.4 the changes are examined in terms of separate categories, and it is found that the increase in the youngest speaker group results from a single category, IN ONE'S CASE. The primary function in Age group I, INTEGRAL/PROXIMATE, is maintained as well, but the Possessive function fades out by Age group III. The CAUSE & REASON and OTHER categories do not occur in the final age group, either.

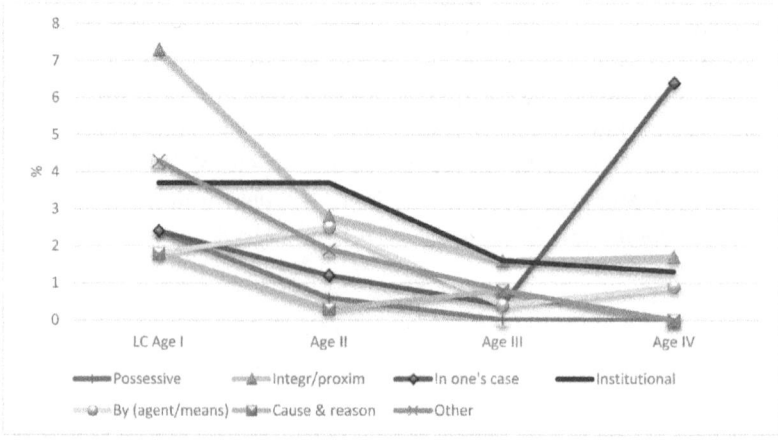

Figure 3.4: Apparent-time change in vernacular functions in LC.

The apparent-time results from LC show that although vernacular *with* constructions remain productive in present-day WelE, definite functional narrowing and standardization can be attested, and the concept of possession is increasingly replaced by more loosely defined relationships.

Preposition replacement and addition
Parry (1999: 118–119) lists a number of prepositional features in the SAWD data, some of which can be considered more typical and characteristic of WelE than others. None are, however, as distinctive or frequent in present-day WelE as the extended use of *with*. The following description focuses on features of replacement or addition which are found in the more recent corpora as well as in *SAWD*, or which are not discussed in *SAWD*.

Nonstandard uses of *on* are discussed by several scholars, both in North Wales (Penhallurick 1991: 207–208) and in the South (Connolly 1990: 128, Parry 1979: 161). Typical instances concern the phrase *name on* (*yr enw ar* 'the name on' in Welsh; Parry 1999: 119) and other types of "possessive" relationships (e.g. *what's on this?* 'what is the matter with this'; Connolly 1990: 128), but there are various others as well, as listed in Parry (1999: 119). The present-day WelE corpora and *Voices* commentaries contain the following types of expression, indicating, for example, some form of possession (56a-b), temporal expressions (*on* = *at*; 56c), or locative expressions (*on* = *at/in*; 56d-e). These are not highly common in the corpora, however, and mainly confined to elderly speakers.

(56) a. you don't think "oh I got a Welsh name *on my street*" (TC: 6b)
 b. "Some of you know, you got your spare time *on you*. Why don't you write?" (LC: 2e)
 c. it does annoy me that um *on times* you know (*Voices*: Builth Wells)
 d. our parents have a go *on us* (*Voices*: Bethesda)
 e. what we do is, most of us gather the- o- on- we're *on the same group* (LC: 2d)

For and *of* are also prepositions with Welsh-induced usages. The phrase *know for sth* produces the majority of nonstandard instances of *for* in *SAWD*, mentioned in the southwestern volume (Parry 1979: 161) and recorded in Clwyd as well. It is also found in LC (57a). King (1993: 307) gives a parallel construction in Welsh which is used with relative clauses. The Welsh preposition *i* has functions of both *to* and *for* (among some others; King 1993: 281–282), which may well explain situations where a bilingual L1 Welsh-speaker uses one in place of another (57b). Most quantity expressions, then, employ the preposition *o* 'of, out of' in

Welsh (King 1993: 125), producing some transfer effects in WelE. There are numerous occurrences of *enough of* recorded in SAWD, particularly in the south (Parry 1999: 118). LC contains examples (57c-d) which operate according to the same principle.

(57) a. Do you *know for Saron*? (LC: 1a)
 b. But funny enough erm, just be- prior *for me-* f- me going to the- to the- to the grammar school... (NWC: 2b; cf. *cyn i mi fynd*, King 1993: 282)
 c. ...there was *hundred and ninety of cows* that were milked. (LC: 1c)
 d. I- well, both of us still do *a little of walking* now. (LC: 2e)

Welsh *o* induces the complex preposition 'out of' in a few cases recorded in the SAWD corpus (58a-b). The only occurrence in the more recent corpora may result from a combination with the phrasal verb *die out*; however, *of* is ungrammatical in this context (58c).

(58) a. [But you'd use slots *>or shalots..]
 Slots, slots<* and when slots is growing innit, you get four or five *out of a slots*, don't you.
 [Yeah.]
 But *out of spring onions* you won't get- only one, it's a seed that it would come. (SAWD: Gn 9: 1)
 b. There's a tremendous big bog *in there*, but you can't do anything *out of it*. (i.e. 'it's useless'; SAWD: Gn 7: 2)
 c. I cannot see Welsh being dying, absolutely dying *out of Wales*, oh no. (LC: 1d)

Off is used in place of *from* in some dialects. The following instances are recorded in the *Voices* interviews, this time in Mid and North Wales. Penhallurick (1991) and Parry (1999) make no mention of these, which together with similar findings in SED suggests that this is an EngE dialect contact feature. However, with the broad semantic scope of *o* and related prepositions, definitive explanations cannot be given.

(59) a. it's just the sort of saying I've picked up *off someone else* you know (*Voices*: Builth Wells; 0:55:32)
 b. you come '*off*' Flint you don't come 'from' Flint (*Voices*: Flint)
 c. I certainly don't want a cwtch *off you* then (*Voices*: Holyhead)

Paulasto's notes on northern SAWD interviews contain a number of instances, where the adverbials *here/there* are accompanied by *in* in contexts where it is not required in StE (see 58b and 60a). Similar instances are again recorded in *SED*, and there is no apparent (structural) counterpart for this construction in Welsh. Southeastern WelE, however, contains the regionally distinctive phrase *by here/ by there*, not used in the bilingual regions. The informants in Tonypandy are highly aware of this feature in their dialect and it is discussed during several interviews (60b-c). The construction is accompanied by a regionally salient pronunciation /bəɪˈjøː/ (and /bəˈðɛː/), which is highlighted in the interviews (e.g. 60d).

(60) a. Well when you're cutting- cleaning the hedges *in here* you use a hook. (SAWD: Gn 7: 2)
 b. you know H. doesn't sound any different to when she lived *by here* so... (TC: 5a)
 c. ...you came through a place called Porth, did you see that?
 [That's right yeah.]
 It's just *by there*. (TC: 3a)
 d. A: Yeah they don't- they don't say come *by here*. <laughs>
 [Yeah.]
 A: They don't- they- they- they pronounce things
 B: Differently.
 A: pro- more, you know, correctly, properly. (TC: 6b)

Unlike the Welsh-induced prepositional features in the bilingual regions, which are confined to the elderly speaker generation, *by here/there* is used by middle-aged Tonypandy informants as well (a total of 17 instances, 3.41 pttw). Although children or young adults are not recorded in TC, this feature is productive enough in the Rhondda dialect that we would, nevertheless, expect it to be used by the younger generations, too. However, its use may be affected by its status as a dialectal, low-prestige feature (see 60d).

Coupland (1988: 37) finds *by here/by there* to be used in Cardiff English in "phonologically standardized realizations". He also mentions the interrogative form *where by?* used in other (presumably southeastern) varieties of WelE, while Cardiff English has the "well-known" variant *where to?* in both positional and directional contexts: *where to's the hammer?* or *where's my wallet to?* (Coupland 1988: 37). The compound forms trigger the following anecdote about the TV series *Gavin and Stacey* (with southeast Welsh characters) in TC:

(61) A: and in the wedding this man was talking to her- and the- she was saying about her boyfriend, and the- and he s- or he said about his girlfriend rather, and she said, "*Where to is she by* now then?" <laughter>
[Mm. <laughter>]
A: and he said to her then, to the one who wrote the film you know,
B: Aye.
A: the fat one Smithy they called him,
B: Aye that's right.
A: and he said "Why don't you learn to speak English?" <laughter> *Where's he to by* then.
B: <laughs> *Where's he to by* then.
A: *Where's he to by* now.
[Would people actually say that then?]
A: Yeah.
B: Yeah. (TC: 2, 3b)

In fact, the informants in (61) exaggerate the construction by adding the *by* preposition used locally; the actual quote is *Where to is she now?*[1] The extract illustrates the salience of these prepositional features in southeastern WelE, however.

Another positional preposition in present-day WelE is *at* used with place names (62a-b, 62a spoken by an informant originating from the Rhondda). *At* also occurs in place of *to* in the expression *listen at*, recorded in South Glamorgan in Parry (1999: 118) and in Flint in the *Voices* interviews (62c).

(62) a. but I'm now quite happy and proud to live and work *at Holyhead* (*Voices*: Holyhead)
b. they probably converse in Welsh in the house then, say, well my relations out *at America* (LC: 2c)
c. let's have a listen *at you!* (*Voices*: Flint)

Further prepositions which in *SAWD* are occasionally used in nonstandard contexts are *about* (e.g. *the English/Welsh name* about), *by* (e.g. *we see* by *our eye*), *over* (e.g. *an old proverb* over *that*) and *to* (e.g. *I'm very cross* to *you*; Parry 1999: 118–119). These are not found in LC, NWC, TC or the *Voices* commentaries. Based on the research materials available, our general impression is that Welsh-induced preposition replacement occurs in the speech of the elderly generation only, and

---

[1] BBC *Gavin and Stacey* Episode #1.6 (30 Sept 2008). See a clip in YouTube: https://www.youtube.com/watch?v=-T-100FEomg (accessed 9 Apr 2020).

StE prepositions have subsequently taken over. Prepositional features which survive in present-day WelE are either superstratal or regional innovations relatively independent of Welsh contact influence.

Preposition omission

In *SAWD*, loss of prepositions is noted in a few, varied contexts (63a; Parry 1999: 118–119). More typically, however, omission occurs in WelE with days of the week (63b) and in complex prepositions such as *up/down at/to/in* and *out of* (63c-d), especially in combination with a place name:

(63) a. the other side Ø *Mold* (Cl 3; Parry 1999: 118)
 b. then I'm back to work Ø *Monday* (LC: 7e); they flew out Ø *Tuesday morning* (TC: 2); we go for meals Ø *Saturday night* (NWC: 8c)
 c. I always thought it's a bit camp, "going *up* Ø *the loo*", to hear a fellow say that "I'm going *up* Ø *the loo*" (TC: 6a); We tend to go *down* Ø *Ammanford* or Swansea. (LC: 7a)
 d. I'm going back *in and out* Ø *the car* (LC: 2f); years ago we'd be em, *out* Ø *the street* down on the corner (TC: 4); when I came *out* Ø *the army* I worked away (NWC: 2a)

Coupland (1988: 35) observes the reduction of complex prepositions in Cardiff, but as this feature is shared by varieties of EngE, he categorizes it as a British social dialect feature rather than a regional Welsh one. True enough, similar instances (including omission with days of the week) can be found aplenty in ICE-GB (Meriläinen & Paulasto 2015). Coupland (1988: 35) records *run out* Ø *the door; round* Ø *Dave's place; over* Ø *Canton; up* Ø *Ely;* and Windsor Lewis (1990c: 117) and Connolly (1990: 127) give similar examples from Glamorgan and Port Talbot English. In the present corpora, these instances are particularly common in TC, although a few can be found in LC and NWC, as well. Preposition omission with days of the week also seems to be somewhat more common in the south than north of Wales.

Types of omission which are not shared by ICE-GB are few in the WelE corpora. These are illustrated by (64):

(64) a. But still as I'm *saying* Ø *you*, they are bit difficult for us to understand. (LC: 2c)
 b. my mother was born Ø *next farm* (NWC: 2c)
 c. Might get mild winters if you go to the peninsula.
 [Yeah.]
 Cause Ø *the sea*, you know (NWC: 6d)

Example (64a) may well be triggered by the internal irregularity of English on the one hand and Welsh contact influence on the other. English has pairs of semantically similar expressions, such as *say to* vs. *tell*, where one requires a preposition while the other does not (see Nesselhauf 2009). Moreover, the Welsh verb *dweud* translates as both 'say' and 'tell'. Contact-induced explanations are unlikely for the other two types of omission. Rather, they may have to do with associated phrases (e.g. *live next door*) or semantic redundancy (also affecting complex prepositions in ex. 63).

3.5 Vernacular features shared with English English

In addition to the above grammatical features, which are more or less distinctive of varieties of WelE and typically (or potentially) originate from Welsh contact influence, spoken English in Wales exhibits features which clearly arise from vernacular EngE. These may be traditional dialect features with long regional histories, particularly in the longstanding English-speaking areas of Wales, or they may be general vernacular features of modern BrE which are used across the country. The former tend to be receding from present-day WelE. Indeed, there is hardly any evidence of them in the recent corpora. The latter, on the other hand, are of common currency. Both types are examined in the following subsections.

3.5.1 Plural marking

We begin by examining a feature where Welsh contact influence is a possibility, but not a strong candidate. Zero plural marking (ZPM) in measure nouns (e.g. *two foot, five mile, four pound*) is a feature of BrE and IrE (see below). It is also attested in several American varieties and a number of pidgins and creoles (Kortmann et al. 2020). *SAWD* indicates that WelE speakers, too, may use the feature in measure nouns following cardinal numerals. Parry (1999: 107) gives several instances of zero marking in the survey item *two year ago* from various parts of Wales. Gwynedd is excluded, however, and it is noteworthy that all of these instances have been recorded along the English border or in the longstanding English regions in Pembrokeshire, the Gower, or the southeast of Wales. The non-morphological and incidental materials collected for *SAWD* contain further instances with diverse measure nouns. The geographic spread is wider, extending into the bilingual Welsh regions, but the majority are again recorded in the east and south of the country (Parry 1999: 107):

(65) *two gallon* (Gn 10); *three acre big* (Dy 24); *two or three ton* (Dy 3/10, Gw: Newport); *four ounce* (Dy 23); *two inch* (Cl 5); *twenty-odd mile away* (Cl 6); *(eight) foot (long)* (P 15–16/20, WG 2/4/6, MG 1, SG 4, Gw: Newport)

ZPM is also a feature of Cardiff English (Coupland 1988: 35). Parry (1999: 107) points out that it is widespread in the traditional dialects of England, although there is also potential for Welsh contact influence, Welsh having no plural marking for nouns after cardinal numerals (see Thorne 1993: 149–50). Based on the geographic distribution of the above findings, it is more likely that this feature results from EngE influence.

Filppula, Klemola and Paulasto (2009: 234–37) carry out a quantitative investigation ZPM in traditional EngE (SED Spoken Corpus), traditional IrE (Filppula 1986), and WelE represented by twelve elderly informants from the Llandybie Corpus (LC age group I plus one; see Section 1.6). Despite similar age ranges, the SED informants were born in the final decades of the nineteenth century and the IrE and WelE informants some 30–50 years later. The normalized frequencies of ZPM are very different: while the SED and IrE corpora yield 11.98 and 10.82 instances per 10,000 words (pttw), respectively, the WelE corpus contains only 3.75 instances. The percentages of ZPM in the three corpora give similar results: 51.5% for SED, 34.1% for IrE and 15.1% for WelE. These figures are further evidence of the EngE origin of the feature in WelE, and possibly also in IrE (Filppula et al. 2009: 236–237). In traditional EngE, then, the feature is likely to originate from Old English measure nouns uninflected for the plural (e.g. *gēar* 'year', *pūnd* 'pound').

There is vast lexical variation in the percentages of ZPM (Filppula et al. 2009: 236). The research data behind the article show that in the WelE corpus, the typical items that lack plural marking are *pound* and *foot*, both of which yield high percentages. *Year* and *mile* make a few appearances as well:

(66) a. I mean, if you had ten *pound* in those days you were a millionaire. (LC: 1a)
   b. ...an iron ring, about, wouldn't be two- somewhere around two *foot*, not quite two *foot* in diameter. (LC: 4c)
   c. Years ago, everybody used to walk.
      [M-hm.]
      Even, two or three *mile*, some of them. (LC: 2e)

The younger generations from Llandybie display very little use of ZPM. The only noun that systematically attracts this feature is *pound*, with a few instances of *foot* and *year* in age groups II and III (for the age groups, see Section 1.6). In NWC, too, there are very few instances overall, but interestingly, the majority occur with *year* rather than *pound*, in spite of a total opposite in Welsh: *blwyddin* 'year' is one of the few nouns which actually take the plural form (*blynedd*) following numerals (Thorne 1993: 150). *SAWD* indicates that ZPM has never been a feature of northern WelE and the present results from North Wales support this. In the Tonypandy Corpus (TC), *mile* has explicit plural marking in the majority of cases, and other items are too few in number for any robust conclusions. The WelE corpora indicate that this feature is receding from these dialects, coming only to be associated with particular lexical items. This trend aligns with general BrE: 4.4% of all instances investigated in the unscripted spoken sections of ICE-GB contain ZPM, and it is basically restricted to two nouns: *stone* and *foot* (Filppula et al. 2009: 238).

3.5.2 Pronouns

There is very little information on nonstandard pronoun usage outside *SAWD* and some historical sources (see Penhallurick 1994: 163–165), which is telling of the marginal status of these features at present. Pronouns are not affected by Welsh contact influence in WelE, and thus, any irregularities that occur arise from EngE dialect contact affecting the longstanding English regions in the south and east of Wales. Along with the gradual loss of distinctive Gower and south Pembroke dialects and the levelling and standardization of traditional EngE dialects across the border, this set of features is bound to fade out (see also Penhallurick 2008b: 363–365).

The nonstandard vernacular usages in *SAWD* described by Parry (1999: 108–109) can be divided into a few different types. Firstly, there are the archaic singular pronouns: nominative *thou* (Cl 3, Dy 14/20), objective *thee* (Cl 3, P 15–16, Dy 14/20, WG 5–6), and possessive *thy* (Dy 20/25, WG 4–6). The second type involves usages where the subject and object forms are switched: nominative *thee* (Cl 3, P 15–16, Dy 21, WG 5–6, SG 3), nominative *her* (Cl 3, P 10/13/17–18/20, Gw 1), objective *we* (P 15–17/20) and objective *they* (MG 3). Morgan (1886: 51) also attests objective *I* ('*help I!*') in the Gower. The distribution of the above localities indicates that these usages are restricted to the specific areas mentioned above: South Pembrokeshire, the Gower peninsula, South Glamorgan, and the eastern border area, with an inland wedge in Radnorshire, Powys, which also Anglicized relatively early on (see Chapter 5). Pronoun exchange is a feature of the traditional Southwest and West Midlands dialects (e.g. Klemola 2003), with limited use (mainly *we/wor* for *us*) in the Northeast (Beal et al. 2012: 51–54). In Welsh, the same forms of personal pronouns are used in both subject and object positions (e.g. Thorne 1993: 154–159), but Welsh is unlikely to have influenced this feature in WelE. Filppula et al. (2008: 114) point out, however, that historical Celtic contact should be considered a possibility in the development of pronoun exchange in EngE.

Linked to the above types are uninflected possessive determiners *it* 'its' (Dy 19), *us* 'our' (Cl 3, WG 3) and *they* 'their' (SG 1/4) and the dialectal possessive pronouns (called "disjunctive" by Parry 1999: 109) *yourn, he's, ourn, theirn* and *they's*, which primarily occur in Radnorshire (as well as *thine*, attested somewhat more widely in the longstanding English regions). In *SED*, these forms are used quite widely in the North, West Midlands and South (especially the southwestern counties).

Pronominal features which originate specifically from the southwest of England include the 3sg masculine nominative *a* and objective *en* (Parry 1999: 109). The latter is also used of inanimate objects (e.g. *put en down*; Cl 3, Dy 12–13/19/24–25, WG 3/5). These are recorded in South Pembrokeshire and the Gower, as well as, curiously, in Cl 3 (Buckley), near the English border in Flintshire. Also earlier descriptions of the Gower dialect by Morgan (1886), Davies (1920) and Tucker (1950, 1957) mention the pronouns *a* (or *ah*) and *en* (or *un*). Parry (1999: 109) points to Old English *hine* as the source for *en* in southwest English. An alternative explanation has, however, been sought in Brythonic contact influence (see Filppula et al. 2008: 114–117, also Klemola 2003: 270–273).

Reflexive pronouns are regularized primarily in the southeast. The following examples are from TC:

(67) a. I don't know whether he knows *hisself* <laughs> (TC: 4)
 b. they present *theirselves* different (TC: 3b)

Coupland (1988: 35) notes these forms in Cardiff English and categorizes them as British social dialect features rather than regional ones.

WelE relative pronouns are subject to some variation, too. *SAWD* indicates that zero relative in a subject position (as in 68a) and *as* for *that/who* (68b) are primarily used in Powys, while there are a few instances with *what* and *which* from South Wales as well as with the possessive relative *that his* (68c) from Powys and West Glamorgan (*SAWD*, Parry 1999: 109–110):

(68) a. I know a man Ø will do it for you
 b. He's the man *as* looks after the cows
 c. That's the man *that his* uncle has drowned

The distribution of these instances, too, points to EngE influence, and their present-day role in WelE is likely to be small, based on the corpora. In fictional representations of WelE they emerge rather often (Section 5.6), but this may result from their distinctly dialectal sound rather than actual use (see below). The only corpus and location where relative *what* and *as* have been spotted is the dubious Talbot Green in the BBC *Voices* data (69a-b). A few zero relatives (69c) and *that* for *who* (69d) are found elsewhere, indicating that these are somewhat more frequent:

(69) a. you might get the odd showman *what* is really Scotch (*Voices*: Talbot Green)
 b. and he died on the same piece of ground *as* my wife was borned on (*Voices*: Talbot Green)
 c. there's a lot of English um Ø come here to live now (*Voices*: Holyhead)
 d. I'm the one *that*'s there normally (*Voices*: Builth Wells)

In EngE, relative *what* is characteristic of southeastern and southwestern dialects (e.g. Trudgill 2008: 410, Wagner 2008: 429, Szmrecsanyi 2013: 63–64), although it is found to occur in the north as well (Tagliamonte et al. 2005: 86–88, Beal et al. 2012: 54–56). Relative *as*, on the other hand, appears to be disappearing even from its primary region in the southwest (Wagner 2008: 429, Britain 2007: 101–102). *That* for a human antecedent, on the other hand, is a frequent choice in most parts of the west and north of England, and zero subject relatives occur practically everywhere to some extent (see Britain 2007: 99–100).

3.5.3 Verb inflection

Agreement
Nonstandard agreement features concern the extension or absence of third person singular *-s* and past tense *was/were* variation. As regards *SAWD*, the most informative volumes are the southwestern (Parry 1979) and northern ones (Penhallurick 1991: 194–206), both of which provide a rich variety of instances. The information from the southeast (Parry 1977) is more limited, especially on 3SG *-s* usage, but it is hard to believe that this feature would not occur in the southeastern counties as well. In the present-day data, nonstandard agreement features emerge primarily in the southeast. A third type, default singular *is/was* with existential/presentational *there*, is discussed in brief below.

Parry (1979: 147) lists extension of *-s* (also known as verbal *-s*; see, e.g. Godfrey and Tagliamonte 1999) under the heading "Present tense habitual", and it seems indeed that most usages mentioned here and in Penhallurick (1991: 194) occur in a generic-habitual (or stative) context. The instances include (70a-b), while (70c) is found in the transcribed SAWD data.

(70) a. I *believes* you (Dy/Pem 10); we *calls* it (Dy/Pem 3/10); bulls *bellows* (Dy/Pem 4; Parry 1979: 147)
 b. things like that sometimes *comes* along (Cl 2); the people *wants* to see them (Gn 1; Penhallurick 1991: 194)
 c. If you *goes* on the mountain now there'll be a- sheep paths all over the place there. (SAWD: Fro 1)

The above sources record extension of -*s* primarily in Pembrokeshire and the northeast of Wales. A very few instances concern the verbs *be* and *do* (e.g. *is they*, Penhallurick 1991: 199; *they does*, Parry 1979: 158). Coupland (1988: 33–34) mentions this feature in Cardiff English, calling it the "central aspect of non-standardness" as regards present-tense verbs. It concerns both lexical verbs (e.g. *I likes it; we lives in Splott*) and *be* and *do* as main verbs (e.g. *they's awful; we does it often*), occasionally including *have* (*we never has homework*; Coupland 1999: 35). Further observations are made in Glamorganshire, "frequently observed in the least sophisticated speakers" (Windsor Lewis 1990c: 118), and Port Talbot (Connolly 1990: 127).

In the present corpora extension of -*s* is low in frequency. TC contains a single instance (71a), while in LC some of the elderly speakers employ extended -*s* in narrative contexts, as in (71b), or in a habitual-general context (as in 71a). Windsor Lewis (1990c: 118), too, finds that extension of -*s* in Glamorgan English is connected to the habitual (or iterative) function.

(71) a. I *goes* in the club and the first thing they say to me if I'm in there is er "is P. coming down tonight" (TC: 4)
 b. I was reading in the church now, you know [...] and they *says* "can you read without glasses", "yes I can" I said (LC: 1d)

There are no instances in the NWC. The distribution indicates that this is a regionally restricted and most likely an English dialect feature: It is attested quite widely in EngE, particularly in the southeast (Kortmann et al. 2020, Anderwald 2008: 451) but also in the southwest of England (see, e.g. Godfrey & Tagliamonte 1999, who also discuss the habitual and narrative functions of the feature).

The opposite case, absence of -*s* with a 3SG subject, is also attested in WelE. Based on the *SAWD* volumes, this feature does not concern lexical verbs but rather the auxiliaries *do* and *have*: Uninflected lexical verbs are few (ex. 72a from the southwest), while uninflected *do* is widespread in both southern volumes and *have* makes a few appearances also in the north (see, e.g. Parry 1977: 173–177; 1979: 158–160). The incidental materials include the examples in (72b).

(72) a. At four o'clock, school *finish* (Dy/Pem 7, Dy/Cth 2–3); the man that *look* after the cows (Dy/Cdg 1; Parry 1979: 147)
 b. My clock *have* stopped (Dy/Cth 3; Parry 1979: 159); a cow that *have* seen the bull (Cl 5; Penhallurick 1991: 206)

In the present-day corpora, absence of *-s* is largely confined to the southeast, Tonypandy and Cardiff/Splott (BBC *Voices*), and to the verbs *do* and, in particular, *have*:

(73) a. well his mother th- I don't know she er, she *don't* speak like some of them do speak up there (TC: 3b)
 b. he*'ve* still got the Rhondda accent but he*'ve* got that Newport- to me they don't sound Welsh (TC: 5a); K.*'ve* ordered them (TC: 2)

Coupland (1988: 34), too, notes the absence of *-s* with *have* in Cardiff English, as does Connolly (1990: 126–127) for Port Talbot, and it is a widespread feature in *SED* (see, e.g. Parry 1979: 159–160).

Other present tense agreement features described in *SAWD* are by now archaic. They concern, for example, the dialectal 2SG inflectional forms (and pronouns; e.g. *thee art/bist/beest; thee artn't*) and the *be*-paradigm (e.g. *I be, thee be, her be, they be; I bain't, she bain't, they bain't*; Parry 1999: 114). These forms are also recorded in older sources describing traditional South Pembrokeshire and Gower English (see Penhallurick 1994: 165–167), but they have no bearing on present-day WelE.

In the past tense, the most notable agreement feature is that of *was/were*-variation, *was/wasn't* being used with plural subjects and *were/weren't* with 1SG and 3SG. The former feature is considerably more widespread in *SAWD*, being recorded in all three volumes (see Parry 1999: 114 for a summary). The instances are more sporadic in the north than the south, however.

Unlike the present-tense agreement features, generalized *was* occurs in all WelE corpora: LC, NWC, TC and *Voices* (in, e.g. Bon-y-maen, Treorchy and Cardiff). It is thus in current use throughout Wales, as illustrated by the following examples, but the instances are nevertheless too few for a quantitative analysis. Most informants using this feature are middle-aged or older.

(74) a. we *was* in a Welsh class for two years, the first and second year (NWC, Llwyngwril: 6a)

b. I thought you *was* off K., like a pint of sour milk (TC: 2)

Was-generalization takes place quite frequently in BrE and varieties of English worldwide (see, e.g. Tagliamonte 2009).

The second type, *were*-generalization, is much less common in WelE, according to both *SAWD* and corpus evidence. The instances are few and far between, recorded in all corners of the country bar the northwest (Parry 1999: 114, Penhallurick 1991: 202). In TC this feature occurs in the negative form only (75a-b), while LC and NWC have a few random occurrences (75c).

(75) a. your gym was up there *weren't* it (TC: 2)
     b. her father *weren't* in good health (TC: 3b)
     c. Well after the Roman period *were finished*, then a gentleman by the name of Mitchell came there... (LC: 2g)

The dialectal distribution of *were*-generalization in EngE is described by, for example, Trudgill (2008: 349–350), who finds it characteristic of many northern and central Midlands counties, along with the southwest of England.

The above instances do not include existential/presentational *there is/was* with plural subjects, which is a highly productive "common core" feature in spoken British English, WelE included (see, e.g. Britain 2007: 78, Szmrecsanyi 2013: 61–62). The eWAVE ranks it as pervasive or obligatory in most L1 varieties of English, both traditional and high-contact ones (Kortmann et al. 2020).

(76) a. Then opposite to my mom *there's two new bungalows* there as well (NWC: 8d)
     b. at the time *there was no mobile phones* so they couldn't go like that and turn away (TC: 5c)

In the present corpora, *there is/has been* (nearly always in the contracted form *there's [been]*) is the default choice with a notional plural subject in 68–74% of all occurrences in LC (with the exception of 30% in Age group II), while in NWC the figures are 26–70%, rising steadily towards the youngest speakers, and 68% in TC. Past tense *was* is the less common variant in LC (8–61%) and NWC (4–38%) but the more common one in TC (74%). This difference may result from a more widespread acceptance of *was*-generalization in the southeast.

Verb morphology

Dialectal features of verb morphology in WelE concern mainly regular, zero, or otherwise nonstandard forms of past tense and past participle inflection of irregular verbs, for example, *bringed, come, lied* and *speaked* instead of *brought, came, lay* and *spoke*, or *ate, drank, give* and *knowed* instead of *eaten, drunk, given* and *known* (Parry 1999: 112–113). Globally speaking, regularization of irregular verb paradigms is a feature of many vernacular L1 Englishes, whether traditional and low-contact ones or high-contact varieties (Kortmann et al. 2020). It is less frequent in L2 varieties and pidgins and creoles. Unmarked forms, then, are a feature of pidgins and creoles, but also of L1 varieties in the British Isles and the US (Kortmann et al. 2020). Parry's account for *SAWD* shows that the majority of instances have been recorded in the longstanding English regions, which is indicative of EngE influence, particularly as similar forms are common in traditional EngE dialects (based on, e.g. *SED* and *EDG* data; see also Anderwald 2009). Nonstandard forms are, however, also used in *SAWD* localities where the informants are L1 Welsh speakers, in which case they may result from EngE influence or regularization strategies adopted by speakers with incomplete command of English verbal paradigms.

In the contemporary WelE corpora, uninflected past tense forms are recorded in the south and east (*Voices*: Builth Wells, Cardiff, Talbot Green; and TC). Most of them concern the verb *come*, with one instance of *run*. Both dialect forms are described in detail by Anderwald (2009: 149–182), who finds past tense *come* especially frequent in EngE, including West Midlands.

(77) a. I *come* back here then er nineteen ninety . em . and I've been here ever since (TC: 5c)
 b. and he *run* into the caravan (*Voices*: Talbot Green)

Coupland (1988: 34–35), too, notes that zero past tense marking is found in Cardiff English (e.g. *he give me a quid; they run off; he come over here*). However, he does not find "over-generalized" past tense forms such as *gived, holded, swinged* being used in Cardiff, nor are they attested in the present corpora apart from a few instances in *Voices*/Talbot Green (*borned, growed*; for the questionable representativeness of the Talbot Green interview, see Section 1.6). Roller (2016: 47, 103) examines the frequencies of zero marking of regular past tense forms in FRED and RWC and finds them to be highly infrequent (0.23 pttw in FRED and 0.15 pttw in RWC).

Other types of nonstandard forms, either simple past for past participle (ex. 78a) or vice versa (78b), are recorded in some of the southern and eastern *Voices* localities and TC, the latter variant being more common (for the EngE distribution, see Anderwald 2009: 98f). These are scarcely found at all in the interview corpora from the bilingual Welsh regions.

(78) a. and some haven't *spoke* a word of English have they? (*Voices*: Bon-y-Maen); we've *sang* with the best we've *sang* with Bryn Terfel (*Voices*: Flint)
 b. and I went back and I *done* two years (*Voices*: Bon-y-Maen); and I *sung* 'Delilah' by Tom Jones (*Voices*: Builth Wells); I *seen* him on the front of the Rhon- (TC: 3a)

SAWD contains a few instances of the now-extinct *a*-prefixing with past participle forms (e.g. *a-had, a-found, a-fetched, a-got, a-lost*; Parry 1999: 113). These are recorded in Pembrokeshire and the Gower, as also noted in Penhallurick (1994: 167), which points to EngE dialect origin. There is no evidence of these forms in any of the recent corpora.

3.5.4 Negation

Vernacular negation features in WelE are of three main types: multiple negation, *never* as a past tense negator, and distinctive forms of negative auxiliaries. None of these are found to be highly frequent in the corpora, however, and the final type, negative auxiliary forms *canna* 'can't', *couldna* 'couldn't', *munna* 'mustn't', *shanna* 'shan't' and *oona* 'won't' (see Parry 1999: 118) are confined to the traditional dialects of Powys. They therefore have little relevance in present-day WelE.

Parry (1999: 119) finds multiple negation or negative concord widespread in *SAWD*. Indeed, it occurs in all present corpora too and in various localities from Tonypandy to Llanuwchllyn, although the frequencies are low. The *Voices* commentaries also indicate that this feature is not associated with any particular region or type of community. There may be some functional variation, however. For instance, an elderly L1 Welsh informant in Llandybie uses it to reinforce the negation (79d), while for other informants this is a neutral construction.

(79) a. I *don't* like it *neither* (*Voices*: Flint)
 b. jewellery is *not* called jewellery *no* more, you've got to call it 'bling' (*Voices*: Splott)
 c. there's *no* grant or *nothing* that you have now like (NWC, Llanuwchllyn: 6b)
 d. I like the English people, I *haven't* got *nothing* against them.

>[*>Well that's good.]
>I have <* *not* got *nothing* against them.
>[Mm.]
>Nothing. (LC: 1c)

Never is used to some extent as a past tense negator in varying contexts. It is recorded with definite time reference, as in BrE (see Britain 2007: 86), primarily in the south and east (80a-b; see also Coupland 1988: 35). In some cases, *never* occurs with the simple past where the present (or past) perfect would be expected (81a-b).

(80) a. they'd ask me to go up and help in the school as well so I was offered a job but I never- I *never took* that either. (TC: 5b)
  b. but we *never kept* the tape unfortunately, would have done really good for this program (*Voices*: Flint)

(81) a. [Have you- what about *ffodrwm*?]
   No I *never heard* the word. (SAWD: Bot 2)
  b. [Pobol y Cwm?]
   No.
   [No?]
   No, *I never liked* it, no. I don't watch things like that. (NWC: 8d)

The latter instances are recorded from L1 Welsh speakers only, which raises the question of Welsh input. As pointed out by Kallen (2013: 95) with regard to the "indefinite anterior perfect" in IrE, the distinction between the past and perfect time references in English is not a straightforward matter. The eWAVE indicates that the simple past for the (experiential) present perfect is fairly common in Englishes worldwide (Kortmann et al. 2020), but in WelE this feature seems to be restricted to expressions involving *never*. Besides LC and NWC, the construction is used in two North Welsh localities of the SAWD corpus, which points to a home-grown origin. The semantics of the simple past and perfect in Welsh basically correspond to those of English, but the perfective time adverb *erioed* 'ever, never' is used in the preterite as well as the perfect tenses (King 1993: 247, Thorne 1993: 418), and this may have an effect on the WelE usages. However, matters are complicated by other vernacular BrE uses of *never*, as in (80a-b), and some degree of overlapping between the simple past and perfect.

3.5.5 Adverbs

Manner adverbs can sometimes remain unmarked in WelE. Again, this is a relatively common characteristic of EngE in the south as well as north of the country (Britain 2007: 93–94) and considered by Coupland (1988: 35) an urban vernacular BrE feature in Cardiff English. The majority of instances in the present-day WelE corpora are recorded in TC and, unlike in Tagliamonte and Ito's (2002) study on York English (reported in Britain 2007: 93–94), the intensifier *real(ly)* does not play a large role in the findings. It does occur in LC to some extent, particularly in older speakers' interviews. *Proper* also functions as an intensifier (e.g. *proper annoyed*; Jones 2016b: 27). In example (82e) the speaker, in contrast, employs an adverb where an adjective would be expected in StE.

(82) a. ...he's doing it *regular*. (TC: 2)
 b. A: Well some some people do, perhaps they're just speaking *proper*,
 B: Innit?
 A: you know what I mean,
 [Yeah.]
 B: Innit? My- and my father's er, sisters they spoke *nice* didn't they?
 [Okay.]
 B: They were like- my father's sisters, they all spoke *nice* they did. (TC: 5b & 3b)
 c. That's you know, really low isn't it?
 [Mhm.]
 Low ability and *real* sloppy. (TC: 6b)
 d. And our doctor now, er, well, he was *real* English but he's learnt Welsh, speaks Welsh as *good* as I- me. (LC: 2c)
 e. I think we sound *differently* and we got different phrases too. (TC: 6b)

In NWC this feature is rare. However, it is reported in the linguistic commentaries for the *Voices* interviews in Flint and Holyhead in the north, Builth Wells, Newtown and Tregaron in mid-Wales, and Bon-y-Maen, Risca, Talbot Green and Treorchy in the south. It is clearly geographically widespread, although the frequencies may vary.

4 Lexis and discourse features

4.1 Introduction

In general accounts of the variety (e.g. Penhallurick 1993: 38–40; Thomas 1994: 142–144), it is pointed out that, unlike phonology, WelE lexicon is not strongly affected by the Welsh language. Thomas (1994: 142), for example, states that Welsh loanwords of general currency are "less than a handful". The situation is very different from IrE, where Irish-derived lexicon has a firm current as well as historical standing (see Kallen 2013: 132–143). The comparatively meagre number of Welsh items results from the more recent Anglicization and formal acquisition of English in Welsh-speaking Wales on the one hand, and of the strong impact of EngE in the longstanding English regions on the other. The combined effect seems to have left fairly little room for Welsh loanwords in general usage. The above authors draw attention to the numerous geographically restricted loanwords, however. Penhallurick (1993: 38–40) also observes that in *SAWD*, in the heavily Welsh-speaking areas, their emergence may well signify the informants' status as L1 Welsh speakers. Rather than being established and common dialect words in the English spoken in the area, Welsh words are used to fill in lexical gaps, as the English words for many of the questionnaire items may be completely unfamiliar to the respondents (see also Parry 1985a: 51–56). This issue is discussed further below.

Instead of Welsh, the majority of dialect lexicon in WelE is of English origin: In the *SAWD* glossary (Parry 1999: 121–201) they constitute c. 95% of all lexical entries. *SAWD* also indicates geographic patterns of distribution of EngE dialect vocabulary, which align well with the history of Anglicization and dialect contact in Wales. The longstanding English regions of South Pembrokeshire, Gower, and the southeast and border areas have historical depth of English lexicon not found in other parts of the country, and hence the density and regional distinctiveness of the dialect words is also greater in these parts. In contrast, some EngE items in *SAWD* have spread across the entire country, while others occur nearly everywhere, only the westernmost areas excepted.

Because of the regional differences, the following sections will examine WelE dialect lexis from the perspectives of source language (Welsh, English, other) and geographic distribution. The focus is on present-day rather than historical usage, but it is important to note the role of Welsh in older regional dialect vocabulary, be it that much of this lexicon has fallen out of active use or is associated with "fairly consciously picturesque speaking" (as commented by Windsor Lewis 1990c: 110). It is impossible, of course, to give a comprehensive description of WelE dialect lexicon here, and hence, we refer you to the sources below for further

https://doi.org/10.1515/9781614512721-004

information. We shall also take a closer look at select lexical items and their distributions in the research data.

Lexicon is the most salient domain of language, and thus is it a central target of traditional dialect research. Studies and documents of WelE dialect lexicon can be broadly divided into four types: traditional rural dialect lexicon studies as represented by *SAWD*, historical as well as recent descriptions focusing on regional lexicon, popularized accounts, and the BBC *Voices* survey. A recent addition to the above is *Welsh English Dialect* (Jones 2016a), an accessible yet research-based booklet focusing on WelE dialect lexis. The main sources for the following sections represent all of these to an extent. Findings in *SAWD* (Parry 1977, 1979, 1999, and Penhallurick 1991) are referred to whenever the item in question is included in the survey or its incidental material. Regional dialect descriptions which are accessible to us and most relevant for the present purposes are consulted as well; these include Windsor Lewis (1964) on Glamorganshire, George (1990) on the Rhondda, Penhallurick (1994) on the Gower, and Jones (2013, 2016b) on Gwent, as well as other smaller or older contributions.

By popularized accounts we refer to the publications depicting the dialect of the southeastern Valleys: *Talk Tidy: The Art of Speaking Wenglish* (1985) and *More Talk Tidy* (1986) by John Edwards, and *Wenglish: The Dialect of the South Wales Valleys* (2008) by Robert Lewis. As the titles may indicate, neither book approaches its subject purely academically but is intended for the enlightenment and entertainment of the general public. The glossaries in the books are long and comprehensive, containing not only dialect words of Welsh and English origin, but also expressions and idioms, nonstandard grammar items and regionally distinctive pronunciations of specific words. As such, they offer an interesting window into the dialect of the Valleys, coloured by the region's bilingual past as an industrial hotspot. Both Edwards and Lewis are local to the area, which is an advantage but also a problem, as they base their glossaries and descriptions on their own knowledge and experience of the dialect rather than systematic data collection or corpus evidence: no further references or sources of information are given. The glossaries are also uninformative on the frequencies and time frames of the words, and thus it is likely that there is a great deal of quantitative, regional and diachronic variation in their actual use. The authors do not contextualize "Wenglish" or its features as part of English in Wales more generally but present it as an independent development.

Welsh English Dialect (Jones 2016a) is likewise intended for a wide audience, and although concise, it is more systematic in its approach and regionally comprehensive. Besides a general word list, the booklet includes lexical case studies and thematic sections on, for example, the language of children's games, food, work, music, and the home, as well as WelE phraseology.

WelE dialect lexicon has recently been charted alongside EngE dialects, in the BBC *Voices* project (BBC Voices 2014) through an online "Language Lab" survey and a radio survey (2004–2005; see Penhallurick 2013). The Language Lab results are available in the form of lexical maps at the BBC Voices website. The *Voices* radio survey, in turn, involved groups of informants who were gathered together to discuss the topic of dialects and accents in various parts of the country. They were furthermore presented with a list of lexical items, and the outcomes of the discussions have been worked into linguistic commentaries which are availed of in the present description (see Section 1.6 and Chapter 6). The *Voices* word list formed the basis for the lexical questionnaire in Jones (2013, 2016b) as well as in the Tonypandy interviews in 2012. Central observations from TC are included below as well.

4.2 Welsh lexicon in Welsh English

Parry (1985a: 51–56) discusses the position of Welsh loanwords in WelE from the technical perspective of compiling the SAWD dialect atlas. In areas which are primarily English-speaking and lacking in heavy Welsh input in phonology and grammar, it is not difficult to perceive Welsh responses to the lexical questionnaire as fully established "importations", as Parry calls them. In this category, he lists, for example, *twp* 'silly, stupid', *pentan* 'the hob of a grate' and *ach-y-fi!* 'exclamation of disgust', all recorded in long-standing English regions as well as bilingual areas (1985a: 52). However, when English is the informant's second language, it is harder to discern whether the Welsh responses are genuine dialect words or "intruders", that is, words drawn from the informant's Welsh word-stock to fill gaps in the English one. In such cases, Parry (1985a: 52–53) finds that one must seek further support from dialect-external evidence (such as the geographic distribution of the word outside the locality), dialect-internal evidence (such as the general linguistic characteristics of the speaker's dialect), and one's own intuition (such as recognizing the role of *tŷ bach*, lit. 'little house', as a useful euphemism for 'toilet, outhouse').

Parry is thus essentially describing the distinction between borrowing and code-switching, a matter of considerable amount of debate in contact-linguistic literature (e.g. Matras 2009: 106–114). Let us pause on this issue for a moment, as it is relevant to multilingual practices and language contact phenomena in Wales. The current evidence suggests that code-switching in the form of spontaneous insertions from the speaker's L1 Welsh is quite infrequent in WelE. Margaret Deuchar (personal e-mail communication, Feb 2017) observes that in the *Siarad* corpus of bilingual Welsh-English communication, only 1% of all bilingual clauses can be identified as having English as the matrix language. (Only 4% of the words in the corpus are English overall; Deuchar et al. 2016: 223.) Moreover, she concludes that Welsh insertions tend to occur in clause-peripheral positions, which "suggests that the English grammar of our speakers is in some sense more impervious to the influence of Welsh than their Welsh grammar is to English" (p.c.).

Further reasons why code-switching is not observed in the present-day WelE corpora are functional (as the interviewer or at least one of the discussants is non-Welsh-speaking), contextual (as highly specific lexical items are not sought), as well as proficiency-related (as bilingual speakers' English language competence today is higher than that of the L1 Welsh *SAWD* informants). This does not mean that it does not take place, but the fact is that the entire body of literature on code-switching in Wales concerns English input into Welsh rather than vice versa (see Deuchar et al. 2016: 215–216).

We concur with Matras (2009: 110–114) that code-switching and borrowing form a continuum rather than a strict dichotomy and operate across various dimensions that are related to the speaker, the structural and functional attributes of the items in question, and their frequency. The interaction of these dimensions can certainly be observed in the use of the Welsh loanwords below. Another relevant factor is the concept of listedness (as in Muysken 2000: 71–72): "the degree to which a particular element or structure is part of a memorized list which has gained acceptance within a particular speech community." This, too, is a scalar rather than binary property.

4.2.1 General currency items

Despite being described as "general currency items", the Welsh words below are used in WelE (and general English usage) for different reasons. Some are cultural loans, which means that there is no meaningful English word for them and hence their use is independent of individual or community-based bilingualism (see Myers-Scotton 1993: 168–172): *Eisteddfod* and *Cymanfa* are Welsh cultural festivals, *penillion* is a traditional Welsh way of performing a song and *crwth* a Welsh instrument. The list also includes words or expressions which are culturally well known, such as *cariad* or *tŷ bach*, although they may be seldom used in actual English discourse. *Mam-gu/nain* 'grandmother' and *tad-cu/taid* 'grandfather', then, are the southern and northern counterparts for the same term, and their distribution in WelE follows the Welsh dialect divide. Neither is thus of "general currency", but overall, one may say that the Welsh terms for grandparents continue to be used in present-day WelE in the north as well as south.

Cariad [ˈkariad] n. 'love, sweetheart'. This term of endearment is well-known in Wales, even for monoglot English speakers, although it is used fairly little in WelE discourse. Windsor Lewis (1964: 213) finds it rare in Glamorganshire, "used chiefly by those more or less familiar with W". Tonypandy informants comment that *cariad* is a word older people would use. In the *Voices* data it appears as a word for 'female partner' in Bethesda but not elsewhere. It is, however, something of a stereotypical Welsh word, also covered by *OED* Online and the *Urban Dictionary*. Jones (2016a: 40) notes that many Welsh businesses, such as wedding planners, cafés, cake makers or other random types utilize the loving aura of *cariad* in their advertising.

Cawl [kaul] n. 'broth, mixed leek/vegetable soup', which may also include lamb. According to *SAWD* this is mainly a southern word in both Welsh and WelE, being recorded in Dyfed and South Glamorgan (Parry 1999: 140). It is also mentioned by the Glamorganshire authors Windsor Lewis (1964: 215), Edwards (1985: 14) and Lewis (2008: 74). In fact, the word is well-known enough across Britain to elicit a number of recipes for "Welsh cawl" on the internet. Food terms can be considered cultural loans; other similar ones are *teisen lap* 'flat currant cake' (Windsor Lewis 1964: 336; Parry 1999: 192), *bara brith* 'fruit loaf', lit. 'speckled bread' (Thomas 1994: 143) and *bara ceirch* 'oatcake' (SAWD Drefach). See Jones (2016a: 50–54) for a fuller description of the distinctive Welsh cuisine.

Crwth [kruːθ] n. 'archaic string instrument', played with a bow. Both the original Welsh *crwth* and the Anglicized form *crowd* are in use, but as this is not a dialect word in any sense, it is not recorded in any of the sources used here. What distinguishes *crwth* from globally widespread Welsh words such as *corgi* is its regional cultural context. Another historical Welsh instrument is *pibgorn* 'hornpipe', a reed instrument made of wood or bone. These are both listed in *OED* Online, unlike *pibau cyrn*, Welsh bagpipes. (See also Jones 2016a: 59)

Cymanfa (Ganu), Gymanfa [kəˈmanvaˈganɨ] n. 'meeting or festival of singing', more specifically a "singing festival held in the (usu. Welsh) non-conformist chapels, often at Easter" (George 1990: 312). This cultural loan is occasionally mentioned by the LC and NWC informants, although it may also be dubbed as "the Welsh singing festival".

Cwtch, cwtsh [kʊtʃ] n. either 'hug, cuddle' or 'small storage space (pantry, potato-clamp etc.), hiding place', both meanings associated with closeness and tight spaces. It also appears in the compounds *cwtsh-dan-staer* (or hybrid form *cwtsh-under-the-stairs*) and *cwtsh glô* 'coal storage' (George 1990: 283–284, also Parry 1979: 221–222). *Cwtch* is a highly enregistered word in WelE, known and used across South Wales and further north too, although as Parry (1985a: 56) points out, it is not strictly-speaking a Welsh word despite native-speaker intuitions to the contrary. The [tʃ] affricate is alien to Welsh, which may be why its spelling varies: Parry and George favour *-tsh*-spelling, while Tonypandy informants (and *OED* Online) spell the word with *-tch*. Its origin is in an (Old) French loanword *couche*, borrowed into both Middle English as *couch* and Welsh as *cwts/cwtsh* n. 'recess, kennel, hiding-place', 'cuddle' (Penhallurick 1991: 352, Parry 1985a: 56, *Geiriadur Prifysgol Cymru* [*GPC*] Online). *SAWD* finds the word used in its second meaning throughout the southern counties, as far north as southern Gwynedd (Parry 1999: 147; the first sense 'cuddle' probably did not arise in the survey). TC informants use both meanings and clearly associate it with Welsh (e.g. *give us a cwtch*, 6a; *where's the sweeping brush, go in the cwtch and fetch it now*, 3c). They find that younger people would not say *cwtch* for 'hug', but this view is contradicted by the young Gwent informants, for whom *cwtch* is the most frequent choice (Jones 2013: 71). Beyond survey and corpus data, it seems that *cwtch* in the sense of 'hug, cuddle' – whether a noun or a verb – has found a new life in public domains with its culturally significant, positive connotations. Jones (2016a: 39) points out that in 2013 *cwtch* was voted as the favourite word in Wales and increasing numbers of businesses, including cafés, crechés and shops, are adopting it in their advertising. Recent observations confirm that rather than fading out, the word is evolving both grammatically and semantically: in October 2017 the Welsh tourism site visitwales.com ran a story on Facebook listing "10 cwtchy Welsh pubs" or pubs with "serious cwtch appeal".

Cwtch, cwtsh v. 'hug, cuddle', 'squat down, hide', the verbal counterpart of the noun. The verb is common in *SAWD* in the meaning 'to squat down on the haunches', but interestingly, it is not used in Gwent and Glamorganshire but in Dyfed and eastern parts of Powys (Parry 1999: 147). This is perhaps indicative of its French language contact origins in both English and Welsh; however, Parry indicates that in *SED* neither the verb nor noun is found in any sense beyond Monmouth and Herefordshire. (There is nevertheless some evidence of its use in Gloucestershire through Michelle Braña-Straw, p.c.) Other meanings are recorded sporadically across South Wales, and the word is used in the sense 'to cuddle' by the older informants of TC (e.g. *to cwtch a baby*, TC: 3c). See above.

Eisteddfod [ə(i)ˈstɛðvɔd] n. 'Welsh festival of the arts', i.e. music, literature, drama and the Welsh language, involving performances and competitions. In addition to the annual National Eisteddfod, there are numerous smaller, regional ones held every year. *OED* Online only gives the historical definition 'a congress of (Welsh) bards'. Eisteddfod is a cultural institution which is discussed in the LC and NWC interviews quite often.

Hiraeth [ˈhiraɪθ] n. 'longing, homesickness', associated with the Welsh cultural experience and frequently considered a word that has no exact translation in English. *GPC* Online gives it the definition 'grief or sadness after the lost or departed, longing, yearning, nostalgia, wistfulness, homesickness, earnest desire'. It is telling of the cultural significance of the term that a non-Welsh-speaking informant in Carmarthen uses it in defence of his Welsh identity: *I am still as much Welsh as he is [...] I'm full of hiraeth, full of it. I'm full of my native country* (Urban SAWD, Carm). The word crops up in *Voices* Flint and TC as well but is absent in the dialect descriptions of Windsor Lewis (1964) and Parry (1999).

Hwyl [huɪl] n. 'gusto, enthusiasm, spiritedness' (Thomas 1994: 142). *Hwyl* is the closest WelE equivalent to IrE *craic*, and its exact meaning varies according to the context. In the *Voices* commentaries it simply means 'fun': e.g. *we were there it was* hwyl *and we were having a great time* (Flint); *for 'fun', I think most people use* hwyl *around here you know... they... it's just part of the language* (Newtown). *GPC* Online gives two related meanings in Welsh which involve either 'fervour (esp. religious), ecstasy, unction, gusto, zest' or 'jollity, mirth, gaiety, amusement, fun'. *Hwyl* is also listed in *OED* Online, where it is interpreted as 'impassioned eloquence; also, the fervour of emotion characteristic of gatherings of Welsh people'.

Mam-gu [mamgɨ] n. 'grandmother' (lit. 'cherished mother') in South Welsh. *SAWD* (Parry 1999: 167–168) records the word as widespread in Dyfed (the item 'granny' is omitted from the southwestern volume; Parry 1979) and Hengoed (southeast). *Mam-gu* and a variant *old mam Jones* are also found in southwestern and southeastern localities of the *Voices* survey (Llanelli, Treorchy, Pontypridd) and in Tonypandy.

Moel [mɔil], *moiled, moiling* adj. 'hornless', used of cows or sheep. This traditional dialect word is found to be highly common in *SAWD*, occurring throughout the country apart from the extreme southeast (Parry 1999: 169). *Moil* and *moiled* are also used in western EngE dialects, and *OED* Online derives the terms from Welsh *moel* 'bald, beardless' and Irish *maol* 'bald'. Other related terms in regional BrE and AmE, *mull* 'heifer' and *muley* 'hornless cow', appear to have similar origins.

Nain [nain] n. 'grandmother', a child's term of address in North Welsh. Recorded in *SAWD* in Gwynedd and Clwyd (north; Penhallurick 1991: 339–340) and North Powys (southeast; Parry 1977: 236). It is a well-known word also to the North Welsh informants in the *Voices* survey (Flint, Holyhead, Llangollen). Much as it resembles *nan, nana*, and *nanny*, the relationship is unclear. In Holyhead, *nain* is described as "really Welsh", while *nana* is the "new, posh" term. *Nana, nan, nanny* and *nanno* are widespread in southwestern and southeastern localities, as well as in Tonypandy, while *nain* is not. *OED* Online derives *nan* and *nana* from *nanny* 'child's nurse', yet the similarity with the Welsh term may influence its frequent use in Wales.

Penillion [pɛnɨɬjɔn] n. 'originally improvised but now usually traditional Welsh verses and melody sung (as in an eisteddfod) in counterpoint to a familiar tune played on the harp', as comprehensively defined by the Merriam-Webster Dictionary Online. The term more commonly used of this style of music today is *cerdd dant* (see http://www.cerdd-dant.org/, accessed 9 April 2020), but again, there is no English term equivalent of these cultural loans.

Sut mae, shumai [ʃʊ'maːɨ] 'how are you', a greeting. Reported in the elderly Rhondda informants' speech, where George (1990: 315) states that it "appears to have been used more by men than women" but "seems to be falling out of use". The pronunciation [ʃʊ] for *sut* is characteristic of South Welsh, while the north favours [sɪt].

Tad-cu [tadkɨ] n. 'grandfather' in South Welsh. *SAWD* finds it used primarily in the southwest (Parry 1999: 192; the item is not included in the southeastern volume), but the *Voices* informants in the southeast (Treorchy) as well as southwest (Llanelli) mention this word. It is also used in Tonypandy, alongside many other terms.

Taid [taid] n. 'grandfather' in North Welsh. Similar to *nain*, *taid* appears in *SAWD* in Gwynedd, Clwyd (north) and northern Powys (southeast; Parry 1999: 192). It is widely known also to northern *Voices* informants, some of whom (in Llangollen) comment that it is used even by the English.

Twp [tʊp] adj. 'silly, stupid'. Recorded in *SAWD* as widespread in South Wales (Dyfed, West Glamorgan and south Powys; Parry 1999: 197) but not in the North. George (1990: 333–335) gives an interesting description of both generational and semantic shifts in the use of the word in the Rhondda. On the one hand, it is associated with bilingual Welsh-speakers' dialect, where the term is quite derogatory, but the younger, monoglot English generation of informants has to an extent adopted it into their WelE idiolect, using it "in a more indulgent and affectionate sense". The term appears in expressions such as *don't be so twp* or *twp as a bicycle* (George 1990: 333–335) and the idiomatically WelE *there's twp you are* (LC: 2c; see also Section 5.6).

Tŷ bach [tɨː'baːx] n. 'outhouse', 'toilet' (lit. 'little house'). The Rhondda informants in both George (1990: 291) and TC point out that although the word is known to them, they do not use it themselves. It is something "the typically Welsh person would say" (George 1990: 291) or only used when speaking English at school. This is a well-known euphemism across the country: in *SAWD* it occurs in all parts of Wales bar Gwent and south Powys (Parry 1999: 197). It is also recorded in LC and several localities in the *Voices* survey (Holyhead, Bethesda, Flint, Newtown, Risca & Llanelli).

Toasting for health or in someone's honour tends to be associated with indigenous language and culture. As the Irish *Sláinte!*, the Welsh toast for good health, *Iechyd da!*, is well-known and used throughout the country, although it makes no appearance in the sources used here apart from Lewis (2008). Besides cultural loans such as those listed above, many Welsh institutions are regularly referred to by their Welsh rather than English names, even when they have both. These include *Plaid Cymru* 'The Party of Wales' and *Cymdeithas yr Iaith Gymraeg* 'Welsh Language Society'. Other organizations, too, which are strongly associated with Welsh-language culture, are typically discussed by their Welsh names in the LC and NWC interviews; for example, *Urdd (Gobaith Cymru)* 'The Welsh League of Youth', *Mentrau Iaith (Cymru)* lit. 'language initiatives', community-based Welsh language organizations, and *Merched y Wawr* lit. 'Daughters of the Dawn', the Welsh language Women's Institute. The National Assembly of Wales, on the other hand, is best known as the Welsh Assembly; not even the stoutest Welsh activists in the corpora use its Welsh name *Cynulliad Cenedlaethol Cymru* when speaking English.

4.2.2 Welsh dialect words with limited use

Sources which focus on specific dialect areas may include Welsh words with regional use only. However, as most older English dialect descriptions in Wales examine the longstanding English areas (e.g. Owen 1871–78, Morgan 1886, Matthews 1913, Howse 1949), the numbers of Welsh loanwords are modest. Penhallurick (1994: 123) mentions Davies (1877–94) as "almost unique" among scholars of Gower English in drawing attention to Welsh lexis in the regional dialect with his list of five items (*ach-a-fi*, *Gŵrac*, *mapsant*, *mochyr* and *pentan*). *SAWD* lists numerous words which only occur in the predominantly Welsh-speaking areas but as pointed out in the introductory section, they may be used by the L1 Welsh informants as lexical gap-fillers rather than established dialect words. The following words are ones which occur in the present research materials or which are relatively common in *SAWD* and other sources.

Bach, fach [baːx, vaːx] adj. 'little', 'dear'; *bachgen* n. 'boy'; South Welsh terms of address or endearment. *Bachgen* ("a term of address used by boys or coalminers of each other", Parry 1999: 129) is unlikely to be used in present-day WelE, but *bach* is occasionally slipped into the conversation, typically by a L1 Welsh-speaker (e.g. in Llandybie). It is also mentioned in TC (e.g. *you know B. always says oh bach, innit*; 6b), listed in Windsor Lewis (1964: 196) and in the popularized accounts of Valleys English lexicon by Edwards (1985) and

Lewis (2008). Thomas (1994: 143) mentions the northern counterpart *del*, which occurs in northern localities of the *Voices* survey meaning 'pretty, attractive'. The sources indicate that the gender references of these terms are changeable.

Bopa ['bopa] n. 'aunty', Mid Glamorgan (Parry 1999: 135; also Windsor Lewis 1964: 205). George (1990: 275–276) states that in her elderly Rhondda informants' lexicon the term also has "wider application as a term of respect for an older lady", such as the lady next door.

Crachach ['kraxax] n. 'the elite; posh people, snobs'. Recorded in southeast Wales by, for example, Windsor Lewis (1964: 226–227) and Connolly (1990: 127), as well as Edwards (1985) and Lewis (2008). The word is also mentioned in *Voices* Pontypridd, which indicates that it continues to be used at present. The word also appears to have experienced a slight semantic shift: Hitt (2006) writes that "the term used to denote local gentry but 21st century crachach is the Taffia, the largely Welsh-speaking elite who dominate the arts, culture and media of Wales and to a lesser extent its political life". Other online sources suggest that the term may be used of practically anyone that the speaker wishes to label as a snob, whether Welsh-speaking or English-speaking elite.

Duw! [dɪʊ] excl. 'God!'. Repeated *Duw duw* translates roughly as 'good God', 'oh dear', 'dear me'. In *SAWD*, *Duw!* is recorded in Gwynedd (e.g. *Duw! I don't know*; Penhallurick 1991: 353), but *Duw duw* also occurs as a comment to the interlocutor in TC (e.g. A: *I must have gone up there about twenty odd times*. B: *Duw duw duw*). It seems to be mainly elderly people who use the word, but in their speech it is quite well integrated into the English language (e.g. *Oh Duw and you could recognize them straight away*; LC: 3g). We have also heard *duw* used by younger people in Swansea but in a rather tongue-in-cheek or facetious manner.

Llawchwith ['ɬauxwɪθ] adj. 'left-handed', *llaw bwt* 'left-handed', lit. 'hand stump'. Neither word is recorded in *SAWD*, but the *Voices* survey has *llawchwith* in Holyhead and Risca and *llaw bwt* in Treorchy and Glyn Neath. The use of both is restricted: *llawchwith* is a Welsh speaker's term, while *llaw bwt* is a case of retention in the southeastern dialect. Tonypandy informants use it in derogatory contexts, e.g. "*come on you old llaw bwt*" *I'd say that to the kids* (TC: 6b), and the same apparently applies to *llawchwith*: e.g. "*bach y bwtchwr llawchwith*" *my father used to call people who were doing things wrongly* (lit. 'left-handed butcher's hook'; *Voices*: Risca). See the following sections.

Mochyn ['moxɪn] n. 'pig', a term of abuse or scolding. Similar to terms of endearment, this word does not appear in *SAWD*, but it is used in TC: e.g. *you say "oh mochyn mawr du", you big black pig* (TC: 6b). Windsor Lewis (1964: 419) and Lewis (2008: 153) observe this word in the southeast as well.

Mwnci [mʊnkɪ] n. 'hames', lit. 'monkey'. This is a word which in *SAWD* has a very neat geolinguistic distribution, being used in all of North Wales bar the eastern border area, and in the heart of Dyfed in the southwest, Carmarthenshire and Ceredigion (Parry 1999: 266).

Other rural items used across the rural north and west include *bargod* 'eaves of the haystack', *beudy* 'cow-house'; and *col, cola* 'bristles of barley' (Parry 1999: 128–201). Welsh loanwords with regional dialectal variation in *SAWD* are, for example, *bwbach, bubbock* (south) v. *bwcci bra(i)n, bwgan bra(i)n* (north) 'scarecrow'; and *cardidwyn, credidwyn, cardottyn, cardodwyn* (south) v. *cull, cwlin* (north) 'weakling of a litter of pigs' (English *neskwal, nisgal* being used along the eastern border). Other south Welsh words include *bwl, bwlyn, bwlcyn* 'hub of a wheel' and *pentans* 'hobs of a grate', while north Welsh ones are, for example, *pistyll* 'water welling from a hill or rock-face' and *twrch ddaear* 'mole' (Parry 1999). This lexicon does not emerge in the present-day corpora, nor in the Glamorganshire accounts (Windsor Lewis 1964, Edwards 1985, Lewis 2008). Although these loanwords are some of the most common ones in *SAWD*, it is safe to say that their presence in today's WelE is limited.

The lexis recorded in the extensive Glamorganshire dialect description by Windsor Lewis (1964) mainly comprises words of English origin. However, Welsh dialect words with an apparent established status in the area are *didoreth* 'lazy, shiftless', *twti/tooty down* 'squat down', and *wus/was/gwas* [wʌs, was] "a not particularly polite term of address" to a male (Windsor Lewis 1964: 236, 395, 413). These are listed also in Edwards (1985) and Lewis (2008), alongside many other, possibly more local or idiolectal items.

A Welsh expression which is mentioned in many of the sources (and recorded in WelE literature, for example, Allen Raine's *Queen of the Rushes* and Dylan Thomas' *Under Milk Wood*) but which does not emerge in any of the corpus data is *ach-y-fi!* 'exclamation of disgust, i.e. ugh' (Parry 1999: 128; Windsor Lewis 1964: 186). Jones (2016b: 27-28; 2013) finds the expression used in Gwent to some extent, and several current online dictionaries of English – bar *OED* Online – recognize the term despite few occurrences in the data.

Some dialect words and expressions, especially in the dialects described by *SAWD*, are Welsh loan translations and hence also the outcome of language contact. These are discussed under Section 4.5 on Welsh English phraseology.

4.3 English dialect lexicon in Welsh English

The accounts of English-derived dialect lexicon in WelE are so abundant in their numbers of entries that it is not feasible to cover them here. This section will therefore describe the general sources of this dialect lexicon, draw patterns of regional distribution, and focus on the results of the recent BBC *Voices* survey, accompanied by respective data from the Tonypandy Corpus.

4.3.1 Origins and geographic patterns of English-derived dialect lexicon

This area of WelE requires a bit of framing. First, there is the history of Anglicization in Wales, which began with the longstanding English regions in the eight to twelfth centuries. This era was followed by a long period of relative stability between the monoglot Welsh and early English-speaking areas and increasingly heavy diglossia. The Anglicization of the Welsh-speaking areas gained momentum along with population growth and industrialization from the late eighteenth century onwards, intensified by free and compulsory English education a century later. From this period onwards, the mobility of population, goods, ideologies and linguistic influences was sped up, resulting in English becoming either the first or an important second language in all parts of the country (see Chapter 5 for details). These processes have left their mark also in the distribution of English dialect lexicon in Wales.

A second introductory point concerns the complexity of this language domain, which has been implied in the section above, but which is all the more tangible, when WelE dialect lexicon is investigated in its entirety. In the following extract, Parry (1985a: 58) describes the historical layeredness and change in the dialect lexicon recorded in SAWD, while also illustrating the diversity through dialect words of the same reference:

> The old-established (1300) compound *cow-house* itself spreads into the eastern borders of Wales from the English West Midlands; the modern (nineteenth-century) *cow-shed* is ousting Welsh *beudy* in Dyfed after having securely established itself in the longstanding-English territory of South and Southwest Wales; *beast-house* in Mid-Wales extends from a very small Herefordshire enclave of the same (SED found part of Monmouthshire to belong to this enclave, but SAWD has not found the word there); Gower has *cow-stall* that is recorded sporadically in Somerset, Surrey, Dorset and Sussex; North Powys *cow-bay* is apparently unique in the whole of Wales and England. The Southwest English enclave of *shippon* has had no apparent influence on South Pembrokeshire/Gower, where it might have been expected, but the Lancashire/Cheshire enclave of *shippon* spreads right across North Wales into Anglesey.

Cow-house is not an extreme example of the variability of dialect lexicon; some of the SAWD Questionnaire items elicit over twenty different responses (Parry 1999: 121–127). They may arise from EngE dialects or they may be unique to the region, as is the case with many South Pembrokeshire words (see Parry 1990b: 160). Moreover, English and Welsh-derived dialect words are often in competition with each other. Such is the case, for example, with 'weakling of a litter of pigs', which displays regional variation in both languages. As shown by Parry (1999: 285–286), the Welsh and English items are in near-complete complementary distribution across the country, and the isoglosses of the English variants are neatly linked to their neighbouring English counties: *rit* is found in Cheshire and eastern Clwyd, *ratling* in Shropshire and north Powys, *neskwal/nisgal* in Herefordshire and the eastern parts of south Powys and Gwent, and *nestle-tripe* in the Somerset-Dorset area and the Gower (for the variation in Welsh, see the section above).

Parry's (1999: 261–307) interpretive maps reveal yet another matter which adds to the complexity: the isoglosses of each survey item tend to look very different. Whereas phonological variation has a certain amount of systematicity, co-alignment of lexical isoglosses is much less consistent, which indicates that regional dialects have notable fluidity across their lexical inventories. One reason for this is the open-endedness of lexicon: the numbers of possible variants are, in theory, infinite. Another is the salience of lexicon for the speakers, which leads to conscious choices, creativity and shifting usages more easily than in the case of language structure (see Chambers & Trudgill 1998: 97). These factors also mean that much of the dialect lexicon described in *SAWD*, whether in Welsh or English, is no longer in use.

However, it is possible to draft certain broad geographic patterns based on *SAWD* and other studies. The most consistent use and the highest number of EngE dialect words are found in areas where English has been spoken the longest. The history of Anglicization also intertwines with regionally more or less specific dialect contacts. The longstanding English pockets of South Pembrokeshire and the Gower peninsula, for example, have maintained distinctive traditional lexicon which has its roots in southwest English dialects. Some of these words are *culm* 'slack of coal' (*EDD*: Somerset, Devon, Hampshire), *evil* 'agricultural fork' (*SED*: Cornwall; *EDD Online*: South West, Hrf., Shr.), *nuddock* 'neck' (*SED*: Cornwall, Devon), *foriers/voriers* 'headlands of a field' (*SED*: Cornwall, Devon), and *oavese/offis* 'eaves of a stack of corn' (*SED*: southeast England; Parry 1999, also 1990b).

Both of these regions also have characteristic lexicon of their own. Words which have not been recorded outside South Pembrokeshire are, for example, *hantries* 'hames', *moil* 'to root' (of pigs; elsewhere in Wales *moel/moil* is used of hornless cows or sheep; see above), *preen* 'to butt' (of cows), *labigan* 'a gossiping woman', and *scaddly* 'greedy' (Parry 1990b: 160, Parry 1999). The traditional Gower dialect, then, has adopted words such as *angle-touch* 'a worm' (*EDD*: *angle-twitch* in Cornwall and Devon), *brims* 'a horsefly' (*EDD*: Kent), *cammit* 'clumsy' (*EDD*: *cammed* 'crooked' in Northern England, also *cam* 'crooked' in Welsh), *clup (pit)* 'broody' (of hens), etc. (Parry 1999, Penhallurick 1994). Despite their distinctiveness, both South Pembrokeshire and the Gower nevertheless share much of their dialect lexicon with other parts of England and Wales, as can be seen when comparing the regional descriptions in Parry (1990b) and Penhallurick (1994) against survey data (*SAWD* and *SED*).

Southeast Wales and the eastern border areas also attracted dialectologists' attention early on (for an overview of the research on the Border country, see Awbery 1997: 93). As pointed out above, the Welsh heartlands Anglicized so late that one can barely speak of so-called traditional dialects of English in this context. Along the border, however, the language shift began in the Old/Middle English period and proceeded at a moderate pace for several centuries, the lexicon of the neighbouring English counties thereby diffusing into a new environment. Parry's (1999) maps yield abundant evidence of the impact of English lexicon on the Welsh border counties, so let us mention a few examples. For the item *stye*, the isogloss for *wisp* extends from Gloucestershire along the south coast to Gwent and Glamorganshire, while *powk* from West Midlands occurs in Brecknockshire, South Powys. Of the variants for *bread-bin*, *(bread-)mug* occurs in the Cheshire-Lancashire region, extending to Flintshire; *(bread-)stean* is used in the West Midlands and all across eastern Mid-Wales; while the widespread southern English *(bread-)pan* has only spread along the south coast of Wales (Parry 1999: 302, 305).

Other EngE dialect words which in have been attested in southeast Wales or near the English border include *(a-)brimming* 'on heat' (of sows; *SED*: all regions of England), *eft/evet* (and *asker/askgel*) 'newt' (*SED*: Midlands and central South), *pleach/glat* 'to plash' (*SED*: lower North West and West Midlands), *(potato-)tump* 'potato-clamp' (*SED*: West Midlands), *quist* 'wood-pigeon' (*EDD*: Scotland, Ireland, West Midlands and southern England), *sally* 'willow' (*SED*: Yorkshire, Man & West Midlands), and *want/oont* 'mole' (eastern South West; Parry 1999). It is noteworthy that, to the west of these isoglosses, the word chosen by the informants is often the standard one: *newt, clamp, pigeon, willow, mole*, etc. (Parry 1977: 189–210). This is clearly indicative of a different mode and period of English language transmission.

As to the southeastern Valley dialects, which are described at length by Windsor Lewis (1964), Edwards (1985) and Lewis (2008), there is relatively little information in the *SAWD* compilation volume. Parry (1999: 1) points out that many of the localities in the original volumes (Parry 1977, 1979) were omitted from the final publication either due to being "comparatively urban" or because of the time lapse between the earliest and more recent field work. The Valley dialects are, of course, urban rather than rural, as they have evolved in the late nineteenth-century industrial hotspots. *SAWD* largely circumvents these areas with its focus on traditional rural dialects, the 1977 volume being a little more informative. The aim of the above dialect descriptions (i.e. Windsor Lewis 1964, Edwards 1985, Lewis 2008) is to give a comprehensive idea of a specific regional variety through extensive word-lists, which however make it difficult to assess the roles and distributions of the words cited. Glamorganshire English words which nevertheless appear in both *SAWD* (Parry 1999) and one or several of the above are, for example, *butty* 'friend, workmate', *cag(gy)/cack/coggy-handed* 'left-handed' (possibly also 'clumsy, stupid'), *chute(s)* 'drainpipes, guttering', *fry* 'pluck of a slaughtered animal', *gambo* 'farm-wagon, cart' (also used in Powys), *jibbons/ gibbons/ shibwns* 'spring onions', *pikelet* 'crumpet, drop scone', *scram(b)* 'to scratch', *tamp* 'to bounce', also *tamping* or *tamping-mad* 'very angry', *tooty down* 'squat down', and *wisp* 'stye'. Some of the above are used in South and East Wales or neighbouring English counties more generally.

English dialect words with wider regional distributions in Wales have often spread primarily to the South or North. From Parry (1999) we can deduce that general South Welsh items include *bakestone* 'iron plate on the stove for baking on', *pikel* 'agricultural fork', *rip(per)/ripe/rib/riff* 'whetstone', *spreader* 'stretcher on a harness keeping traces apart', and *tun-dish* 'domestic funnel'. In North Wales, particularly along the coast, we find, for example, *launders* 'guttering', *lay* 'to plash a hedge', *shippon* 'cow-house', and *starved/starving* 'of a person; very cold'. Widespread EngE dialect words may also have made their way into Wales along both northern and southern coastlines and the border area; these are, for example, *fiddle* 'container used when sowing seeds by hand', *hogget* 'male or ewe-lamb, wether, or ewe-hog', and *learnt* 'taught'. Practically all over Wales bar the westernmost parts we find *poll* 'hornless cow', *rig* 'ridgel', *tack* 'hired pasturage', and *yorks* 'knee-straps for trousers'. A word which appears to be ubiquitous is *gilt* 'young sow', but because of the great regional variability, such words are extremely infrequent. The wave-like patterns of distribution indicate that the strongly Welsh-speaking counties of Gwynedd and Dyfed have not received high numbers of EngE dialect lexicon overall. The reasons for this are the recency of the language shift and, in consequence, the mode of language transmission: English has largely entered these areas through formal education from the late nineteenth century onwards.

Over the centuries, English spoken in Wales has also absorbed influences from languages other than Welsh. However, their impact on WelE dialect lexicon is minor and mainly based on secondary sources: loanwords from Old Irish, Old Norse or (Anglo-Norman) French have first entered regional dialects of English in

England and later WelE as well. The same applies to words with German or Dutch ancestry.

Words in *SAWD* which Parry (1999) identifies as Old Norse in origin are, for example, *haggard* 'stackyard for storing hay' (southern Dyfed; *EDD*: Scotland, Ireland, Man, Carmarthenshire), *segs* 'callosities on the hands', *skrike* 'to scream' (both in Clwyd; *SED*: North West, Yorkshire and West Midlands), and *speel* 'splinter' (Clwyd; *SED*: Northern England). The examples indicate that many of these words occur in the northeast of Wales, connecting to the Northern English dialect area. *Haggard* is an interesting exception in this respect and may originate from the Norse settlement in the area (see Thomas 1994: 104). Windsor Lewis (1990c: 111) mentions also other Scandinavian items in Glamorganshire English, each of them with an EngE dialect origin. Of French origin are, for example, *launders* 'guttering' (North Wales), *leagers* 'gently, in a leisured manner' (South Pembrokeshire and Gower), *scarifier* 'implement for rooting up weeds' (Gower), and *skew* 'diagonal bar of a gate' (Gwent).

The word *jibbons/gibbons/shibwns* 'spring onions', mentioned above as a southeastern dialect word, shares its roots most likely with both Welsh and French. The respective Welsh word is varyingly *sibwns, sibwls, sibol* or *chibol* (*GPC* Online), probably from French *ciboules* 'spring onions'. A Google search of the word produces some discussions on its dialectal distribution, the majority opinion being that it is associated with South Wales. *EDD*, however, finds *jibbole* or *jibble/gibble* used in Southwest England, too (Windsor Lewis 1964: 287; *EDD* Online). Secondary language contact through Welsh is therefore also a possibility, as in the case with *cwtch*, discussed above.

Few of the above dialect words seem to be considered salient in present-day WelE, at least when it comes to Cardiffians or British Twitter users. Coupland (1988: 38–39) reports on the results of street interviews carried out in Cardiff. Items which some of the respondents recognized, but wouldn't necessarily use, were, for example, *pine-end* 'gable-end', *tump* 'hillock, bump in the road, mound of grass', *lose* 'miss' (e.g. *lose the bus*; Welsh *colli* 'miss, lose'), *off* 'hostile, angry'. Only *eisteddfod* was considered to be in general use, while the majority of the listed words were not familiar to the respondents. Durham (2015), then, examines tweeters' observations and performance tweets on WelE during 2012–2015. As regards lexicon, the items which draw the most attention are *lush* 'lovely', *tamping* (or *fuming / raging*) 'furious', *tidy* 'nice, decent, excellent', *boyo, butt(y)* 'friend', *cwtch*, and *mun*, a term of address or pragmatic marker 'man'. The phrase *What's occurring?* 'what's going on?' is frequent in the data as well.

Durham points out that many of the tweeters are not Welsh, and hence they mainly draw on TV series and other hearsay in their descriptions. She mentions that shows such as *Gavin and Stacey*, *The Valleys*, or *The Call Centre* mainly depict the accents and dialects of southeast Wales and Swansea. Corpus evidence shows that the results are nevertheless indicative of actual present-day language use in these areas. The words *cwtch* and *butt(y)* are commented on elsewhere in this chapter. *Lush*, then, is one of the terms given for 'attractive woman' by *Voices* informants in Cardiff, Llanelli and Treorchy, and also mentioned several times in Jones's Gwent data (2013: 71). *Tamping* is likewise frequent in southeast Welsh localities, while *fuming* emerges in Cardiff and Bangor. *Tidy* gets a few random mentions in the *Voices* commentaries, but *mun* does not. *Boyo* is in fact rated rather negatively and commented on as a term which the British media like to use of the Welsh, for example, *that's all you've seen in some of the papers, "the boyos have done it"* (*Voices*: Tregaron). *Boyo* is also the only word on Durham's list which is not found in Lewis (2008). It can be considered a linguistic stereotype of the dialect.

The WelE dialect attracts attention also on the Internet, where one can find several lists of miscellaneous words and expressions that are considered specific of Wales. These must be taken with a pinch of salt, but again, they give an idea of what kinds of expressions people consider regionally salient. For example, the news website WalesOnline.com presents its own list of "25 English words and phrases you only hear in Wales" (Rhys 2014). These include, besides the above (and other expressions and language features varyingly discussed elsewhere in this book), words like *chopsing* 'arguing', *gomping* 'nasty, unpleasant', *buzzing* 'really unpleasant' and *dwt* 'a small person'. None of these emerge in the *Voices* or TC data, but Lewis (2008) and Jones (2016a, 2016b) mention *chopsing* as 'gossiping, talking a lot', *chopsy* 'chatty' and *dwt* as 'a small thing, small child' (*dwt* discussed further in Jones 2016b: 28).

Another development worth noting in present-day English in Wales is the impact of ethnic diversity on language use. On the one hand, the numbers of citizens of Asian, African and Caribbean descent are on the increase within Wales itself. On the other, the most influential spoken variety of BrE, London English, is currently adopting features from Multicultural London English especially when it comes to youth language (e.g. Cheshire et al. 2011). Consequently, this input is diffusing into other parts of Britain, including Wales. The development is commented on by McCarthy (2013) in his online article "Forget Butty... it's Bruv now, innit!" The title suggests that words favoured in current British youth language are ousting traditional dialect words in Wales, although this is not explicitly claimed in the article itself. Kerswill (2014: 140–146) examines the use of terms such as *bruv* and *chav* in London youth language, and indeed, *chav* is mentioned by TC informants as a term for 'a young person in cheap trendy clothes and jewellery'. They also point out that mainly young people would use this word. Lexis is subject to trends, however, and although some changes may be under way, there is, as of now, little research on this phenomenon from the WelE perspective.

4.3.2 Lexical surveys in BBC *Voices* and in Tonypandy

This section presents a case study combining data from the BBC *Voices* survey and the Tonypandy corpus. The *Voices* survey consisted of field-recordings made with groups of local informants all across Britain and Northern Ireland in 2004–2005, accompanied by the *Voices* Language Lab, an online lexical questionnaire survey for which responses were collected during 2005–2007 (BBC Voices 2014). The project was originally focused on linguistic and cultural diversity in Britain, but dialectologists and sociolinguists had a major influence on how the survey was ultimately carried out.

Penhallurick (2013) describes the process of creating the survey and the methods of data collection in detail. He also undertakes an effort to conduct a diachronic analysis on changes in WelE dialect lexicon in light of *SAWD* and *Voices*, but concludes that the surveys are too different from each other to allow such a comparison. Continuity is hampered, first, by very different sets of lexical items: rural and agricultural for *SAWD*, general everyday items for *Voices*. The scales and foci of data collection are also quite different: while *SAWD* consists of systematic, questionnaire-based interviews with elderly informants in evenly spaced rural localities, *Voices* involves informal, lexically themed interviews with informant groups of different ages in more scattered and mainly urban localities. However, Penhallurick (2013: 130–131) sees possibilities as well, as some of the lexical items in the surveys are the same (e.g. *grandmother, grandfather, ill, left-handed, living room, (outside) toilet, feeling cold* & some incidental items). The geographic distribution and the linguistic descriptions of the *Voices* interviews (see Robinson et al. 2013) also allow for some comparisons and analyses.

Central for the present purposes are the linguistic commentaries which were written on the basis of the audio recordings by the *Voices of the UK* team at the British Library (Robinson et al. 2009–2012). The commentaries sum up the linguistic findings of the interviews: elicited lexis (survey), spontaneous lexis, phonology, and grammatical dialect features. The results obtained from the commentaries are somewhat varying, however, as the lexical survey was not conducted everywhere or with the same consistency. Overall, the survey involves 23 localities with an uneven distribution (e.g. the rural southwest is largely ignored), 4–7 informants of varying ages in each locality, and 40 lexical items. Of these, the study below focuses on ten localities: three in North Wales (Flint, Holyhead, Llangollen), three near the South/Southwest coast (Bon-y-maen, Llanelli, Milford Haven) and four in the Southeast (Newport, Cardiff Portcanna, Pontypridd, Treorchy).

In parallel with *Voices*, we will be looking into results obtained from the lexical survey in the Tonypandy corpus. The Rhondda is an area which experienced a fast and complete language shift from Welsh to English. The entire southeastern coalfield was still fully Welsh-speaking in late eighteenth century, but by the census of 1921, Welsh speakers were only 38% of the population, 2% being monoglot Welsh. In many families, the language shifted within three generations. According to the census of 2011, 12% of the population speak Welsh in the present county of Rhondda Cynon Taff.

The lexical survey included in the Tonypandy interviews consists of list of 41 words in total, largely the same ones as in the *Voices* survey. Responses were elicited using the indirect method (McDavid 1985), circumventing the item itself so as not to influence the respondents' answers (e.g. *In the middle of July when the sun is beaming down, you feel...* [hot, boiling, roasting, clammy...]). Ten informants aged 43–85 (and some children on the side) participated in the survey, all friends or relatives with each other, and all monoglot English speakers.

Seven of the items were selected for the present study, as they were found to elicit either Welsh language dialect words or regionally distinctive English dialect words. Table 4.1 presents the lexical variants of the first type and the responses recorded for these in the *Voices* linguistic commentaries. Some words are accompanied by comments from the *Voices* informants.

Table 4.1: Items eliciting Welsh language dialect words in the *Voices* survey.

	North: Flint, Holyhead, Llangollen	South/SW coast: Bon-y-maen, Llanelli, Milford Haven	Southeast: Newport, Cardiff Portcanna, Pontypridd, Treorchy
grandmother	nana; **nain** (used even by English) (Fl) **nainey; nain** ("really Welsh"); nana (new, "posh") (Hh) grandma; nana; granny; nanny; **nain** (Lg)	nana; grandma; nan (Bm) mams; nan; **mam-gu** (Ll) grandma; nana; granny (MH)	nan (Np) nan (CP) granny; nan; nanny; old **mam** Jones (Pp) nan; nana; **mam-gu** (Tr)
grandfather	grandad (used by grandson); **taid** (used even by English) (Fl) didey; **taid** (Hh) grandpa; pops; grandad; **taid** (Lg)	bampa; grandad; grandpa; gramps (Bm) grandad; gramps; **tad-cu** (Ll) grandfer; pop; gagga; **bampy**; granddad (MH)	ganker; **grandsire**; granddad (Np) **grampy**; dada; grandpa; bampy; granddad (CP) grandpa; the old man; grandad; grampy (Pp) **grandsire; tad-cu** (Tr)
left-handed	cack-handed (Fl) left-handed; lefty; **llawchwith** 'left handed'	cack-handed ("horrible word"); coochie (Bm)	left-handed (Np) left-handed; flexible (CP) left-handed; southpaw;

Table 4.1: (continued).

	North: Flint, Holyhead, Llangollen	South/SW coast: Bon-y-maen, Llanelli, Milford Haven	Southeast: Newport, Cardiff Portcanna, Pontypridd, Treorchy
	(Hh) cack-handed (Lg)	left; split-brain (Ll) kift; cack-handed (MH)	cag-handed (Pp) lefty; **llaw bwt**, lit.'hand stump'; **llawi** (Tr)
toilet	lav ("pretty universal"); **tŷ bach** (Fl) toilet; lavatory; netty; bog; **tŷ bach** (Hh) bog; loo; toilet (Lg)	lav; bog; ladies; loo (Bm) the bog; loo; **tŷ bach** (Ll) loo; bog; crapper ("not a very nice one") (MH)	lavatory; loo; washroom; lav (Np) loo; bog; ladies; lavatory (CP) loo; toilet; out the back (Pp) lav(atory) (outside toilet); W.C.; ladies; gents; bathroom; little boys/girls room; john; loo; powder room; bog ("crude"); toilet (used now), **tŷ bach** ("very Welsh", not used now) (Tr)

Terms for grandparents have a great deal of diversity within each locality. The Welsh language dialect words *nain, mam-gu, taid,* and *tad-cu* are discussed above in section 4.2.1. The *Voices* data confirm the regional division into northern and southern items as regards these terms; *grandma, grandpa, nana* and related words, on the other hand, are widespread throughout the country. *Bampy* (or *bampi*), then, is a South Welsh dialect term, with variants in Gwent such as *bampa* and *bamp* (Jones 2013: 70). Southeast Welsh informants mention the term *grandsire* ['granʃə], also recorded in *Voices* Risca and Builth Wells as well as in Gwent (Jones 2013) but not elsewhere. *OED* Online first attests the word from c. 1300, describing it at present as archaic or regional. Its origins are in French *grant-sire* and *EDD* Online finds it used in Scotland, Yorkshire and Shropshire. It has not been recorded in *SAWD*, which is why its current existence in southeast Wales is quite interesting.

Llawchwith and *llaw bwt* 'left-handed' are also examined above. Another word of interest is *cack-handed*, listed above under southeastern dialect words in *SAWD* but also extending to northeast Wales. Penhallurick (2013: 128–130) discusses the distribution of this word and related ones at length (*cag[gy]-handed, coochy, gammy-handed, keck-fisted, left-keg*), noting the distributional similarity between *cag(gy)-handed* in Parry (1999) and *cack-handed* in *Voices* Language Lab (*SAWD* not listing the latter word). He notes that, inconclusive as this kind of survey data is, it would appear that *cack-handed*, a majority non-standard form in present-day EngE, has largely taken over this domain from other variants in WelE as well. *Caggy-handed*, however, remains a minority form in southeast and northeast Wales.

The *Voices* commentaries show that *tŷ bach* holds its position as a euphemism for 'toilet' across the country, among a multitude of English ones. The commentaries include a Treorchy informant's observation that the word is "very Welsh" and not used nowadays.

The Tonypandy results for the same items are given in Table 4.2, this time grouped according to the ages of the informants. The category *young* involves sporadic comments obtained from the c. 10-year-old daughter of two of the informants, and the numbers refer to the number of informants who produced the item.

Table 4.2: Items eliciting Welsh language dialect words in Tonypandy.

	Elderly	Middle-aged	Young
grandmother	nanny 2 **mam** Jones, nan, mom, granny, mambo, **mam-gu**, gran (used by some)	nan 3 nanno 2 nanan, gran, grandma, nanny, **mam-gu, mam** Jones	granny, nanny, nanny granny (overheard)
grandfather	**grandsire** 2 dad, **tad-cu**, grandpa (some say)	daddo, dadad, **tad-cu**, dad Jones, **grandsire, bampy**	**bampy**
left-handed	left-handed 4 **llaw bwt** 4 southpaw (boxing term), throwing Swansea (darts term)	left-handed 3 **llaw bwt** 2 (old), left-hander	
toilet	toilet 3 ladies' 2 lav(vie) (used to say) 2 loo, bathroom, bog (men use), gents', **tŷ bach** (a Welsh word)	toilet 4 bathroom 2 bog 2 (some say/used as a teenager) loo 2 (some say) lavatory (some say), WC (some say), **tŷ bach** (a Welsh word)	toilet, **tŷ bach** (used when speaking Welsh at school)

In TC, the South Welsh *mam-gu* and *tad-cu* are known and have been used in the families of the elderly speakers, but they seem to be disappearing; the youngest informant claims not to use these. 'Words for grandparents' is again a highly productive category, but the more widespread *nanny* and *granny* seem to be growing in popularity. *Grandsire* emerges in this survey, too, being used or known in the old and middle age groups, whereas *bampy* is mentioned by the middle-aged and young informants. Shifting usages are emergent.

Llaw bwt is mentioned by several informants in TC. Its distribution in the Rhondda and Glyn Neath implies that it is mainly a Valleys word. Although the TC informants consider themselves monoglot English speakers, they use *llaw bwt* because, as one of them states, *I think it's nice for [the children] to hear the odd Welsh word you know* (TC: 6b). *Tŷ bach*, then, is mentioned as the Welsh word for toilet, but the informants maintain that they do not use it themselves when speaking English. It is restricted to speaking Welsh.

As for (Welsh) English dialect words, the focus is here on three items: *child's soft shoes worn for PE, to play truant,* and *friend*.

Table 4.3: (Welsh) English dialect words in *Voices*.

	North: Flint, Holyhead, Llangollen	South/SW coast: Bon-y-maen, Llanelli, Milford Haven	Southeast: Newport, Cardiff Portcanna, Pontypridd, Treorchy
child's soft PE shoes	pumps; **daps;** plimsolls (Fl) pumps; **daps;** plimsolls (Hh) trainers; pumps (Lg)	gyms; plimsolls; **daps;** gym-shoes (Bm) **daps** (learnt from parents); trainers (used by young people) (Ll) **daps** (used as a child); trainers (used today); plimsolls (MH)	plimsolls; pumps; dappers; **daps** (used as a child); trainers (used now); canvas shoes (Np) trainers; plimsolls (used when younger); **daps** (CP) plimsolls (used in London); **daps** (Pp) **daps;** plimsolls; trainers (Tr)
to play truant	to dodge school; to play wag (Fl) **to mitch;** dodging; **mitsio** ('to mitch'); trwant ('truant') (Hh) skive; wagging (Lg)	**on the mitch;** absent without leave; **to mitch;** skipping school; **mitching** (Bm) **mitch;** skive (Ll) tell lies; hide out; **mitching; mitch** (MH)	mooched, mooching (Np) **mitching;** bunk off (used in London); **go on the mitch;** on the knock (used by 14-year-old niece) (CP) skiving off; skive;

4.3 English dialect lexicon in Welsh English — 155

Table 4.3: (continued).

	North: Flint, Holyhead, Llangollen	South/SW coast: Bon-y-maen, Llanelli, Milford Haven	Southeast: Newport, Cardiff Portcanna, Pontypridd, Treorchy
			mitching (Pp) mitching (used in the past, not heard today); bunking off (used now) (Tr)
friend	**butty; butt**; mate (Hh) pal; bud; friend (Lg)	pal; mate; friend (Bm) mate; buddy; bro (Ll) matey; love; pal; high girl; high maid; oppo (MH)	mate; buddy (Np) mate; my gal; bum chum (used by 14 year old niece) (CP) mates (of males/ females); friends; mate; friend (Pp) **butty**; mate; chum (Tr)

Table 4.3 presents the responses from the *Voices* survey. At first glance, there seem to be few clear patterns for the first item: *daps* and *plimsolls* are used all around, but *pumps* would appear to be mainly a northern word. The map for this item on the *Voices* Language Lab website confirms that *pumps* is indeed a word strongly associated with the Liverpool–Leeds–Birmingham area, although it is also used in London and less frequently across the country. *Daps* is the second favourite, the regional foci this time in London, Bristol area and Southeast Wales. *OED* Online lists *daps* (from 1924) as colloquial and dialectal, with the possible etymology of *dap* v., 'to rebound, bounce; to hop or skip'. Parry (1999: 307) confirms that *dap* 'to bounce' occurs in the area around Bristol and in very southeast Wales.

As to the wide distribution in the *Voices* recordings, we should note that the southwestern localities are not outside the *Voices* area for this word, and the Holyhead response turns out to be deceiving: *daps* is recorded from an informant who has moved to the area from the Rhondda. Another matter is that the informants are in fact using the word for quite different kind of shoes. In many localities, the informants state that *daps* were used as children in the past, whereas present-day children use *trainers*. The TC informants (Table 4.4), however, mention *daps* as the majority variant, and although the elderly speakers perhaps associate the word with an old-fashioned kind of shoe, the middle-aged and youngest informants use it of modern canvas shoes or trainers. The word has in other words shifted its referent to meet present-day fashion standards. This is confirmed by

Jones (2013: 68), whose young Gwent informants choose *daps* (or *dappers, dapes* or *dabs*) as by far the most popular term.

The next word of interest is *mitching* 'to play truant', which has a considerably narrower regional distribution in *Voices* Language Lab than *daps*, being primarily found in southeast (and southwest) Wales and Belfast. It is therefore no surprise that it is also recorded in the same areas in the *Voices* interviews. Again, the Holyhead responses are given by the Rhondda man, as is the case for *butty* below, too. *OED* Online regards *mitching* (from 1672) as a British regional and Irish English word, apparently of Anglo-Norman origins (*muscer, muscier*, etc. and Old French *mucier, muchier* 'to hide, conceal [oneself]'). Jones (2013: 68, also 2016a: 41) finds that in Gwent the word takes the form *mutching* or *muching*; the orthography is from the informants themselves and suggests a vowel sound closer to /ʌ/. *Skiving* is nearly as common. In Tonypandy, *mitching* is the traditional dialect word used by the elderly informants, but it appears to be losing ground to *bunking*, which is widespread throughout southern England.

Finally, the regionally distinctive word for *friend* in Tables 4.3 and 4.4 is *butty*, or *butt*, used by men of their male friends. *EDD* in fact finds that the word occurs all across West Midlands and the Southwest, but the *Voices* Language Lab indicates that its focal area at present is southeast Wales. At the *Voices* website, Susie Dent reports that the use of *butty* to mean a friend or workmate probably comes from the nouns *booty* and *booty fellow*, someone who you share your plunder with. *Butty* is also a nineteenth-century term for the middleman in the mine, whose *butty-colliers* or *butty-gangs* shared a job and divided the proceeds (see also *OED* Online). "Throughout these uses of the word, right up to the present day, the idea of sharing and comradeship is a constant theme" (Dent 2014). The TC informants feel that *butty* is distinctly the elderly generation's word. However, they are a bit averse to *mate*, which is described as alien to the local dialect. The *Voices* interviews indicate that *mate* is, in fact, in use throughout Wales, and the AmE variant *bud(dy)* is emerging as well. There are no responses to this from the youngest informant, but *friend, mate* and *buddy*, in this order, are the most common choices for the young informants in Gwent as well (Jones 2013: 70).

Table 4.4: (Welsh) English dialect words in TC.

	Elderly	Middle-aged	Young
child's soft PE shoes	**daps 6** (*years ago* 2) trainers, plimsoles (used by some)	trainers 4 **daps 4** (used by some 1) pumps, strides	**daps** (canvas) trainers

Table 4.4: (continued).

	Elderly	Middle-aged	Young
to play truant	**mitching** 5 truanting, bunking	bunking 2 bunked off 2 **mitching** 2 playing truant (used by some)	bunking
friend	friend 4 **butty** 2 (male) **butt** (male) mate 2 buddy, pal	friend 4 pal, the boys, **butty**, mate (some say, not local, a Cardiff word 3)	

Overall, the results are indicative of the resilience and covert prestige of WelE dialect vocabulary on the one hand, as well as of the gradual changes taking place across generations on the other. The above words are very different in terms of their distributions and cultural connotations, which will affect their future fates. The Welsh terms for grandparents have cultural significance in the north, which will most likely sustain them, but the southern variants appear to be losing to English alternatives. *Llaw bwt* is highly local and *tŷ bach* associated with the Welsh language. Of the English dialect words, *butty* has the smallest regional spread and heaviest competition from other terms widespread in young people's language. It is hence probably the likeliest one to fade out of use.

4.4 Discourse features

Apart from a few studies involving invariant question tags (Jones 1990a, 1990b, Paulasto 2016, Williams 2003), research on WelE discourse phenomena is close to non-existent. We believe that one of the main reasons for this is the spoken language continuum with EngE, which gives the impression that there is fairly little in this domain of WelE that is genuinely distinctive and worthy of attention. Discourse and pragmatics are not the first domains of language to be examined in traditional dialect descriptions, either, rather the opposite, and hence they do not easily emerge as salient objects of research. Lack of salience, the vast diversity of linguistic forms and functions involved, and deprecation of spoken language have hindered research in this field overall (Pichler 2013: 6–9). In the field of IrE linguistics there are by this stage numerous articles and whole books dedicated to discourse and pragmatics (e.g. Barron & Schneider 2005, Amador-Moreno et al.

2015). However, in the case of IrE, too, the interest has only arisen since the turn of the twenty-first century and there is still "a dearth of research" into sociolinguistic and regional variation in this field (Corrigan 2015: 38). WelE is comparatively new as an object of linguistic interest, and hence, there are many more areas of language as well as language variation that remain unexplored. Discourse and pragmatics are some of these, to a great extent. We will, nevertheless, examine invariant tag usage and give an overview of other existing studies and observations. These mainly concern discourse-pragmatic markers.

4.4.1 Invariant question tags

WelE speakers make frequent and functionally varying use of invariant question tags *isn't it* and *is it*. Along with focus fronting, this is one of the most salient and productive features of WelE, common enough to be considered "stereotypical" (Coupland 1988: 36), although its role as a distinctly Welsh feature of English can be contested: Thomas (1994: 141), for example, categorizes it among general BrE vernacular features. Invariant question tags are common in varieties across the world: 68% of the 77 varieties in eWAVE (mainly high-contact L1, indigenized L2 or P/C) have an invariant non-concord tag of some kind, and *isn't it* and *is it* are among the most frequent ones (Kortmann et al. 2020). In the British Isles, this feature is considered "pervasive or obligatory" only in WelE and Channel Islands English.

The WelE invariant question tags are obviously used alongside the complex question tag system of StE (see Quirk et al. 1985: 810–811) and a large variety of other invariant tags (e.g. *You know? Right? Yeah? OK? Eh?;* Algeo 1988, Columbus 2009). Another invariant tag that is mentioned in WelE literature is *yes/yeah* (Jones 1990a: 19; 1990b: 184–189; Thomas 1994: 141), used in North Wales. Let us begin with the former types, however.

The negative invariant question tag *isn't it* is recorded in *SAWD*, although with considerable geographic delimitations which may of course simply be a by-product of the structured methods whereby morphosyntactic data is often collected. Parry (1977, 1979) makes no note of it, but Penhallurick (1991: 204–205) draws attention to the use of *isn't it* in the northern volume (see also Thomas 1984: 192, Trudgill and Hannah [1982] 1994: 35). The feature is subsequently included in Parry (1999: 115–6), where the negative question tag is considered "fairly widespread except in Gwent". Penhallurick (1991), Parry (1999) and Coupland (1988: 36) find that the tag is broad in scope, applying to the whole of the preceding statement rather than just to the subject NP. They also consider this a Welsh contact feature, although they each cite slightly different Welsh invariant tag forms (see below). Penhallurick's (1991: 204–205) examples include those in (83). This feature is also pointed out in the commentaries to the *Voices* interviews, attested at least in southern and southeastern localities as well as in the northeast (84).

(83) a. You have to rig him up in his clothes, *isn't it?* (*SAWD*: Gwynedd 2)
     b. We saw some the other day, *isn't it?* (*SAWD*: Clwyd 1)

(84) a. you turn round and you say, "tidy" *isn't it?* (*Voices*: Bon-y-maen)
     b. and only now recently can girls wear trousers, *isn't it?* (*Voices*: Risca)

Although the positive invariant question tag *is it* is not mentioned in the above sources, both positive and negative tags are found to be quite common in the present corpora. The positive question tag is discussed in the studies by Jones (1990a, 1990b) and Williams (2003; see also Connolly 1990: 127). Jones (1990b: 174) finds that in his WelE corpus, the positive tag is in fact more common than the negative one. He presents a careful analysis of the linguistic contexts in which variant and invariant tags are used, but the results are clearly influenced by his method of data collection, which involves 5–7-year-old children at play. The majority of the invariant tags occur with directive clauses, such as the following (Jones 1990b: 179):

(85) a. Let's finish this off, *isn't it?*
     b. Fill the boxes up, *is it?*
     c. We'll just leave that there like that, *yeah?*

Directives and imperatives barely emerge in the present corpora, but these instances are an interesting indication of the functional range of the WelE invariant tags: they replace not only canonical question tags and imperative clause tags like *shall we, would you,* but also lexical tags such as *right, alright* or *okay* (see also below).

In the present corpora, these invariant tags have been categorized by four discourse contexts: question tags proper, tags in verbless clauses, follow-ups, and phrasal tags. They frequently occur in constant polarity to the preceding statement, for example, a positive tag following a positive anchor clause (Jones 1990b: 175). This is unusual in StE, where question tags are generally in reverse polarity to the preceding statement (Quirk et al. 1985: 810–811). When constant positive polarity tags as used, they often carry "an emotive meaning of disapproval, reproach, belligerence, or the like", or they can indicate surprise or acknowledgement of the news value contained within the proposition (Huddleston

& Pullum 2002: 895). Constant negative polarity tags, on the other hand, are considered ungrammatical in StE.

The following examples illustrate invariant question tags proper (QUE) in LC, NWC and TC. In accordance with Jones (1990b: 175), WelE positive and negative tags behave very differently in terms of their polarity: positive question tags tend to have constant polarity (76%; 16/21), while negative ones favour reverse polarity (96%; 131/136). This of course results in part from the main clauses usually being positive rather than negative, but it also shows that the two question tags have different functions. In addition to declarative sentences, LC contains a few question tags in interrogative and imperative sentences.

(86) Reverse: a. So you wouldn't have any sheep at all in Finland, *is it?* (NWC, Ruthin: 4e)
Constant: b. You know, thank you, if I've- if- if I've been any help at all, *is it?* (LC: 2f)
c. Our nephew you know he went to- to Stockholm, *is it?* Or Oslo, or elsewhere. (LC: 2b)
Interrogative: d. Oh did you travel by car, *is it?* (LC: 2e)
Imperative: e. Carry on, *is it*, yeah? (LC: 5c)

(87) Reverse: a. That depends on the individual really I suppose *isn' it?* (NWC, Llwyngwril: 6f)
b. He is a Welsh one, you see, from erm, Hendy, *isn' it?* No, Llangennech. (LC: 2c)
Constant: c. Wouldn' say it's worse, *innit?* My own opinion an' that. (LC: 7a)

The present functional analysis is rough in the sense that it is based on context alone, disregarding intonation patterns. Scholars take varying approaches to the functional characteristics of tag questions (e.g. Holmes 1995, Andersen 2001, Pichler 2013), but for the present purposes, we will settle for Algeo's (1988: 180-187) categorization, with the addition of observations made by Williams (2003) and Pichler (2013, 2016).

Out of Algeo's four categories, we find that positive question tags in our WelE corpora tend to be informational, while negative ones are mainly confirmatory. Algeo's negatively coloured peremptory and aggressive tags do not occur, but this may result from the method of data collection. In other words, the informants are quite unlikely to express hostility towards the interviewer in the context in which they are speaking. Both positive and negative question tags (but mostly *isn't it*) can also be used in a generalized, accord-building function, for example, in

(86b, 86e, 87c) and (88) below. In these situations, the interlocutor is not expected to answer the speaker or confirm their viewpoint but the meaning of the question tag is similar to the discourse-pragmatic marker *you know* (see Williams 2003: 209). Pichler (2013: 188–189, 193) defines these types of tags as subjective and non-conducive; they are interactional and attitudinal rather than epistemic or response-eliciting. She also points out (2013: 193) that "unlike the non-conducive tags described in Algeo (1988, 1990) and Cheshire (1981), however, they do not generally carry a hostile or antagonistic overtone." In (88), for example, the speaker uses both *innit* and *you know* to establish rapport with the interviewer and the hedges *I suppose* and *like* are then used to frame the concept "your native tongue", that is, Welsh, and the interviewee's feelings about it.

(88) I suppose, you look back and you regret that you never learnt
[Mhm.]
to speak your- your native tongue *innit* I suppose like you know. (TC: 4)

The above examples also illustrate the scope of the question tag. It is narrow in (86c), (86d) and (87b), with a focus on the adverbials *to Stockholm, by car* and *from Hendy*. Sentences with these kinds of focusing tag could, in theory, be rephrased as clefts (see Section 3.4.2): *Is it Stockholm he went to?* By contrast, the scope is broad in examples (86a; informational) and (87a; confirmatory). In these contexts, the question tag seems to stand for the introductory clause *Is it / isn't it so that...* A similar relationship between clefting and invariant *is it* tags is found to exist in IrE as well. Kallen (2013: 75) states that in cases such as (86a), *is it* functions as "the inverse of a cleft", referring to the whole of the preceding statement. In WelE, this also applies to *isn't it* (ex. 87a), as pointed out by Coupland (1988: 36). It follows that polarity is not at issue in the selection of the question tag. Rather, what is central is the presupposition which the tag expresses: with a neutral presupposition, the tag is positive (*is it so?*) and with an affirmative one, it is negative (*isn't it so?*), regardless of whether the anchor clause is positive or negative.

In addition to question tags proper, invariant *is it* and *isn't it* occur in elliptical verbless clauses (CLAU). This is a subcategory of question tags proper, because as Pichler (2016: 63) points out, often the "ellipted subject and finite verb can be fairly straightforwardly inferred from the surrounding linguistic context". The inference is hampered by the invariability of the tag, however. In (89a), for example, the full sentence in StE could be 'You're going to be a teacher, are you?', but in WelE it might be 'It's a teacher you're going to be, is it?' In other cases, it is unclear what the ellipted elements would be, yet the negative invariant tag seems to have been selected as the default option (90). The tag takes a canonical post-finite position, as in question tags proper. The primary functions are informational (89), confirmatory (90a) and accord-building (90b).

(89) a. [I'm going to be a teacher.]
Teacher, *is it?* (LC: 2e)
b. Where- where are you staying?
[Milo.]
(...) Like an exchanger, *is it?* (LC: 5f)

(90) a. AD: Ryan aye, well his- his son gin- with the ginger hair *innit?*
IB: That's right aye. (TC: 2)
b. Not many of us now. No, of the old Llwyngwril, *isn't it?* (NWC, Llwyngwril: 2c)

Verbless clause tags are utilized particularly in the SAWD sample corpus and TC, where the interviews (or parts of them) are based on a lexical questionnaire format. However, the majority of instances can be considered paradigmatic, for example, Q: *When milk stands, what rises to the top then? A: Oh, the fat* isn' it. (SAWD: Fro4).

Thirdly, Andersen (2001: 101–102) points out that invariant tags can be used as follow-up questions to the preceding statement (FOL). These usually "signal either surprise at or alignment with previous speakers' propositions" (Pichler 2016: 64). In WelE, follow-ups are nearly always positive and informational in meaning. The negative tag in (92) is confirmatory.

(91) a. [Well, you're just a year older than I am then.]
Is it? (LC: 7i)
b. A: So, then er- I- I used to put it here but indeed, I got to-
B: *Is it?*
A: Yeah, I got to put it very very hot... (SAWD: Drefach 4)

(92) [Well thank goodness that's been changing.]
Yes, *isn' it?* (LC: 6f)

Finally, the data include some instances similar to Pichler's (2016: 60–61) non-canonical phrasal tags in the *Linguistic Innovators Corpus* on Multicultural London English (MLE). She points out (Pichler 2016: 64–65) that non-canonical positions have been typically associated with invariant lexical tags, such as *right* or *yeah*, not question tags (see also Stenström et al. 2002: 172ff.). Jones (1990b: 187–188) finds that the North Welsh invariant *yeah* may also be positioned sentence-medially, following a subclause or noun phrase, but *is(n't) it* does not occur in this position in his data:

(93) a. Now when I stop the wheel, *yeah*, (you) don't want no more in
  b. Hey my dad, *yeah*, he goes in rallies through the night

In our corpora, phrasal tags appear in the form *innit* in two informants's speech: a young man in LC IV (2 instances) and an elderly woman in TC (2 instances). An instance of *isn't it* by a middle-aged informant in LC III (94c) can also be categorized in this group. These are all working-class, monoglot English speakers, but there is little point in drawing sociolinguistic generalizations based on just three informants.

(94) a. You know, I think it's probably better- you know like with some people, you know, when they're young, *innit*, young, it's hard enough for them in English then, when you've learnt English then. (LC: 7a)
  b. oh and when I went up to Gloucester mind you and er, my stepdaughter *innit*, she used to speak a bit I used to think er [...] I used to say to her father now "hearken her", she used to put on airs like... (TC: 3b)
  c. As- as I mentioned earlier on about the village, the growth in the village for a start,
    [Yeah.]
    erm, well, jobs again, *isn't it*, back to the collieries, the collieries are closing. (LC: 5a)

Pichler (2016: 70–76) analyses similar instances in MLE and concludes that the primary function of these tags is to mark the information structure of the utterance, activating or identifying referents in the discussion or indicating the referents' discourse prominence. The WelE extracts above align with Pichler's interpretation. In (94a), the speaker comments on Welsh-medium education and uses *innit* to highlight the young age of L1 English students, who may have enough trouble carrying out their studies in English, let alone in Welsh. In (94b), *my stepdaughter* is tagged as the topic of the ensuing story on posh English, and (94c) involves reactivating the topic of *jobs* in order to comment on the fate of the collieries.

Phrasal tags are functionally distinct and so few in the corpora as to make no difference in the results below, but they signal the evolution of *isn't it* from an invariant question tag to a discourse marker, most likely under the influence of London English. In Pichler's words (2016: 80), "real and apparent-time evidence supports the view that these uses are very recent innovations in the neg-tag system of MLE", which indicates that they must also be very recent in WelE.

Figure 4.1 illustrates the normalized frequencies of invariant question tag usage in WelE, including the SAWD sample corpus, LC, NWC and TC. For the category "other" (OTH), see below.

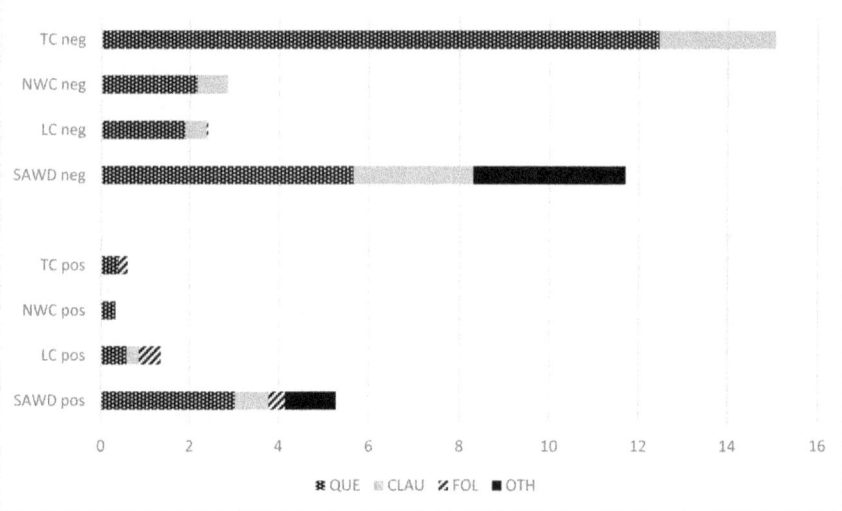

Figure 4.1: Invariant question tags *isn't it* / *is it* as question tags proper (QUE), in verbless clauses (CLAU), follow-ups (FOL), and other nonstandard question tags (OTH) in WelE corpora (instances pttw).

The figure shows that *isn't it* appears in all corpora much more frequently than *is it* does. The differences are particularly great in TC and NWC. What is distinctive about TC is also the form of the negative question tag, that is, the informants tend to say *innit* (77%) rather than *isn't it*, while the opposite is the case in LC (7%) and NWC (1%). Coupland (1988: 36) observes that in Cardiff English, too, the negative tag is frequently realized as /ˈɪnɪt/ rather than *isn't it*. Both forms are used in SAWD (*innit* 44%), indicating that the form itself is not a recent innovation in WelE. Question tags are highly susceptible to the method of data collection, which shows up very clearly in the questionnaire-based SAWD when compared to the others used here. The TC results for verbless clause tags are also affected by the lexical survey section in the interviews, but this does not change the fact that most of the informants use the tag *innit* remarkably often throughout the interviews.

The above frequencies of invariant *isn't it* can again be set against those in Roller (2016), who investigates this feature in the Welsh sections of FRED and in the transcribed Radio Wales Corpus. Interestingly, both corpora yield comparatively low frequencies: 0.9 instances pttw in FRED and only 0.45 pttw in RWC (Roller 2016: 47, 103). Our only explanation for the vast differences is that they must result from actual regional, sociolectal and idiolectal variation combined with the somewhat different kinds of discourse settings in the corpora. Roller (2016: 105) also finds that the low frequencies in her data are curiously out of balance with the high salience which her informants assign to *isn't it* as a feature of WelE. She shows (Roller 2016: 108–111) through the Linguistic Innovators Corpus that in MLE the invariant tag systematically takes the form *innit* and not *isn't it*, which can be interpreted as a possible cause of the salience of *isn't it* as a feature of WelE. However, the high frequencies of invariant *isn't it* in Paulasto (2016) and the present volume suggest that Roller's informants are in fact quite well in tune with the frequency of *isn't it* in WelE, and the usages observed for this particular feature in FRED and RWC are not regionally and situationally fully representative.

The SAWD corpus deviates from the contemporary corpora in its methods of interview, but it also displays types of nonstandard tags not found elsewhere (category "other" in Figure 4.1). Some informants in Gwynedd use the construction '*aren't* + subject pronoun' fairly systematically (95a-b), while there are also other, probably more random types of occurrence (95c-d).

(95) a. Just the same as this one see, but two hooks on it (has?) hangin', see, understand me, *aren't you*? (SAWD: Gn 9: 4)
   b. Been- they been drained *aren't they*, and those been blocked. (SAWD: Gn 9: 1)
   c. ...if you'd burnt some- some timber, it'd be ashes, *will it?* (SAWD: Gn 9: 1)
   d. ...that's gone out, now nobody does it nowadays, *does it?* (SAWD: Dy 5: 4)

Table 4.5, then, gives the percentages of invariant *is it* and *isn't it* in relation to their paradigmatic use. Invariant use is proportionally quite common in most categories, but interesting peaks are found in question tags proper in SAWD and in positive verbless clauses and follow-ups in LC. The latter, in particular, are barely used outside the LC dataset.

Table 4.5: Numbers and percentages of invariant question tags *is it* / *isn't it* in proportion to the total number of invariant and paradigmatic instances (question tags proper (QUE), verbless clauses (CLAU) and follow-ups (FOL)) in four WelE corpora.

	SAWD		LC		NWC		TC	
	N	%	N	%	N	%	N	%
QUE								
is it	8/10	80.0	15/43	34.9	4/10	40.0	2/14	14.3
isn't it	15/29	51.7	49/145	33.8	26/82	29.3	59/127	46.5
CLAU								
is it	2/9	22.2	7/11	63.6	0/1	0.0	3/13	23.1
isn't it	7/23	30.4	12/23	52.2	8/13	61.5	13/52	25.0
FOL								
is it	1/1	100.0	13/29	44.8	0/4	0.0	1/7	14.3
isn't it	–		1/2	50.0	–		–	

An overview of the results confirms the stronger role of positive question tags in SAWD and LC in comparison to NWC and TC. This raises the issue of the role that Welsh contact influence, EngE dialect contact influence and standardization might play in the four types of variety.

Although many sources (e.g. Jones 1990a: 200–201, Parry 1999: 115–116, Williams 2003: 206–209) note that the invariant tag usage in WelE arises from Welsh language influence, the exact Welsh counterparts for the WelE invariant tags can be somewhat difficult to define, as the sources refer to different constructions. Generally speaking, question tags in Welsh inflect according to the tense and person of the preceding statement (Jones and Thomas 1977: 302–303, King 1993: 159–160). However, there are invariant question tags, too, which display some regional variation. Jones (1990a: 200, based on Jones and Thomas 1977) gives the positive variants *ie* (north) and *efe* (south) and negative ones *ynte* (north) and *yntefe* (south), while George (1990: 243) comments that the invariant question tag in Rhondda English "probably arises as a result of the influence of the Welsh generalised confirmatory interrogative *ydy fe?* 'is it?' or the confirmatory negative *ontefe?* 'isn't it?'" (see also Jones 1999: 90–91).

If we compare the four age groups in LC and NWC (Figure 4.2) for diachronic change, we find regional differences between both positive and negative question tags. The positive tags, both invariant and paradigmatic, are disappearing in NWC, while LC indicates a rise resulting, for example, from increased use of *is it* as an invariant follow-up question in Age group IV. In the case of negative tags, LC again displays highly frequent use of the invariant type in Age group IV, while in NWC the respective columns remain fairly level across groups II-IV and the use of *isn't it* in paradigmatic contexts is on the rise. However, the numbers of instances in NWC are too small for definitive conclusions.

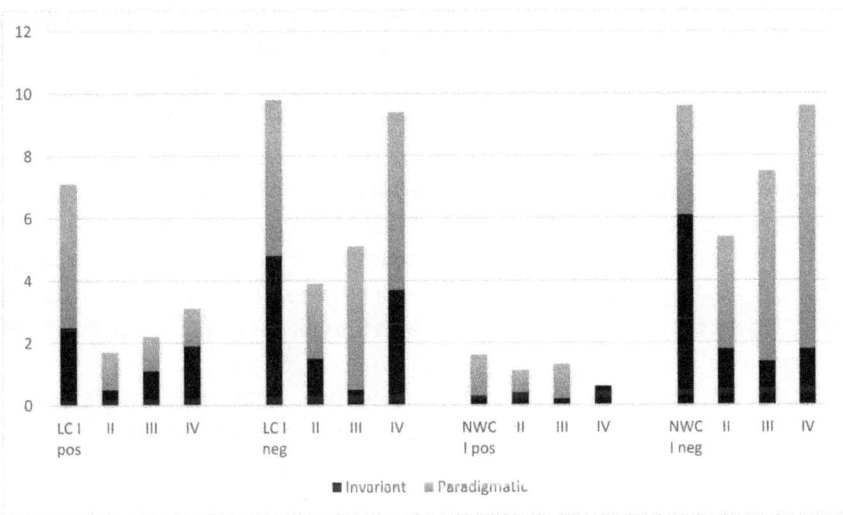

Figure 4.2: Apparent-time change in invariant and paradigmatic question tags, all types included.

Both question tags in LC as well as *isn't it* in NWC experience a considerable drop in Age group II, after which the frequencies rise again. The drop may partly be caused by age-grading, the older middle-aged informants in the second age groups being disinclined to use these question tags in an interview situation. The results also show that the oldest speakers do employ this feature quite frequently.

While Welsh contact influence is a plausible answer for the high frequencies in Age group I, there remains the question of what causes the increasing use in Age group IV in Llandybie but not in NWC. Functionally speaking, there is a clear proportional increase in accord-building negative tags in LC, from 8% in Age group I to 48% in IV. These are not unusual in NWC, either (27% on average), nor in TC (27%). In LC Age group IV, however, the form *innit* tends to co-occur with the accord-building function (5/9, 56%) and especially with phrasal tags, few as they are (2/2, 100%). It is our conclusion that the southern development feeds from the regional Welsh-induced usage, on the one hand, and from London English, on the other.

EngE invariant tags, *innit* in particular, have attracted considerable academic interest in recent decades. In Andersen's (2001: 183–195) study, invariant *innit* is associated primarily with ethnic minorities, which he interprets as the source of the usage, but also with speakers under the age of 30, the greater London area, lower socio-economic backgrounds, and females (albeit males are found to drive the spread of the feature into higher social classes). In other parts of England, *innit* is likely to be used in the south rather than the north, and by young males of lower socio-economic backgrounds (Krug 1998, Cheshire et al. 2005). Functionally, for example, Cheshire (1982) and Krug (1998) suggest that *innit* is used especially in peremptory and aggressive functions (as described in Algeo 1988: 180–187), which are non-conducive and attitudinal. As shown by Pichler (2013: 193) as well as the present data, however, non-conducive invariant tags need not be antagonistic; they can also carry positive interactional significance. Finally, Pichler's (2013: 203–205) results from Berwick English indicate that non-conducive functions strongly correlate with the form *innit* rather than with canonical tags, including the form *isn't it*. This, together with the emergence of phrasal *innit* tags, is a strong indicator of EngE input in the southern WelE usages.

As mentioned above, there is also another type of invariant question tag in WelE which is discussed in, for example, Jones (1990a, 1990b). Studying 5–7-year old children's English across schools with a broad regional range, he finds a clear geographical difference in the use of southern *is it / isn't it* and the northern variant *yes* (1990a: 219–220). He ascribes this to Welsh dialect influence, as the southern and northern invariant question tags are different in the language. Jones (1990b) studies the use of *yes/yeah/aye* in a WelE child language corpus and finds that it is used with directives (see ex. 85), as well as declarative clauses (96a), interrogatives (96b), and zero verb clauses (96c; 1990b: 187):

(96) a. It was good, *aye?*
     b. D'ya want red, *yeah?*
     c. Cleaning the floor (tonight), *yes?*

Yeah is also found in non-canonical sentence-medial positions (see ex. 93), which is befitting to its character as a lexical tag.

Curiously, our data yield little evidence of invariant *yes/yeah* in any part of Wales. There are very few occurrences of in NWC and none in the other corpora, while *isn't it* is quite common in the north, too. The following examples illustrate the findings in NWC:

(97) a. Well, you used erm, paper which was very mutl- much like grease proof paper,
[Mm.]
< > grease proof paper you see that you use to bake a *>cake. *Yeah?*
[Oh, right.<* Yeah.] (NWC, Llanuwchllyn: 4d)
b. I make a point to have the Welsh language.
[That's right. I've tried it sometimes.]
Yes?
[Just- just to see if you c- I can manage, you know.] (i.e. choosing Welsh in cash machines; NWC, Pencaenewydd: 8d)

In example (97a) the question tag can be considered accord-building ('you know?'), while in (97b) it functions as a confirmatory follow-up question ('Have you?'). As these tags are barely used by any informant in any age group in NWC, it is at present difficult to say whether *isn't it* or some pragmatic marker or another has taken their place in North Wales, or whether there is some other reason why they do not show in the corpora.

4.4.2 Other discourse-pragmatic markers

Windsor Lewis (1964: 297–298) draws attention to the word *like* in Glamorgan English, stating that it is "a very characteristic word of the dial often carrying very little meaning and occurring in various positions in the sentence". He lists five different types of *like*, which can in present-day terms be identified as discourse markers (e.g. *to make sure like*), comparative prepositions (e.g. *He had like a cloak on; He acted like he was crazy*), and as a "'suffix to modify the force of adjectives' (EDD)" or adverbs (e.g. *He's daft-like; It happened so sudden-like*). Despite the hyphenated spelling, Windsor Lewis points out that the final type is very similar to the first, discourse marker function. Similar instances can be found in WelE fiction, for example, Lewis Jones's *Cwmardy* (1937) Ron Berry's *So Long Hector Bebb* (1970), which implies that this feature has some salience in the dialect (see also James 2011: 60). The *Voices* commentaries make numerous mentions of *like*, whether as a discourse marker in a clause-medial position (98) or clause-final position (99) or as a quotative (100):

(98) a. it's just we have so many *like* English influences around us (*Voices*: Bethesda)
b. women *like* want to be more socially aware (*Voices*: Rhos-on-Sea)

(99) a. little bit... common mm a bit too um sharp *like*, not smooth *like*, um (*Voices*: Bethesda)
b. I won't go any further, *like* (*Voices*: Flint)

(100) I'm *like*, "no I haven't," and she's *like*, "yeah," and I'm *like*, "well what kind of accent have I got then?" and she's *like*, "well Welsh," and I'm *like*, "oh right" (*Voices*: Bon-y-Maen)

(101) and you *go*, "crumbs did I just say the f-word?" and your friends *go*... (*Voices*: Splott)

The evidence available at present is somewhat sporadic and hence a closer functional examination is not feasible. It is safe to say that discourse functions of *like* which occur in spoken EngE can also be found in WelE, but the potential patterns of regional or sociolinguistic variation and change in these usages are yet to be uncovered. *Like* in its different functions has been studied extensively in various Englishes (e.g. Andersen 2001, Buchstaller 2001, D'Arcy 2008, Schweinberger 2012), and quotatives make another interesting variable in themselves. The *Voices* commentaries include a few instances of quotative *go* as well, as in (101). WelE perspectives into these features would be very welcome.

Now is also used in WelE as a discourse marker or pragmatic marker. It has distinctive functions as an adverb, too, according to Edwards (1985) and Lewis (2008), as the temporal span of *now* can be quite flexible (e.g. *I'll see to it now, when I get home*; Edwards 1985: 29). Migge (2015) describes the discursive functions of *now* in IrE and other Englishes and states that that as a discourse marker, it occurs utterance-initially, while as a pragmatic marker, for example, with an affective or intensifying meaning, it can also take other positions. WelE usages, however, appear to deviate from this pattern. Williams (2003: 209–212) investigates *now* in the Miners' Library and Ceri George's interview data from southeast Wales, and concludes that it operates primarily as a thematic marker, frequently positioned after the theme (102). It can also be highly prolific in the elderly informants' speech (103), which Williams interprets as a means of organizing one's thoughts in an unfamiliar interview setting. Example (103) furthermore illustrates the interrelatedness of temporal and discursive functions pointed out by Migge (2015: 396, with reference to Schiffrin 1987).

(102) My brother *now* that died, Dai, when I started work, er, he was driving from [sic] my father, driving a horse then. (CG: TS; Williams 2003: 209)

(103) And I got a sister older than me *now* she haven't had a voice *now* eight years *now* coming this month. (CG: KL; Williams 2003: 210)

Williams (2003: 211–212) discusses the possibility that the thematic function is a result of the rheme-theme information structure commonly employed by Welsh and WelE, leading to an impulse to mark initial thematic elements explicitly. There is thus far no definitive explanation however.

A related discourse-pragmatic marker, which appears to be more characteristic still in WelE, is *now then*. It is particularly common in LC but occurs in other corpora as well and displays similar functions to *now*, as an adverbial (104), discourse marker (105; e.g. thematic, introductory or indicating a shift in the narrative) or pragmatic marker (106; e.g. affective, emphatic or intensifying). The functions can overlap.

(104) a. what was the other one I was thinking *now then* you know (TC: 6b)
b. I ended my mining days about- 'bout six years ago, yes. And I'm now, of course, retired *now then*. (LC: 3d)

(105) a. Right. Ah, Milo *now then*, there's a thing. That's a prime example of a little village that's been totally changed... (LC: 5f)
b. *Now then*, the minority language there is Slovenian. *Now then* I met some- some teachers out there... (NWC, Pencaenewydd: 6e)

(106) a. whereas with me *now then*, my mother is Welsh-speaking (LC: 7i)
b. we only speak English *now then* to someone who doesn't understand Welsh. (LC: 3d)

A comprehensive examination of the whole range of discourse-pragmatic variables in the above functions would most likely reveal patterns that are quite distinctive of WelE.

TC contains another phrase, *now just* (107), which however clearly functions as an adverbial. Lewis (2008: 160) records it in the Rhondda, too, as indicating a time point in the near future or recent past. Although the TC informants discuss *now just* during the interview – and comment on the curious semantics – there are no instances in the corpora where informants would in fact be using it (also *now in a minute*, e.g. Lewis 2008: 159).

(107) A: they've got . there's a lot who say I'll do it *now just* I'll do it *just now* or now ju-
[Mm]

A: instead of *now just* though
B: Aye
A: I don't know which is right <laughter>
B: No . that's right
A: How can you do it *now just* <laughter> (TC: 2, 3a)

A superficial search through the WelE corpora at hand shows that *you know* is extremely frequent. Searching for *you know* without a manual extraction of non-discursive instances gives frequencies of 121 pttw (NWC), 127 pttw (LC), and 133 pttw (TC). Palma-Fahey (2015: 355), using the very same method, arrives at frequencies from 40 to 51 pttw in three corpora of fictionalized IrE dialogues, and Kallen's (2005: 65) figures of the discourse marker *you know* in ICE-Ireland and ICE-GB are lower as well. In his study, which also involves formal spoken language, the total normalized frequencies are 61.6 pttw for Northern Ireland, 33.4 for the Republic of Ireland, and 28.9 for Great Britain, and the highest frequencies of 105.4 pttw arise from Northern Irish telephone conversations. The WelE figures have been obtained from interview corpora, which perhaps raises the frequencies along with the "quick and dirty" search method, but one can nevertheless conclude that the Welsh are active users of this item.

The discourse marker *you see* appears to have been studied much less in varieties of English. The above type of dirty search in the WelE corpora produces normalized frequencies of 8 pttw (NWC), 20 pttw (LC) and 5 pttw (TC) for the chunk *you see*. The reduced variant, *see*, seems to be considered quite salient in WelE, as it appears relatively often in fictional accounts of the dialect. The data suggest that there is age-related variation regarding this discourse marker; it seems to be used by older rather than younger speakers. Like *you know* or *you see*, *see* can be positioned utterance-finally or initially. In (108b) it combines with the invariant tag *innit*.

(108) a. I remember going to Avonmouth [...] em . my wife had an auntie living in Avonmouth docks *see* (TC: 6b)
b. there's Welsh schools opening *see* innit (TC: 2)
c. *See* once the limestone became- once they became bigger, more efficient,
[Yeah.]
then there was no work for them so they- they just moved away. (LC: 4c)

A further item, mentioned in the *Voices* commentaries, is *mind* or *mind you*, whose main function is discourse-structural, highlighting and positioning a piece of information against the prior context. *Mind* is a tag-like utterance-final element (109), whereas *mind you* can also take an introductory, initial position, and on some rare occasions even a medial one (110). *Mind (you)* emerges to some extent in all present WelE corpora, perhaps more so in the south than north, but a closer examination of the usages against other varieties of English remains to be carried out.

(109) a. and I had the AA 4 man out the front... out the back there... only to mend my car, *mind* (*Voices*: Bon-y-Maen)
b. I used to catch lobsters too, *mind* (NWC: 2c)

(110) a. *Mind you*, having said that, my father was never against me having an education or anything like that. (LC: 6f)
b. I never bothered then
[Yeah yeah]
although I liked going *mind you* to work (TC: 3b)

Older WelE fiction contains instances, where *mind (now)* is used as an imperative clause rather than a discourse marker (e.g. *But, mind, do not say it after me*, Ceredig [Owen Parry], *Among the Mountains* 1870; *Mind now what I am telling you*, Margiad Evans, *Country Dance* 1937). This is indicative of the origins of the discourse marker function.

General extenders are another type of tag which might be of interest in WelE. The variant which is brought up in the *Voices* commentaries is *and that*, but many others are of course used as well. In her study on adolescent speech in EngE, Cheshire (2007) finds that *and that* is associated with working class speech, whereas middle class informants prefer, for example, *and stuff* or *and things*. In the present WelE corpora, *and that* emerges primarily in the northern, eastern and southern edges of Wales.

(111) a. I feel much better with myself *and that* (*Voices*: Splott)
b. and they were on about these 'mutations' *and stuff* (*Voices*: Builth Wells)
c. a lot of people are playing on their computers *and stuff like that* aren't they (TC: 4)
d. most people my age go on holiday now, they go in a big group *or something* (LC: 7d)
e. he goes occasionally to places like Barcelona *and things like that* (NWC: 2b)
f. And I suppose I've got time to see friends *and things*... (LC: 6e)

4.5 Welsh English phraseology

When addressing the phraseology of WelE, focus here is placed upon local expressions and coinages rather than those that may have wider currency amongst other English varieties. The distinctive phraseology of Welsh English has received little treatment or analysis in the literature, although Jones (2016) provides a short list of phrases largely taken from material such as the SAWD, as well as Gower material from Penhallurick (1994). Currently, there are two strands from which WelE phraseology can be interrogated. The first concern phrases that are a result of the language contact situation, in that they were likely translated from a Welsh source. Indeed, these phrases may well be some of the more contemporary examples of WelE phraseology, deriving from the late nineteenth- and twentieth-century contact situation. The second concern the phrases coined in regions in which there have been long-standing traditions of English within speech communities, for example, the Gower and the Border country.

First are several phrases recorded that have analogous meaning in Welsh. For example, *pulling one's tongue out* 'putting one's tongue out' (*tynnu tafod*, found in Gwynedd & Clwyd in Parry 1999: 177); *in the bone* 'fundamentally' (*yn y bôn*, South Wales; Lewis 2008: 66); and *keep (the dishes)* 'put dishes away after washing up' (*cadw [llestri]*, Gwynedd, Clwyd, North Powys; Parry 1999). The phrase *keep the dishes* arises in *Voices* (Holyhead), but the present corpora reveal nothing further about the current use of these expressions. The use of *stop* in place of *stay* is recorded from a Llandybie informant in collocations such as *stop indoors* and *stop up for me* (LC: 2c), likely deriving from Welsh *sefyll* 'stop, wait, stand'. Several noun phrases recorded in SAWD also result from loan translations, for example *dog's grass* 'couchgrass' (*porfa ci*, Gwent & Dyfed) and *white lady* 'bindweed' (*ladi wen*, Dyfed; both in Parry 1999).

The second category concerns WelE phrases that have developed from a long-established settlement of English-speaking communities, namely in the regions descendent of the Welsh Marches, such as the Gower peninsula, and eastern border regions such as Monmouthshire and Flintshire.

Penhallurick's *Gowerland and its Language* (1994), being a repository of numerous dialect glossaries since the seventeenth century, includes over thirty-five phrases, many distinct to Gower (this is reproduced as an independent listing in Jones & Penhallurick 2018). Some of the earliest come from 1697, such as the idiom *blesse ye windowe* 'to fasten the window tight' and a religious oath *god and our lady keepe us*. Proverbs were also in use in Gower such as *if Candlemas day is fair and fine, there's forty days of winter behind*, a weather adage recorded from Llanmadoc in 1879.

Of importance to a discussion of WelE lexis overall is that several Gower phrases incorporate local lexis, for example *zemmit* 'sieve' in another proverb noted in 1951: *if thee cast make a zemmit wi'out acrinkle, thee't git a husband wi'out a wrinkle*, i.e. 'hard work pays off'. There is also *hyst thee calks* 'make an escape' (Tucker 1957) derived from *hyst* 'hoist' and *calk* 'a part of horse-shoes', and *toad under the harass* 'a lively person' (Upton 1969) derived from *harass* 'a harrow, a farming instrument for turning soil'.

Dennis Griffiths also notes some phrase usages for the "Buckley dialect", a northern Borders variety supposedly formed around the end of the twelfth century when English-speaking miners and potters emigrated to Buckley mountain (Griffiths 1969). Several lexical items in Griffiths' *Talk of My Town* are unique to the area like *above a bit* 'a great deal', 'substantial'. Most of them however share similarity with West Midlands EngE varieties, being phonetic respellings of the phrase structure, such as *haud/owd thee naise*, a declarative 'be quiet', lit. 'hold your nose'; *a pair for neets* 'pyjama bottoms', lit. 'pair for nights'; as well as *fane and wet* 'very wet', lit. 'fine and wet' (although there is a possibility that *fane* here refers to *weather-fane* rather than a respelling of *fine*). Two prepositional phrases for location exist too, *o'er the 'ills* 'to send somebody to Denbigh Lunatic Asylum' and *on the bonk* 'a Pithead waste bank'.

Correspondingly, Ivor Waters' observation of the southern Borders variety (east Gwent) provides several phrases in his *Folklore and Dialect of the Lower Wye Valley* (1973). Waters states that this dialect "resembles the dialect of Gloucestershire rather than that of West Monmouthshire" (Waters 1973: 21). He records *have it to go* 'to quarrel noisily' and both *a bit of* and *bits of* in the sense 'barely' in *he's a bit of a foreman* or *they're only bits of girls* (1973: 22). Some phrases are attested in other sources like *all of a bodge* 'untidy' (Parry 1999: 134) derived from *bodge* 'to mend clumsily' (*EDD*) and *a Bristolman's sleep* 'watchful, cunning' (also in Jack Windsor Lewis' database below) derived from Bristol tradesmen cunningly sleeping with one eye open. Waters (1973: 22) also alludes to a Wye custom of adding determiners to nouns and pluralization to their stems, as in the phrase *a touch of the shorts* 'to have no money' where *the shorts* likely derived from being 'short of money'. This modification of nouns with determiners is attested in east Gwent in reference to headaches: *I got the headache / I got the toothache* (Parry 1999: 108; see also Section 3.2).

There is also the case of Jack Windsor Lewis' (1964) database of material for Glamorganshire. This differs from the above material in that the speech communities here were Anglicized at a later period. Windsor Lewis lists over sixty phrases, of which about half are distinct in that they do not appear in other dialectological records. To what degree this wealth of unique phraseological material corresponds with phrases from Welsh is currently unclear. Windsor Lewis does note that in the phrase *to have one's pang out* 'to vent one's temper', *pang* may derive from the Welsh 'spasm, attack' (*GPC*), whilst *over the bottle* 'drinking from the bottle' might derive from the Welsh *dros y bottel*. In the material there are oaths like *damn my rags*, simile constructions like *black as the hob* 'very dirty', and numerous verbal phrases like *to bath the baby* 'get things done', *to not care whether it snows* 'to be indifferent', *to feel like a bloated cockroach* 'very full' (Cardiff in origin), and *to have one's heart up* 'being severely bilious' (similar sense to *turn one's heart over* in *EDD*).

Finally, there are a number of phrases which are relatively recent to WelE. Some of these are discussed in connection with discourse-pragmatic markers in the above subsection 4.4.2, such as *now just*. A related adverbial phrase is *now in a minute* for 'relatively soon'. Much like *cwtch* and *cariad*, the expression has a degree of enregisterment in South Wales, appearing on lay wordlists (e.g. Pay 2015) and dialect merchandise such as T-shirts. Its specific origins are unclear, although its popularity may have been boosted by Welsh singer-songwriter Donna Lewis' platinum certified 1994 album *Now In a Minute*.

Popular culture has also done much to popularize one final expression, *what's occurring*? 'what's going on?', a phrase from the television show *Gavin and Stacey*, where it serves as a catchphrase for the character Nessa (Ruth Jones). Although the popularity of the term may lead it to be used facetiously by fans who are WelE speakers, confusion as to whether it is a genuine WelE term may exist for those outside Wales.

5 History of Welsh English

5.1 Introduction

Although from year to year we know more about the historical and social developments of the Welsh varieties of English, on the whole there is still much about the variety's history we have yet to learn, especially regarding early WelE. Throughout its history, one consistent feature of WelE has been the impact of the Welsh language on English usage.

The study of WelE history is limited by the unfortunate dearth of first-hand evidence of the variety before the twentieth century (Thomas 1994: 109). Before that century, the degree of English language literacy amongst the native Welsh was low; those that could write in both languages, used Standard English for their model, whether it was personal letters or official documents. Much of this chapter discusses the perceived notion of this "Welsh English" by commentators and writers within sociohistorical contexts.

We now have the beginnings of a detailed account of the representation of Welsh English in fictive contexts (see Jones 2018), therefore this chapter is designed to canvas, for the first time in sociolinguistic and dialectological discussion of the dialect, the history of the variety from its early inception until present day through such means. Most of what we know of the historical nature of WelE comes from written texts, both fictive and non-fictive, and thus these modes will take precedence here, informing us of the forms in which earlier renditions of WelE may have taken. It should be noted that in using historical examples from fictive sources (e.g. plays, novels, film), dialect writers take artistic liberties when depicting dialect. Krapp (1926: 525) emphasizes that such linguistic observers are "dialect artists" rather than trained linguists, and produce content for casual readers or viewers. That being said, dialect depictions from such sources constitute important linguistic evidence (Shorrocks 1996: 385, Sullivan 1980: 205), especially in perceived commonality of particular linguistic forms, but also in the larger metalinguistic awareness that the variety had value for its speakers. Therefore, in supplement to these illustrative examples of WelE in primary written texts, the larger socio-historical context of the usage of English in Wales will also inform this chapter's discussion.

We should perhaps begin by discussing the history of the term used of the variety, that is, how scholars and laymen have named the Welsh variet(ies) of English. *Welsh English* is the term used by linguists today to cover all (spoken) English usage in Wales. As an umbrella term, we are really referring to the plural, Welsh Englishes, in that there are several geographic variations within this variety (Garrett, Coupland and Williams 1999: 325–237). Most of these dialect zones correspond with historical periods of Anglicization, where, as Welsh language diminished to be supplanted by English, new contact Englishes emerged. The Englishes of the Gower and south Pembrokeshire were the earliest, followed by the varieties found along the English–Welsh border. These date back to the Norman invasions of the eleventh century. Later, during the nineteenth century, the Industrial Revolution that brought English-speaking migrants to Wales led to English becoming widespread throughout south Welsh valleys. Even the cities and their environs, like Cardiff, Swansea, and Wrexham today have complex, distinct linguistic makeups. Unlike southern varieties, which have completed a language shift to English, northern varieties of WelE could be classified as being in a shift process due to L1 Welsh language influence. Few of these speech communities have *designations*, however. Though we may hypothetically label them with names such as Gower English, Welsh Borders English, Valleys English, or Cardiff Conurbation English, the borders of such regions are uncertain (Thomas 1984: 178–179), and few lay speakers of these Welsh Englishes even acknowledge that Welsh English could be classified as a dialect (see also Sections 1.4 and 1.5).

The term Welsh English was used by philologist A.J. Ellis (1882) in passing in his nineteenth-century dialectological survey. It referenced the use of English along the borders of Wales and England: "[the] southern part of Shropshire was a Welsh speaking country, on which English was forced hundreds of years ago. It is therefore an old English speaking region, but the English was always a *Welsh English*" (emphasis present authors'; Ellis 1882: 18). However, Ellis preferred to use the term "Cambrian English" to refer to English in Wales, using a Latinate adjective. He also acknowledged a divide between North and South Cambrian English (Ellis 1882: 20). During the twentieth century, dialectologist David Parry (1977, 1979, and 1999) used the term *Anglo-Welsh*, in doing so highlighting an Anglicized quality to a speech from Wales. At the time, Parry's decision corresponded with popular usage in other academic circles, primarily the literary movement of English writers from Wales, and the labelling of Irish varieties of English as "Anglo-Irish" (see Henry 1957: 3–4).

More recently, lay investigators in the southeast Valleys' dialect have adopted the term "Wenglish" to refer to English speech in Wales. This blend parallels other lay movements around the world that have coined terms for contact varieties like Chinglish (Chinese English) or Konglish (Korean English). Subsequent usage of the term by the public can be controversial: Hadikin (2014) notes that these terms can be "disparaging", presenting speakers of these varieties as comical or unable to master a Standard "global" English, although the variety's users may also find solidarity with the blend (Bae 2014). All of this is true of Wenglish. Layman glossaries (Edwards 1985, Lewis 2008) that use the term treat the variety

5.2 The Anglo-Saxon period

The history of WelE can be said to begin with the first contacts of Britons and Anglo-Saxons. Current research (see Filppula et al. 2008) shows that the contacts were not exclusively devastating to the Britons, as traditionally believed, but that large numbers of Britons remained in place in central England, where there was most likely a long period of bilingualism. English was possibly spoken in the eastern Radnorshire plain in Mid-Wales as early as the eighth century (Williams 1935, Watkin 1964), but in all other respects Wales was thoroughly monoglot Welsh.

Although classical thought (e.g. Venerable Bede and later nineteenth-century biased historians) suggested the invaders exterminated the native Britons, driving them to the northern and westerly regions, modern historians suggest that, although raids did occur (Tristam 1999: 5, 8–9; Jackson [1953] 1994: 198–219), Britons and Germanic tribes assimilated their societies. Eventually, the early English language gained prominence (Higham 1992: 229). This was the first contact between a Brythonic [Welsh] language and a Germanic [English] one. The archaeological record demonstrates the Germanic impact in culture-specific burial rites and paleobotantical findings, but the influence was mutual, evidenced in the linguistic record. There was likely widespread bi/multi-lingualism throughout the speech communities (German 2000: 368–369), and the survival of large numbers of Brythonic place names in England indeed suggests a successful coexistence between the two groups (Coates & Breeze 2000).

The question of the effect of Brythonic on the morphosyntactic component of Old and Middle English is a matter of growing interest, recent research indicating that the substrate language affected the superstrate (see Tristram 2000, 2003, 2006; Filppula et al. 2002, 2008). Celtic impact on the development of English as a whole is relevant for present-day WelE in regards to the historical layeredness of Celtic contact influence in WelE. Some of these features are discussed further in Chapter 3, the complementary distribution of habitual periphrastic *do* (representing the "old" Brythonic layer) and habitual extension of the progressive (arising from "new" Welsh contact influence) being the most obvious case.

During this early contact era, the Anglo-Saxons referred to the Britons as *wealas* 'foreigners', and this term would later become the English language's adjectival demonym, Welsh (Germanic speakers semantically expanded the term's usage for all Romanized Celtic peoples, for example, Walloons of Belgium and the Welsch of the Italian Tyrol; Davies [1993] 2007: 69). Conversely, the Welsh called themselves *Y Cymry* 'the compatriots', and their language *Cymraeg*, referring to the Anglo-Saxons as *Saesneg* 'Saxons', a term still used of the English today.

5.3 The Norman Conquest and the Late Middle Ages

If the previous period marked the foundation of English in Wales, the Norman Conquest of 1066 led to establishing the contact between the two languages, which then remained fairly stable for several centuries. The area today known as Wales was undergoing considerable changes. Following the Norman invasion of Britain in 1066, Marcher Lordships were formed along its border regions with the English kingdoms and southern coastline to repel the Welsh kingdoms from gaining territory outside the Welsh peninsula. This formed a dichotomy: the *Marchia Wallie* ruled by Anglo-Norman Marcher Lords and the *Pura Wallia* ruled by the Welsh princes.

To consolidate the claim to the land, Henry I ordered English and Flemish peasants to settle in South Pembrokeshire and the Gower peninsula; in reference to this method, John Davies (1993: 111) elaborates that "a dense settlement of peasants [was] always a more effective way of consolidating conquest than a thin layer of gentry". These regions were the first English language settlements in Wales (bearing in mind that the structure of Flemish was similar to English at this time) and remained pockets of English with dialects of their own well into the twentieth century (see Parry 1990 for discussion of South Pembrokeshire English and Penhallurick 1994 for discussion of Gower English). In the late medieval period, topological names were given to the south Pembrokeshire region: *Anglia Transwalliana* and Little England Beyond Wales.

Most of the Marches, however, remained largely Welsh-speaking until their disestablishment and well into the industrial age (Williams 1985: 65). During the late medieval period, the Marches were controlled by Anglo-Norman Marcher Lords. The regional distinctions and factions that controlled the Marches were numerous and complex (see Lieberman 2008: 129). What we know of the March today encompasses the historic Welsh counties of Denbighshire, Montgomeryshire, Flintshire, Brecknockshire, Radnorshire, Monmouthshire, Glamorganshire, Carmarthenshire and Pembrokeshire.

Despite Anglo-Norman rulers subjugating much of Welsh culture, thus leaving us with little record of Welsh life under Anglo-Norman authority, these Anglicized Marcher Lordship communities were not devoid of a Welsh culture and language (Meecham-Jones 2008: 30). The Welsh Marches were very much a frontier region. Although the area housed both Welsh and Anglo-Norman armies, they shared it with the local peasantry. Consequently, these were regions of rich linguistic diversity (Meecham-Jones 2008: 30–31). The native Welsh speech community was joined by immigrants from Norman possessions in England, Norman-controlled France, and Flanders, thereby bringing French, Anglo-Norman and Flemish to the Marches. Eventually, English too began gaining footholds in the region (German 2009: 27), however, the native Welsh language remained a central language amongst peasantry. As Meecham-Jones (2008: 31) states, "the pattern of conquest and appropriation in the March ensured that Welsh functioned as a crucial linguistic and cultural substrate in the development of Marcher culture".

Take for example the ancient Brythonic kingdom of Ergyng (later known as Archenfield) which lies today between English Herefordshire and Welsh Monmouthshire. Before the Norman Conquest it was often passed between Welsh royal houses, belonging to either Gwent, Glywysing or Morgannwg. As part of the Welsh March, it remained a prominently Welsh-speaking area. A collection of Middle English texts known as the Katherine Group detail that Welsh lexical items were clearly influencing the English written texts of the region. Both *Ancrene Wisse* and *Sir Gawain and the Green Knight* contain borrowed Welsh language lexical features; indeed, it is these features that helped historians locate the texts' origins to present-day Herefordshire (Meecham-Jones 2008: 31–32). The English dialect of Herefordshire circa 1200 contained at least three Welsh words. *Cader* 'candle' featured in both *Ancrene Wisse* and *Hali Meiðhad*, *genow* 'mouth' was used in *Ste Margarete*, and *keis* was used for both 'satellites' and 'henchmen' in *Sawles Warde* (Dobson 1976: 115–16).

Although Welsh law was distinct from English law, Welsh law still influenced the Marcher system. This can be evidenced in the Welsh legal words *galanas*, a word to do with homicide, and *anghyfarch*, a word associated with thievery. In Marcher texts, these were often left untranslated in both English and Latin translations within the territories, perhaps because the concepts could not be directly translated (Roberts 2008: 89).

As is expected, the cross-linguistic influence was not a one-way system. English loanwords found their way into the territory's Welsh too. For example, the Welsh *edling* is a loan from Old English *aetheling* 'male heir' (Roberts 2008: 89). Though these examples are not strictly instances of early WelE, they tell us that the Marcher languages were malleable; lexical items were borrowed across the speech communities. The cross-linguistic practices of the Marches represent one of the cornerstones for the development of Welsh English as variety in its own right.

After two centuries, the many conflicts between the Welsh princes and the Anglo-Norman lords saw the defeat of the last indigenous Prince of Wales, Llywelyn ap Gruffudd, in 1282. With Llywelyn's defeat, political power was transferred to the English, which marked the beginning of the cultural subjugation of Wales

(John Davies [1993] 2007: 158–161). Effectively, Wales may be seen as the "first colony of an expanding British state" (Williams 1990: 19).

The Late Middle Ages were marked by a clear-cut separation between the English-speaking gentry and the monoglot Welsh peasants. English became the language of law and administration by the fifteenth century replacing Anglo-French and Latin, and found usage among the upper classes, including the Welsh gentry (Janet Davies 1993: 22). With the gentry learning English as a second language, the beginnings of Welsh English as a contact variety had emerged. Geographically, of course, the language situation was stable: English was seeping in extremely slowly from the east but already had widespread usage in Gower and South Pembrokeshire, albeit it derived largely from the English used by colonising peasants centuries before. Individual bilingualism was therefore only found in towns along the borders.

The 1400s saw Wales featuring as a backdrop for various Middle English romance tales. One notable tale, the anonymous *Sir Cleges*, featured two Welsh characters conversing in English language discourse in "Cardyff syde" (Davenport 2008: 141–142). There is little of note regarding any semblance of a distinct Welsh Marcher language variety of English besides one character possibly using focus fronting, a Welsh-induced feature (e.g. "Tomorrow to Cardyff, I will go") (see Section 3.4.2.), bearing in mind, however, that this is a feature common in other English varieties, too.

But what of Welsh writers of English in this period? During the late medieval period, there are few examples of Welsh people writing in English. The most notable was William Salesbury, a scholar and translator born in 1520 in Denbighshire, who likely received education in both Wales and Oxford (Evans 2008a: 255). First active in Edward VI's reign, Salesbury made good use of the printing revolution in London, printing Welsh language material. At this time, London's Welsh population was far greater than any Welsh urban settlement (Evans 2008a: 250–253). Of the four works he wrote in English, two are notable: *A Dictionary of Englyshe and Welshe* (1547) and *A brief and a Playne Introduction [to] the Brytysh Tongue* (1550). Both texts' aims were to help non-Welsh clergy to practise their faith in Wales; whether his native Welsh influenced his English writing or orthography is debatable.

There is, fortunately, record of one Welsh person, Ieuan ap Hywel Swrdwal, whose English writing matches the manner in which he pronounced it, that is, with a Welsh accent. His poem *Hymn to the Virgin* (1480) was notably written as a retaliation to his English classmates who claimed the Welsh had no worthwhile culture (Dobson 1953: 112, cited in German 2009: 28).

The poem, reproduced in Chapter 7, uses Welsh orthography, and its conservative written Welsh means that we are able to view the precise phonetic values of the English phonemes perceived by L1 Welsh speakers of English in 1480 (German 2009: 28). Most notable is that fricative phonemes such as /z/, /ʒ/, and /ʃ/, and affricates such as /tʃ/, and /dʒ/, are absent from the poem, as are initial glides like /j/, with /w/ often represented as a long vowel (these exist in Welsh and WelE today). For example, *dazzle* is rendered <taslio>, *wish* <wys>, *such* <sits>, *your* <iur>, and *would* <uld>. Another feature is the absence of voiced stops and fricatives, so that *band* becomes <bant> and *of* <off> (see Section 2.5.1.; Penhallurick 1991 and Thomas 1984 attest to this in some WelE varieties today). German (2009: 33) quite rightly believes that this text is of "utmost sociolinguistic significance", being the first text in which a Welsh language influenced English variety is used by a Welsh person to commend Welsh national identity.

Ieuan ap Hywel Swrdwal was early to the game, however. The idea of WelE users using their variety in a text to mark social solidarity would not prosper until the nineteenth century, over three hundred years later (Section 5.5). Not long after Ieuan's inventive dialectological experiment, users of other varieties began to use his template for the creation of their own fictive, stock characters. The earliest of which was a collection of English jests called *A Hundred Merry Tales* (1526; see Zall 1963: 131). Here, the Welsh were discriminated against both culturally and linguistically, notably in Tale 31, which saw devoicing of several plosives and the rendering of possessive pronouns solely as 'her' which may have erroneously derived from EngE users overhearing WelE users referring to concepts like the weather as female, for example, *mae hi'n bwrw glaw*, lit. 'she is raining' (Blank 1996: 134; Bartley 1954: 73). Take for example: "Master, by Cot's bloot [God's Blood] and her [his] nail I have stand yonder this two hours and I could see never a male [deer] but a little male that a man had hanging at his saddle bow" (quoted in Zall 1963: 93–94). These linguistic features would become stereotyped staples in the then-imminent era of Elizabethan theatre.

Some writers, like Sussex-born Andrew Borde (b. 1490), also wrote non-fictional texts that mentioned the variety in its earlier years. Borde's *Fyrst Boke of the Introduction of Knowledge* (1547; Evans 2008b: 89) set out to be a linguistic guidebook for merchants travelling in Europe and Asia Minor, with vocabulary items illustrated as they might sound to EngE users. The Welsh chapter contains 164 lines, the longest in the guidebook. Like Salesbury, Borde included the Welsh language in his writing, the first Englishman to do so, providing set phrases for English speakers to use in the Welsh language. Though Borde deserves commendation here, there are also 24 lines devoted to a first-person poem written in a (stock) WelE. It highlights various cultural stereotypes like loving roasted cheese and walking barefoot, and adheres to linguistic stereotypes. *Cawse* 'cheese' is left untranslated, as is *metheglin* 'mead' which was well-known as a drink associated with Wales at this time (Warner 1897: 55). The habitual periphrastic *do* emerges as well: "I am a Welshman, and do dwel in Wales". Although highlighted as a feature of WelE, it should be noted that the periphrastic *do* in affirmative declaratives was, to some extent, used more generally in EModE than at present. Borde also attempted to render Welsh language and WelE phonemes, though this is of mixed result. He mishears the voiceless lateral fricative /ɬ/, a sound not found in English in his era nor today, as <cl> in *llety* and *lletywraig*, and <kl> in *Llundain*, although he does pick up on the devoicing of final stops, such as /d/ becoming /t/ and /g/ becoming /k/.

The second chapytre treateth of Wales. And of the natural disposicion of Welshmen. Teaching an Englyshman to speake some Welsh.

I Am a Welshman, and do dwel in Wales,
   I haue loued to serche boudgets, & looke in males;

Figure 5.1: A print from Andrew Borde's *Fyrst Boke* (1547 [1870]: 125). Public domain.

5.4 Acts of Union, Elizabethan theatre, and the early industrialization

Between 1535 and 1542, English parliamentary measures were known as the Laws in Wales Act (also the "Acts of Union"). The English government's underlying language ideology suggested that English should replace Welsh, and the policy that followed asked for English to be used in all legal matters and that English should be the official language of Wales. Thus, monoglot users of Welsh were barred from legal courts and administrative activity unless they learnt English (Janet Davies 1993: 23). The Welsh Marches were dissolved, as was the remaining Principality of Wales, thereby annexing Wales into England proper.

This created a new period in the political history of Wales as well as in the history of the Welsh language. The diglossia was deepened into an official division of roles, English being the unequivocal High domain language while Welsh remained in vigorous use in the Low domain; though stripped of any public or administrative functions, it still fulfilled literary and religious ones. Indeed, the religious aspect of Welsh usage was perhaps what led to its longevity of use, with Welsh being the first non-state European language to complete and print its own translation of the Bible in 1588 (Williams 1990: 21).

During the Tudor period, the profitable venture of London continued to entice Welsh people. They attended English universities, studied law and became tradesmen (Lloyd 2010: 59). Owen (1962: 68) writes that "there was hardly one sphere of [trading] activity into which Welshmen did not penetrate". They became an integral part of the community, distinguishable perhaps only by their use of English. The Welsh language had a widespread distribution amongst the London Welsh, with non-Welsh Londoners likely recognizing the odd Welsh lexical item (Bartley & Richards 1947: 40, cited in Lloyd 2010: 60). On the other hand, some of the Welsh in London were critical of their compatriots who chose to abandon their Welsh usage in favour of the prestige, preferment or power associated with a Standard London English. One Welsh person, Gruffydd Robert, notes that "you will find some people, who as soon as they see the Severn, or the bell-towers of Shrewsbury, and once hear an Englishman say 'Good Morrow', they begin to let their Welsh fall away" (cited in Morgan 1966: 14).

Although it cannot be determined how removed these Welsh were from the Welsh language, some sources cited in Owen (1962: 60) indicate that the Welsh were very self-conscious about their English speech, with some even perceiving it as a disadvantage or physical disability. In 1598, a Captain Thomas Madryn apologized for his "false [accented] English" to the Earl of Essex: "If I have in anywise offended you, either in speaking false English or otherwise in my simple manner of speech, I beseech you to consider that I am a Welshman" (Williams 1987:

464). Such a remark by a Welsh person may have been spurred on by cultural attitudes. One anonymous English writer associated WelE with mental disabilities caused by cultural and even racial differences (Blank 1996: 130), whilst a seventeenth-century source said the Welsh in Abergavenny could not speak English "without corruption from [their] mother tongue", stating the accent was full of "vicious pronunciation [and] idiotisms" therefore being an "infection" upon England (cited in Williams 1987: 465).

It should come as little surprise that WelE speakers were then easy targets of early English language purists who sought to "improve" (i.e. level or standardize) linguistic features of dialect speakers. In 1603, the Welsh from the former Marches and London had come into contact with this form of Anglicization. (Blank 1996: 128). Though efforts were made to ensure that political and legal written representation was denied to Welsh language speakers, forcing many to outwardly seek education in English, Welsh language usage remained dominant in most Welsh areas, creating a community of Welsh people who wrote in English, yet spoke in Welsh (Blank 1996: 131). Ultimately, such language planning led to transfer between the two languages, and consequently, to more WelE speakers. Although the purpose of English language ideologies had been to convert Welsh language users to English language users *and* to eradicate dialectal features of WelE, the unexpected result was that the variety was catapulted into then-mainstream entertainment: that of Early Modern Elizabethan theatre.

Despite the lack of worth some of the Welsh felt about their English speech, playwrights from England put WelE to use in many plays (Lloyd 2010: 61), and such representations are the quintessential description of the variety during this era. Many other foreign varieties were transcribed by playwrights; whether French or Dutch, accented speech served the purpose of providing local colour and realism to the multicultural urban centre (Griffiths 2010: 111). Celtic (i.e. non-Anglic) characters were common, and during the Elizabethan era, Welsh characters far exceeded representations of the Irish and Scottish (Lloyd 2010: 61). For Griffiths (2010: 116), the singling out of the Welsh fulfilled two reasons. First, the cadence and musicality of the accents was "amusing" to London audiences and drew in audiences, and second, depicting WelE as "nonsense" fulfilled the underlying language ideology of the era: that WelE and other varieties were exemplars of "poor English".

The principal text of this era that used WelE features was William Shakespeare's *Henry V* (1599), which featured the comedic Welsh captain Fluellen. The representation chiefly "relies on ethnic humour" with dialect jokes and comic stereotyping (Powers 1994: 120). German (2009: 34) argues that Shakespeare's representation of WelE was remarkably close to then-contemporary records, and to ridicule it as "unrealistic" or dismiss it as "stage Welsh" is not wholly justified. He continues that Shakespeare "was a much better dialectologist than most people might believe today" (Powers 1994: 120). Indeed, several of the linguistic features match those used by Ieuan ap Hywel Swrdwal. We should not forget, however, that Shakespeare did utilize the dialect for comedic purposes. A key scene from *Henry V* concerns Fluellen's translation of the name Alexander the Great from the Welsh *Alexander Fawr* to "Alexander the Pig" [Big]. When corrected, he responds: "Why, I pray you, is not pig great? The pig, or the great, or the mighty, or the huge, or the magnanimous, are all one reckonings, save the phrase there is a little variations" (Shakespeare 1599: Act 4, Scene 7). The underlying humour here is that Fluellen understands synonymy, yet does not realize the discrepancies of meaning created by his WelE pronunciation, producing a devoiced bilabial plosive /p/ rather than /b/ (Section 2.5.1). Indeed, this is a North Walian feature that was recorded as late as the twentieth century; therefore, either devoiced bilabials were common in southeast Wales in the sixteenth century, or maybe Shakespeare was taking some artistic liberties.

Fluellen is not always the butt of every joke; in some scenes he offers worldly advice. Shakespeare also approximates several linguistic features of this WelE era including glidal omission (*'orld* 'world') and an alveolarized production of post-alveolar sibilants (*sall* 'shall'). *Henry V* also contains the first documentation of the discourse marker *look you*, a well-known linguistic stereotype of WelE even today. Popularized by Fluellen's character, later playwrights also adopted the discourse marker for Welsh characters, despite the marker also being used by other characters in the play.

Shakespeare's *Merry Wives of Windsor* (1597), too, features examples of WelE, but it is perhaps most notable for its attitudinal metalinguistic commentary regarding the variety. In a scene where two learned men (one Welsh – Sir Hugh Evans, one French – Doctor Caius) argue in English, the English host disarms the combatants, stating: "Let them keep their limbs whole, and hack our English" (Shakespeare 1597: Act 3, Scene 1). This scene suggests that the pretence of the underlying language ideology was in place: to use WelE was to "hack" at "good" English. In another scene, an English character, Falstaff, takes offence to Welsh accented English, he proceeds to mock the WelE user's pronunciation of *cheese* and *butter* concluding with: "Have I liv'd to stand at the taunt of one that makes fritters of English?" (Shakespeare 1597: Act 4, Scene 7).

Shakespeare's representation of WelE was very influential. Many of his contemporaries used the forms he introduced, and several added additional linguistic features, quite likely transcribed from genuine WelE users. Plays which use WelE include Thomas Dekker's *The Welsh Embassador* (1597) and *The Patient Grissill* (1600), Anonymous *Sir John Oldcastle* (1600), Robert Armin's *Two Maids of More-Clacke* (1606), Thomas Middleton's *A Chaste Maid in Cheapside* (1613), and

Ben Jonson's *For the Honor of Wales* (1618). Phonetic respelling was a large focus for playwrights using "theatrical WelE". The most common features are summarized in Table 5.1. For example, along with devoicing bilabial stops, alveolar and velar stops were also devoiced, as were labiodental fricatives and sibilant alveolar fricatives. Other techniques included writing palato-alveolar fricatives as alveolar fricatives, omission of initial glides, and affricate sounds becoming sibilantized alveolar fricatives or palato-alveolar fricatives. For a detailed discussion per text see Jones (2018: 82–96).

Table 5.1: Summary of Elizabethan era Welsh English phonetic respelling

Phonological feature	English English phonemes	Theatrical WelE phonetic respelling	Example quotation
Bilabial, alveolar, and **velar plosives**	Initial /b/, /d/, and /g/	/p/, /t/, /k/	**Prave** (brave)
	Medial or final /p/, /t/, and /k/	/b/, /d/, and /g/	**Tawge** (talk)
Labiodental **Fricative**	Initial and medial /v/	/f/	**Falorous** (valorous)
Sibilant **alveolar fricative** Sibilant **palato-alveolar fricative**	Medial & final /z/ /ʃ/ \<sh\>	/s/ /s/	**Asse** (as) **Welse** (Welsh)
Affricate 1 **Affricate 2**	/tʃ/ \<ch\> /dʒ/ \<j\>	/s/	**Sarles** (Charles) **Sentilman** (gentleman)
	/tʃ/ \<ch\> /dʒ/ \<j\>	/ʃ/ \<sh\>	**Shallenge** (challenge) **Sheshu** (Jesus)
Glides	Initial /w/	Omitted	**Urld** (world)

Because some of these features match Ieuan ap Hywel Swrdwal's fifteenth-century poem (Section 5.3), and others were recorded as late as the twentieth century, it is likely that these playwrights were making accurate linguistic enquiry into the variety, but whether all their recorded features can be validated is uncertain. What we do know is that the popularity of these linguistic forms created a subset of linguistic stereotypes for Elizabethan WelE, many of which were utilized tirelessly over the next few centuries alongside the character stereotype of a "comic" Welsh person (Bartley 1954: 154, 144). New plays that were produced during the 1700s continued to use Elizabethan forms, suggesting that popularity took precedence over realism; indeed, writers added no new linguistic forms to their texts during this period. Examples include Lacy Ryan's *Cobler's Opera*

(1730), John Hippisley's *Journey to Bristol* (1730), Richard Cumberland's *Fashionable Lover* (1772) and Charles Dibdin's *Liberty-Hall* (1785), all of which were more concerned with using an antiquated (possibly erroneous in places) WelE to create comical characters.

Despite the sociopolitical changes and the full-scale Anglicization of the gentry, the language situation changed very little geographically in this period. There was little migration within the country and the advance of English from the east was slow up until the beginning of the industrial era. Pryce (1990) examines Church in Wales Records that contain details on the language of religious service from the eighteenth century, and concludes that the River Usk in southeast Wales formed a language boundary in 1771 (Pryce 1990: 52). Some parishes recorded both English and Welsh speakers, however, Pryce believes that this does not denote large-scale bilingualism but rather the presence of two separate speech communities with odd bilingual parishioners acting as mediators between the speech groups, considering that there is no evidence of a sort of pidgin in Wales (Pryce 1990: 54). Thomas (1994: 96), too, points out that the Welsh gentry acted in a mediator position in the earlier Elizabethan period. As bilingualism continued to be rare, the English language in Wales kept its exonormative status. That is not to say that the English speech along the borders was not in some way affected by both bilingualism and the language shift from Welsh.

Exterior perceptions of WelE users at this time are largely unknown. We do know that one traveller, Rev. Richard Warner, perceived the variety favourably around 1798/1800 (cited in Ellis 1882: 189–190). Speaking of bilingual children in Flintshire, Warner states: "all the children of Flintshire speak English very well, and were it not for a little curl, or elevation of the voice, at the conclusion of the sentence (which has a pleasing effect), one should perceive no difference in this respect between the North Walians and the natives of England." The "little curl" Warner describes likely references the observation of WelE's suprasegmental phonological features (see Section 2.6).

5.5 The language shift

5.5.1 Changes in society

It is remarkable, considering the fate of other Celtic languages in Britain, that although English began to be spoken in parts of Wales in the eighth century, it took over a thousand years for it to become the dominant language.

The dawn of industry in the 1770s had profound long-term effects for the Welsh linguistic and cultural landscape (Pryce 1978: 229–230). Urban settlements were expanding, and in-migration drew rural workers to the coalmining seams in the south; consequently, administration became centralized to the south as well as the northeast close to the English port, Liverpool. Migration to Wales from other European locales contributed to a staggering population growth; indeed, before the First World War, Wales was the only nation outside the U.S. to register net immigration (Williams 1985: 178). Between 1770 and 1851, the population soared from 500,000 to 1,188,914. By 1911, it was 2,442,041 (Jenkins 1998: 1; statistics from Jones 1998). John Davies (1993: 322–323) argues that Wales also saw great emigration to England and the Americas in this time and therefore suggests that the growth in population likely corresponds with a decrease in death-rate and increase in birth-rate and quantity of offspring, being spurred on by the confidence in economic prospects.

The linguistic situation was understandably complex, and there is still much we have to learn about it. Jenkins (1998: 11) describes the South Wales coalfield as a "huge, complex, amorphous, even chaotic, sprawl of intensely divergent linguistic communities". By the closure of the nineteenth century, a paradoxical linguistic situation had occurred that saw the actual number of Welsh speakers reach an all-time high (below 600,000 in 1801 to 977,366 in 1901), yet the proportion of the population speaking Welsh begin to fall (95% in 1801 to 44.6% in 1911) (Jenkins 1998: 3). Perhaps most damaging to the survival of Welsh was the sudden decline in monolingual speakers. In less than twenty years monoglot Welsh speakers declined from 30.4% in 1891 to 15.1% in 1901 and to 8.7% in 1911. At the start of the twentieth century, the majority (55.2%) of the population living in Wales were English monoglots, with the remainder being bilingual (35.9%). The bilingualism became widespread; Welsh users learnt English, and monoglot English users learnt Welsh to communicate with their co-workers. This is particularly evidenced in that, at this time of increasing English usage, Welsh periodical publications also abounded.

Besides the Industrial Revolution's notable effects on the language situation, another significant event that led to rapid Anglicization was the 1847 publication of the *Reports of the Commissioners of Inquiry into the State of Education in Wales* (attributed in Welsh as "The Treachery of the Blue Books", Roberts 1996: 190), an action that was instrumental in turning popular opinion against Welsh usage. The earlier part of the nineteenth century saw many civil unrests in South Wales, where the working class revolted against various institutional organizations that had cut wages and dismissed workers. Industrial and rural areas of South Wales from West Wales to eastern Newport witnessed mining strikes, protests and even riots. Pressured with the development of the political movement of Chartism and the "Newport rising" riots, English commentators believed one solution to remedy social disaffection would be to provide a more thorough English language education, whilst critically side-lining the importance of Welsh. For English commissioners, "English not only emphasized the official status of Wales as incorporated into, and subordinate to, England, it was also perceived as the means by which English culture and civilization could be internalized" (Roberts 1996: 175).

Interesting to this discussion on the emerging WelE variety is that in the report, the Commissioners made clear their linguistic prejudices even against the phonological quality of this new "Welsh" English. The classroom recital of English material is likened by one commissioner as "a Welsh screech which seems expressly devised to annihilate all chance of expression or modulation of tone" (cited in Roberts 1996: 187). The conclusion was that the Welsh language influence was a barrier to "progress" for the Welsh. To quote the commissioners' report (as cited in Roberts 1996: 185):

> the Welsh language is a drawback to Wales, and a manifold barrier to the moral progress and commercial prosperity of the people. It is not easy to over-estimate its evil effects [...] Good schools would remove ... this disastrous barrier to all moral improvement and popular progress in Wales.

Later into the century, the educational reform of 1870 made English-medium education compulsory, although free for all at the elementary level, and Welsh usage was banned from classrooms; those found speaking it were subject to the infamous Welsh Not, a humiliating placard placed around their necks (although its infamy likely outranks any sort of widespread use; Janet Davies 1993: 48–49). The combined impact of the above developments would lead to English becoming the majority language by the census of 1911, when Welsh speakers would fall from 49.9 per cent in 1901 to 43.5 per cent 1911 (Janet Davies 1993: 56). This period marks the establishment of "new" Wales – industrial and urbanizing, with its administration and population centring in the southeast – and the birth of Welsh English as a nativized variety.

5.5.2 Writers' use of Welsh English

Features of WelE were rare in personal letters and legal documents, as the bilingual Welsh used StE as their model for writing in English (thereby reducing phonological, lexical, and morphosyntax features), but some features nevertheless made it to written documents, likely covertly. Thomas (1994: 110–111) quotes a letter written by a W. Davies in 1826, which features some structural features affected by Welsh.

(112) "I am *against* you to *come*"
cf. 'wyf yn *erbyn* ichwi *ddod*' (lit. am(-I) *against* for-you *come*)

(113) "I *think* to be at Newtown..."
cf. 'wyf yn *meddwl* bod yn...' (lit. am(-I) 'in' *think/expect/intend* be in...)

Paulasto (2006: 16) examines further the Voelas Estate correspondence from Anglesey, including writings that contain short notes in Welsh English. They differ stylistically from personal letters, being brief notes or marginalia written between farmhands and estate owners. Some of her examples feature nonstandard agreement:

(114) "...my later neighbours there *knows* this..."
"...I suppose the landlord and tenant together *reaps* the benefit." (C 782–3)

Another example potentially results from Welsh language contact: in Welsh, existential sentences are formed using an existential form of the verb BOD 'be' (here *mae* 'is'), which may have led to the lack of existential *there* in English. Example (115) also features article omission:

(115) "All is finished inside but painting , roof is on the chaff house"
cf. '*mae* to ar y tŷ' (lit. is roof on the house)

The nineteenth century saw the prominent beginnings of the Welsh writing in English movement (otherwise known as Anglo-Welsh literature). With literacy in the English language increasing in Wales, WelE users, like the fifteenth-century poet Ieuan ap Hywel Swrdwal before them, were beginning to represent their regional English speech in writing. Identifying WelE forms present in writing before the nineteenth century was difficult largely because Welsh writers of English often clung to the English written standard. Garlick & Mathias (1982: 36) comment upon this, concluding that this meant that a lot of writing was "the English of the Welsh professional class".

Bilingualism affected writers and poets' linguistic identities and written styles, and the Welsh were beginning to recognize English as a language of Wales. Ieuan Ddu (John L. Thomas, 1795–1871), a Carmarthen schoolmaster, argued in 1867 that English *was* a language of Wales (Garlick & Mathias 1982: 35). Ddu's writing reflected this, as lexis borrowed from Welsh often featured in his English verse. In his poem *Harry Vaughan*, Ddu created a rhythmic coupling that rhymed English *history*, with Welsh *Llyfr du*, a couplet that only works if the English speaker also knows Welsh colour-adjectives:

(116) A place that once could boast, **Saith** history / [Seven history]
A castle proud which kept the **Llyfr Du**. [Black book, pronounced: /diː/, not /duː/]
(in Garlick & Mathias 1982: 111)

Ruthin-based Thomas Hughes (1818–1865) similarly used Welsh lexis within his English poetry. In *A Cheese for the Archdeacon*, Hughes uses two Welsh phrases, perhaps demonstrating the lexical borrowing in his speech community: *bara a chaws* 'bread and cheese' and *chroesaw*, a phonetic respelling of *croeso* 'welcome'. Rather than English playwrights misappropriating WelE usage, Welsh people used what they knew of WelE to form a new "literary dialect", thus handing WelE depiction back to the Welsh.

The first novelist who used WelE literary dialect was T.J.L. Prichard in *The Adventures and Vagaries of Twm Shon Catti* (1828). Not only was it the first to feature WelE, but Prichard's *Twm Shon Catti* was the first English language novel of Welsh origin to be published (Mathias 1987: 65; Knight 2004: 8). Prichard was from the Welsh borders, and he was fascinated with English outlaw folk tradition, taking it upon himself to write a Welsh outlaw analogue from Welsh folk tales of the sixteenth century. Evans and Knight (2011: 91–93) consider Prichard's work a "major text" in the canon of Welsh writing in English; even if it is chronologically distinct from the canon's later works (see Section 5.6), it heralded the incoming potency of Anglophone culture in Wales.

Prichard's preface indicates his awareness of both linguistic inquiry, helping us to understand the method behind his writing technique. His chief concerns were that non-Welsh writers mispronounced and mistranscribed phonemic inventory used in Welsh speech communities (whether Welsh or English). Prichard notes that London playwrights were mispronouncing the eponymous Welsh highwayman, and that it was his duty to make amends (Prichard 1828: 3).

Lexically, Prichard had an awareness of the Welsh loans that were present in the English-speaking community. For example, he uses the endearment term *vach*, *ystavell* 'floor', and *eisteddvod*, a Welsh festival, phonetically respelling the Welsh <f> (/v/) to English orthography <v>. Also present are words that were recorded in Wales and its borders in later systematic surveys (e.g. EDD, SAWD). One is *bwlch* 'gap', later recorded in Mid-Wales and Dyfed (the setting of *Twm Shon Catti*), and others are found in EngE varieties (and present in later WelE surveys) too, such as *tump* 'hill', *shift* 'chemise', and *sidling* 'shimmying'. Prichard even used forms that do not appear in surveys, such as *rusties* 'drunkards', and *weazon-faced* 'wheezy-faced'. And, grammatically, Prichard is the first writer of WelE to capture in writing a grammatical staple for future writers of WelE: exclamative *there* ("There's an impious rascal, for you!" Prichard 1828: 50; see 3.4.4).

Prichard's text also highlights the sociolectal attitudes of his era (1790–1820). In one skit, Twm shifts his speech to a working class register of WelE to mock the naiveté of the Welsh gentry, for example: "Twm answered [the Welsh gentleman] in broken English, imitating the dialect of the lower class" (Prichard 1828: 218), suggesting that Twm (i.e. Prichard) viewed several class-divisions in the usage of WelE: lower-class, his own variety, and an "upper-class". Prichard viewed this lower-class English, that takes the form of Shakespeare's stage Welsh, as "broken", possibly inferring commentary upon Prichard's opinion that earlier non-Welsh writers had done the dialect disservice in writing.

The next important depictions of WelE in fictive texts were those of Amy Dillwyn and Allen Raine, two women who though built upon previous conventions, set the foundations for Welsh writing in English fiction. Both novelists aimed to depict the variety of WelE that was forming in west Wales bilingual communities (Gramich 2008). Inspired by George Eliot's *Middlemarch*, Dillwyn's *The Rebecca Rioter* ([1880] 2008) was to be a "real novel, about real people", their "racy slang" included (Painting 1987: 72–75).

Although implied in-text that all speech in the novel was Welsh, it was "translated" by Dillwyn from Welsh into a WelE proxy, the kind Dillwyn professed to have heard. Called a "striking […] experiment" by Gramich, it thus represented the qualities of the early contact variety of WelE around west Wales.

Like in Prichard's work, both exclamative *there* and focus fronting were present, with Dillwyn recording some grammatical forms that would later show up in dialect surveys such as the use of *us* in the subject position ("suppose if us was to take it", Prichard 1828: 33) as well as habitual *do* and *as* as a relative pronoun ("there was a boy here as was very like what you do say", Prichard 1828: 52).

Raine further developed Dillwyn's method, writing her dialogue with her own experience with Welsh, English, and the emerging contact variety. Indeed, Mathias (1987: 7–8) describes the dialogue in *Queen of the Rushes* ([1906] 1998) as "an advance on the efforts of previous writers [from Wales]". Gramich (1998: 7) notes that Raine "[balanced] on that bridging hyphen between a Welsh Wales which she knew first hand and an Anglicized or English reading public".

Raine's discourse featured familiar and newly attested literary dialect usages for both lexis (e.g. *whintell* 'wooden basket', *ach-y-fi* 'expression of disgust') and grammar (e.g. focus fronting), and she left many Welsh words for concepts "untranslated" in discourse, a likely testament to the shifting language situation. To avoid "reader resistance" (see Toolan 1992) or opaqueness in her text, Raine was the first WelE writer to provide a comprehensive paratextual glossary detailing 28 terms.

Similar to Shakespearean phonetic respelling (see 5.4), Raine also used extensive phonetic respelling to capture the sounds of her contact variety. Respellings such as *pwr* 'poor' and *fforwel* 'farewell' match their Welsh language equivalents, whilst *dono* and *oction* render RP diphthong /əʊ/ as a half-close back vowel /ɒ/, a sound that matches *SAWD* records (See section 2.4.1.: FACE/STAY and GOAT/SNOW). Table 7.5 documents some of these items, noting their standardized spelling, followed by phonetic respelling of the standard (by way of RP) and a speculative dialectal representation.

Table 7.5: List of phonetic respellings in Raine ([1880] 1998)

Respelling	Standard form	RP IPA	Dialectal IPA
Well, I **dono** (p. 29)	Dunno	/dʌnəʊ/	/dɒnɒ/
Oction at poor Jinni Owen's to-day (p. 31)	Auction	/ɔːkʃʌn/	/ɒkʃʌn/
Hai (p. 32)	Hi	/haɪ/	/haɪː/
Oh **fforwel!** (p. 43)	Farewell	/feəwɛl/	/fɔːwɛl/
Alreit, alreit! (p. 49)	Alright	/ɔːlraɪt/	/ɔːlreɪt/
Pwr fellow (p. 60)	Poor	/pɔː/	/puːə/
I told **mestress** (p. 213)	Mistress	/mɪstrɪs/	/mɛstrɪs/ or /mɛstrɛs/

5.6 From the twentieth to the twenty-first century

The primary developments in the twentieth century have been the continued decline of the Welsh language, particularly in the rural areas which were sheltered from Anglicization earlier, and the rise of the Anglo-Welsh ethnolinguistic community, bringing questions of nationalism and identity to the fore in politics and culture.

Several factors led to the dominance of English in Wales during the twentieth century. First, the Great War was devastating for the Welsh economy, and resultant class wars in the coalfields led to unemployment and emigration (Thomas 1987: 437; cited in Aitchison & Carter 2000: 38). Janet Davies (1993: 59) states that perhaps some 390,000 people left Wales for southeast England and the Midlands. After this, the industrial valleys became bastions of Marxism, catering to nonconformist and liberalist Welsh traditions; here, many adopted English, which gave workers the possibility to unite labour movements across the country (Jones 1980). We must also consider the growth of mass media in the 1920s and 1930s, which aided English proliferation in the nation. English newspapers outnumbered weekly or monthly Welsh language papers, and the BBC's English language programming started its broadcasting from Cardiff and Swansea (Janet Davies 1993: 60).

Census figures show that the decline of Welsh halted at a little under 20 per cent of the nation's population in the 1980s and the numbers of speakers are now relatively level. The end result is a language maintenance situation and a bi-cultural country, as described in Chapter 1 above. Varieties of Welsh English are spoken throughout, but the term itself is not well-known, nor do the Welsh necessarily recognize WelE as a distinct English dialect although they do recognize the Welsh accent, as discovered in the interviews conducted by Penhallurick and Paulasto (see Section 1.5). Towards the end of the twentieth century, however, lay observers and users of the dialect began to identify, or enregister, several linguistic features of the dialect. Agha (2007: 81) defines the process as "performable signs [becoming] recognized (and regrouped) as belonging to distinct, differentially valorized semiotic registers by a population". This led to several enregistered features dominating popular media, early examples of which are John Edwards' *Talk Tidy* books (1985, 1986).

As will be seen below, the variety begins to see greater depiction in modes of fiction literature and film during the twentieth century, through the stylistic mode of "literary dialect". Although writers, actors, and producers may not explicitly know the term Welsh English, many have clear conceptions of the words, grammar, and phonology that constitutes WelE.

As regards the present-day relationship between the two languages of Wales, Welsh as the indigenous minority language holds a high level of prestige and national significance. It has received administrative support through several Language Acts over the past century, and today, its "official" status parallels that of English with bilingual language policy encouraged by the Welsh government (Welsh Government 2012). The Welsh language is also widely supported by the people, although symbolic support and everyday use may not go hand-in-hand (Durham & Morris 2016: 10–12). English remains the first language of over eighty per cent of the Welsh people, hence being the language of the majority. Yet considering the history of the two languages, acceptance of English as a cultural and historical language of Wales in its own right can be a charged topic (Coupland and Thomas 1990; Penhallurick 1993, 1998). The language attitude studies examined in Section 1.5 nevertheless indicate that Welsh English, too, is seen as a medium of national and linguistic identity.

The regional variation within WelE began to receive systematic attention in the 1960s, notably with David Parry's *Survey of Anglo-Welsh Dialects*, which commenced in 1968. The survey focused on residents of 60 years and above, thereby examining WelE variation as it existed from the beginning of the twentieth century (see Chapter 6). When compared with Orton's *Survey of English Dialects*, evidence from the Gwent network (a.k.a. Monmouthshire; Parry 1985c: 83–90) showed that many lexical, phonological, and grammatical items were shared with neighbouring western English counties, which indicated a longstanding relationship between eastern WelE varieties and the west of England. For example, *r*-colouring (see subsection 2.4.1) in the region likely stems from the southwest Midlands and southwest England, and the intrusive initial /j/ in, for example, *ears* [jœːz], common throughout South Wales, arrived in WelE from southwestern dialects as early as the late medieval era (Parry 1985c: 85). There is also lexis that point to this relationship along the borderland, for example *dap* 'bounce' and *gammy-handed* 'left-handed' arrived from the Southwest and *tine* 'fork prong' and *fitchet* 'polceat' from the West Midlands.

Parry (1985c: 85) concludes that:

> distinctively English influences on the sounds – such as R-colouring – appear only on the eastern borders. The chief influences on lexis and grammar are those of the neighbouring English [dialects], a good deal of linguistic material having been imported from Somerset and from the south-west midlands.

Such influences led scholars such as Thomas (1984: 178) to hypothesize that this close proximity to England would result in southern Welsh Englishes eventually shedding all Welsh linguistic influence, adopting West Midlands and South-West English features as a result. This prediction has of yet not come to pass, likely because the cultural identity of the Anglo-Welsh is very much tied to the dialect (see also Paulasto 2016).

From the earliest years of the twentieth century, the Anglo-Welsh have fought to have their variety of English legitimized. One of the prominent means for this was through representation in English media such as novels and film. The salient variety of Welsh English that dominated the southern coalfield began to gain recognition in its speech community. Following in the wake of early Welsh writers of English such as T.J. Prichard, Amy Dillwyn, and Allen Raine (Section 5.5.2), a movement that literary critics dub "The First Flowering" introduced further methods through which the WelE variety could be represented. This meant not only writing in a literary dialect but also providing metalinguistic insights into the changing speech communities.

One early example was Jack Jones, a Merthyr-born novelist, public speaker and politician, who in 1935 published *Black Parade*, a text situated in Merthyr between 1905 and 1926. Jones expressed interest in capturing the Anglicization of South Wales, in particular its "hybrid culture and [its] peculiar linguistic habits" (Edwards 1974: 20). Like Dillwyn's approach, the novel's dialogue is implied at first to be Welsh, translated into Welsh English for the reader. As the novel progresses, Jones provides metalinguistic observations from his characters that there has been a language shift from Welsh to English throughout the younger generation and across various modes both written and spoken. The character Saran laments:

> [the new generation] thought differently, and talked differently, in the English tongue. And they read books and papers – couldn't live without the Merthyr Express and The Echo – and shouting themselves hoarse and in English at the football matches on Saturday afternoons. (Jones [1935] 2009: 205)

Other writers were intrigued by specific domains of language use in WelE during this period. One such writer was Glyn Jones. Just one decade before systematic dialect surveying began (i.e. SAWD etc.), Jones incorporated a lifetime of dialect enquiry into his novel *Island of Apples* ([1965] 1992), recording both dialectal usages and even schoolyard sociolectal ones. In a 1992 edition of the text, Jones even provides a paratextual glossary in the novel's preface, highlighting 35 forms, some of which are of Welsh origin, others with EngE etymologies, positioning Jones as an accomplished lay observer of WelE's lexicography. Ron Berry's *So Long Hector Bebb* (1970) also depicts the southern variety. Unique to Berry's literary dialect is not only his depiction of fourteen unique idiolects of the variety, but also first-person commentary about how the WelE community perceived their own variety and other related varieties. For example, one character metalinguistically observes of another that: "his voice sounds [...] loud and fast, the way they gab [talk] up the valleys" (Berry 1970: 29). Similar lay contemplations on the variety are evident in Joe Dunthorne's *Submarine* (2008), where protagonist Oliver Tate provides numerous prescriptivist comments of the variety. The character, whose parents are from England, also focuses upon concerns of linguistic prestige, recognising that the WelE speech community is an in-group that he does not belong to, as he is bullied for not sharing the accent of his classmates.

What we can surmise from such commentary is that laymen during this period in the history of WelE began to write about the way in which the variety had become endonormative by offering metalinguistic commentary on generational language shift, sociolectal or regional differences, and ideas of covert prestige. In creating their renditions of WelE literary dialects, many of the aforementioned writers as well as others (for a comprehensive list and detailed description per text, see Jones 2018) utilize a subset of familiar forms that we can consider to be highly enregistered, that is, "enshrined" and overtly recognisable within the community. Whether lexical, grammatical, or phonological, the forms were likely to be familiar to Welsh readers. Lexically, Welsh-derived words were common, such as endearment term *bach/fach*, expression of disgust *ach-y-fi*, *mam* 'mother', and *cwtch* 'cuddle'. Although many lexical items are English in origin, such as affirmative *aye*, adjective *tidy* 'decent', verbs *mitch/mouch/mwch* 'to truant' and *tamping* 'raging', they are distinctive of WelE (see Section 4.3.). For grammar and discourse features, by far the most common linguistic forms present in this literary dialect movement were exclamative *there* (e.g. "There's ungrateful, Mr. Davies"; Jones [1965] 1992: 30) and focus fronting (e.g. "Pretty to watch, Sammy was"; Berry [1970] 2006: 7). Other salient features include discourse markers *see* and *like*, as well as use of *as* as a relative pronoun (e.g. "They'll be saying as I'm stuck up"; Jones [1935] 2009: 94).

These Anglo-Welsh "dialect artists" also attempted to render WelE phonology in writing. Common methods include treating the RP diphthong /əʊ/ as a monophthong /ɒ/ or /ɔː/ (e.g. rendering *postcards* as *posscards*, i.e. /pəʊskɑːdz/ to /pɒskɑːdz/ (Goodwin [1936] 2008: 15), dropping the glottal fricative /h/, (e.g. *home* as *ome*, Goodwin [1936] 2008: 107) and spelling the WelE diphthong /ɪu/ as <ew> or <iw> (e.g. *you* as *yew*, Dunthorne 2008: 149; see *Tuesday* in Section 2.4.1).

Furthermore, it should be noted that the southern Valleys variety of WelE was not the only variety represented in literature. Authors such as Margiad Evans and Geraint Goodwin also attempted to write the WelE variety common along and across the Welsh border with England. Both Evans and Goodwin utilized lexis, grammar, and phonology familiar from their southern contemporaries, such as Welsh loanwords and grammatical structures, they also incorporated forms that the *EDD* and later *SAWD* attributed to the Welsh-English border counties. For example, Evans in *Country Dance* [1932] 2006) included the verb *tan* 'strike' (Evans [1932] 2006: 78), as well as archaic features of grammar such as 2sg pronoun *thou* and the respective inflectional verb form *art*. Goodwin in *The Heyday in the Blood* [1936] 2008) likewise uses 2sg objective pronoun *thee* and 3sg negative contractions *inna* '(he) is not' and *dunna* '(he) does not' (Goodwin [1936] 2008: 152–153) – forms that are recorded in *SAWD* in the Welsh borders (Parry 1999: 108–109, 114, 116).

Indeed, when compared to the material collected in later systematic surveys, it becomes evident that the fiction writers who chose to use WelE used it with some degree of accuracy. Unsurprisingly, there are also linguistic items in this body of work hitherto undiscovered in dialect surveys. From Prichard's *rusties* 'drunkards' and *weazon-faced* 'wheezy-faced', to Goodwin's *robin-run-the-hedge cleaver plant* and Glyn Jones' *horse-tods* 'horse manure', writers were able to record such items because they were keen observers of the variety's usage. By the twentieth century, at the latest, speakers of WelE especially in the south recognized the features of their dialects, and a process of enregisterment was arguably underway.

With the emergence of film came another medium through which creative writers could display an awareness, appreciation and/or application of WelE. Although there have been many WelE-speaking characters in minor roles (some portrayed with contrived performances), some of the best-received Welsh films have featured attested users of WelE in prominent roles, providing audiences with an insight into English language speech communities from Wales.

Early films such as Charles Frend's BAFTA-nominated *A Run For Your Money* (1949) (section 7.1) prominently placed two Welsh protagonists at the forefront of his comedy and ran the gamut of attested lexical and grammatical forms, whilst phonological features were authentically represented through the casting of Donald Houston and Meredith Edwards. Later, films such as J. Lee Thompson's *Tiger Bay* (1959) and Andrew Grieve's *On the Black Hill* (1987) offered audiences insight in the usage of specific WelE varieties such as Cardiff English and Borders WelE respectively, but it was not until Kevin Allen's *Twin Town* (1997) that southern Welsh cinemagoers had a quintessential "Welsh" film. Set in Swansea, the dark comedy uses the Swansea variety of WelE, performed largely with a southern Welsh cast (bar the protagonist twins' actors, who are natives of North Wales).

Filmmakers use similar lexico-grammatical forms in their screenplays as novelists in literature, thus making similar linguistic observations about the variety. Lexically, *bach, mam,* and *aye* are common, the vocative *mun/man*, focus fronting, invariant question tags *is it/isn't it*, and exclamative *there* are all common markers of "dialect" in the filmic sphere.

Of course, film being a visual medium offers a new means in which WelE can be defined for viewers both familiar and unfamiliar with the variety. Fascinatingly, paralinguistic gestures are used in both *Twin Town* (1997) and Christopher Monger's *The Englishman Who Went Up A Hill...* (1995). *Twin Town* uses a paralinguistic gesture, hands crossed across the chest, for the noun *cwtch* 'cuddle', and *Englishman* elaborates the adjective *twp* 'stupid' with the speaker's index finger pointed at his temple.

5.7 Changes in progress

Like many languages and varieties, Welsh English is in a process of change. Continued in-migration to large urban areas like Cardiff and Swansea brings along new linguistic features. The "conservative rural" data from Parry's SAWD is now long out of date, and the changes that can be witnessed in spoken English in different parts of the country are of ongoing interest.

There are no large-scale studies on diachronic developments in the phonology of WelE. However, Podhovnik's (2010) apparent-time study on segmental features in Neath English indicates that, if anything, phonological features characteristic of WelE (e.g. monophthong /eː/ in FACE/STAY and semi-vowel realizations /auwə/ and /aijə/ in POWER and FIRE) are strengthened or at least maintained in her youngest informants' speech. Hejná (2015: 248–249), too, observes that pre-aspiration of consonants is more frequent and longer among her younger than older Aberystwyth informants. Rowan Campbell's (forthc.) PhD research charts ongoing accent and dialect change in Cardiff English. This area of WelE sociolinguistics is however in need of further study.

As regards morphosyntax, some of the earlier research (notably Paulasto 2006, 2016) has uncovered apparent-time changes that indicate levelling in Welsh contact-induced features: younger generations of speakers are employing, for example, focus fronting and the habitual progressive less frequently than elderly speakers and in forms and functions which approach general vernacular BrE. The apparent-time (and, as regards the Rhondda, real-time) research into the dialect grammar of WelE is continued in the present volume, specifically in Llandybie English and on those features which are frequent enough to enable the analysis. All Welsh-induced features experience a drop in use from the oldest towards the younger age groups in Llandybie, which is unsurprising considering the socioeconomic and educational backgrounds of the speakers as well as the societal changes enabling StE and spoken EngE input in all corners of the UK. However, apart from the extended progressive usages, there is some indication that the youngest speaker group is maintaining WelE dialect features in some forms or contexts. Extended definite article use is quite frequent with names of languages (subsection 3.2), and embedded inversion rises slightly in WH-questions (3.4.1). Focus fronting, too, is maintained by young WelE speakers (3.4.2). Extended uses of the preposition *with* are declining in the most "Welsh" POSSESSIVE and INTEGRAL/PROXIMATE functions but there is a sharp increase among the youngest speakers in the function IN ONE'S CASE, not far removed from the INTEGRAL/PROXIMATE (3.4.5). The invariant tags *isn't it* and *is it* are also on the rise among young Llandybie informants, accompanied by increasing use of the form *innit* and the accord-building function of the tag (4.4.1). Together with the maintenance of phonological characteristics of WelE, these findings are indicative of a level of covert prestige and regional or national linguistic significance of WelE; hence the dialect is not likely to merge with neighbouring EngE dialects any time soon (see also Paulasto 2016).

Lexical changes in WelE are examined in Chapter 4, which is in fact one of the few descriptons of this topic in existence. Penhallurick (2013) is another source drawing together evidence on lexical change based on the survey data in SAWD and *Voices*. Lexicon is the most salient domain of language and hence changes and usages are also observed and reported by the dialect speakers themselves. Chapter 4 indicates that there are relatively few Welsh words in general use in WelE; of these, for example, *cariad*, *cwtch* and *hiraeth* have clear and identifiable cultural value. Many other Welsh dialect words, however, are regionally restricted or used primarily by older generations of speakers, and thus, possibly fading out of use (e.g. *bach, bopa, Duw!*). The same goes for the vast majority of English dialect words recorded in SAWD (e.g. Parry 1999). On the other hand, specific English language items, including *lush, tamping, mun*, and *tidy*, have been found to represent present-day Welsh English in TV programmes and social media (e.g. Durham 2015).

A recent trend of change which can be witnessed across different domains of language involves the increasing impact of Estuary English. Certain features emerging especially in the southeast of the country can be traced back to London. These include TH-fronting (e.g. *think* [fɪŋk], *with* [wɪv]) discussed in subsection 2.5.2, the structural and discourse-pragmatic alignment of the Welsh invariant tag *isn't it* with *innit* (4.4.1) and words such as *chav* and *bruv* becoming a part of the WelE lexical inventory (4.3.1). The change is gradual and clearly spreading geographically from the southeast, hence indicating that Estuary English continues to extend its sphere of influence towards the north and west, and across the border from England to Wales.

There is no question that globalization is also having significant effects on WelE along with all other varieties of English and hundreds of other languages of the world. The introduction of the internet and electronic communication as well as the influence of audio-visual media have led not only to increased exposure to other varieties of English but also to computer-mediated vernaculars merging with the notion of WelE especially for young people. For example, Jones's (2016b: 30–31) survey of young people's use of dialect in Gwent inadvertently elicited several forms of computer-mediated vernacular initialisms like *WTF* 'what the fuck' and *LMAO* 'laughing my ass off', although it is uncertain whether such forms derived from written lects are part of young people's spoken discourse. It would also be interesting to gain further insight into the impact that AmE is currently having on varieties of WelE.

Although some studies demonstrate that attitudes and perceptions towards WelE were mixed during the late twentieth century, the variety has since gained prestige amongst other British varieties (subsection 1.5.1), as also shown by a contemporary study into WelE language attitudes by Durham (2016), utilizing metalinguistic evidence from Twitter. This upward social prestige regarding WelE dovetails into its acceptance, interest, and visibility on the world stage. We will turn to other contemporary representations of the dialect in fiction and metalinguistic commentaries for some further discussion on this. Although for much of cinematic history, demand for the Welsh accent on-screen was negligible (and this was not helped by a considerable dearth of Welsh actors), by the twenty-first century the desire for screen-presence of WelE has been changing.

A highly influential contemporary narrative form that has been making use of the variety is the videogame. This relatively young media form has dominated creative industries in the twenty-first century; in 2011 revenues were $55.5 billion with 8.2% increase per year, higher than the film industry's 5.9% (Egenfeldt-Nielsen, Smith & Tosca 2013), demonstrating a significant potential as a mass media product. Here, game developers have not only sought the authenticity of WelE voice-actors for their narratives, but have also invited them to collaboratively shape the stories. One critically acclaimed title was *Assassin's Creed: Black Flag* (2013), a historical pirating adventure with a Swansea-born protagonist (Matt Ryan). When Ryan auditioned and was cast in *Black Flag*, the developers chose to rewrite the story to better suit his Welsh accent; so influential was this decision that the creators were later inundated with gamers worldwide asking to know more about WelE, a variety many were unfamiliar with (Williams 2013).

It should be mentioned in the closing of this chapter that today WelE is also being used to index, or semiotically stand in for, several underlying character stereotypes of the Welsh people. The first is "The Fantastical", a character stereotype that has long been associated with Celtic nations like Wales and Ireland. Literary Romanticists like William Wordsworth made reference to Wales' otherworldly qualities (Jones 2018: 61), whilst twentieth-century fantasy authors such as J.R.R. Tolkien cemented the idea of a "Welsh" elf/fairy by constructing an Elven language largely based on Welsh. Tolkien himself stated that Welsh "seemed to fit the rather 'Celtic' type of legends and stories told of [my Elven] speakers" (Tolkien 1981: 176). Two prominent examples that use a fairy/elven trope in recent videogames are *Ni No Kuni: Wrath of the White Witch* (2013), a fantasy tale that depicts members of a WelE-speaking fairy race as supporting characters (the lead being voiced by Steffan Rhodri), and *Dragon Age II* (2011), where actress Eve Myles plays a subjugated resistance fighter in a community of WelE and IrE-accented Elves. Both actors were headhunted by producers for their accent.

The second stereotype is "The Comic", where WelE as a nonstandard accent (as is often the case with many varieties in the English-speaking world) is contrasted, perhaps discriminatively, with StE to evoke negative qualities (see Lippi-Green 1997 on linguistic discrimination in the media). As seen above, Shakespeare and contemporaries (Section 5.4) used the dialect to generate humour in the Elizabethan period, and today we continue to see similar uses in videogaming narratives. In *Ni No Kuni*, not only are the fairies WelE-accented, but every fairy is a bumbling comedian. Arguably, other videogames like *Timesplitters: Future Perfect* (2005), *Fable III* (2010), and *Star Wars: The Old Republic* (2011) have all used WelE to signify WelE speakers as Comedians.

Although from textual evidences we can discern that the form and representation of WelE has changed greatly over the centuries, some habits associated with WelE, such as linguistic and character stereotyping, have persevered. Nevertheless, by using both historical commentary as well as evidences from fictional texts, this chapter has demonstrated that we today have a more complete picture of the way that the Welsh English dialect has developed during the last six hundred years. There is still much more to be done in this emerging historical field of Welsh English studies.

6 Survey of essential works and resources

In this chapter we provide a guide to the main larger-scale works and resources on Welsh English (WelE) and to a concise selection of the more locally focused studies as well as to some interesting lesser-known publications. In the Welsh context, contemplation of the bonds between language, identity, politics, and policy has produced abundant discussion, but here we focus on research which deals with varieties of spoken English in Wales. For a complete bibliography and webography of all the sources used in the writing of the present book, including those discussed here, please turn to the end of the volume.

6.1 Large-scale works and resources, and national overviews

There have been some national-scale surveys of WelE. The most extensive is the Survey of Anglo-Welsh Dialects (SAWD), directed by David R. Parry between 1968 and 1995.

SAWD was begun in October 1968 at Swansea University, conceived by Parry as an inquiry into the English speech of Wales in the philological tradition and inspired by his experience as a postgraduate student under Harold Orton and Stanley Ellis at Leeds University between 1959 and 1961, and as a fieldworker in Monmouthshire in 1960 for Orton's Survey of English Dialects (SED). As Parry (1975: 1) himself put it: "It is because the editor of the Survey of Anglo-Welsh Dialects was privileged to be a pupil of Professor Orton that the Survey of Anglo-Welsh Dialects exists at all." Parry's choice of the label *Anglo-Welsh* rather than *Welsh English* for his Survey reflects the customary use of the term to refer to the English-speaking community of Wales or to the English language as employed by Welsh speakers and writers, as in phrases such as "Anglo-Welsh literature" – in fact, David Parry's use of it features as a citation in the *OED*'s entry for the term.

The aims and methods of SAWD emulated those of the SED, with the intention being "to provide material for Wales that is directly comparable with that obtained in England" (Parry 1999: 1), a comparison that would include the construction of composite maps from SAWD and SED data. The SAWD questionnaire (Chesters, Upton & Parry: 1968) was a modified version of the Dieth-Orton SED questionnaire (1962), with 33 of the original 1,092 numbered questions edited out, 23 new ones added, and a further 75 amended. Like many of its predecessors in philological dialectology, the questionnaire was lengthy and designed to elicit a large quantity of lexical, grammatical, and pronunciation features. Up to 1982, postgraduate and undergraduate student fieldworkers trained by Parry travelled to all parts of rural Wales to interview and audio-record speakers of WelE, until a network of 90 SAWD localities was chosen from the nearly 120 investigated. The Survey relied on a judgement sample of informants. A handful per locality were sought, the questionnaire being asked once in each locality. Parry (1999: 1) lists the criteria for SAWD's standard informant: "(i) aged over 60; (ii) knowledgeable about agricultural life and work; (iii) not formally educated beyond the age of 15; (iv) resident in the native area without significant interruption; (v) free from speech impediments."

By 1982, two print volumes of data and analysis had already been edited and published by Parry: *The Survey of Anglo-Welsh Dialects*, Vol. 1: *The south-east* (1977), containing material from 34 localities; and *The Survey of Anglo-Welsh Dialects*, Vol. 2: *The south-west* (1979), covering 25 localities. Each volume includes a description of methodology, details of localities and informants, a comprehensive account of the recorded WelE vowels and consonants of the region, a discussion of non-standard features of morphology and syntax, a glossary of non-standard lexis, and a selection of isogloss-and-display-symbol maps showing the geographical distribution of features and variants. The volumes combine a historically framed consideration of the data with the aim of making as much of the elicited basic material as possible available to scholars wishing to use it for their own research, though this can be a painstaking process for researchers used to searchable electronic databases. A third volume following the same format and encompassing 17 northern localities was published in 1991: *The Anglo-Welsh dialects of North Wales* (Penhallurick).

While there has been no SAWD atlas to date, in 1985, in a chapter by Parry in the collection of essays on linguistic geography edited by Kirk, Sanderson and Widdowson, the first composite maps of England and Wales appeared, six in all (Parry 1985a). Another 50 were published (along with 90 maps of Wales only) in Parry's *A grammar and glossary of the conservative Anglo-Welsh dialects of rural Wales* (1999), which was an in-depth overview of all the rural SAWD data. For the first time, a cartographic view of the patterns of regional continuity and difference in features of the traditional WelE and English English dialects was available. (See also *Voices* and Gabmap, below.) This later volume by Parry is important in another way too, for it presents complete sound-systems for each of the 90 localities, and shows the regional distribution of each phonemic unit and its realizations in 144 keywords. In his own history of SAWD (2008), Parry says: "Although the collected material contained no 'minimal pairs' (unless fortuitously), it still seemed worthwhile to attempt a grouping, a systematization, a kind of 'tentatively proposed phonemicization' based on intuition and upon our own observational experience of what sound-differences appear to be phonemically significant to native speakers and what do not." In 2015, Parry finished a typescript which adds further phonetic detail to his modestly designated "tentatively proposed phonemicization" of the full rural network of Anglo-Welsh dialects, including an informative table of the SAWD/SED phonological keywords cross-referenced to John Wells's lexical sets (1982). As yet unpublished, the 2015 typescript was generously given to the authors of the present volume and we draw upon it in our Chapter 2.

A second phase of SAWD was begun in 1985 using a more sociolinguistic methodology to collect material from a number of age-groups in urban areas of Wales. For this purpose, a short phonological questionnaire was compiled by Parry (1985b), and a more casual style was used for the rest of the interview, centred upon discussion of the personal histories of the informants and their perceptions of local speech in relation to other varieties. Four broad age-groups were interviewed in each locality visited: teenagers; 20–30 years old; 30–60 years old; and over 60 years old. In total, 54 informants were interviewed, with ages ranging from 12 to 82. All were natives of the locality in question, and very few had gone through higher education. Total interview time of the resulting audio recordings was nearly 24 hours. The localities were Caernarfon and Wrexham in the north, and Carmarthen and the Grangetown district of Cardiff in the south. The recordings remained unexploited until Heli Paulasto used them in her research on WelE grammar – see Paulasto (2006) discussed below.

The archives of SAWD – including all of the original field transcriptions and surviving analogue audio recordings – are now in the care of Rob Penhallurick. Among those scholars who have consulted the archives for their work are Gary German, Heli Paulasto, and Malcolm Williams, all of whom feature below. In 2008, 502 digital audio transfers from 151 audio compact cassette recordings (dating from 1965–1991) were deposited by Penhallurick at the British Library. These recordings (which include those from urban Wales) can be listened to on site at the BL via the Library's catalogue and a selection, together with transcripts and commentaries by Jonnie Robinson, is available online at the BL's *British accents and dialects* web pages: https://www.bl.uk/british-accents-and-dialects.

The British Library possesses several other audio resources that contain WelE material of value to researchers and students, three of them deriving from national-scale surveys. These are the Millennium Memory Bank (MMB), BBC *Voices*, and the SED.

The MMB was a large oral history project by the BBC, based on recordings made by its local radio stations in the UK of all age-groups in 1998–1999. The authors of the present volume had access to unpublished linguistic commentaries by the BL's Jonnie Robinson on 20 of the MMB localities in Wales. These localities are: Bangor, Bethesda, Llanwnda, and Trefor in the north; Aberhosan and Rhayader in Mid Wales; and Aberbeeg, Aberporth, Brynamman, Cardiff, Cwmfelinfach, Gorseinon, Maerdy, Monmouth, Mumbles, Mynydd-y-Garreg, Newport (Monmouthshire), Resolven, Swansea, and Tremorfa (Cardiff) in the south. The audio recordings can be accessed on site at the BL via the Library's catalogue, and a selection from the Welsh localities together with commentaries is available online at the BL's *British accents and dialects* web pages and via the MMB tab of the *Accents and dialects* page of British Library *Sounds*: https://sounds.bl.uk/Accents-and-dialects.

The BBC *Voices* project originated in the New Media department at BBC Wales. Its aim was to tap into the linguistic and cultural diversity of Britain, making productive use of the BBC's regional resources. Scholars from dialectology and sociolinguistics were consulted, the preliminary discussions taking place in Cardiff. The project offered the opportunity to collect a substantial amount of data in a small period of time – a goal beyond the means of previous national linguistic surveys. By the time the BBC journalists started interviewing informants in 2004, *Voices* had adopted a methodology developed by Clive Upton and others at Leeds and Sheffield Universities (Elmes 2013). Focused on lexis, and informed by the SED questionnaire, this used a set of prompts designed to guide conversations with informants (nearly 1,300 in over 300 locations in total), aiming to create a more informal environment than the traditional field interview. The same set of lexical prompts was used for the online *Voices* Language Lab survey, which by 2006 had received over 62,500 submissions from users.

The *Voices* website was launched in 2004 to coincide with a wave of national and local radio broadcasts (Jaffe 2013: 51). In that they contained links to many local glossaries, the *Voices* web pages were in tune with the long tradition of dialect lexicography, but the centrepiece was cartographic, a series of Word Maps, displaying responses to a selection of the lexical prompts. Although the website stopped being updated in 2014, one can still use its interactive mapping facility, which accesses *Voices* data for the whole of the UK. There is scope to compare the data from Wales with SAWD material, as approximately 50 per cent of the lexical notions targeted by the *Voices* methodology have an equivalent in the SAWD questionnaire. Furthermore, by means of the free web-based application for dialectometry, *Gabmap*, Martijn Wieling and his collaborators at the University of Groningen have developed a website where users can construct linguistic maps of various types based on the *Voices* data.

The *Voices* audio interviews are held at the British Library, where from 2009–2012 the follow-up *Voices of the UK* project catalogued the recordings and the team of Robinson, Gilbert and Herring compiled detailed linguistic descriptions of the majority of interviews for online access via British Library *Sounds*. Audio and commentary are available for 21 Welsh locations: Bangor, Bethesda, Flint, Holyhead, Llangollen, Rhosgadfan, Rhos-on-Sea, and Wrexham in the north; Builth Wells, Newtown, and Tregaron in Mid Wales; and Bonymaen (Swansea), Glyn

Neath, Llanelli, Milford Haven, Newport (Monmouthshire), Pontcanna (Cardiff), Pontypridd, Risca, Talbot Green, and Treorchy in the south. The authors of the present volume had access to the draft unpublished versions of the linguistic descriptions for the Welsh *Voices* locations, including an additional commentary for Splott (Cardiff).

Although the *Voices* recordings focused on elicitation of lexis, 13 of the *Voices of the UK* linguistic descriptions also list all non-standard grammar used by informants in the interviews, and give vowel inventories and notes on non-standard consonants, using standard lexical sets.

And finally, the British Library Sound Archive holds 288 audio recordings from SED localities investigated from the early 1950s to 1974. These are of significance –as are the data and publications of the SED generally – to any scholar wishing to compare the features and regions of WelE with those of English English, but of particular interest are six SED localities in Monmouthshire, which include two where the original fieldwork was done by David Parry in the summer of 1960, Llanfrechfa and Newport, though the audio dates from 1974. The remaining localities are Llanellen, Raglan, Shirenewton, and Skenfrith, all represented by audio from 1955. Linguistic descriptions by Jonnie Robinson and samples of the audio are available online via the SED tab of the *Accents and dialects* page of British Library *Sounds*: https://sounds.bl.uk/Accents-and-dialects.

For her PhD study, Katja Roller compiled and transcribed a corpus of present-day spoken WelE by combining material from the two BBC radio collections, the BBC *Voices* Radio Wales interviews and Welsh-locality recordings from the MMB, and titled it the Radio Wales Corpus (see Roller 2016: 78–87). The first component includes 110 informants born 1923–1989 and 20 hours of speech. The MMB component is smaller, comprising nine hours of recordings and 22 speakers, who are aged 25–35 or 60–70. These are mainly single interviews, in contrast to the *Voices* section, where the number of informants participating in the conversations varies between three and eight. The *Voices* conversations in Roller's corpus comprise c. 191,000 words and the MMB interviews c. 78,000 words, that is, 269,000 in total. Together they represent the present-day WelE dialects spoken in all parts of Wales and all decades of birth from 1920s to 1980s (Roller 2016: 84–85).

Another corpus with a WelE component is the Freiburg English Dialect Corpus (FRED), a database of audio recordings and transcripts in ordinary orthography totalling 300 hours of speech and 2.5 million words of text. The sound recordings were made mainly in the 1970s and 1980s of 432 English-dialect-speaking informants from England, Scotland, and Wales, the majority born before 1920 (see Hernández 2006). The compilers of FRED, Bernd Kortmann and his team, had research on morphosyntactic variation in mind primarily, but the corpus is suited to a range of interests (see Kortmann & Wagner 2005, Szmrecsanyi 2013). There are

11 WelE localities in FRED, four in Denbighshire and seven in Glamorganshire, providing a total of over 110,000 words of text transcription (FRED does not have sound recordings of these interviews). There is an online free-access sampler version of the database, FRED-S, but the WelE material is not at present available via this, which means that one would normally have to be on site at Freiburg in order to access it.

The studies based on FRED usually account for dialect variation across the board in Britain, rather than focusing on Wales in particular. However, insights into the two regional varieties of WelE represented in FRED can be gleaned from Anderwald (2009) and Szmrecsanyi (2013).

A number of other significant collections and corpora can be mentioned here.

The National Museum of History at St Fagans, Cardiff, houses a collection of oral history recordings in WelE as well as Welsh which has on occasion been used by linguists, for example, Malcolm Williams (2003). The recordings are available by prior arrangement with the archivist. Beth Thomas (personal e-mail communication, February 2015) informs us that some of the recordings have been transcribed in full, but most are simply summarized for content. For further information, see the Museum website: https://museum.wales/curatorial/social-cultural-history/archives.

The South Wales Miners' Library (Swansea University) is home to the South Wales Coalfield Collection (SWCC), which, in addition to documentary records of the mining community, includes a collection of audio-recorded interviews. Huber (2003: 184–186) states that the collection consists of 678 recordings made in 120 localities in southeast Wales, mostly in the 1970s and early 1980s. The informants (75% male) were of varying ages, born between the 1870s and 1960s. Huber initiated a corpus project in 2000 with the aim of transcribing the SWCC recordings and creating a 3.2-million-word corpus of English in Southeast Wales, although the project has not been completed thus far. Recordings of the oldest speakers in the SWCC (born around 1900) have been transcribed, and other recordings are at varying stages of completion (Magnus Huber, personal communication, February 2015).

The Miners' Library staff inform us that the audio collection is available for research purposes, mostly as audio cassettes but increasingly in a digitized format. About a third of the interviews were transcribed shortly after they were conducted in the 1970s and 1980s, but these transcriptions are not available digitally. Catalogues of the collection can be found on the library websites at www.swansea.ac.uk/swcc and www.agor.org.uk/cwm (both accessed in December 2019). The catalogues do not reveal which interviews have been transcribed, but the information is available if needed (Siân Williams, personal communication, February 2015; Joanne E. Waller, personal communication, September 2016).

The ICAME collection includes the Polytechnic of Wales corpus, which has 61,000 words of spoken English collected from children aged 6–12 in the Pontypridd area (Souter 1989). The corpus was compiled with the aim of studying first language acquisition, and thus the methods of data collection and selection of informants are not ideal for dialectological purposes.

Other regionally focused, unpublished corpora collected for masters and doctoral dissertations include those for Schmidt (1990; Darran Valley, southeast Wales), Elton (1994; the Rhondda), Walters (1999; the Rhondda), and Hejná (2015; Aberystwyth).

We return now to a summary of print volumes, chapters, and articles that offer overviews of WelE.

English in Wales: Diversity, conflict and change (1990) is a miscellany edited by two of the major figures of dialect study in Wales, Nikolas Coupland and Alan R. Thomas. It is a wide-ranging collection comprising sections on the Anglicization of Wales, on sociolinguistic processes in WelE (including Coupland on the elusiveness of any "Standard Welsh English", and Howard Giles on the study of social attitudes to WelE), as well as a set of descriptive sketches of some urban and rural WelE dialects. The sketches are inclined towards varieties of southern WelE, including Port Talbot (Connolly), Abercrave (Tench), and the historical rural dialects of north Carmarthenshire and south Pembrokeshire (both by Parry). The lack of material on northern WelE was, we must confess, partly due to one of the present authors. Rob Penhallurick, having completed his doctoral dissertation on northern WelE in 1986 (published as Penhallurick 1991), was invited to submit a chapter, but found himself scurrying between jobs and countries and, not for the first time, he missed the deadline. Also in the collection are chapters on Cardiff English by Collins and Mees, part of a long-term study which they would revisit (Mees and Collins 1999), and by Jack Windsor Lewis. The chapters by Windsor Lewis on Cardiff and Glamorgan English are based on a detailed 420-page typescript from 1964 titled *Glamorgan spoken English*. The typescript is of some significance but it remains unpublished. It contains six chapters on the vowels and consonants of Glamorgan English, two on grammar, and a glossary of over 2,600 entries "based on general observations and informal discussions" (Windsor Lewis 1990c: 109). A copy is in the care of Rob Penhallurick.

A later collection with national breadth is *Sociolinguistics in Wales* (2016), edited by Mercedes Durham and Jonathan Morris, although only one of its three main parts is specifically on WelE, the others dealing with the Welsh language and bilingualism/multilingualism. Of the three chapters on WelE, two are on social attitudes to dialect and accent variation: Chris Montgomery presents the principal findings from a survey that asked respondents in four locations along the Wales-England border to complete a "draw-a-map" task as used in the perceptual dialectology pioneered by Dennis R. Preston in the USA and by Montgomery himself in Britain; and Mercedes Durham analyses material collected in 2012–2013 from Twitter that discusses WelE accents. The study of WelE has been particularly well served by research on attitudes to and perceptions of dialect, and we come back to this shortly, below. The third chapter on WelE in Durham and Morris (2016) is by Heli Paulasto. This is a diachronic review of three Welsh-language-induced features of WelE grammar based on data from four corpora, three of which were collected on separate fieldwork trips to North and South Wales by Paulasto between 1995–2012, with the fourth taken from Ceri George's 1981 Rhondda interviews for a survey (1990) which was an off-shoot of SAWD. The chapter develops from Paulasto's sustained interest in WelE grammar which also yielded in 2006 a rarity in WelE studies, that is, a book-length national-scale investigation of selected characteristic features of WelE. This was *Welsh English syntax: Contact and variation* (2006), which analyses as fully as possible the distributions, functions, history, and causes of focus fronting and non-standard progressive verb constructions in WelE, using corpora collected by Paulasto and SAWD, and adding much detail to preceding research on these features, such as that by Malcom Williams (2000, 2003) in relation to focus fronting, and Rob Penhallurick (1996) and Alan R. Thomas (1984, 1985, 1994) on progressive forms.

Also published in 2016, drawing on academic sources while aiming at accessibility and a general readership, there is Benjamin A. Jones's *Welsh English dialect*, a small volume crammed with examples of WelE vocabulary, pronunciation, grammar, and illustrations of their use.

A good number of shorter descriptive summaries of WelE and its elements exist, several written by Penhallurick, whose output includes a discursive overview (1993), accounts of phonology (2004a, 2008a) and grammar (2004b, 2008b, 2011/2013, 2012), an outline of WelE overall (2007), and an evaluation of the compatability of the SAWD and BBC *Voices* data sets (2013). Other perspectives are available too! Charles V. J. Russ (1982) covers a lot of ground in his summary of the history and variety of English in England as well as in Wales. There are four separate chapters by Alan R. Thomas to note: two on phonology (1983, 1984), one on grammar (1985), and the last one a lengthier, more extensive depiction of the history, social significance, and features of WelE (1994). All of these pieces by Thomas are centred on description of southern WelE, although the last account devotes more space to northern dialects than the earlier chapters do (around three pages in total). Despite its title of "The English language in Wales", Gwenllian Awbery's 1997 contribution (to the first volume of papers produced by the Celtic Englishes project of the University of Potsdam) is more a survey of work on WelE than a survey of WelE itself. As such it is an informative companion to the present chapter, particularly in its references to unpublished dissertations, and in the attention it pays to WelE material in Joseph Wright's *English Dialect Dictionary* (1898–1905), the SED, and that lodged in the sound archive of the National Museum of (Welsh) History at St Fagan's. The tone of Awbery's commentary is at other times somewhat disdainful of "traditional linguistic geography" (Awbery 1997: 99) and reminiscent of the dispute that arose in dialect study in the 1960s-to-1980s between sociolinguists and dialectologists. Awbery's model of WelE is to the fore in Marion Löffler's (2009) short but broadly ranging sketch. At greater length and drawing on a large number of sources, Colin H. Williams (2012) provides an authoritative linguistic history and an outline of Welsh writing in English (or Anglo-Welsh literature), and says more than Löffler on the features of WelE, as well as discussing education and language policy.

Although more concerned with probing the relationship between English-speaking and Welsh-speaking in Wales than with describing WelE, the 1973 essay by Roland Mathias is worth mentioning here. Mathias tells at information-packed length the story of the arrivals and subsequent fluctuations of the Welsh and English languages in Wales, before putting forward his recipe for safeguarding the futures of both "Welsh-speaking Wales" and the "English-only majority" (Mathias 1973: 58). The issues addressed are not a million miles away from those discussed in the 1989 paper by Nikolas Coupland and Martin J. Ball on the sociolinguistic approach to the relative prestige in Wales of differing varieties of Welsh and English. The paper includes a summary of work up until the late 1980s in the research strand on attitudes to varieties mentioned a couple of times above.

It is with this strand that we conclude this section. Much of the profusion of research from 1970 onwards on social attitudes towards WelE has been carried out by a group of scholars based at Cardiff University's Language and Communication section, among them Justine Coupland, Nikolas Coupland, Peter Garrett, Howard Giles, and Angie Williams. Taking cues from the work of William Labov, Wallace Lambert (the matched-guise technique), and Dennis R. Preston (perceptual dialectology), the Cardiff group developed an integrated programme of research that used a battery of procedures to gather data from teachers and teenagers in Welsh schools. There is a comprehensive summing-up of this project in *Investigating language attitudes* (Garrett, Coupland & Williams 2003), the findings of which suggest, among other things, that one should treat attempts to model the major regional linguistic and cultural divisions of Wales as masking some significant perceptual complexities on the part of speakers of WelE (139–140, 214–215). This volume also serves as a review of the field of attitudes research in general and of the Cardiff group's work in particular. An informative earlier book-length exposition of the field is *Speech style and social evaluation* (Giles & Powesland 1975), which includes some reference to Wales as well as an early version of Howard Giles's accommodation theory of linguistic diversity and interpersonal communication. Shorter pieces with WelE relevance include, in rough chronological order, Giles (1970, 1971), Giles & Bourhis (1975), Bourhis & Giles (1976), Coupland, Williams & Garrett (1994, 1999), Garrett, Coupland & Williams (1995, 1999), and Williams, Garrett & Coupland (1996). Later entries are: Bishop, Coupland & Garrett (2005) and Coupland & Bishop (2007), both of which examine data gathered by an attitudes part of the BBC *Voices* survey from respondents across the UK; and Durham (2016) and Montgomery (2016) from the *Sociolinguistics in Wales* collection. From outside this paradigm, but nevertheless relevant, there is also a report on *Attitudes to Welsh and English in the schools of Wales* (1973) by Sharp, Thomas, Price, Francis & Davies.

6.2 Works on individual localities and regions, and other items of interest

A number of the older regional varieties of WelE are relatively well covered by dialect studies.

A major urban variety of WelE is described in Nikolas Coupland's *Dialect in use: Sociolinguistic variation in Cardiff English* (1988). Coupland draws on methods and ideas from dialectology, sociolinguistics, and accommodation theory in order to present a description of the phonology (including intonation), grammar, and distinctive lexis of Cardiff English, and to discuss the semiotic significance of speakers' choices from the range of linguistic variants at their disposal. He collected his data from interviews and less structured recordings of local radio broadcasts and interactions in a travel agency.

The long history of the English dialect of the Gower Peninsula is told in Rob Penhallurick's *Gowerland and its language* (1994), a compendium and analysis of word lists and accounts from the late seventeenth to the late twentieth century. A selection from this volume was recast in 2018 as *The Gower glossary*, a pocket book aimed at a general readership co-authored by Penhallurick and Benjamin A. Jones. (Penhallurick's *Gowerland* aims to be comprehensive, but there is one lesser-known omission in its sources to note: the MA dissertation by Richard Rees Griffiths, *An enquiry into the dialect of Gower* 1923.)

In 1999, a pioneering inquiry into the phonology of the English of the Rhondda Valleys was completed by Rod Walters – pioneering in that it includes the first extensive description of the prosody of any variety of WelE. Originally a doctoral dissertation focusing on working-class male speech, a condensed version is available from: http://phonetics.research.glam.ac.uk, and also from http://phonology.org (2019 edition). Walters also produced a number of shorter pieces that developed out of the main study (Walters 2001, 2003a, 2003b, 2003c).

Another exhaustive survey of prosody – in this case of the WelE of northwest and mid-west Wales – is Stefano Quaino's *The intonation of Welsh English: The case of Ceredigion and Gwynedd* (2011). Using nearly 200 extracts from digitized audio recordings of 19 informants in ten SAWD localities, and with supervisory advice from Rod Walters, Quaino's dissertation painstakingly examines pitch, stress, rhythm, and the alignment of certain pitch movements (such as pitch peak) with segmental features. A subsequent article by Quaino on alignment in the mid-west was published in 2014. Both Walters (for example, 2003a: 82; 2003b: 235) and Quaino (2014: 46–48) indicate that the position and intensity of the pitch peak might be a distinguishing feature of WelE intonation (it can be preceded by a comparatively long delay, to put it rather simply). Also from 2014, there is a small-scale intonation study of Carmarthen English by Marina Arashiro.

One other item about the English of the Valleys of the southeast can be noted: Robert Lewis's *Wenglish: The dialect of the South Wales Valleys* (2008, 2016). *Wenglish* is a label coined by John Edwards for his *Talk Tidy* booklets (1985, 1986) and the accompanying audio cassettes and after dinner speeches, a project very much in the time-honoured tradition of celebratory comic performance of regional dialect. Lewis's volume is considerably more copious and detailed, but is still something of a hybrid. Apparently based on personal observation, as well as on the collections of Edwards, it "sets Wenglish in its rightful place as an authentic regional dialect" (Lewis 2016: 10). One gets what Lewis is fighting against – the perception of non-standard dialects as sub-standard – but the whole premise of "Wenglish" colludes with the problem. Rhondda Valleys English is already an authentic regional dialect, and Welsh English is already a group of authentic regional dialects.

There are glossarial contributions on the English of Pembrokeshire and the borders too, on the dialects of Flintshire, Montgomeryshire, Radnorshire, and Monmouthshire.

For south Pembrokeshire, we have Percy Valentine Harris's *Pembrokeshire place-names and dialect* (1960, 1974), and Bertie Charles's *The English dialect of south Pembrokeshire* (1982), a slim companion to the substantial *Place-names of Pembrokeshire* (1992), also by Charles. Brian John includes a short word-list in his discussion of the historical north/south division of Pembrokeshire into a Welshry and an Englishry (John 1995: 153–164), and Gwen Awbery (1990) provides a convincing case for the Old English origins of the term for the boundary line between the two areas, *landsker*.

For Flintshire, there is *Talk of my town* (1969), by Dennis Griffiths, on the old dialect of the town of Buckley in the northeast corner of Wales, very close to the border with England.

Between 1871–1881, a dozen articles by Elias Owen appeared in the *Montgomeryshire Collections* journal on the "Archaic words, phrases, etc., of Montgomeryshire". Owen, in line with guidance from the English Dialect Society, aimed to compile a full glossary of dialect words occurring in Montgomeryshire, and he followed this series with another on "Folk-lore, superstitions, or what-not, in Montgomeryshire and elsewhere". In total his dialect series amounts to 85 pages. Other contributors to the *Collections* emulated Owen. In 1877, in the eleventh chapter of his "Parochial account of Llanidloes", Edward Hamer gave a list of "Local words and phrases"; and Richard Williams produced a short supplement to Owen's series in 1889, plus a dialogue in 1890 in the dialect of Newton.

The historic county of Montgomeryshire is currently the main part of the north of the principal area and county of Powys. South Powys covers the area that includes the historic county of Radnorshire, and for Radnorshire we have a meticulous consideration of both the English and Welsh languages of the county by William Henry Howse in his topographical and historical guide, *Radnorshire*, published in 1949 (Howse 1949: 274–300, 301–315). The account of Radnorshire English includes a glossary, and builds on previous descriptions by Howse (1944, 1945) and W. E. T. Morgan (1918).

Further south, into Monmouthshire, in 1913 John Hobson Matthews supplied a short glossary of the dialect of the county town, together with descriptions of local grammar, nicknames, idioms, and superstitions. The prolific founding member of the Chepstow Society, Ivor Waters, gave us a ten-page glossary in his *Folklore and dialect of the lower Wye Valley* (1973) that updated his *Chepstow talk* pamphlet (1950). David Parry, writing in the early days of SAWD, delivered a beautifully concise and expert portrayal of Newport English in *The Anglo-Welsh Review* (1971). And in 2016, Ben Jones compared the results of his 2013 *Voices*-questionnaire-based survey of contemporary lexis with SAWD data.

In Chapter 4 of the present book, we offer an analysis of the lexicon of contemporary WelE, but the inventory above surely indicates that there is a wealth of material crying out to be amalgamated into a historical dictionary of traditional Welsh English.

In this chapter, we have aimed to provide a survey of the works and resources that can guide and inform future enterprises. We end by noting three publications on the history of WelE, and one example of research on present-day multilingualism in Wales.

Gary German's (2009) article on Ieuan ap Hywel Swrdwal's fifteenth-century poem *Hymn to the Virgin* and Shakespeare's character Fluellen from *Henry V* (1599) gives us a picture of early perceptions of WelE (see Section 7.1). The 1882 article by the great English dialectologist Alexander J. Ellis and Chapter IX of the 1892 book by John E. Southall (1892: 336–364) both attempt to chart the geographical limits of predominantly English- and Welsh-speaking areas of Wales at the end of the nineteenth century. There is a map associated with each estimation, one at the back of Ellis (1889) and another at the front of Southall (1892), respectively. Southall produced a further map in 1895, using statistics from the 1891 census on percentages of those speaking Welsh in each registration district.

We have indicated elsewhere in the present volume that there is a gap in our knowledge of the interplay between varieties of Welsh English and more recently imported languages (and dialects) of immigrant communities in Wales. Mirona Moraru's research (2016, 2019), using a framework influenced by the work of the sociologist Pierre Bourdieu, analyses the linguistic practices and beliefs of 13 second-generation immigrants in Cardiff. Although not a study of linguistic features, the research provides an insight into the connections between the perceptions, uses, and circumstances of use of English in relation to other languages such as Arabic, Bengali, Hindi, Punjabi, Somali, and Urdu in the communities represented by these participants. Such insight could prove extremely useful to future research on the kinds of English that are emerging in such contexts.

7 Sample texts

The sample texts in this chapter have been selected from depictions of Welsh English in creative works (poetry, literature, and film) as well as from the Llandybie, North Wales, and Tonypandy interview corpora (see Section 1.6). The fictive texts, although literary dialect, give us vital historical information about WelE from time periods predating dialect surveys, whilst the corpus samples represent Welsh English as it emerges in the present-day research data utilized for this volume.

7.1 Fictional text samples

1. Ieuan ap Hywel Swrdwal's *Hymn to the Virgin* (1480) [poem]

Ieuan ap Hywel Swrdwal's fifteenth-century poem *Hymn to the Virgin* is the earliest record of Welsh English. The poem was written primarily using Welsh orthography of the fifteenth century thereby illustrating for readers the manner in which a L1 Welsh speaker theoretically pronounced an L2 English. Perhaps most striking is that Ieuan wrote the poem to mark a sort of social solidarity with other English varieties, having been confronted by his peers that Welsh speakers of English had no cultural worth. This extract is adapted from *Anglo-Welsh Poetry: 1480–1980*, a collection by Garlick and Mathias (1984). Unlike in Garlick and Mathias (1984), the translated version on the right is written to match the original syntactically, and no vocabulary has been altered to any modern equivalent. Glosses for these archaic terms are found below the poem. See Section 5.3 for further discussion.

Table 7.1: Reproduction of Ieuan ap Hywel Swrdwal's Hymn to the Virgin and translation

Original rendering	Modern respelling (adapted from Garlick & Mathias, 1984)
I	1.
O michti ladi, owr leding/tw haf	Oh mighty lady, our leading / to have
At hefn owr abeiding:	At heaven our **abiding**:
Yntw ddy ffest efrlesting	Into the feast everlasting
I set a braents ws tw bring.	Ye set a branch us to bring
II	2.
I wann ddys wyth blys, ddy blessing/off God	Ye won this with bliss, the blessing / of God
Ffor iwr gwd abering,	For your good a'bearing
Hwier I bynn ffor iwr wyning	Where ye been for your winning

Table 7.1: (continued).

Original rendering	Modern respelling (adapted from Garlick & Mathias, 1984)
Syns kwin, and iwr swnn ys king.	Since queen, and your son is king.
III	3.
Owr ffadyrs ffadyr, owr ffiding,/owr pop,	Our father's father, our feeding, / our pope
On iwr paps had swking;	On your **paps** had sucking;
Yn hefn-blys i haf thys thing,	In heaven's bliss ye have this thing,
Atendans wythowt ending.	Attendance without ending.
IV	4.
Wi sin ddy bricht kwin wyth kwning/and blys,	We seen the bright queen with knowing/ and bliss,
Ddy bloswm ffruwt bering;	The blossom fruit bearing
Ei wowld, as owld as ei sing,	I would, as old as I sing,
Wynn iwr lwf on iwr lofing.	Win your love on your loving.
V	5.
Kwin od off owr God, owr geiding/mwdyr	Queen [g]**od***[sole] of our God, our guiding / mother
Maedyn notwythstanding,	Maiden notwithstanding
Hwo wed syts wyth a ryts ring	Who wed such with a rich ring
As God wod ddys gwd weding	As God **wo'd** this good wedding
VI	6.
Help ws, prae ffor ws, preffering/owr sowls;	Help us, pray for us, preferring / our souls
Asoel ws at owr ending.	Absolve us at our ending.
Mak ddat awl wi ffawl tw ffing	Make that all we fall to **fing**
Iwr swns lwf, owr syns lefing.	Your son's love, our sins leaving
VII	7.
As wi mae ddy dae off deiing/resef	As we may the day of dying/ receive
Owr safiowr yn howsling;	Our saviour in **houseling**
As hi mae tak ws waking	As he may take us waking
Tw wwn yn hys michti wing.	To **wone** in his mighty wing
VIII	8.
Michti, i twk, mi ocht tw tel	Mighty he took, me ought to tell
Owt, sowls off hel tw soels off hicht.	Out, souls of Hell to **soels** of height.
Wi aes wyth bwk, wi wys wyth bel,	We ask with book, we wish with bell,
Tw hefn ffwl welt w haf on fflicht	To heaven full well to have on flight
Awl dids wel dwn,	All deeds well done
Tabeit te bwn–	To abide the boon–
A god-mat trwn,	A god-made throne
A gwd, mit wricht;	A good, **mete wright**;

Table 7.1: (continued).

Original rendering	Modern respelling (adapted from Garlick & Mathias, 1984)

And si so swn
And north and nwn
An swnn an mwn
    An swnn on micht.
	And see so soon
	And north and noon
	And sun and moon
	    And the Son on might.

* * * * * * * * * *	* * * * * * * * * *

XII
O trysti Kreist tat werst a krown,
Er wi dei down, aredi dicht
  Tw thank tw thi
  At te rwt-tri
  Dden went awl wi,
    Ddein own, tw licht.
Tw grawnt agri,
Amen, wy mi,
Ddat ei mae si
    Ddi tw mei sicht!
	12.
	Oh trusty Christ that **wearest** a crown,
	Ere we die down, already **dight**
	  To thank to thee
	  At the rood-tree
	  Then wend all we,
	    Thine own, to light.
	To grant agree,
	Amen, with me,
	That I may see
	    Thee to my sight!

XIII
Owr lwk, owr king, owr lok, owr kae–
Mei God, ei prae, mei geid wpricht!
Ei sik, ei sing, ei siak, ei sae,
Ei wer awae, a wiri wicht.
  Agast ei go,
    Mei ffrynds mi ffro
Ei ffond a ffo,
  Wy ffynd ei fficht;
Eil sing awlso
Yn welth an wo
(ei kann no mo)
    Tw kwin o micht.
	13.
	Our luck, our king, our lock, owr key–
	My God, I pray, my guide upright!
	I seek, I sing, I shake, I say,
	I wear away, a weary **wight**.
	  Aghast I go,
	    My friends me fro
	I found a foe,
	  With fiend I fight;
	I'll sing also
	In wealth and woe
	(I can no more)
	    To queen of might.

Translations of archaic terms (**bold**): Verse 1 (abiding – abode); Verse 3 (paps – breasts); Verse 5 (wo'd – to will, ordain), ([g]od – euphemistic use of the Christian God); Verse 6 (fing – trust/accept); Verse 7 (houseling – communion), (wone – dwell); Verse 8 (soels – site/foundation of a city), (mete – suitable), (wright – divine creator); Verse 12 (wearest – 2nd person sing. pres. of wears); (dight – adorned); Verse 13 (wight – spectre).

2. William Shakespeare's *Henry V* (1599) [play]

William Shakespeare's *Henry V* featured the second significant literary iteration of a Welsh English. Though not penned by a Welsh person, and laced with a mocking character stereotyping of the Welsh, Shakespeare's (and his Elizabethan playwright contemporaries) efforts were the result of careful inquiry into what was at the time a common variety of English especially amongst the London Welsh. In this extract from Scene VII of Act IV, Welshman Fluellen (lit. Llewelyn, for Shakespeare could not either hear or mark down the fricative distinction in the Welsh language phoneme <ll> [ɬ]) uses a sort of WelE that focuses on devoiced plosives, notably devoicing of bilabial plosives /b/ to /p/. It is also the source of the discourse marker *look you*, a well-known linguistic stereotype of WelE today.

See Section 5.4 for further discussion.

SCENE VII. Another part of the field

Enter FLUELLEN and GOWER

> FLUELLEN
> Kill the poys and the luggage! 'tis expressly
> against the law of arms: 'tis as arrant a piece of
> knavery, mark you now, as can be offer't; in your
> conscience, now, is it not?
>
> GOWER
> 'Tis certain there's not a boy left alive; and the
> cowardly rascals that ran from the battle ha' done
> this slaughter: besides, they have burned and
> carried away all that was in the king's tent;
> wherefore the king, most worthily, hath caused every
> soldier to cut his prisoner's throat. O, 'tis a
> gallant king!
>
> FLUELLEN
> Ay, he was porn at Monmouth, Captain Gower. What
> call you the town's name where Alexander the Pig was born!
>
> GOWER
> Alexander the Great.
>
> FLUELLEN
> Why, I pray you, is not pig great? the pig, or the
> great, or the mighty, or the huge, or the
> magnanimous, are all one reckonings, save the phrase
> is a little variations.

GOWER
I think Alexander the Great was born in Macedon; his
father was called Philip of Macedon, as I take it.

FLUELLEN
I think it is in Macedon where Alexander is porn. I
tell you, captain, if you look in the maps of the
'orld, I warrant you sall find, in the comparisons
between Macedon and Monmouth, that the situations,
look you, is both alike. There is a river in
Macedon; and there is also moreover a river at
Monmouth: it is called Wye at Monmouth; but it is
out of my prains what is the name of the other
river; but 'tis all one, 'tis alike as my fingers is
to my fingers, and there is salmons in both. If you
mark Alexander's life well, Harry of Monmouth's life
is come after it indifferent well; for there is
figures in all things. Alexander, God knows, and
you know, in his rages, and his furies, and his
wraths, and his cholers, and his moods, and his
displeasures, and his indignations, and also being a
little intoxicates in his prains, did, in his ales and
his angers, look you, kill his best friend, Cleitus.

GOWER
Our king is not like him in that: he never killed
any of his friends.

FLUELLEN
It is not well done, mark you now take the tales out
of my mouth, ere it is made and finished. I speak
but in the figures and comparisons of it: as
Alexander killed his friend Cleitus, being in his
ales and his cups; so also Harry Monmouth, being in
his right wits and his good judgments, turned away
the fat knight with the great belly-doublet: he
was full of jests, and gipes, and knaveries, and
mocks; I have forgot his name.

GOWER
Sir John Falstaff.

FLUELLEN
That is he: I'll tell you there is good men porn at Monmouth.

GOWER
Here comes his majesty.

3. Geraint Goodwin's *The Heyday in the Blood* (1936) [novel] (pp.106–109)

Written in just two months, Montgomeryshire-born Geraint Goodwin intended *Heyday* to be a contemporary piece that captured both Welsh and English borderland cultural identity. Commended by critics for its naturalistic dialogue yet also criticized by some for his dialect-writing potentially alienating readers, Goodwin's linguistic contribution is today finally coming to light amongst linguists studying literary dialect as one of the key WelE dialect texts.

In the extract below, Goodwin's "naturalistic dialogue" is depicted as Dici, Wati, and Twmi, three men of the borders, strike up conversation with several *shonihois* (a derogatory Welsh language term for south-Walian miners) on their way to Liverpool. Besides non-standard verb agreement, several distinctly WelE morphosyntax is represented, for example exclamative *there* in *there's a boy, for you*, *see* as discourse marker, and focus fronting in *ignorant, he iss*. Phonologically, we see phonetic respellings used to render devoicing of consonants in *ploody* and *wass*, as well as respellings used to convey vowels occurring higher in the mouth in *murdah*, *laf* and *shutapp*. Goodwin also experiments with including both rhoticity in *arr* and *farr* for the Borders speakers and hyphenization for the shonihois to render intonational differences in *men-shun*, *cuck-oo* and *work-ahs*. Lexically we see loaned Welsh lexis *myn uffern i* (lit. 'by hell', an interjection), affirmative *aye*, *tamping* to denote 'furiously', and both *mun* and *gwas* used vocatively.

They were two shonihois from the South, one could see at a glance, even if the little blue streaks of coal dust, worked under the skin like tiny veins, did not give them away.

The one man went over to look for the bar and the other took his seat beside 'rhen Shacob.

"Cardiff City – going down an' down", he said confidentially.

Shacob went on moving his toothless gums. But the stranger was not deterred.

"Things is bad down South," he said again in the same easy confidential tone. But still Shacob did not answer. In a final effort the man spoke again.

"Jack Petersen – there's a boy for you!"

There was still no answer, and he was now vaguely alarmed. "Hey, Ianto!" he called to his butty and cocked his head at the old man. "Ploody waxworks, myn uffern i!"

Dici leaned across. He had not heard what was going on in the general hubbub. He tapped his ear knowingly.

"Hard of hearing, he iss," he said apologetically. The man's face lightened.

"Don't men-shun," he answered waving his hand affably.

"You come a long way?" broke in Wati, making conversation.

"Down South," he said briefly and then, to be more explicit. "You know that murdah – how long ago, Ianto, aye two yeahs sure to be – when they found the girl on the tip. That's our 'ome," he said with finality.

"Never?" Dici answered in astonishment.

"Aye aye, mun. Knew him well." He wiped a hand backwards across his mouth. "Little pugah he wass, too."

They crowded round the men as if they had been monkeys. Their ways, their talk, their dress were all different. "Down South" was another world.

"Arr you going farr?" asked Wati anxiously. He looked down at his feet. Their boots, patched and tied with string, were hanging from their feet.

"Farr enough," he replied. "What you say, Ianto? It's all done down there." He cocked his finger over his shoulder and shook his head hopelessly. "Thirty-four yeahs of it mun. Look at me now! Look at 'im."

He did not want to say any more. They were men who did not parade their sorrows. He took a gulp at his beer and his face brightened.

"Plenty jobs in London. So they say."

"You come a long way round," broke in Twmi. He stood there a moment facing them, the same old changeless expression on his face.

"Wrong for you, mun," said the old miner looking from the fire. "Up 'eah we got it," and he tapped his head knowingly.

"We goin' to try the Mersey Tunnel," broke in his mate, a thin, hatchet-faced man, with bright quick eyes.

"We wass only saying," said Wili in his most ponderous way. "We wass only saying as how Wales iss all done and finished for."

"Done, you say?" The miner lifted his face, gone haggard, put his hands on his knees and spat in the fire. He was deep in thought.

"Damn it all mun, what do you know?" he said, a light in his eye. "You come down South and see." He dropped his voice: and the light went out in his eye. "We gone past been done for," he said after a while. He put his hands to his head and looked at the floor. He had gone beyond words.

"The Rhondda..." He could say no more. "One end to the other. Tonypandy, Ton Pentre, Treorchy... worse than death; not as quick."

But now it was Ianto's turn. He was a different type altogether.

"Four yeahs I been out. Laf that wan off! I go to the overman. He got a down on me – I'm a communist, see? 'What about it now, boss?' He looks me up and down as though I was a bit of dirt. 'Come back in Spring' he says. Diawl ario'd – up comes the lamp. 'What do you think I am, gwas – a ploody cuck-oo.' No more work for me. That done it."

The older man, his head whitened, his eyes tired and hopeless, let him have his head. He was like the jackal after the lion.

"There was Iddy Pryce now…" went on the younger man in his shrill high voice. "A sort of relation of mine…"

"Shutapp, mun," said his mate, roused from out of himself. "Sort of relation! No relation at all."

"Yess, yess, he iss," went on the other in his shrill way. "Ignorant, he iss." Then dropping his voice to a confidential whisper. "My wife wass haf a kid by him, see?"

The company looked down their noses, and moved uneasily in their seats.

And Ianto, having disposed of the point, went scampering off.

"When the work-ahs get together, you wait! Ploody ruckshuns I tell you! I'm on the committee, see?" He nodded knowingly.

"What iss he?" asked Wili pointing to the older man who had sunk back into himself.

"He's labah," he said apologetically. "But he's tamping to the left fast."

4. Charles Frend's' *A Run for your Money* [film] [00:16:56–00:19:23]

Directed by Charles Frend, *A Run for Your Money* was one of the earliest films to feature Welsh protagonists, as well as to have been written by Welsh writers, Clifford Evans, Richard Hughes, and dialogue writer, Diana Morgan. It was also thereby one of the earliest depictions of WelE in a motion picture.

In the transcript below, Twm and Dai sit at a table after serving themselves breakfast at a London café. There are numerous WelE features. Morphosyntactic elements include the vocative usage of *mun*, focus fronting (*diddled, you've been*) exclamative there (*there's money for you*), *see* as a discourse marker, and omission of the suffix *-ly* for adverbial (*see it proper*), as well as lexis such as affirmative *aye*, and Welsh loans *twp* 'stupid' and expletive *duw* 'god'. The discourse is particularly remarkable due to its metalinguistic and socially perceptual elements. Although con-woman Jo's ears prick up at their comment of two hundred pounds, it could be argued that her recognition of their Welsh English performances make them easy targets to con.

Twm:	Huh. Thought I'd lost you, **mun**.
Dai:	Don't talk nonsense.
Twm:	Not nonsense at all. Nearly lost each other on the train didn't we? Well then – much easier in London. Suppose we do. If it's the morning: each go to Twickenham. Meet at the entrance outside. If it's

	after the match, we meet at Paddington, under the clock, **see**. Now, we must have a plan. Suppose, we go there first, see it **proper**.
Dai:	**Aye**, and then *The Echo*. Two hundred pounds, **there's money** for you. We might even have some over at the end of the day.

[Con-woman Jo's ears prick up. Begins listening to the conversation]

Twm:	Talking of money, did you count your change?
Dai:	Ah, don't be so **twp**, they wouldn't cheat you in a place like this.
Twm:	ha ha
Dai:	I'm supposed to have four pounds seventeen.

[Counts money and unknowingly drops some on the floor, Jo notices]

	I'm ten-bob short!
Twm:	What did I tell you. **Diddled, you've been**.
Dai:	Ah! **Duw**. What's ten-bob to a man with two hundred pounds? Chicken feed is ten-bob!
Twm:	Chicken feed's to be counted as well as chickens.

[Jo picks up Dai's misplaced money]

Jo:	Is this yours?
Dai:	Really? Why yes it is. Thank you very much.
Twm:	Very decent of you I'm sure, miss.
Jo:	Pleasure. You're Welsh aren't you?
Dai:	Yes
Twm:	How did you guess?
Dai:	**Aye**, we are.
Twm:	Won't you sit down and join us, miss? Have a cuppa coffee.
Dai:	**Aye**. Indeed.
Jo:	Well, I've finished really
Twm:	Gooo-on!
Jo:	I'll just sit down for a minute then. Is this your first visit to London?
Dai:	**Aye**, first visit to England.
Jo:	But ... Wales is part of England?
Dai & Twm:	Oh! Ho-ho ho!
Dai:	Shame on you! [Laughing]
Twm:	It's easy to see you've never been to Wales, miss.
Jo:	That's right, never been further west than the West End.

[All laugh]

Twm:	See, Dai, this is one of those young ladies you were warned **against**.
Jo:	Oh. Really?
Twm:	Oh it's alright, miss. **Only joking, I was**. Back home, they were saying that Dai would lose his heart up here.

Jo:	Depends how long you're going to be here.
Twm:	Ah well, only up for a day, **see**.
Jo:	I see, well you can't come to much harm in that time, can you?
[Jo begins to leave]	
Dai:	Hey, not going, are you?
Jo:	Yes, I'm afraid I must. Well, have a good time. And if you can't be careful, be clever. Bye-bye.
Twm:	So long now.
Dai:	Goodbye.
Dai:	Well, **there's a nice girl for you**.
Twm:	Very nice indeed. No side, either.
Dai:	No, plenty of everything else though.
Waitress:	Is this yours? [Holds Jo's misplaced purse]
Twm:	**Diawl**! It must be hers, that young lady.
Dai:	Here, I'll take it to her!

7.2 Spoken Welsh English in the interview corpora

To represent spoken language we have selected three short extracts from Heli Paulasto's corpora: one from Llandybie in the southwest of Wales, one from Llanuwchllyn in the north, and one from Tonypandy in the southeast. The informants thus come from different parts of Wales but they share some characteristics in other respects: they were all born prior to the 1940s and they have worked in fields which require fairly little vocational or professional education.

Three short clips cannot be expected to illustrate the scope of regional or sociolinguistic diversity of Welsh dialects of English, nor include every feature of WelE examined in this book. They do, however, give a fair idea of the data used as the basis for the analysis of morphosyntactic and discourse features. They also show that WelE speakers rarely use dialect features systematically. These are variants, which the speakers may have at their disposal, but for the most past, their English is not structurally or lexically highly distinctive.

1. **LC. Llandybie, Carmarthenshire. Informants aged 72 and 73, both L1 Welsh-speakers. Interviewed and transcribed by Heli Paulasto in 1995.**

The Llandybie sample was among the first set of interviews recorded by Heli Paulasto. The speakers are an elderly couple, who seem a bit uncertain as to how much their Finnish interviewer in fact understands of what they say. E, in particular, speaks slowly and carefully. Their concern is somewhat justified, as C's accent presents occasional difficulties for the interviewer. Despite the somewhat formal air of the discussion, the interview includes many characteristics of southwestern WelE both in terms of structure and discourse.

In this extract, the most prominent feature is the habitual use of the progressive. However, only the expressions related to miners' bathing habits (recurring events) have been classified as extended use. Other instances concern, for example, the collieries as significant employers in the area (a state) or Londoners flocking into the area to work as "Bevin boys" (a trend), meaning work force conscripted into the mines by the war-time Minister of Labour and National Service, Ernest Bevin. What is and is not considered "extended use" is certainly a somewhat subjective matter, but it is safe to say that the informants favour the progressive in imperfective habitual/generic contexts.

Of other Welsh-induced features, the sample also includes focus fronting (*Bevin boys we used to call them*), but all other vernacular features are of EngE origin: generalized *was* and *wasn't*, the discourse marker *like* and the *be* perfect (*they are settled down*). C is, furthermore, an avid user of the adverbial/discourse marker *then*, which is functionally similar to *now* and *now then*, discussed in Chapter 4 in the context of discourse-pragmatic markers.

C: but during when I was starting work in nineteen thirty-six, there **was** about seven collieries down here
E: yes, **wasn' it?**
C: only about two miles from each other
E: yes.
C: and **they were all employin'** about- well, at least three hundred men
I: mm
C: up to five hundred men
E: and at that time there were no baths in the [collieries
I: oh!]
C: [oh no!
E: **they were] comin' back** black as [anything
C: oh aye], bathin' ho-, bathin' home
E: bathin' home
C: big erm, tin baths
E: yeah, because there **wasn't** any bathrooms
C: no
I: well, of course not, no
E: you know, at that time . in front of the fire.
C: oh aye.

E: mm . **they were comin' home**, black as anything
I: mm
E: but of course they had baths then in the collieries, so **they were changin'** into clean clothes, comin' home
I: I see, yeah
<pause>
E: mm . everything is changin' . you know
C: an' ah, I was called up when I was eighteen
E: yes, because
C: [the war
E: your] colliery, where you were workin', Pencae, in [Llandybie,
I: yeah]
E: it had [closed, hadn't it
C: yes, it closed] (that time?) (2), well they didn' want any coal, (well it was the?) government whatyoucall, I don' know, then more people **then** had to go in the forces **like** you know (the?) . they'd shut the colliery down and I was called up then, eighteen, so I went into the air force . so I- there for- till nineteen forty-four . then, you (1) they wanted coal then, so they released me back to go into the colliery then
I: mhm
C: see they- they they wanted it both ways
I: yeah
C: they released me then to go back to the colliery . they wanted miners then, for the coal, to get coal
E: well of course the boys from London and those places, England, **they were comin' here** as Bevin [boys
C: oh yes]
E: (int?) . not to go into the forces,
I: [mm
E: **they**] **were comin' here** as Bevin boys
C: yes, (2) [(attracted them?)
I: I see]
E: [yes
C: into the] coal mine, (you know they were?) short of coal, then . now they wanted coal . and **they were closin' 'em down** before that .
E: [so
C: well a] lot of- lot of people **then**- you know, we call them in- in Welsh *saesneg*, were Cockneys and all that, (you probably [know?)
I: yeah I]
C: and lot of them **now are . settled** down here now er

E: yes
C: and the **Bevin boys we used to call them**

2. NWC. Llanuwchllyn, Gwynedd. Informant aged 61, L1 Welsh-speaking. Interviewed and transcribed by Heli Paulasto in 2000.

The North Welsh informant was interviewed at her house, accompanied only by her cat. The speaker's English shares some dialectal characteristics with the previous interview, such as focus fronting (*three an' a half we went to school; to Bermaw we used to say*). The invariant question tag *isn't it* is also used in both interviews, although it makes no appearance in the specific extract above. G, however, uses the habitual modals *would* and *used to* instead of the progressive form. Other vernacular features are shared with EngE: *them* for determiner *those* (*in them days*), *off* instead of *from* and reduction of the indefinite article (*I had a card off her [a] fortnight ago, birthday card*). As to the preposition *with* (*we enjoyed it and the sandwiches with him*), it is difficult to say whether its scope extends to the man, indicating accompaniment, or simply to the preceding *sandwiches*, indicating possession (i.e. *his sandwiches*). The latter usage would reflect the respective Welsh language construction, but similar instances are in fact quite rare throughout the corpora. We suggest that the former interpretation is likelier; there is also the possibility of a functionally mixed case.

Of the discourse features, *now* appears here as a discourse marker, indicating a new topic of conversation (*now, in them days*) or acting as a thematic marker on some occasions (*goin' back to J–P– Old Goat now*).

I: mm, well, having lived here just about all your life, can you remember any stories relating to the village or village characters or things like that?
G: not really
I: Mm.
<pause>
G: well yes, this should interest you really, erm, there's a lane that goes u- past the back of the house you know I'll [show you
I: yeah]
G: before you go
I: [okay
G: and it goes] up to four farms in the (1)
I: mhm
G: **now**, in **them** days the council workers were on foot with their wheelbarrows an' their brushes an' their spades,

I: yeah
G: an' not machinery as they are today. an' there was a little ditch running down this side of this lane, so every Friday morning old J–P– Old Goat, as we called him,
I: mm
G: it was his duty to clear this road an' clean it . so just- well during the war, really, erm, a lady had lived on the front here . her sister lived in London an' she had a daughter, an'- A–N–, she is four days older than me . so because of the bombing et cetera in London, A– came here to h- her aunt as an evacuee, an' she [came to
I: mm]
G: school with me at four, or **three an' a half I think we went to school** because we were a nuisance by the gate watching the children
I: mhm
G: and erm- so we used to play **now up the lane** here, all the children in the village, an' my grandmother **now** had said to me- the only holiday we had was a day in Barmouth by the sea,
I: [yeah
G: which is] what, thirty odd miles on the train, right up the coast . so my grandmother said to me, "ask the little girl if she'd like to come with you" . A– couldn' work- speak a word of Welsh,
I: mm
G: an' I couldn't speak English either then, really . so goin' back to J–P– Old Goat **now**, my grandmother had told him, "tell her to ask that little girl if she wants to come to Barmouth" . well J–P– he said- we were havin' a cup of tea an' then he always **used to** s- share his erm, tin of tea
I: yeah
G: with us, you know, we'd have a sip of tea, oh we enjoyed it an' the sandwiches **with him** . now he said, "you **wanna** ask this little girl if she's coming with you to- to Barmouth" . **to Bermaw we used to say**, not Barmouth
I: okay
G: the version, Bermaw alright? an' A– still remembers to this day, I had a card **off her (a)** fortnight ago, birthday card . "Will you come Barmouth to me?" an' that's the way I asked it an' she understood me . and old J–P– Old Goat, he's died now, but every time I saw him, he **would** mention this, you know

[...]

I: well talkin' about the English language then, erm, do you think that there's a Welsh variety of English that is different from English in England?
G: yes, definitely
I: is it just the accent or is it shom- something else as well?

G: no I think the culture comes into it as well, **isn' it?**
I: mhm
G: erm, yes, definitely there is a... I would think so, yes
I: what do you mean by the culture coming into it?
G: oh I know there's a culture in England as well,
I: mm
G: but erm, English people do tend to be more sort of independent, don't they?
I: mhm
G: more sort of self... what's the word I'm looking for?
I: reliant?
G: probably, yes,
I: [right
G: whereas] in Wales, even South Wales as well, erm, if you've moved in, if you want to be on your own and not mix,
I: yeah
G: yes, fine, but if you want a life that's friendly an' full of- you know, you've got to
I: yeah
G: mix in an' I don't think it really matters with the language really,
I: [okay
G: erm] not so much

3. TC. Tonypandy, Rhondda Cynon Taff. Informants aged 84 (B) and 80 (C), L1 English-speaking. Interviewed by Heli Paulasto (A) in 2012, transcribed by Marja Kilpiö.

These Tonypany informants, two old friends, were interviewed at a local café, which produced a lot of background noise. The situation was fairly informal though, as Heli Paulasto had already been chatting with the men in a larger group for a while.

The extract includes many vernacular features typical of the Tonypandy area, some of which are distinctly Welsh English, while others originate from EngE dialect input. The Welsh-induced features below are primarily focus fronting (*only one phrase he come out with*), the invariant tags *is it* and *innit*. As discussed in Sections 3.4.2 and 4.4.1, both features appear in spoken EngE as well. The mixed sentence structure in *he was speaking English he was* with its two SV-clauses can be considered an instance of "edited" focus fronting or emphatic tag use, common in spoken EngE (Paulasto 2006: 169–170). It is possible that the EngE propensity for the latter combines with the WelE tendency for contrastive focus fronting here.

The positive invariant tag *is it* appears in the unusual confirmatory rather than informational function, while the negative question tag takes the form *innit*, echoing London English. Note that the Finnish interviewer has by now adopted the invariant follow-up tag *is it* and is using it quite fluently! The extract also includes an instance of extended use of the definite article with names of languages (*the Welsh*).

EngE dialect features are more numerous still. These include an unmarked adverb (*it comes natural*), generalized *was* (*we was*) and default singular *there's*, uninflected past tense of *come*, zero copular *be* (*you from Scotland?*), omission of the subject pronoun (*sound Scottish*), left dislocation (*one kid he said to me*), and addition of the preposition *in* (*in there*). The interview includes the local expression *by there* as well, although it does not appear in this clip. Discourse-pragmatic markers in this extract are, for example, *like*, *see*, and *then*.

<A> you don't . well how do you feel about the Rhondda dialect of English then </A>
<B> pardon </B>
<A> the Rhondda accent of English </A>
<B> well . it's what I've been used to **then is it** </B>
<A> (mm) </A>
<B> great <laughs> </B>
<A> yeah it's the best thing to- yeah yeah alright </A>
<C> aye . yeah well I . I told you before (then?) . we are very attached to it </C>
<A> (mm) </A>
<B> you know </B>
<C> so it comes a- **natural** to us </C>
<A> yeah </A>
<C> and we enjoy it . because it's the only way we know how to speak </C>
<A> that's right </A>
<B> when I was in Scotland when . when C– was with us . and we **was staying** in this woman's house </B>
<A> (mm) </A>
<B> and there was a kiddy **in there** . and he was speaking and the kiddy would say to his mother "what did he what did he say" </B>
<A> yeah </A>
<B> cos the mother could understand . and he spoke he said something in Welsh one day . and he said "what . wha=" em . "what did he say" and his mother said the mother said to the little boy . "he spoke in Welsh then" . and the kiddy said "I thought he was speaking Welsh all the time" <laughter> and only and **only one phrase he come out with** </B>
<A> yeah </A>

\<C\> aye . aye \</C\>
\<B\> and the boy thought he was speaking Welsh \</B\>
\<C\> [there you are \</C\>
\<B\> **he was speaking]** English he was \</B\>
\<C\> there you are \</C\>
\<B\> but er . different accent in Scotland [altogether **innit** \</B\>
\<C\> that's right] that's right yeah . I remember going to Evenmouth \</C\>
\<B\> (eh) \</B\>
\<C\> (em) . my wife had an auntie living in Evenmouth dock **see** . in the council area council (3) (**like**?) . and I went out on the . outside her house one day **we was** up there for about a . three or four days staying there **like** \</C\>
\<A\> (mm) \</A\>
\<C\> and (eh) . **there was** two children . two boys playing \</C\>
\<A\> yeah \</A\>
\<C\> so I spoke to the kids we got we talked (with the kid?) we talked a bit (3) . and I spoke to these kids and then . **one kid he** said to me . **"you from Scotland?"** \</C\>
\<laughter\>
\<C\> "are you from Scotland" I said "no from Wales" . "sound Scottish" \</C\>
\<B\> yeah \</B\>
\<A\> yeah \</A\>
\<C\> and nothing like (1) sound Scottish \</C\>
\<A\> how weird . (em) how far do you have to go from the Rhondda to . find that people are speaking differently . people have a different kind of accent \</A\>
\<B\> you can stay in the Rhondda \</B\>
\<C\> \<laughter\> \</C\>
\<A\> yeah \</A\>
\<B\> you know\<?\> \</B\>
\<A\> \<overlap /\> but if you \</A\>
\<B\> \<overlap /\> fur= further up the valley they're more Welshy still \</B\>
\<A\> **is it** \</A\>
\<B\> yeah \</B\>
\<C\> yeah \</C\>
\<A\> oh . it's that close by then \</A\>
\<C\> yeah \</C\>
\<B\> yeah \</B\>
\<C\> that was the last place that **used the Welsh** were up there \</C\>
\<A\> yeah . okay \</A\>
\<B\> my father . father-in-law said something about the the alphabet he . where we would say A B C he'd say /e:/ . instead of /eɪ/ he'd say /e:/ \</B\>
\<A\> okay \</A\>

<B> he was always . that's only . about six miles up . from where we are now </B>
<A> yeah </A>
<B> it changes as you as you as you go up and </B>
<A> alright </A>
<B> but I don't know where the borderline is </B>
<A> yeah </A>
<C> no . and they say (2) . is from up there from . Treherbert </C>
<B> yeah </B>
<C> that's (near here?) </C>
<B> yeah </B>
<C> the closer you go to Cardiff the more English you become </C>
<A> yeah </A>
<B> down (1) through the cities **innit** </B>
<C> yeah </C>
<A> okay </A>
<C> it's it is right because you know </C>
<A> but the Cardiff people speak differently from the English </A>
<C> oh yes </C>
<B> yeah . it's Caediff </B>
<A> Caediff </A>
<C> it's a hard accent </C>
<A> (mm) </A>
<C> hard old accent </C>
<A> so how does the Cardiff accent sound to you </A>
<B> yeah . and yet there's a lot of Welsh back in Cardiff now through the school </B>
<A> (mm) </A>
<B> **there's** Welsh schools opening **see innit** </B>
<C> **there's** more Welsh schools in Cardiff </C>
<B> yeah </B>
<C> than in other any other city . now </C>

References

Agha, Asif. 2007. *Language and social relations*. Cambridge: Cambridge University Press.
Aitchison, John & Harold Carter. 2000. *Language, economy and society: The changing fortunes of the Welsh language in the twentieth century*. Cardiff: University of Wales Press.
Aitchison, John & Harold Carter. 2004. *Spreading the word: The Welsh language 2001*. Talybont: Y Lolfa.
Algeo, John. 1988. The tag question in British English: it's different, i'n' it? *English World-Wide* 9 (2). 171–191.
Algeo, John. 1990. It's a myth, innit? Politeness and the English tag question. In Christopher Ricks and Leonard Michaels (eds.), *The state of the language*, 443– 450. London: Faber & Faber.
Allen, Kevin (director) & Peter McAleese (producer). 1997. *Twin town*. United Kingdom: Agenda, Aimimage Productions & Figment Films.
Altendorf, Ulrike & Dominic Watt. 2008. The dialects in the south of England: Phonology. In Bernd Kortmann & Clive Upton (eds.), *Varieties of English 1: The British Isles*, 194–222. Berlin & New York: Mouton de Gruyter.
Amador-Moreno, Carolina P., Kevin McCafferty & Elaine Vaughan (eds.). 2015. *Pragmatic markers in Irish English*. Amsterdam & Philadelphia: John Benjamins.
Andersen, Gisle. 2001. *Pragmatic markers and sociolinguistic variation. A relevance-theoretic approach to the language of adolescents*. Philadelphia: John Benjamins.
Anderwald, Liselotte. 2008. The varieties of English spoken in the Southeast of England: Morphology and syntax. In Bernd Kortmann & Clive Upton (eds.), *Varieties of English 1: The British Isles*, 440–462. Berlin: Mouton de Gruyter.
Anderwald, Liselotte. 2009. *The morphology of English dialects: Verb formation in non-standard English*. Cambridge: Cambridge University Press.
Arashiro, Marina. A descriptive study of intonation in Welsh English: Preliminary investigation of statements and yes/no questions. *Tokyo University of Foreign Studies Journal*, 2014. 172–192. Available at: http://repository.tufs.ac.jp/bitstream/10108/81176/1/lacs020011.pdf (December 2019).
Awbery, Gwenllian M. 1990. The term 'landsker' in Pembrokeshire. *Journal of the Pembrokeshire Historical Society* 4. 32–44.
Awbery, Gwenllian M. 1997. The English language in Wales. In Hildegard L.C. Tristram (ed.), *The Celtic Englishes*, 86–99. Heidelberg: Universitatsverlag C. Winter.
Bae, So Hee. 2014. Complexity of language ideologies in transnational movement: Korean jogi yuhak families' ambivalent attitudes towards local varieties of English in Singapore. *International Journal of Bilingual Education and Bilingualism* 18. 643–659.
Ball, Martin J. 1988. The study of pronunciation patterns. In Martin J. Ball (ed.), *The use of Welsh: A contribution to sociolinguistics*, 49–57. Clevedon, England & Philadelphia: Multilingual Matters.
Balsom, Denis. 1985. The three-Wales model. In John Osmond (ed.), *The national question again: Welsh political identity in the 1980s*, 1–17. Llandysul: Gomer Press.
Barron, Anne & Klaus P. Schneider (eds.). 2005. *The pragmatics of Irish English*. Berlin & New York: Mouton de Gruyter.
Bartley, J.O. 1954. *Teague, shenkin, and sawney*. Cork, Ireland: Cork University Press.
Bartley , J.O. & Melville Richards. 1947. The Welsh language in English plays. *Welsh Review* 6 (1). 40.

https://doi.org/10.1515/9781614512721-008

Beal, Joan. 2008. English dialects in the North of England: Morphology and syntax. In Bernd Kortmann & Clive Upton (eds.), *Varieties of English 1: The British Isles*, 373–403. Berlin: Mouton de Gruyter.

Beal, Joan. 2010. *An introduction to regional Englishes: Dialect variation in England*. Edinburgh: Edinburgh University Press.

Beal, Joan, Lourdes Burbano-Elizondo & Carman Llamas. 2012. *Urban North-Eastern English: Tyneside to Teesside*. Edinburgh: Edinburgh University Press.

Berry, Ron. 2006 [1970]. *So long Hector Bebb*. Library of Wales edition. Cardigan: Parthian.

Biber, Douglas, Stig Johansson, Geoffrey Leech, Susan Conrad & Edward Finegan. 1999. *Longman grammar of spoken and written English*. London: Longman.

Birner, Betty J. & Gregory Ward. 1998. *Information status and noncanonical word order in English*. Amsterdam: Benjamins.

Bishop, Hywel, Nikolas Coupland & Peter Garrett. 2005. Conceptual accent evaluation: Thirty years of accent prejudice in the U.K. *Acta Linguistica Hafniensia* 37 (1). 131–154.

Blank, Paula. 1996. *Broken English*. London: Routledge.

Borde, Andrew. 1870 [1547]. The fyrst boke of the introduction of knowledge made by Andrew Borde, of physycke doctor. A compendyous regyment; or, A dyetary of helth made in Mountpyllier. London: Pub. for the Early English Text Society, by N.T. Trübner & Co. Available at: https://archive.org/details/fyrstbokeintrod01boorgoog/page/n132 (December 2019).

Bourhis, Richard Y. 1977. *Language and social evaluation in Wales*. Bristol: University of Bristol PhD dissertation.

Bourhis, Richard Y. & Howard Giles. 1976. The language of cooperation in Wales: A field study. *Language Sciences* 42. 13–16.

Bourhis, Richard Y. & Howard Giles. 1977. The language of intergroup distinctiveness. In Howard Giles (ed.), *Language, ethnicity and intergroup relations*, 119–135. London: Academic Press.

Bourhis, Richard Y., Howard Giles & Wallace E. Lambert. 1975. Social consequences of accommodating one's style of speech: A cross-national investigation. *International Journal of the Sociology of Language* 6. 55–72.

Bourhis, Richard Y., Howard Giles & Henri Tajfel. 1973. Language as a determinant of Welsh identity. *European Journal of Social Psychology* 3 (4). 447–460.

Bowen, E. G. 1959. Le Pays de Galles. *Transactions of the Institute of British Geographers* 26. 1–23.

Bowen, E. G. 1964. Daearyddiaeth Cymru fel cefndir i'w hanes. London: BBC (Radio lecture).

Britain, David. 2007. Grammatical variation in England. In David Britain (ed.), *Language in the British Isles*, 75–104. Cambridge: Cambridge University Press.

Brown, Bruce. L., Howard Giles & Jitendra N. Thakerar. 1985. Speaker evaluations as a function of speech rate, accent and context. *Language and Communication* 5. 207–222.

Buchstaller, Isabelle. 2001. An alternative view of *like*: Its grammaticalization in conversational American English. *Edinburgh Working Papers in Applied Linguistics* 11. 21–41.

Campbell, Rowan. Forthcoming. *Dialect levelling in Cardiff*. Cardiff: Cardiff University PhD dissertation.

Carter, Harold. 1986. Population movements into Wales: An historical review. In Peter S. Harper & Eric Sunderland (eds.), *Genetic and population studies in Wales,* 31–53. Cardiff: University of Wales Press.

Chambers, J.K. & Peter Trudgill. 1998 [1980]. *Dialectology*. 2nd edn. Cambridge: Cambridge University Press.

Charles, Bertie George. 1982. *The English dialect of south Pembrokeshire: Introduction and word-list*. Haverfordwest: Pembrokeshire Record Society.
Charles, Bertie George. 1992. *The place-names of Pembrokeshire*. Aberystwyth: National Library of Wales
Cheesman, Tom & Filiz Çelik. 2017. Introduction. In Tom Cheesman, Jeni Williams & Filiz Çelik (eds.), *My heart loves in my language: Poems & stories from Swansea*, 11–16. Swansea: Hafan Books.
Cheshire, Jenny. 1981. Variation in the use of *ain't* in an urban British English dialect. *Language in Society* 10 (2). 365– 381.
Cheshire, Jenny. 1982. *Variation in an English dialect. A sociolinguistic study*. Cambridge: Cambridge University Press.
Cheshire, Jenny. 1999. Spoken standard English. In Tony Bex & Richard J. Watts (eds.). *Standard English: The widening debate*, 129–148. London & New York: Routledge.
Cheshire, Jenny. 2007. Discourse variation, grammaticalisation and stuff like that. *Journal of Sociolinguistics* 11 (2). 155–193.
Cheshire, Jenny, Viv Edwards & Pamela Whittle. 1993. Non-standard English and dialect levelling. In James Milroy & Leslie Milroy (eds.). *Real English: The grammar of English dialects in the British Isles*, 53–96. London & New York: Longman.
Cheshire, Jenny, Sue Fox, Paul Kerswill & Eivind Ness Torgersen. 2008. Ethnicity, friendship network and social practices as the motor of dialect change: Linguistic innovation in London. *Sociolinguistica* 22. 1–23. Special issue on Dialect Sociology, edited by Alexandra Lenz & Klaus J. Mattheier.
Cheshire, Jenny, Paul Kerswill, Sue Fox & Eivind Torgersen. 2011. Contact, the feature pool and the speech community: The emergence of Multicultural London English. *Journal of Sociolinguistics* 15 (2). 151–196.
Cheshire, Jenny, Paul Kerswill & Ann Williams. 2005. Phonology, grammar, and discourse in dialect convergence. In Peter Auer, Frans Hinskens & Paul Kerswill (eds.), *Dialect change. convergence and divergence in European languages*, 135– 167. Cambridge: Cambridge University Press.
Chesters, Anne V., Clive S. Upton & David R. Parry. 1968. *A questionnaire for a linguistic atlas of England, modified for use in Welsh localities*. Swansea: privately published.
Coates, Richard & Andrew Breeze. 2000. *Celtic voices, English places: Studies of the Celtic impact on place-names in England*. Stamford: Shaun Tyas.
Collins, Beverley & Inger M. Mees. 1990. The phonetics of Cardiff English. In Nikolas Coupland (ed.), *English in Wales: Diversity, conflict and change*, 87–103. Clevedon: Multilingual Matters.
Columbus, Georgie. 2009. A corpus-based analysis of invariant tags in five varieties of English. In Antoinette Renouf & Andrew Kenoe (eds.), *Corpus linguistics: Refinements and reassessments*, 401–414. Amsterdam: Rodopi.
Comrie, Bernard. 1976. *Aspect: An introduction to the study of verbal aspect and related problems*. Cambridge: Cambridge University Press.
Connolly, John H. 1990. Port Talbot English. In Nikolas Coupland (ed.), *English in Wales: Diversity, conflict and change*, 121–129. Clevedon: Multilingual Matters.
Corrigan, Karen. 2003. *For-to* infinitives and beyond: Interdisciplinary approaches to non-finite complementation in a rural Celtic English. In Hildegard L. C. Tristram (ed.), *The Celtic Englishes III*, 318–338. Heidelberg: Universitätsverlag C. Winter.
Corrigan, Karen P. 2010. *Irish English – Volume 1, Northern Ireland*. Edinburgh: Edinburgh University Press

Corrigan, Karen. 2015. "I always think of people here, you know, saying 'like' after every sentence": The dynamics of discourse-pragmatic markers in Northern Irish English. In Carolina P. Amador-Moreno, Kevin McCafferty & Elaine Vaughan (eds.), *Pragmatic markers in Irish English*, 37–64. Amsterdam & Philadelphia: John Benjamins.
Coupland, Nikolas. 1980. Style-shifting in a Cardiff work-setting. *Language in Society* 9 (1). 1–12.
Coupland, Nikolas. 1985. 'Hark, hark, the lark': Social motivations for phonological style-shifting. *Language and Communication* 5 (3). 153–171.
Coupland, Nikolas. 1988. *Dialect in use: Sociolinguistic variation in Cardiff English*. Cardiff: University of Wales Press.
Coupland, Nikolas. 1990a. 'Standard Welsh English': A variable semiotic. In Nikolas Coupland (ed.), *English in Wales: Diversity, conflict and change*, 232–257. Clevedon: Multilingual Matters.
Coupland, Nikolas (ed., in association with Alan R. Thomas). 1990b. *English in Wales: Diversity, conflict and change*. Clevedon: Multilingual Matters.
Coupland, Nikolas. 2001. Dialect stylization in radio talk. *Language in Society* 30. 345–375.
Coupland, Nikolas. 2006. The discursive framing of phonological acts of identity: Welshness through English. In Janina Brutt-Griffler & Catherine Evans-Davies (eds.). *English and ethnicity*, 19–48. Basingstoke & New York: Palgrave Macmillan.
Coupland, Nikolas. 2009. Dialect style, social class and metacultural performance: The pantomime dame. In Nikolas Coupland & Adam Jaworski (ed.). *The new sociolinguistics reader*, 311–325. Basingstoke & New York: Palgrave Macmillan.
Coupland, Nikolas & Martin J. Ball. 1989. Welsh and English in contemporary Wales: Sociolinguistic issues. *Contemporary Wales* 3. 7–40.
Coupland, Nikolas & Hywel Bishop. 2007. Ideologised values for British accents. *Journal of Sociolinguistics* 11 (1). 74–93.
Coupland, Nikolas, Hywel Bishop & Peter Garrett. 2006. One Wales? Reassessing diversity in Welsh ethnolinguistic identification. *Contemporary Wales* 18. 1–27.
Coupland, Nikolas, Hywel Bishop, Angie Williams, Betsy Evans & Peter Garrett. 2005. Affiliation, engagement, language use and vitality: Secondary school students' subjective orientation to Welsh and Welshness. *The International Journal of Bilingual Education and Bilingualism* 8 (1). 1–24.
Coupland, Nikolas & Alan R. Thomas. 1990. Social linguistic perspectives on English in Wales. Introduction to Nikolas Coupland (ed.), *English in Wales: Diversity, conflict and change*, 1–18. Clevedon: Multilingual Matters.
Coupland, Nikolas, Angie Williams & Peter Garrett. 1994. The social meanings of Welsh English: teachers' stereotyped judgements. *Journal of Multilingual and Multicultural Development* 15 (6). 471–489.
Coupland, Nikolas, Angie Williams & Peter Garrett. 1999. 'Welshness' and 'Englishness' as attitudinal dimensions of English language varieties in Wales. In Dennis R. Preston (ed.), *Handbook of perceptual dialectology*, Vol. 1, 333–343. Amsterdam: John Benjamins.
D'Arcy, Alexandra. 2008. Canadian English as a window to the rise of 'like' in discourse. *Anglistik (International Journal of English Studies)* 19 (2). 125–140.
Dartnell, Lewis. 2019. *Origins: How the Earth shaped human history*. London: Vintage.
Davenport, Tony. 2008. Wales and Welshness in Middle-English romances. In Ruth Kennedy and Simon Meecham-Jones (eds.), *Authority and Subjugation in Writing of Medieval Wales*, 137–158. Basingstoke: Palgrave Macmillan.

Davies, Janet. 1993. *The Welsh language*. Cardiff: University of Wales Press.
Davies, Janet. 2000. Welsh. In Glanville Price (ed.), *Languages in Britain and Ireland*, 78–108. Oxford: Blackwell.
Davies, John. 2007 [1993]. *A history of Wales*. Revised edn. London: Penguin.
Davies, John David. 1877–94. *A history of West Gower, Glamorganshire* Parts I–IV. Swansea: The Cambrian.
Davies, D. Witton. 1920. Gowerland: Its people, speech and some of its ways. *Archaeologia Cambrensis* XX Sixth Series. 179–188.
Deuchar, Margaret, Donnelly, Kevin, & Caroline Piercy. 2016. 'Mae pobl monolingual yn minority': Factors favouring the production of code switching by Welsh-English bilingual speakers. In Mercedes Durham & Jonathan Morris (eds.), *Sociolinguistics in Wales*, 209–239. Basingstoke: Palgrave Macmillan.
Dieth, Eugen & Harold Orton. 1962. *A questionnaire for a linguistic atlas of England*. In Harold Orton, *Survey of English Dialects (A) Introduction*, 40–113. Leeds: E. J. Arnold and Son. Reprint, with alterations and additions (6th version), of the edition published by the Leeds Philosophical and Literary Society, January, 1952.
Dillwyn, Amy. 2008 [1880]. *The Rebecca Rioter*. South Glamorgan: Honno Classics.
Dobson, E.J. 1953. *Hymn to the Virgin*. London: Honourable Society of the Commorodorion.
Dobson, E.J. 1976. *The origins of Ancrene Wisse*. Oxford: Clarendon Press.
Dunthorne, Joe. 2008. *Submarine*. London: Penguin.
Durham, Mercedes. 2015. Representations of Welsh English online: What can tweets tell us about salience and enregisterment? Paper presented at NWAVE44, Toronto, 22–25 Oct 2015.
Durham, Mercedes. 2016. Changing attitudes towards the Welsh English accent: A view from Twitter. In Mercedes Durham & Jonathan Morris (eds.), *Sociolinguistics in Wales*, 181–205. London: Palgrave Macmillan.
Durham, Mercedes. 2019. Quantifying potential: Non-canonical word order through a variationist perspective. Paper presented at UK Language Variation and Change 12, London, 3–5 Sept 2019.
Durham, Mercedes & Jonathan Morris (eds.). 2016. *Sociolinguistics in Wales*. London: Palgrave Macmillan.
Edwards, John. 1985. *"Talk Tidy": The art of speaking Wenglish*. Cowbridge: D. Brown and Sons.
Edwards, John. 1986. *More Talk Tidy*. Cowbridge: D. Brown and Sons.
Edwards, Keri. 1974. *Jack Jones: Writers of Wales*. Cardiff: University of Wales Press.
Egenfeldt-Nielsen, Simon, Jonas Heide Smith & Susana Pajares Tosca. 2013. *Understanding videogames: the essential introduction*. New York: Routledge.
Ellegård, Alvar. 1953. *The auxiliary do: The establishment and regulation of its use*. Gothenburg Studies 2. Stockholm: Almqvist & Wiksell.
Ellis, Alexander J. 1882. On the delimitation of the English and Welsh languages. *Y Cymmrodor* 5. 173–208.
Ellis, Alexander J. 1889. *On Early English pronunciation, with especial reference to Shakspere and Chaucer*. Part V: *Existing dialectal as compared with West Saxon pronunciation*. London: Trübner for the Philological Society, the Early English Text Society, and the Chaucer Society.
Elmes, Simon. 2013. *Voices*: A unique BBC adventure. In Clive Upton & Bethan L. Davies (eds.), *Analysing twenty-first century British English: Conceptual and methodological aspects of the "Voices" project*, 1–11. Abingdon, Oxfordshire & New York: Routledge.
Elton, Helen T. 1994. *Sound bites. Rhondda 1993*. Swansea: Swansea University BA dissertation.

Emery, F. V. 1965. Edward Lluyd and some of his correspondents: A view of Gower in the 1690s. *The Transactions of the Honourable Society of Cymmrodorion Session* 1965 Part I. London: The Honourable Society of Cymmrodorion, 59–114.

Evans, Dafydd. 2007. How far across the border do you have to be, to be considered Welsh? National identification at the regional level. *Contemporary Wales* 20. 123–143.

Evans, Geraint. 2008a. William Salesbury and Welsh printing in London before 1557. In Ruth Kennedy & Simon Meecham-Jones (eds.), *Authority and subjugation in writing of medieval Wales*, 251–266. Basingstoke: Palgrave Macmillan.

Evans, Geraint 2008b. Wales and the Welsh language in Andrew Borde's fyrst boke of the introduction of knowledge. *Studia Celtica*, (42). 87–104.

Evans, Jonathan & Stephen Knight. 2011. The hand at the window: Twm Siôn Cati, the Welsh colonial trickster. In Audrey L. Becker & Kristin Noone (eds.), *Welsh mythology and folklore in popular culture: Essays on adaptations in literature, film, television and digital media*, 91–107. Jefferson: McFarland & Company.

Evans, Margiad. 2006 [1932]. *Country Dance*. Library of Wales edition. Cardigan: Parthian.

Fife, James. 1990. *The semantics of the Welsh verb: A cognitive approach*. Cardiff: University of Wales Press.

Fife, James & Gareth King. 1991. Focus and the Welsh 'abnormal sentence': A cross-linguistic perspective. In James Fife & Erich Poppe (eds.), *Studies in Brythonic word order*, 81–153. Amsterdam: John Benjamins.

Filppula, Markku. 1986. *Some aspects of Hiberno-English in a functional sentence perspective*. Joensuu: University of Joensuu.

Filppula, Markku. 1999. *The grammar of Irish English: Language in Hibernian style*. London & New York: Routledge.

Filppula, Markku, Juhani Klemola & Heli Paulasto. 2008. *English and Celtic in contact*. London & New York: Routledge.

Filppula, Markku, Juhani Klemola & Heli Paulasto. 2009. Digging for roots: universals and contact in regional varieties of English. In Markku Filppula, Juhani Klemola & Heli Paulasto (eds.), *Vernacular universals and language contacts: Evidence from varieties of English and beyond*, 231–261. New York & London: Routledge.

Filppula, Markku, Juhani Klemola & Heli Pitkänen (eds.). 2002. *The Celtic roots of English*. Studies in Languages 37. Joensuu: University of Joensuu.

Foulkes, Paul & Gerard J. Docherty (eds.). 1999. *Urban voices: Accent studies in the British Isles*. London: Arnold.

Frend, Charles (director), Michael Balcon (producer) & Leslie Norman (producer). 1949. *A Run for Your Money*. United Kingdom: Ealing studios.

Garlick, Raymond & Roland Mathias. 1984. *Anglo-Welsh poetry: 1480–1990*. Bridgend: Seren.

Garrett, Peter, Nikolas Coupland & Angie Williams. 1995. 'City harsh' and 'the Welsh version of RP': Some ways in which teachers view dialects of Welsh English. *Language Awareness* 4 (2). 99–107.

Garrett, Peter, Nikolas Coupland & Angie Williams. 1999. Evaluating dialect in discourse: Teachers' and teenagers' responses to young English speakers in Wales. *Language in Society* 28 (3). 321–354.

Garrett, Peter, Nikolas Coupland & Angie Williams. 2003. *Investigating language attitudes: Social meanings of dialect, ethnicity and performance*. Cardiff: University of Wales Press.

George, Ceri. 1990. *Community and coal: An investigation of the English-language dialect of the Rhondda Valleys, Mid Glamorgan*. Swansea: Swansea University PhD thesis.

German, Gary. 2000. Britons, Anglo-Saxons and scholars: 19th century attitudes towards the survival of Britons in Anglo-Saxon England. In Hildegard L. C. Tristram (ed.), *The Celtic Englishes II*, 347–374. Heidelberg: C. Winter.

German, Gary. 2009. Two early examples of Welsh English as a marker of national identity: Ieuan ap Hywel Swrdwal's *Hymn to the Virgin* and Shakespeare's Fluellen. In Anne Hellegouarc'h-Bryce, Gary German & Jean-Yves Le Disez (eds.), *Pays de Galles: quelle(s) image(s)? What Visibility for Wales?* Actes du colloque de Brest, 25–26 janvier 2007, Brest, CRBC-UBO. 23–38.

Giles, Howard. 1970. Evaluative reactions to accents. *Educational Review* 22 (3). 211–227.

Giles, Howard. 1971. Patterns of evaluation in reactions to R.P., South Welsh and Somerset accented speech. *British Journal of Social and Clinical Psychology* 10 (3). 280–281.

Giles, Howard. 1990. Social meanings of Welsh English. In Nikolas Coupland (ed.), *English in Wales: Diversity, conflict and change*, 258–282. Clevedon: Multilingual Matters.

Giles, Howard & Richard Bourhis. 1975. Linguistic assimilation: West Indians in Cardiff. *Language Sciences* 38. 9–12.

Giles, Howard & Patricia Marsh 1979. Perceived masculinity and accented speech. *Language Sciences* 1 (2), 301–305.

Giles, Howard & Peter F. Powesland. 1975. *Speech style and social evaluation*. London & New York: Academic Press in cooperation with the European Association of Experimental Social Psychology.

Giles, Howard, Pamela Wilson & Anthony Conway. 1981. Accent and lexical diversity as determinants of impression formation and employment selection. *Language Sciences* 3 (1). 92–103.

Givón, Talmy. 2001. *Syntax: An introduction, vol. II*. Amsterdam: Benjamins.

Godfrey, Elizabeth & Sali Tagliamonte. 1999. Another piece for the verbal *-s* story: Evidence from Devon in southwest England. *Language Variation and Change* 11 (1). 87–121.

Goodwin, Geraint. 2008 [1936]. *The Heyday in the Blood*. Library of Wales edition. Cardigan: Parthian.

Gramich, Katie 1998. Introduction to Allen Raine, *Queen of the rushes: A tale of Welsh revival*, 1–23. South Glamorgan: Honno Classics.

Gramich, Katie. 2008. Introduction to Amy Dillwyn, *The Rebecca Rioter*, v–xxi. South Glamorgan: Honno Classics.

Grieve, Andrew (director) & Jennifer Howarth (producer). 1987. *On the Black Hill*. United Kingdom: British Film Institute.

Griffiths, Dennis. 1969. *Talk of my town*. Buckley, Flintshire: Buckley Young People's Cultural Association.

Griffiths, Huw. 2010. "O, I am ignorance itself in this!": Listening to Welsh in Shakespeare and Armin. In Willy Maley & Philip Schwyzer (eds.), *Shakespeare and Wales: From the Marches to the Assembly*, 111–126. London: Routledge.

Griffiths, Richard Rees. 1923. *An enquiry into the dialect of Gower*. Cardiff: University College of Cardiff MA thesis.

Hadikin, Glenn. 2014. *A, an*, and the environments in spoken Korean English. *Corpora* 9 (1). 1–28.

Hamer, Edward. 1877. Parochial account of Llanidloes: Chapter XI: Local words and phrases. *Montgomeryshire Collections* 10. 277–312.

Harris, Percy Valentine. 1960, 1974. *Pembrokeshire place-names and dialect*, 1st & 2nd edns. Tenby: H. G. Walters.

Heinecke, Johannes. 1999. *Temporal deixis in Welsh and Breton*. Heidelberg: C. Winter.

Hejná, Michaela. 2015. *Pre-aspiration in Welsh English: A case study of Aberystwyth*. Manchester: University of Manchester PhD dissertation. Available at: https://www.escholar.manchester.ac.uk/uk-ac-man-scw:277156 (December 2019).

Henry, Patrick Leo. 1957. *An Anglo-Irish dialect of North Roscommon*. Dublin: University College, Department of English.

Higgs, Gary, Colin Williams & Danny Dorling. 2004. Use of the census of population to discern trends in the Welsh language: an aggregate analysis. *Area* 36 (2). 187–201.

Higham, Nicholas. 1992. *Rome, Britain and the Anglo-Saxons*. London: Seaby.

Hilbert, Michaela. 2008. Interrogative inversion in non-standard varieties of English. In Peter Siemund & Noemi Kintana (eds.) *Language contact and contact languages*, 261–89. Amsterdam: John Benjamins.

Hilbert, Michaela. 2011. Interrogative inversion as a learner phenomenon in English contact varieties: a case of angloversals? In Joybrato Mukherjee & Marianne Hundt (eds.) *Exploring second-language varieties of English and learner Englishes: Bridging the paradigm gap*, 125–44. Amsterdam & Philadelphia: John Benjamins.

Holmes, Janet. 1995. *Women, men and politeness*. London & New York: Longman.

Howse, William Henry. 1944. *Radnor old and new*. Hereford: Jakemans.

Howse, William Henry. 1945. *Presteigne past and present*. Hereford: Jakemans.

Howse, William Henry. 1949. *Radnorshire*. Hereford: E.J. Thurston.

Huber, Magnus. 2003. The Corpus of English in South-East Wales and its synchronic and diachronic implications. In Hildegard L. C. Tristram (ed.), *Celtic Englishes III*, 183–200. Heidelberg: C. Winter.

Huddleston, Rodney & Geoffrey K. Pullum. 2002. *The Cambridge grammar of the English language*. Cambridge: Cambridge University Press.

ap Hywel Swrdwal, Ieuan. 1984 [1480]. Hymn to the virgin. In R. Garlick & Roland Mathias (eds.), *Anglo-Welsh poetry: 1480–1980*, 45–48. Bridgend, Wales: Poetry Wales Press.

Ihalainen, Ossi. 1976. Periphrastic *do* in affirmative sentences in the dialect of East Somerset. *Neuphilologische Mitteilungen 77*. 609–22.

Ihalainen, Ossi. 1994. The dialects of England since 1776. In Robert Burchfield (ed.), *The Cambridge history of the English language, vol. V. English in Britain and overseas: Origins and development*, 197–274. Cambridge: Cambridge University Press.

Jackson, Kenneth. 1994 [1953]. *Language and History in Early Britain*. Republication. Dublin: Four Courts Press.

Jaffe, Alexandra. 2013. Diverse voices, public broadcasts: Sociolinguistic representations in mainstream programming. In Clive Upton & Bethan L. Davies (eds.), *Analysing twenty-first century British English: Conceptual and methodological aspects of the 'Voices' project*, 48–90. Abingdon, Oxfordshire & New York: Routledge.

James, Allan. 2011. English(es) in post-devolution Wales: The sociolinguistic reconstruction of late modern Valleys Voice. *AAA – Arbeiten aus Anglistik und Amerikanistik* 36 (1). 47–63.

Jenkins, Geraint H. 1998. Introduction to Geraint H. Jenkins (ed.) *A social history of the Welsh language: Language and community in the nineteenth century*, 1–20. Cardiff: University of Wales Press.

John, Brian S. 1995. *Pembrokeshire: Past and present*. Newport, Pembrokeshire: Greencroft Books.

Jones, Benjamin A. 2013. *A comparative investigation of Gwent's contemporary dialect*. Swansea: Swansea University BA essay.

Jones, Benjamin A. 2016a. *Welsh English dialect*. Sheffield: Bradwell Books.
Jones, Benjamin A. 2016b. Gwent English: A comparative investigation of lexical items. *Tradition Today: Journal of the Centre for English Traditional Heritage* 5. 20–34. Available at <http://centre-for-english-traditional-heritage.org/TraditionToday5/TT5_Jones_Gwent_English.pdf>. Accessed 21 August 2017.
Jones, Benjamin A. 2018. *A history of the Welsh English dialect in fiction*. Swansea: Swansea University PhD dissertation.
Jones, Benjamin A. & Rob Penhallurick. 2018. *The Gower glossary*. Swansea: Gower Landscape Partnership.
Jones, Bob Morris. 1990a. Welsh influence on children's English. In Nikolas Coupland (ed.), *English in Wales: Diversity, conflict and change*, 195-231. Clevedon: Multilingual Matters.
Jones, Bob Morris. 1990b. Constraints on Welsh English tags: Some evidence from children's language. *English World-Wide* 11. 173 – 93.
Jones, Bob Morris. 1999. *The Welsh answering system*. Berlin: Mouton de Gruyter.
Jones, Dot. 1998. *Statistical evidence relating to the Welsh language 1801–1911 / Tystiolaeth ystadegol yn ymwneud a'r iaith Gymraeg 1801–1911*. Cardiff: University of Wales Press.
Jones, Glyn. 1998 [1965]. *The Island of Apples*. 2nd edn. Cardiff: University of Wales Press.
Jones, Glyn E. 1984. The distinctive vowels and consonants of Welsh. In Martin J. Ball & Glyn E. Jones (eds.), *Welsh phonology: Selected readings*, 40–64. Clevedon, England & Philadelphia: Multilingual Matters.
Jones, I. G. 1980. Language and community in nineteenth century Wales. In David Smith (ed.), *A people and a proletariat: Essays on the history of Wales 1780-1980*, 47–71. London: Pluto Press in association with Llafur, the Society for the Study of Welsh Labour History.
Jones, Jack. 2009 [1935]. *Black Parade*. Cardigan: Parthian.
Jones, Lewis. 2010 [1937]. *Cwmardy*. Cardigan, Wales: Parthian.
Jones, Megan. 2002. "You do get queer, see. She do get queer...": Non-standard periphrastic *do* in Somerset English. *University of Pennsylvania Working Papers in Linguistics* 8 (3). 117–132.
Jones, Morris & Alan R. Thomas. 1977. *The Welsh language: Studies in its syntax and semantics*. Cardiff: University of Wales Press.
Jones, Rhys & Huw Lewis. 2019. *New geographies of language: Language, culture and politics in Wales*. London: Palgrave Macmillan/Springer Nature.
Jones, Stephen. 1926. *A Welsh phonetic reader*. London: University of London Press.
Jones, W. R. 1949. Attitudes towards Welsh as a second language: a preliminary investigation. *British Journal of Educational Psychology* 19, 44–52.
Kachru, Braj B. 1992. World Englishes: approaches, issues and resources. *Language Teaching*, 25 (1). 1–14.
Kallen, Jeffrey L. 2005. Silence and mitigation in Irish English discourse. In Anne Barron & Klaus P. Schneider (eds.), *The pragmatics of Irish English*, 47–71. Berlin & New York: Mouton de Gruyter.
Kallen, Jeffrey L. 2013. *Irish English volume 2: The Republic of Ireland*. Berlin & Boston: De Gruyter Mouton.
Kerswill, Paul. 2013. Identity, ethnicity and place: The construction of youth language in London. In Peter Auer, Martin Hilpert, Anja Stukenbrock & Benedikt Szmrecsanyi (eds.), *Space in language and linguistics: Geographical, interactional, and cognitive perspectives*, 128–164. Berlin & Boston: De Gruyter.

King, Gareth. 1993. *Modern Welsh: A comprehensive grammar*. London: Routledge.
Kirk, John M., Stewart Sanderson & J.D.A Widdowson (eds.). 1985. *Studies in linguistic geography: The dialects of English in Britain and Ireland*. London: Croom Helm.
Klemola, Juhani. 1994. Periphrastic do in South-Western dialects of British English: a reassessment. *Dialektologia et Geolinguistica* 2. 33–51.
Klemola, Juhani. 1998. Semantics of do in southwestern dialects of English English. In Ingrid Tieken-Boon van Ostade, Marijke van der Wal & Arjan van Leuvensteijn (eds.), *Do in English, Dutch and German: History and present-day variation*, 25–51. Amsterdam: Stichting Neerlandistiek VU / Münster: Nodus Publikationen.
Klemola, Juhani. 2002. Periphrastic *do*: dialectal distribution and origins. In Markku Filppula, Juhani Klemola & Heli Pitkänen (eds.), *The Celtic roots of English*. Studies in Languages 37, 199–210. Joensuu: University of Joensuu.
Klemola, Juhani. 2003. Personal pronouns in the traditional dialects of the South West of England. In Hildegard L. C. Tristram (ed.), *Celtic Englishes III*, 260–275. Heidelberg: C. Winter.
Klemola, Juhani & Jones, Mark J. 1999. The Leeds Corpus of English Dialects – project. In Clive Upton & Katie Wales (eds.), *Dialectal variation in English: Proceedings of the Harold Orton centenary conference 1998*, 17–30. Leeds: Leeds Studies in English, N.S. XXX.
Kolbe, Daniela & Andrea Sand. 2010. Embedded inversion worldwide. *Linguaculture* 2 (1). 25–42.
Kortmann, Bernd & Benedikt Szmrecsanyi. 2004. Global synopsis: morphological and syntactic variation in English. In Bernd Kortmann, Edgar W. Schneider, Kate Burridge, Rajend Mesthrie & Clive Upton (eds.), *A handbook of varieties of English, vol. 2*, 1142–1202. Berlin & New York: Mouton de Gruyter.
Kortmann, Bernd & Susanne Wagner. 2005. The Freiburg English Dialect project and corpus. In Bernd Kortmann, Tanja Herrmann, Lukas Pietsch & Susanne Wagner (eds.), *A comparative grammar of British English dialects: Agreement, gender, relative clauses*, 1–20. Berlin & New York: Mouton de Gruyter.
Knight, Stephen. 2004. *A hundred years of fiction: Writing Wales in English*. Cardiff: University of Wales Press.
Kranich, Svenja. 2010. *Progressive in Modern English: A corpus-based study of grammaticalization and related changes*. Amsterdam: Rodopi.
Krapp, George P. 1926. The psychology of dialect writing. *The Bookman*, July 1926. 522–527.
Krug, Manfred. 1998. British English is developing a new discourse marker, *innit?* A study in lexicalisation based on social, regional and stylistic variation. *Arbeiten aus Anglistik und Amerikanistik* 23 (2). 145–197.
Kytö, Merja. 1994. BE vs. HAVE with intransitives in Early Modern English. In Francisco Fernández, Miguel Fuster & Juan José Calvo (eds.), *English historical linguistics 1992*, 179–190. Amsterdam: John Benjamins.
Leech, Geoffrey & Jan Svartvik. 1994 [1975]. *A communicative grammar of English*. 2nd edn. London & New York: Longman.
Leech, Geoffrey, Marianne Hundt, Christian Mair & Nicholas Smith. 2009. *Change in contemporary English: A grammatical study*. Cambridge: Cambridge University Press.
Lewis, Robert. 2008/2016. *Wenglish: The dialect of the South Wales Valleys*, 1st and 2nd edns. Talybont: Y Lolfa.
Lieberman, Max. 2008. *The March of Wales 1067–1300: A borderland of medieval Britain*. Cardiff: University of Wales Press.
Lindstromberg, Seth. 2010. *English prepositions explained*. Amsterdam: Benjamins.

Lippi Green, Rosina. 1997. *English with an accent: Language, ideology, and discrimination in the United States*. London: Routledge.
Lloyd, Megan. 2010. Rhymer, Minstrel Lady Mortimer and the power of Welsh words. In Willy Maley & Philip Schwyzer (eds.), *Shakespeare and Wales: From the Marches to the Assembly*, 59–73. London: Routledge.
Löffler, Marion. 2009. English in Wales. In Haruko Momma & Michael Matto (eds.), *A companion to the history of the English language*, 350–357. Chichester: Wiley-Blackwell.
Maley, Willy & Philip Schwyzer (eds.). 2010. *Shakespeare and Wales: From the Marches to the assembly*. London: Routledge.
Mathias, Roland. 1973/1979. The Welsh language and the English language. In Meic Stephens (ed.), *The Welsh language today*, 1st and 2nd edns, 32–64. Llandysul: Gomer Press.
Mathias, Roland. 1987. *Anglo-Welsh literature. An illustrated history*. Bridgend: Poetry Wales Press.
Matras, Yaron. 2009. *Language contact*. Cambridge: Cambridge University Press.
Matthews, John Hobson. 1913. The folk speech of Monmouth and the neighbourhood. *Archaeologia Cambrensis*, Vol. XIII, 6th series, Part II, 165–172.
Mayr, Robert. 2010. What exactly is a front rounded vowel? An acoustic and articulatory investigation of the NURSE vowel in South Wales English. *Journal of the International Phonetic Association* 40 (1). 93–112. Doi:10.1017/S0025100309990272
Mayr, Robert, Jonathan Morris, Ineke Mennen & Daniel Williams. 2017. Disentangling the effects of long-term language contact and individual bilingualism: The case of monophthongs in Welsh and English. *International Journal of Bilingualism* 21 (3). 245–267.
McDavid, Raven I. 1985. Eliciting: Direct, indirect, and oblique. *American Speech* 60, 309–317.
McEwan, Ian. 2019. *The Cockroach*. London: Jonathan Cape.
McWhorter, John H. 2009. What else happened to English? A brief for the Celtic hypothesis. *English Language and Linguistics* 13. 163–191. Doi:10.1017/S1360674309002974
Meecham-Jones, Simon. 2008. Erasure of Wales in medieval culture. In Ruth Kennedy & Simon Meecham-Jones (eds.), *Authority and subjugation in writing of Medieval Wales*, 27–55. Basingstoke: Palgrave Macmillan.
Mees, Inger M. 1977. *Language and social class in Cardiff: A survey of the speech habits of schoolchildren*. Leiden: University of Leiden MA thesis.
Mees, Inger M. 1983. *The speech of Cardiff schoolchildren: A real time study*. Leiden: University of Leiden PhD dissertation.
Mees, Inger M. 1987. Glottal stop as a prestigious feature of Cardiff English. *English World-Wide* 8 (1). 25–39.
Mees, Inger M. 1990. The phonetics of Cardiff English. In Nikolas Coupland (ed.), *English in Wales: Diversity, conflict and change*, 167–194. Clevedon: Multilingual Matters.
Mees, Inger M. & Beverley Collins. 1999. Cardiff: A real-time study of glottalization. In Paul Foulkes & Gerard Docherty (eds.), *Urban voices: Accent studies in the British Isles*, 185–202. London: Arnold.
Meriläinen, Lea & Heli Paulasto. 2017. Embedded inversion as an angloversal: Evidence from Inner, Outer and Expanding Circle Englishes. In Markku Filppula, Juhani Klemola & Devyani Sharma (eds.). *The Oxford handbook of World Englishes*, 676–696. Oxford & New York: Oxford University Press.
Meriläinen, Lea & Heli Paulasto. 2015. "One day we can go karaoke": Preposition omission as an angloversal across Englishes? Paper presented at ChangE 2015: Integrating cognitive, social and typological perspectives. Helsinki, 8–10 June 2015.

Meriläinen, Lea, Heli Paulasto & Paula Rautionaho. 2017. Extended uses of the progressive form in Inner, Outer and Expanding Circle Englishes. In Markku Filppula, Juhani Klemola, Anna Mauranen & Svetlana Vetchinnikova (eds.). *Changing English: Global and local perspectives*. Topics in English linguistics, 191–216. Berlin: Mouton de Gruyter.

Mesthrie, Rajend. 2008. Synopsis: Morphological and syntactic variation in Africa and South and Southeast Asia. In Rajend Mesthrie (ed.). *Varieties of English vol. 4: Africa, South and Southeast Asia*, 624–635. Berlin & New York: Mouton de Gruyter.

Mesthrie, Rajend & Rakesh M. Bhatt. 2008. *World Englishes: The study of new linguistic varieties*. Cambridge: Cambridge University Press.

Migge, Bettina. 2015. *Now* in the speech of newcomers to Ireland. In Carolina P. Amador-Moreno, Kevin McCafferty & Elainen Vaughan (eds.). *Pragmatic markers in Irish English*, 390–407. Amsterdam: John Benjamins.

Milroy, Jim. 2003. When is a sound change? On the role of external factors in language change. In David Britain & Jenny Cheshire (eds.), *Social dialectology: In honour of Peter Trudgill*, 209–221. Amsterdam & Philadelphia: John Benjamins.

Monger, Christopher (director) & Sarah Curtis (producer). 1995. *The Englishman that went up a hill and came down a mountain*. United Kingdom: Miramax Films.

Montgomery, Chris. 2014. Perceptual dialectology across the Scottish-English border. In Dominic Watt & Carmen Llamas (eds.), *Language, borders and identities*, 118–136. Edinburgh: Edinburgh University Press.

Montgomery, Chris. 2016. The perceptual dialectology of Wales from the border. In Mercedes Durham & Jonathan Morris (eds.), *Sociolinguistics in Wales*, 151–179. London: Palgrave Macmillan.

Moraru, Mirona. 2016. *Bourdieu, multilingualism, and immigration: Understanding how second-generation multilingual immigrants reproduce linguistic practices with non-autochthonous minority languages in Cardiff, Wales*. Cardiff: Cardiff University PhD dissertation. Available at: http://orca.cf.ac.uk/98458.

Moraru, Mirona. 2019. Toward a Bourdieusian theory of multilingualism. *Critical Inquiry in Language Studies*, DOI: https://doi.org/10.1080/15427587.2019.1574578. Vol. 17 (2) (2020), 79–100.

Morgan, C. D. 1886 [1862]. *Wanderings in Gower: A perfect guide to the tourist, with all the lays, legends and customs, and glossary of the dialect*. 2nd edition. Swansea: The Cambrian.

Morgan, Gerald. 1966. *The Dragon's tongue*. Cardiff: Triskell press.

Morgan, Kenneth O. 1981. *Rebirth of a nation: A history of modern Wales*. Oxford: Oxford University Press.

Morgan, W. E. T. 1918. Radnorshire words. *Archæologia Cambrensis*, Vol. XVIII, 6th series, Part I. 89–100.

Morris, Jonathan. 2010. Phonetic variation in Northern Wales: preaspiration. In Miriam Meyerhoff, Chie Adachi, Agata Daleszynska & Ana Strycharz (eds.). *Proceedings of the Second Summer School of Sociolinguistics, The University of Edinburgh*. Edinburgh: University of Edinburgh, 1–16.

Morris, Jonathan. 2013. *Sociolinguistic variation and regional minority language bilingualism: An investigation of Welsh-English bilinguals in North Wales*. Manchester: University of Manchester PhD dissertation. Available at https://www.escholar.manchester.ac.uk/uk-ac-man-scw:205563 (accessed on 12 March 2018).

Moylan, Seamas. 2009. *Southern Irish English: Review and exemplary texts*. Dublin: Geography Publications.

Muysken, Pieter. 2000. *Bilingual speech: A typology of code-mixing*. Cambridge: Cambridge University Press.
Myers-Scotton, Carol. 1993. *Duelling languages: Grammatical structure in codeswitching*. Oxford: Clarendon Press.
Nesselhauf, Nadja. 2009. Co-selection phenomena across New Englishes: Parallels and differences to foreign (learner) varieties. *English World-Wide* 30 (1). 1–26.
Orton, Harold. 1962. *Survey of English Dialects (A): Introduction*. Leeds: E. J. Arnold; repr. Routledge, London, 1998.
Orton, Harold, Michael V. Barry, Wilfrid J. Halliday, Philip M. Tilling & Martyn F. Wakelin (eds.) (1962–1971). *Survey of English Dialects (B): The Basic Material* (4 vols in 12 parts). Leeds: E. J. Arnold; repr. Routledge, London, 1998.
Owen, Elias. 1871–1881. Archaic words, phrases, etc., of Montgomeryshire. A series of articles contributed to the *Collections historical and archaeological relating to Montgomeryshire [and its borders]*, issued by the Powys-Land Club for the use of its members. Vol. IV, 49–54, 433–440; Vol. V, 199–202; Vol. VI, 243–248; Vol. VII, 117–124; Vol. VII, 393–404; Vol. VIII, 117–122, 351 –358; Vol. IX, 402–410; Vol. X, 207–220; Vol. XI, 317–324; Vol. 14, 139–146.
Owen, G. D. 1962. *Elizabethan Wales: The social scene*. Cardiff: University of Wales Press.
Painting, David. 1987. *Writers of Wales: Amy Dillwyn*. Cardiff: University of Wales Press.
Palma-Fahey, Maria. 2015. "Yeah well, probably, you know, I wasn't that big into school, you know": Pragmatic markers and the representation of Irish English in fictionalised dialogue. In Carolina P. Amador-Moreno, Kevin McCafferty & Elaine Vaughan (eds.), *Pragmatic markers in Irish English*, 348–369. Amsterdam & Philadelphia: John Benjamins.
Parry, David R. 1964. *Studies in the linguistic geography of Radnorshire, Breconshire, Monmouthshire and Glamorganshire*. Leeds: University of Leeds MA thesis.
Parry, David R. 1971. Newport English. *The Anglo-Welsh Review* 19 (44). 228–233.
Parry, David R. 1975. Editor's letter. *Sawdsheet Five*. 1–2a.
Parry, David R. (ed.). 1977. *The Survey of Anglo-Welsh Dialects, vol. 1: The South-East*. Swansea: David Parry, privately published.
Parry, David R. (ed.). 1979. *The Survey of Anglo-Welsh Dialects, vol. 2: The South-West*. Swansea: David Parry, privately published.
Parry, David R. 1985a. On producing a linguistic atlas: The Survey of Anglo-Welsh Dialects. In John M. Kirk, Stewart Sanderson & John D.A. Widdowson (eds.), *Studies in linguistic geography: The dialects of English in Britain and Ireland*, 51–66. London: Croom Helm.
Parry, David R. 1985b. *The short phonological questionnaire*. Swansea: David Parry, privately published.
Parry, David R. 1985c. The English of Gwent. *Planet – The Welsh Internationalist* 53 (9). 82–90.
Parry, David R. 1990a. The conservative English dialects of North Carmarthenshire. In Nikolas Coupland (ed.), *English in Wales: Diversity, conflict and change*, 142–150. Clevedon: Multilingual Matters.
Parry, David R. 1990b. The conservative English dialects of South Pembrokeshire. In Nikolas Coupland (ed.), *English in Wales: Diversity, conflict and change*, 151–161. Clevedon: Multilingual Matters.
Parry, David R. (ed.). 1999. *A grammar and glossary of conservative Anglo-Welsh dialects of rural Wales*. NATCECT. Occasional Publications, No. 8. Sheffield: University of Sheffield.
Parry, David R. 2015. Untitled, unpublished typescript on the vowels, consonants, sound-systems, vocabulary, and grammar of Anglo-Welsh dialects. 132 pp.

Parry, Owen "Ceredig". 1870. *Among the mountains, or life in Wales*. Ebbw Vale, Wales: J. Davies & J. Clarke.
Paulasto, Heli. 2006. *Welsh English syntax: Contact and variation*. Joensuu: Joensuu University Press. Available online at: http://epublications.uef.fi/pub/urn_isbn_952-458-804-8/index_en.html
Paulasto, Heli. 2009. Regional effects of the mode of transmission in Welsh English. In Esa Penttilä & Heli Paulasto (eds.). *Language contacts meet English dialects: Studies in honour of Markku Filppula*, 211–229. Newcastle-upon-Tyne: Cambridge Scholars Publishing.
Paulasto, Heli. 2013a. There's variation with *with* in Welsh English: a case of context extension. Paper presented at the CROSSLING Symposium: Language Contacts at the Crossroads of Disciplines, Joensuu, Finland, 28 Feb–1 Mar 2013.
Paulasto, Heli. 2013b. Invariant tags in Welsh English. Paper presented at IAWE 19, Tempe AZ, 16–18 Nov 2013.
Paulasto, Heli. 2013c. English in Wales. In Tometro Hopkins & John McKenny (eds.). *World Englishes, vol I: The British Isles*, 241–262. London, New Delhi, New York & Sydney: Bloomsbury Academic.
Paulasto, Heli. 2014a. Extended uses of the progressive form in L1 and L2 Englishes. *English World-Wide* 35 (3). 247–276. https://doi.org/10.1075/eww.35.3.01pau
Paulasto, Heli. 2016. Variation and change in the grammar of Welsh English. In Mercedes Durham & Jonathan Morris (eds.), *Sociolinguistics in Wales*, 123–150. London: Palgrave Macmillan.
Penhallurick, Robert. 1991. *The Anglo-Welsh dialects of North Wales*. University of Bamberg Studies in English Linguistics, Vol. 27. Frankfurt am Main: Peter Lang.
Penhallurick, Robert. 1993. Welsh English: a national language? *Dialectologia et Geolinguistica* 1, 28–46.
Penhallurick, Robert. 1994. *Gowerland and its language*. University of Bamberg Studies in English Linguistics, Vol. 36. Frankfurt am Main: Peter Lang.
Penhallurick, Robert. 1996. The grammar of northern Welsh English: Progressive verb phrases. In Juhani Klemola, Merja Kytö & Matti Rissanen (eds.), *Speech past and present. Studies in English dialectology in memory of Ossi Ihalainen*. University of Bamberg Studies in English Linguistics, Vol. 38, 308–342. Frankfurt am Main: Peter Lang.
Penhallurick, Robert. 1998. Dialect and the nation's future. *Planet: The Welsh Internationalist* 127. 82–87.
Penhallurick, Robert. 2004a. Welsh English: Phonology. In Edgar W. Schneider, Kate Burridge, Bernd Kortmann, Rajend Mesthrie & Clive Upton (eds.), *A handbook of varieties of English, Vol. 1: Phonology*, 98–112. Berlin & New York: Mouton de Gruyter.
Penhallurick, Robert. 2004b. Welsh English: Morphology and syntax. In Bernd Kortmann, Kate Burridge, Rajend Mesthrie, Edgar W. Schneider & Clive Upton (eds.), *A handbook of varieties of English, Vol. 2: Morphology and syntax*, 102–113. Berlin & New York: Mouton de Gruyter.
Penhallurick, Robert. 2007. English in Wales. In David Britain (ed.), *Language in the British Isles*, 152–170. Cambridge: Cambridge University Press.
Penhallurick, Robert, 2008a. Welsh English: Phonology. In Bernd Kortmann & Clive Upton (eds.), *Varieties of English 1: The British Isles*, 105–121. Berlin & New York: Mouton de Gruyter.
Penhallurick, Robert. 2008b. Welsh English: Morphology and syntax. In Bernd Kortmann & Clive Upton (eds.), *Varieties of English 1: The British Isles*, 360–372. Berlin & New York: Mouton de Gruyter.
Penhallurick, Rob. 2012. Welsh English. In Bernd Kortmann & Kerstin Lunkenheimer (eds.), *The Mouton world atlas of variation in English*, 58–69. Berlin & Boston: Mouton de Gruyter.

Penhallurick, Rob. 2013. *Voices* in Wales: A new national survey. In Clive Upton & Bethan L. Davies (eds.). *Analysing twenty-first century British English: Conceptual and methodological aspects of the 'Voices' project*, 124–135. Abingdon, Oxfordshire and New York: Routledge.
Perks, Rob. 2001. The century speaks: A public history partnership. *Oral History* 29 (2). 95–105.
Pichler, Heike. 2013. *The structure of discourse-pragmatic variation*. Amsterdam: John Benjamins.
Pichler, Heike. 2016. Uncovering discourse-pragmatic innovations: *Innit* in Multicultural London English. In Heike Pichler (ed.). *Discourse-pragmatic variation and change in English: New methods and insights*, 59–85. Cambridge: Cambridge University Press.
Pitkänen, Heli. 2003. Non-standard uses of the progressive form in Welsh English: an apparent time study. In H. L. C. Tristram (ed.), *The Celtic Englishes III*, 111–128. Heidelberg: C. Winter.
Podhovnik, Edith. 2008. *The phonology of Neath English: A socio-dialectological survey*. Swansea: Swansea University PhD dissertation.
Podhovnik, Edith. 2010. Age and accent-changes in a southern Welsh English accent. *Research in Language* 8. 1–18.
Price, Mary. 1979. *A modern geography of Wales*, 2nd ed. Swansea: Christopher Davies.
Price, Stephen, Manfred Fluck & Howard Giles. 1983. The effects of language of testing on bilingual preadolescents' attitudes towards Welsh and varieties of English. *Journal of Multilingual and Multicultural Development* 4. 149–161.
Prichard, T. J. L. 1828. *The adventures and vagaries of Twm Shon Catti, descriptive of life in Wales: Enterspersed with Poems*. Aberystwyth, Wales: Printed for the author by John Cox.
Pryce, W. T. R. 1978. Wales as a culture region: patterns of change 1750–1971. *Transactions in the Honourable Society of Cymmrodorion*, Session 1978. 229–261.
Pryce, W.T.R. 1990. Language shift in Gwent, c. 1770–1981. In Nikolas Coupland (ed.), *English in Wales: Diversity, conflict and change*, 48–83. Clevedon: Multilingual Matters.
Quaino, Stefano. 2011. *The intonation of Welsh English: The case of Ceredigion and Gwynedd*. Klagenfurt: Alpen-Adria-University Klagenfurt PhD dissertation.
Quaino, Stefano. 2014. Pitch alignment in Welsh English: The case of rising tones in Ceredigion. *Dialectologia* 13. 27–48.
Quirk, Randolph, Sidney Greenbaum, Geoffrey Leech & Jan Svartvik. 1985. *A comprehensive grammar of the English language*. London: Longman.
Raine, Allen. 1998 [1906]. *Queen of the Rushes: A tale of Welsh revival*. South Glamorgan, Wales: Honno Classics.
Ranta, Elina. 2013. *Universals in a universal language? Exploring verb-syntactic features in English as a lingua franca*. Tampere: University of Tampere PhD dissertation.
Rissanen, Matti. 1991. Spoken language and the history of *do*-periphrasis. In Dieter Kastovsky (ed.). *Historical English syntax*, 321–342. Berlin & New York: Mouton de Gruyter.
Roberts, Gwyneth Tyson. 1996. "Under the hatches": English Parliamentary Commissioners' views of the people and language of mid-nineteenth-century Wales. In Bill Schwarz (ed.), *The expansion of England: Race, ethnicity and cultural History*, 171–197. London: Routledge.
Roberts, Sarah Elin. 2008. "By the authority of the devil": The operation of Welsh and English law in medieval Wales. In Ruth Kennedy & Simon Meecham-Jones (eds.), *Authority and subjugation in writing of Medieval Wales*, 85–98. Basingstoke: Palgrave Macmillan.
Robinson, Jonnie. 2004. SED (Survey of English Dialects) at the British Library: unpublished commentaries.
Robinson, Jonnie. 2004–2007. Millennium Memory Bank (MMB) at the British Library: unpublished commentaries.

Robinson, Jonnie, Holly Gilbert & Jon Herring. 2010. *Voices of the UK*. British Library, Social Sciences Collections and Research, project funded by the Leverhulme Trust. Unpublished linguistic descriptions of English in Wales.

Roller, Katja. 2016. *Salience in Welsh English grammar: A usage-based approach*. PhD Dissertation, Albert-Ludwigs-Universität Freiburg . Freiburg: University Library Press. DOI: 10.6094/ 978-3-928969-67-3. Available at <https://freidok.uni-freiburg.de/data/11437> (accessed on 16 Apr 2018).

Rouveret, Alain. 1996. Bod in the present tense and in other tenses. In In Robert D. Borsley & Ian Roberts (eds.), *The syntax of the Celtic languages: A comparative perspective*, 125–170. Cambridge: Cambridge University Press.

Rupp, Laura & Hanne Page-Verhoef. 2005. Pragmatic and historical aspects of Definite Article Reduction in northern English dialects. *English World-Wide* 26 (3). 325–346.

Russ, Charles V. J. 1982. The geographical and social variation of English in England and Wales. In Richard W. Bailey & Manfred Görlach (eds.), *English as a world language*, 11–55. Ann Arbor: University of Michigan Press.

Sabban, Anette. 1982. *Gälisch-Englischer Sprachkontakt. Zur Variabilität des englischen im gälischsprachigen Gebiet Scottlands. Eine empirische Studie*. Heidelberg: Julius Groos.

Sand, Andrea. 2003. The definite article in Irish English and other contact varieties of English. In H. L. C. Tristram (ed.), *Celtic Englishes III*, 413–430. Heidelberg: C. Winter.

Schiffrin, Deborah. 1987. *Discourse markers*. Cambridge: Cambridge University Press.

Schmidt, Christa. M. 1990. *Das English der Darran-Valley (Südost-Wales). Eine phonologische Untersuchung unter Berücksichtigung des kymrischen Substrats*. PhD thesis, Freiburg i. Brsg. (privately published).

Schneider, Edgar W. 2007. *Postcolonial English: Varieties around the world*. Cambridge: Cambridge University Press.

Schweinberger, Martin. 2012. The discourse marker LIKE in Irish English. In Bettina Migge & Máire Ní Chiosáin (eds.). *New perspectives on Irish English*, 179–201. Amsterdam: John Benjamins.

Scragg, D. G. 1974. *A history of English spelling*. Manchester: Manchester University Press; and New York: Barnes & Noble.

Shakespeare, William. 1599. *Henry V*. Available at Project Gutenberg http://www.gutenberg.org/ cache/epub/1784/pg1784.txt (March 2019).

Sharp, Derrick, Beryl Thomas, Eurwen Price, Gareth Francis & Iwan Davies. 1973. *Attitudes to Welsh and English in the schools of Wales: A full report with appendices in Welsh and English from the Schools Council project on attitudes to and motivation for the learning of Welsh and English in Wales, based at the Department of Education, University College of Swansea*. London & Cardiff: Macmillan/University of Wales Press.

Shorrocks, Graham. 1996. Non-standard dialect literature and popular culture. In Juhani Klemola, Merja Kytö & Matti Rissanen (eds.), *Speech past and present. Studies in English dialectology in memory of Ossi Ihalainen*. University of Bamberg Studies in English Linguistics, Vol. 38, 385–411. Frankfurt am Main: Peter Lang.

Shorrocks, Graham. 1999. *A grammar of the dialect of the Bolton area. Part II: Morphology and syntax*. Frankfurt am Mein: Peter Lang.

Shuken, Cynthia. 1984. Highland and Island English. In Peter Trudgill (ed.), *Languages in the British Isles*, 152–166. Cambridge: Cambridge University Press.

Smitterberg, Erik. 2005. *The progressive in 19th-century English: A process of integration*. Amsterdam: Rodopi.

Souter, Clive. 1989. *A short handbook to the Polytechnic of Wales Corpus*. ICAME, Norwegian Computing Centre for the Humanities, Bergen University, Norway.

Southall, John E. 1892. *Wales and her language considered from a historical, educational and social standpoint with remarks on modern Welsh literature and a linguistic map of the country*. Newport, Monmouthshire: J. E. Southall; London: E. Hicks Jr.

Southall, John E. 1895. *The Welsh language census of 1891, with coloured map of the 52 registration districts into which Wales is divided*. Newport, Monmouthshire: John E. Southall.

Stalmaszczyk, Piotr. 2007. Prepositional possessive constructions in Celtic languages and Celtic Englishes. In H. L. C. Tristram (ed.), *The Celtic languages in contact: Papers from the workshop within the framework of the XIII International Congress of Celtic Studies, Bonn, 26–27 July 2007*, 126–145. Potsdam: Potsdam University Press.

Stenström, Anna-Brita, Gisle Andersen & Ingrid Kristine Hasund. 2002. *Trends in teenage talk: Corpus compilation, analysis and findings*. Amsterdam: John Benjamins.

Stuart-Smith, Jane, Gwilym Pryce, Claire Timmins & Barrie Gunter. 2013. Television can also be a factor in language change: Evidence from an urban dialect. *Language* 89 (3). 501–536.

Sullivan, James P. 1980. The validity of literary dialect: evidence from the theatrical portrayal of Hiberno-English forms. *Language in society* 9 (2). 195–219.

Szmrecsanyi, Benedikt. 2013. *Grammatical variation in British English dialects: A study in corpus-based dialectometry*. Cambridge: Cambridge University Press.

Tagliamonte, Sali. 2000. The grammaticalization of the present perfect in English: Tracks of change and continuity in a linguistic enclave. In Olga Fischer, Anette Rosenbach & Dieter Stein (eds.), *Pathways of change: Grammaticalization in English*, 329–354. Amsterdam & Philadelphia: John Benjamins.

Tagliamonte, Sali. 2009. "There was universals; then there weren't": a comparative sociolinguistic perspective on "default singulars". In Markku Filppula, Juhani Klemola & Heli Paulasto (eds.), *Vernacular universals and language contacts: Evidence from varieties of English and beyond*, 103–129. New York & London: Routledge.

Tagliamonte, Sali & Rika Ito. 2002. Think *really different*: Continuity and specialization in the English dual form adverbs. *Journal of Sociolinguistics* 6 (2). 236–266.

Tagliamonte, Sali A. & Rebecca V. Roeder. 2009. Variation in the English definite article: Socio-historical linguistics in t'speech community. *Journal of Sociolinguistics* 13 (4). 435–471.

Tagliamonte, Sali A., Jennifer Smith & Helen Lawrence. 2005. No taming the vernacular! Insights from the relatives in northern Britain. *Language Variation and Change* 17 (1). 75–112. doi:10.1017/S0954394505050040

Tench, Paul. 1990. The pronunciation of English in Abercrave. In Nikolas Coupland (ed.), *English in Wales: Diversity, conflict and change*, 130–141. Clevedon & Philadelphia: Multilingual Matters.

Thomas, Alan R. 1983. The English language in Wales. In Y. Matsumura (ed.), *The English language around the world*, 137–193. Tokyo: Kenkyusha.

Thomas, Alan R. 1984. Welsh English. In Peter Trudgill (ed.), *Language in the British Isles*, 178–194. Cambridge: Cambridge University Press.

Thomas, Alan R. 1985. Welsh English: a grammatical conspectus. In Wolfgang Viereck (ed.). *Focus on: England and Wales*, 213–221. Amsterdam & Philadelphia: Benjamins.

Thomas, Alan R. 1994. English in Wales. In Robert Burchfield (ed.), *The Cambridge history of the English language, vol. V. English in Britain and overseas: Origins and development*, 94–147. Cambridge: Cambridge University Press.

Thomas, Dylan. 1977 [1954]. *Under Milk Wood: A play for voices*. London: J. M. Dent & Sons Ltd.
Thomason, Sarah G. 2001. *Language contact: An introduction*. Edinburgh: Edinburgh University Press.
Thompson, J. Lee (director) & John Hawkesworth (producer). 1959. *Tiger Bay*. United Kingdom: Rank Organisation.
Thorne, David A. 1993. *A comprehensive Welsh grammar*. Oxford: Blackwell Publishers.
Tolkien, J.R.R. 1981. Letter 144: To Naomi Mitchison. In Humphrey Carpenter & Christopher Tolkien (eds.), *The letters of J.R.R. Tolkien*, 173–181. Hammersmith, England: HarperCollins.
Toolan, Michael. 1992. The significations of representing dialect in writing. *Language and Literature* 1 (1). 28–46.
Tristram, Hildegard L. C. 1997. *The Celtic Englishes*. Heidelberg: C. Winter.
Tristram, Hildegard L. C. 1999. How Celtic is Standard English? (The Annual Celtic Lecture). Nauka, St. Petersburg.
Tristram, Hildegard L. C. (ed.). 2000. *The Celtic Englishes II*. Heidelberg: C. Winter.
Tristram, Hildegard L. C. (ed.). 2003. *The Celtic Englishes III*. Heidelberg: C. Winter.
Tristram, Hildegard L. C. (ed.). 2006. *The Celtic Englishes IV: The interface between English and the Celtic languages*. Potsdam: Universitätsverlag Potsdam.
Trudgill, Peter. 1974. *The social differentiation of English in Norwich*. Cambridge: Cambridge University Press.
Trudgill, Peter. 1988. Norwich revisited: Recent linguistic changes in an English urban dialect. *English World-Wide* 9 (1). 33–49.
Trudgill, Peter. 1999 [1990]. *The dialects of England*. Second edition. Oxford: Blackwell.
Trudgill, Peter. 2008. The dialect of East Anglia: Morphology and syntax. In Bernd Kortmann & Clive Upton (eds.), *Varieties of English 1: The British Isles*, 404–416. Berlin: Mouton de Gruyter.
Trudgill, Peter. 2009. Vernacular universals and the sociolinguistic typology of English dialects. In Markku Filppula, Juhani Klemola & Heli Paulasto (eds.), *Vernacular universals and language contacts: Evidence from varieties of English and beyond*, 304–322. New York & London: Routledge.
Trudgill, Peter & Jean Hannah. 1994 [1982]. *International English: A guide to the varieties of standard English*. Third edition. London, New York, Sydney & Auckland: Edward Arnold.
Tucker, H. M. 1950. The dialect speech of Gower. *Gower: Journal of the Gower Society* 3. 26–29.
Tucker, H. M. 1957. *My Gower*. Neath: Rowlands & Company.
Upton, Clive. 1969. Dialects of Gower. *Gower pageant and fair: Souvenir programme* (Penrice Castle August 30 1969). 14–16.
Van der Auwera, Johan & Inge Genee. 2002. English *do*: On the convergence of languages and linguists. *English Language and Linguistics* 6 (2). 283–307.
Visser, G. J. 1955. Celtic influence in English. *Neophilologus* 39. 267–293.
Wagner, Susanne. 2008. English dialects in the Southwest: morphology and syntax. In Bernd Kortmann & Clive Upton (eds.), *Varieties of English 1: The British Isles*, 417–439. Berlin: Mouton de Gruyter.
Walters, J. Roderick 1999. *A study of the segmental and suprasegmental phonology of Rhondda Valleys English*. Pontypridd: University of Glamorgan PhD dissertation. Available at: http://phonetics.research.glam.ac.uk, and also from http://phonology.org (2019 edition).
Walters, J. Roderick. 2001. English in Wales and a 'Welsh Valleys' accent. *World Englishes* 20 (3). 285–304.

Walters, J. Roderick. 2003a. 'Celtic English': Influences on a South Wales Valleys accent. *English World-Wide* 24 (1). 63–87.
Walters, J. Roderick. 2003b. On the intonation of a South Wales 'Valleys Accent' of English. *Journal of the International Phonetics Association*, Vol. 33, No. 2. 211–238.
Walters, J. Roderick. 2003c. A study of the prosody of a South East Wales 'Valleys Accent'. In Hildegard L. C. Tristram (ed.), *Celtic Englishes III*, 224–239. Heidelberg: C. Winter.
Warner, C. D. 1897. *The people for whom Shakespeare wrote*. New York, NY: Harper & Brothers.
Waters, Ivor. 1950. *Chepstow talk*. Chepstow: The Chepstow Society.
Waters, Ivor. 1973. *Folklore and dialect of the lower Wye Valley*. Chepstow: The Chepstow Society.
Watkin, Morgan. 1964. English and Welsh racial elements in western Shropshire and in the adjacent Welsh Borderland: ABO blood group evidence. *The Journal of the Royal Anthropological Institute of Great Britain and Ireland* 94. 52–65
Watkins, T. Arwyn. 1991. The function of cleft and non-cleft constituent orders in Modern Welsh. In James Fife & Erich Poppe (eds.), *Studies in Brythonic word order*, 329–351. Amsterdam: John Benjamins.
Wells, J. C. 1982. *Accents of English. 1: An Introduction. 2: The British Isles*. Cambridge: Cambridge University Press.
Weltens, Bert. 1983. Non-standard periphrastic *do* in the dialects of South-West Britain. *Lore and Language* 3 (8): 56–64.
Williams, Angie, Peter Garrett & Nikolas Coupland. 1996. Perceptual dialectology, folklinguistics, and regional stereotypes: Teachers' perceptions of variation in Welsh English. *Multilingua* 5 (2). 171–199.
Williams, Colin H. 1990. The anglicisation of Wales. In Nikolas Coupland (ed.), *English in Wales: Diversity, conflict and change*, 19–47. Clevedon: Multilingual Matters.
Williams, Colin H. 2012. English in Wales. In Alexander Bergs & Laurel J. Brinton (eds.), *English historical linguistics: An international handbook*, Vol. 2, 1977–1994. Berlin & Boston: De Gruyter Mouton.
Williams, Glanmor. 1987. *Recovery, reorientation and reformation: Wales c. 1415–1642*. Oxford: Clarendon Press/University of Wales Press.
Williams, Gwyn A. 1985. *When was Wales? A history of the Welsh*. London: Penguin.
Williams, Malcolm. 2000. The pragmatics of predicate fronting in Welsh English. In Hildegard L. C. Tristram (ed.), *The Celtic Englishes II*, 210–230. Heidelberg: C. Winter.
Williams, Malcolm. 2001. *Interférences syntaxiques et pragmatiques en anglais du Pays de Galles.*' Unpublished PhD thesis, Université Stendhal Grenoble-III.
Williams, Malcolm. 2003. Information packaging in Rhondda speech: a second look at the research of Ceri George. In Hildegard L. C. Tristram (ed.), *Celtic Englishes III*, 201–223. Heidelberg: C. Winter.
Williams, Richard. 1889. Archaic words, phrases etc. of Montgomeryshire. A supplement. *Montgomeryshire Collections* 23. 59–65.
Williams, Richard. 1890. Montgomeryshire dialect (Newton). *Montgomeryshire Collections* 24. 233–236.
Windsor Lewis, Jack. 1964. *Glamorganshire spoken English*. Unpublished typescript on the phonetics, phonology, morphology, syntax and vocabulary of Glamorgan English. 420 pp.
Windsor Lewis, Jack. 1990a. Transcribed specimen of Cardiff English. In Nikolas Coupland (ed.), *English in Wales: Diversity, conflict and change*, 104. Clevedon: Multilingual Matters.
Windsor Lewis, Jack. 1990b. The roots of Cardiff English. In Nikolas Coupland (ed.), *English in Wales: Diversity, conflict and change*, 105–108. Clevedon: Multilingual Matters.

Windsor Lewis, Jack. 1990c. Syntax and lexis in Glamorgan English. In Nikolas Coupland (ed.), *English in Wales: Diversity, conflict and change*, 109–120. Clevedon: Multilingual Matters.

Wright, Joseph (ed.). 1898–1905. *The English dialect dictionary*. Six vols. London: Henry Frowde.

Zahn, Christopher & Robert Hopper. 1985 Measuring language attitudes: the speech evaluation instrument. *Journal of Language and Social Psychology* 4 (2). 113–123.

Zall, P. M. 1963. *A Hundred Merry Tales and other jestbooks*. Lincoln: University of Nebraska Press.

Website references

Armstrong, Edward. 2016. *Welsh farming facts and figures*. Cardiff: National Assembly for Wales Research Service. Available at: https://seneddresearch.blog/2016/09/26/welsh-farming-facts-and-figures/ (December 2019).

BBC News online: Born abroad: Wales. Available at: http://news.bbc.co.uk/1/shared/spl/hi/uk/05/born_abroad/around_britain/html/wales.stm (December 2019).

BBC News online: EU Referendum 2016 results. Available at: https://www.bbc.co.uk/news/politics/eu_referendum/results (September 2019).

BBC *Voices*. 2004–2014. Available at: http://www.bbc.co.uk/voices/. (December 2019).

BBC Wales History. 2008. The 20th century. Available at: https://www.bbc.co.uk/wales/history/sites/themes/society/industry_coal03.shtml (September 2019).

British Library resources (accessed in December 2019):
  BL Sounds. 2004 onwards. *British Library Sounds*. Available at https://sounds.bl.uk.
  MMB and SAWD at the BL via the *British accents and dialects* web pages, 2019 onwards: https://www.bl.uk/british-accents-and-dialects. Curated by Jonnie Robinson.
  MMB, SAWD, SED and *Voices* at the BL via the Library's catalogue: http://www.bl.uk/reshelp/findhelpsubject/socsci/socioling/soundrec/sociolingsound.html.
  Voices of the UK, 2009–2012: http://www.bl.uk/voicesoftheuk.

Dahlgreen, Will. 2014. 'Brummie' is the least attractive accent. (YouGov survey). Available at: https://yougov.co.uk/news/2014/12/09/accent-map2/ (March 2018).

Dent, Susie. 2014. The story behind *butty*. *BBC Voices Language Lab Word Map*. Available at: http://www.bbc.co.uk/voices/results/wordmap/ (January 2018).

Frampton, Ben. 2019. BBC News online, Wales: Why is Wales used as a unit of measurement? Available at: https://www.bbc.co.uk/news/uk-wales-46737277 (September 2019).

Freiburg English Dialect Corpus (FRED). 2000–2005. Corpus compiled by Bernd Kortmann (project supervisor), Lieselotte Anderwald, Tanja Herrmann, Lukas Pietsch, Susanne Wagner, Nuria Hernández & Benedikt Szmrecsanyi. Website, 2000–2008: http://www2.anglistik.uni-freiburg.de/institut/lskortmann/FRED/ (December 2019).

Freiburg Corpus of English Dialects (FRED) – Interactive Database (FRED Sampler/FRED-S). 2016. Freiburg: Universitätsbibliothek Freiburg. https://fred.ub.uni-freiburg.de (December 2019).

German, Gary. 2009. Two early examples of Welsh English as a marker of national identity: Ieuan ap Hywel Swrdwal's *Hymn to the Virgin* and Shakespeare's Fluellen. Available at Hyper Article en Ligne – Sciences de l'Homme et de la Société: http://hal.univ-brest.fr/docs/00/47/44/20/PDF/German_PDGalles_.pdf (December 2019).

Hall, Phil. 2018. Patterns of migration: the Welsh context. Cardiff: WJEC/CBAC. Available at: https://resources.wjec.co.uk/Pages/ResourceSingle.aspx?rlid=2810.

Harries, Bethan, Bridget Byrne & Kitty Lymperopoulou. 2014. *Who identifies as Welsh? National identities and ethnicity in Wales. Dynamics of diversity: Evidence from the 2011 census*. Manchester: Centre on Dynamics of Ethnicity. http://hummedia.manchester.ac.uk/institutes/code/briefings/dynamicsofdiversity/code-census-briefing-national-identity-wales.pdf (August 2019).

Hernández, Nuria. 2006. *User's guide to FRED*. Freiburg: English Dialects Research Group, Albert-Ludwigs-Universität Freiburg. Downloadable from: https://freidok.uni-freiburg.de/data/2489 (December 2019).

Hitt, Carolyn. 2006. So just who are 'the crachach'? BBC News, 1 March 2006. Available at: http://news.bbc.co.uk/2/hi/uk_news/wales/4754896.stm (April 2018).

ICE Project. 2009. The International Corpus of English. Available at http://ice-corpora.net/ice/ (May 2018).

Jones, Hywel M. 2012. *A statistical overview of the Welsh language*. The Welsh Language Commissioner. Available at: http://www.comisiynyddygymraeg.cymru/English/Publications%20List/A%20statistical%20overview%20of%20the%20Welsh%20language.pdf (December 2019).

Jones, Luned. 2013. *2011 Census: Welsh Language Data for Small Areas*. Knowledge. https://gweddill.gov.wales/statistics-and-research/census-population-welsh-language/index9ed2.html?lang=en (September 2019).

Kerswill, Paul, Eivind Ness Torgersen & Susan Fox. 2007. Phonological innovation in London teenage speech: Ethnicity as the driver of change in a metropolis. Oxford Graduate Seminar, 12 November 2007. Available at: http://www.lancaster.ac.uk/fss/projects/linguistics/innovators/documents/Oxford_Kerswill_Nov07_000.ppt (December 2019).

Kortmann, Bernd, Kerstin Lunkenheimer & Katharina Ehret (eds). 2020. The Electronic World Atlas of Varieties of English [eWAVE]. Zenodo. DOI: 10.5281/zenodo.3712132. Available at: http://ewave-atlas.org (June 2020).

Linguistic Innovators. 2004–2007. The English of adolescents in London. Available at: http://www.lancaster.ac.uk/fss/projects/linguistics/innovators/index.htm. Jenny Cheshire, Sue Fox, Paul Kerswill and Eivind Ness Torgersen. (December 2019).

Llywodraeth Cymru / Welsh Government. 2017. *Cymraeg 2050: A million Welsh speakers*. Cardiff: Welsh Language Division. http://www.assembly.wales/laid%20documents/gen-ld11108/gen-ld11108-e.pdf (September 2019).

McCarthy, James. 2013. Forget Butty… it's Bruv now, innit! Behind the new 'Jafaican' dialect on the streets of Wales. WalesOnline.com (17 Nov 2013). Available at: http://www.walesonline.co.uk/news/wales-news/forget-butty-its-bruv-now-6311555_(January 2018).

Monmouthshire.gov, 2019a. Monmouthshire and the Welsh language. Available at: https://www.monmouthshire.gov.uk/monmouthshire-welsh-language/ (September 2019).

Monmouthshire.gov, 2019b. Our schools. Available at: https://www.monmouthshire.gov.uk/our-schools/ (September 2019).

Monmouthshire.gov, 2019c. *Monmouthshire County Council Annual Welsh Language Monitoring Report 2017-2018*. Available at: https://www.monmouthshire.gov.uk/monmouthshire-welsh-language/mcc-wl_ann-mon-rep-wlb-201718-eng/ (September 2019).

Museum Wales. 2010. *Wales's other languages*. Available at https://museum.wales/articles/2010-02-01/Wales-other-languages/ (December 2019).

National Museum of History at St Fagans: https://museum.wales/curatorial/social-culturalhistory/archives/ (December 2019).

ONS [Office for National Statistics]. 2012. *International migrants in England and Wales: 2011*: regional geography of non-UK born and non-UK nationals. Newport, Titchfield and London:

Office for National Statistics. Available at: https://www.ons.gov.uk/peoplepopulationand community/populationandmigration/internationalmigration/articles/internationalmigrant sinenglandandwales/2012-12-11#toc (July 2020).

One Wales. 2007, June. *A progressive agenda for the government of Wales: An agreement between the Labour and Plaid Cymru Groups in the National Assembly*. Available at: http://news.bbc.co.uk/1/shared/bsp/hi/pdfs/27_06_07_onewales.pdf. (August 2019).

Pay, Amy 2015. 25 phrases you'll only hear in Cardiff. Wow 24/7. Available at: http://www.wow247.co.uk/2015/06/19/only-hear-cardiff/ (November 2019).

Parry, David R. 2008. The Survey of Anglo-Welsh Dialects: History. Online, no page numbers. Edited by Rob Penhallurick, and published on the Archive of Welsh English website (2008–2019): http://www.swansea.ac.uk/riah/researchgroups/lrc/awe/storyofsawd/. Site no longer active.

Penhallurick, Robert. 2011/2013. Welsh English. In Bernd Kortmann & Kerstin Lunkenheimer (eds.), *The Electronic World Atlas of Varieties of English*, 1st and 2nd versions. Leipzig: Max Planck Institute for Evolutionary Anthropology. Available online at http://ewave-atlas.org (December 2019).

Rhys, Steffan. 2014. '25 English words and phrases you only hear in Wales'. WalesOnline.com (14 May 2014). Available at: http://www.walesonline.co.uk/lifestyle/fun-stuff/25-english-words-phrases-you-7071496 (January 2018).

Robinson, Jonnie, Jon Herring & Holly Gilbert. 2009–2012. Voices of the UK linguistic descriptions. Online. Available at: http://sounds.bl.uk/Accents-and-dialects/BBC-Voices (June 2017).

Size of Wales website: https://sizeofwales.org.uk (September 2019).

South Wales Miners' Library, Swansea: catalogues available at www.swansea.ac.uk/swcc and www.agor.org.uk/cwm (December 2019).

StatsWales. 2012. Welsh speakers by local authority and broader age groups, 2001 and 2011 census. Welsh Government. Available at: https://statswales.gov.wales/Catalogue/Welsh-Language/Census-Welsh-Language/welshspeakers-by-la-broaderage-2001and2011census (December 2019).

Vision of Britain Through Time website, 2009–2017: http://www.visionofbritain.org.uk, University of Portsmouth et al., accessed September 2019. Table 127: *1911 Census of England and Wales, General Report with Appendices*, Table 127: Wales and Monmouthshire. – Proportional numbers speaking English only, Welsh only, and both English and Welsh, 1901 and 1911: http://www.visionofbritain.org.uk/census/table_page.jsp?tab_id=EW1911GEN_M127&show=DB. Local Distribution: *1911 Census of England and Wales, Census Returns of England and Wales, 1911, giving details of Areas, Houses, Families or separate occupiers, and Population:- Languages Spoken in Wales and Monmouthshire* (1913): http://www.visionofbritain.org.uk/census/EW1911WEL/4. (December 2019).

Welsh Government. 2012. A living language: A language for living. Available at: http://www.assembly.wales/laid%20documents/gen-ld10769/gen-ld10769-e.pdf (December 2019).

Wieling, Martijn. 2013 onwards. BBC *Voices Explored*. Available at: http://www.gabmap.nl/voices/ (December 2019).

Williams, Kathryn. 2013. Shiver me timbers! Pirate hero in new Assassin's Creed is a Welshman! WalesOnline. Available at: http://www.walesonline.co.uk/lifestyle/pirate-hero-new-assassins-creed-6074652 (March 2019).

WorldAtlas online: Wales geography. 2017. Available at: https://www.worldatlas.com/webimage/countrys/europe/wales/ukwland.htm#page (September 2019).

Index

Aberystwyth 2, 10, 31, 211
acquisition of English 19–20, 23, 38, 71, 91, 98, 133, 211
agreement 124–127, 192, 224
American English 86, 93, 96, 99, 120, 139, 156
Anglesey 6–8, 13, 144, 192
Anglicization 1, 4, 6–7, 9–12, 15, 17, 20–21, 23–24, 26, 39, 42, 50–51, 56–58, 68, 71–72, 94, 102, 108, 122, 133, 137, 144–146, 175, 178, 180, 186, 189–190, 194–195, 197, 211
apparent-time research 31, 37–38, 78–79, 92, 97–99, 105–106, 114–115, 163, 167, 200–201
articles 24, 71, 73, 81, 192
– definite 73–81, 201, 234
– indefinite 79–81, 231
aspect, *see* habituality; progressive (form)

Bala 66
BBC *Voices* 27, 29, 36, 38, **41, 45–48**, 52, 55, 72, 106, 124, 126, 134–135, 144, **206–209**, 212, 214, 216
– Language Lab 38, 135, **150**, 153, 156, **208**
– *Voices of the UK* **41, 46–47**, 55, 150, **208–209**
bilingual speakers, Welsh-English 5, 15, 19–20, 23, 27, 31, 37–39, 71, 86, 115, 135–136, 140, 189, 191
bilingualism 5, 7, 11–12, 26, 134, 136, 179, 182, 189–190, 192, 211
Border country 3–4, 6, 8, 10, 15, 17, 20–21, 24–25, 28, 50, 53, 56, 58, 66–67, 72, 80, 120, 122–123, 133, 146–147, 174–175, 178, 189, 193, 197, 199, 202, 224
borrowing 23, 135–136, 138, 181, 192–193
– *see also* loanwords
Brecknockshire/Breconshire 146, 180
Bristol 175, 179
British English 19, 27, 42, 69, 71–73, 77, 82, 86, 91, 93, 96, 109–110, 112, 114, 120, 122, 127, 130–131, 139, 158, 201
Brythonic contact influence 86, 123, 179

Caernarfon 31, 40, 207
Cardiff 63, 209
– demographics 2, 4, 6–8, 15, 17, 19
– dialect area 21, 25, 178, 200
– discourse 164, 176
– lexis 148–150, 157
– morphosyntax 117, 119, 121, 123, 125–126, 128, 131
– phonology 52, 55–57, 61–62, 64, 67, 69
– research locality 40, 46, 207–208, 210, 211
– sociolinguistics 27–28, 30–31, 33, 217, 236
Cardiganshire/Ceredigion 7–8, 13, 68, 76, 83, 106, 143, 215
Carmarthen 40, 139, 192, 207, 215
Carmarthenshire 7–8, 13, 27, 32, 36, 143, 148, 180, 211, 228
Ceri George Corpus 23, **40**, 86–87, 90–91, 99–102, 170, 212
cleft constructions 99, 103, 106–107, 161
Clwyd 2, 7, 115, 139–140, 145, 148, 174
code-switching 23, 135–136
creole 74, 79, 83, 86, 99, 120, 128

Denbighshire 7–8, 13, 180, 182, 210
devoiced stops 62, 183, 187–188, 222
dialect contact, *see* dialects of English English
dialect levelling 23–24, 64, 71, 105, 122, 201–202
dialect onomastics 178
– Anglo-Welsh 178, 205
– Welsh English 33, 177–178, 205
– "Wenglish" 33, 134, 178, 215
dialect regions, Welsh English 6, 20–24, 27–28, 30, 41, 46, 177–178
– bilingual north and southwest Wales 6, 20–21, 23–24, 28, 33, 37, 39, 51, 67, 72, 82, 86, 95, 108, 100, 110, 117, 120, 133, 135, 143, 194, 228–229
– longstanding English regions 20, 24–25, 53, 81, 108, 120, 122–123, 128, 133, 141, 144–145
– mid-Wales 21, 24, 28, 45–46, 50, 53, 60, 62–63, 65–66, 131, 144, 146, 193

- north 20–21, 24, 31, 37, 39, 46, 60–63, 65, 77, 107, 116, 139, 147–148, 150, 157–158, 162, 168, 179, 187, 211, 231
- northeast Wales 21, 24, 28, 51, 125, 148, 153, 159, 176, 215
- south Wales 24–25, 28, 46, 52, 58–59, 65, 69, 75, 82, 123, 137–140, 147–148, 150, 157, 168, 176, 197, 211–212
- southeast Wales 20–21, 23–25, 28–29, 31–33, 38–39, 50, 57, 59, 61–63, 67–68, 72, 83, 85–87, 97, 99, 102, 108, 117–118, 120, 123–124, 126–127, 133–134, 139–140, 142, 146, 148–150, 153, 156, 159, 170, 176, 178–179, 187, 191, 202, 210–211, 215, 228
- *see also* Anglesey; Border country; Brecknockshire; Cardiganshire; Cardiff; Carmarthenshire; Clwyd; Denbighshire; Dyfed; Flintshire; Glamorganshire; Gower Peninsula; Gwent; Gwynedd; Merionethshire; Monmouthshire; Montgomeryshire; Pembrokeshire; Powys; Radnorshire; Rhondda; the Valleys

dialects of English English 4, 20, 23–25, 28, 183, 201, 212
- discourse and phraseology 157, 166–168, 170, 173, 175
- eastern 94
- lexis 133, 135, 145–148, 153, 193, 198
- morphosyntax 71–73, 75, 78, 80–81, 89–91, 94, 98–100, 108, 116, 119–124, 128, 131. 229, 231, 233–234
- northern 51, 64, 74–75, 79, 94, 122, 124, 127, 148
- phonology 51–54, 56, 63–65
- research data 42, 206, 209
- southeastern 64, 124–125
- southwestern 4, 51, 80–85, 94, 122, 124–125, 127
- western 51, 55, 57, 59, 63, 67, 110, 113, 124, 127–128, 139, 175

discourse functions 84–85, 99, 101–104, 106, 109–111, 113–114, 157–160, 162–163, 165, 167–171, 201–202, 229, 234
- *see also* focus fronting; invariant question tags

discourse-pragmatic markers 148, 158, 163, 169–173, 187, 199, 222, 229, 234
- *like* 161, 169–170, 199, 229, 234
- *mind (you)* 172–173
- *now (then)* 170–171, 229, 231
- *see* 224, 226
- *you know* 161, 172
- *(you) see* 172, 199, 234

Dyfed 7, 95, 137–140, 143–144, 147–148, 174, 193

electronic World Atlas of Variation in English (eWAVE) 29–30, 73–74, 79, 83, 85–87, 94, 99, 108, 127, 130, 158
embedded inversion 29–30, 71, 95–98, 201
emphasis 60, 66, 68, 72–73, 81–82, 84–85, 91, 102–103, 171
- *see also* stress
emphatic tags 29, 100, 233
England 11, 18
English
- Early Modern 82, 93–95, 184, 186
- Middle 81, 86, 138, 146, 179, 181–182
- Old 86, 121, 123, 146, 179, 181, 215
enregisterment 17, 26, 28, 137, 176, 196, 198–199, 201
- *see also* salience
ethnicity 17–18, 31, 41, 47, 149, 168
- Anglo-Welsh 11, 192, 195, 197, 199, 205
exclamative *there* 29, 109, 193–194, 199–200, 224, 226
existential *there* 106, 124, 127, 192
extension of
- definite article, *see* articles
- *-s* (i.e. verbal *-s*) 29, 124–125
- progressive, *see* progressive (form)
- *with* 24, 109–115, 201

first language, *see* L1
Flemish 180
Flintshire 7–8, 46, 61, 123, 146, 174, 180, 189, 208, 215
focus fronting 23–24, 29, 71, 98–106, 182, 194, 199–201, 212, 224, 226, 229, 231, 233
Freiburg English Dialect Corpus 29–30, 39, 91, 94, 97, 101, 108, 128, 165, **209–210**

French
- Anglo-Norman 4–5, 156, 180–181

Glamorganshire 4–7, 10, 15, 20–21, 25, 53, 63, 81, 83, 87, 108, 118–120, 122–123, 125–126, 129, 133–134, 137–138, 140–141, 142–148, 169, 174–175, 178, 180, 182, 210–211, 214
Gower Peninsula 3–4, 9, 45, 50, 66–67, 83, 174, 180, 214
Gwent 7–8, 15, 25, 36, 83, 87, 134, 138, 140, 143, 145–146, 148–149, 156, 158, 174–176, 181, 197, 202
Gwynedd 7–8, 13, 68, 79, 94–95, 120, 138–140, 142, 147, 165, 174, 215, 231

H-dropping 30, 65, 81
habituality 24, 29–30, 81–92, 179, 183, 194, 201, 229
- *see also* periphrastic *do*; progressive (form)
Hebrides English 78, 106

ICE-Great Britain **43**, 93–96, 110–111, 113, 119, 122, 172
ICE-India 43, 89
ICE-Ireland 43, 95, 98, 110–111, 113, 172
identity 1, 6, 17–21, 26–28, 31, 33–34, 139, 183, 195–197, 224
immigrant languages and communities 5–6, 18–19, 25, 45, 217
Industrial Revolution 4–5, 10–11, 178, 190
information structure 98, 100–104, 163, 171
- *see also* focus fronting; right dislocation; discourse markers
intonation 19, 24, 45, 68, 160, 189, 215
invariant question tags 24–25, 29–30, 71, 157, 159–168, 172, 200–202, 231, 233
Ireland 5, 11, 94, 114, 146, 148, 172, 203
- Northern 150, 172
Irish English 27, 71, 73–74, 77–78, 83, 93–94, 98, 104, 106, 108, 110–114, 120–121, 130, 133, 139, 156–158, 161, 170, 172, 178, 186, 203
- Northern 78, 172
Irish language 71, 94, 98, 111, 133, 139, 147

L1
- English speakers 32, 34, 37, 39, 163, 233
- varieties of English 86, 98, 127–128, 158
- Welsh speakers 23, 32, 34, 37–39, 71, 80, 91–94, 106–107, 115, 128–130, 133, 135–136, 141, 183, 219, 228, 231
- *see also* bilingual speakers; monoglot; Welsh contact influence
L2
- English speakers 12, 19, 219
- varieties of English 23, 86, 98–99, 128, 158
- Welsh speakers 38
language competence
- English 12, 30, 86, 92, 136
- Welsh 13, 16, 31–32, 37–38
- *see also* bilingual speakers; L1; L2
language legislation and policy 10, 12, 15, 20, 26, 182, 185–186, 190–191, 196, 213
language shift 1, 11–12, 26, 71, 73, 146–147, 151, 178, 185, 189, 198
- *see also* Anglicization
learner English 33, 96, 98, 109
linguistic stereotype 21, 137, 149, 158, 183, 186–188, 203, 222
literary dialect 31, 62, 102, 192–194, 196–198, 219, 222, 224, 226
- *see also* Welsh English representation in the media
Liverpool 21, 24, 179, 190
Llandybie Corpus 23, 32–33, **36–38**, 78, 97, 100, 121, 129, 141, 174, 201, 212, 219, 228
Llanelli 2, 4, 32, 46–47, 61, 106, 139–140, 149–150, 209
loan translations 143, 174
loanwords
- cultural 136–137, 140–141
- English in Welsh language 62–63, 181
- French 65, 138, 147–148, 156, 176
- Scandinavian 147–148
- Welsh 15, 48, 62, 133, 135–136, 141, 143, 181, 193, 198–199, 201, 226
London 29, 64, 168, 182, 185–186, 193, 202, 222, 226
London English 23, 25, 34, 64, 149, 167, 179, 185, 234

Manchester 3
Merseyside 3
Merthyr Tydfil 7, 10, 19, 197–198
metalinguistic commentary 32–35, 117, 171, 177, 187, 197–198, 202, 226
Middle Welsh 86, 106
migration 1, 5, 7, 11, 15–17, 19, 178, 189–190, 195, 200
Millennium Memory Bank 29, 36, **41–42**, 45–48, 55, 207, **208–209**
modal auxiliaries *will, would, used to* 87–88, 90–92, 231
Monmouth 46, 207
Monmouthshire 3–5, 7, 15, 25, 32, 46, 63, 85, 138, 144, 174–175, 180–181, 197, 205, 209, 215–216
monoglot
– English-speaking 5, 11, 19, 27, 33, 38, 89, 91, 137, 140, 151, 154, 190
– Welsh-speaking 10–12, 144, 151, 179, 182, 185, 190
– *see also* L1; L2
monophthongs /e:/ and /o:/ 53–55, 200
Montgomeryshire 180, 215–216, 224
Multicultural London English 135, 149, 162–165
– *see also* London English
multilingualism 19, 25, 179, 181, 211, 216

Neath 4, 7–8, 200
Newport 2–4, 7–8, 10, 17, 19, 21, 32, 34, 46, 76, 80, 150, 190, 208–209, 216
North Wales Corpus 32–33, **37–38**, 91, 100, 212, 219

Pembrokeshire 4–10, 13, 20–21, 25, 32, 50–51, 53, 63, 66–67, 83, 94, 108, 120, 122–123, 125–126, 129, 133, 144–146, 178, 180, 182, 211, 215
perceptions and attitudes, Welsh English 1, 20–22, 26–35, 41, 69, 138, 189, 194, 202, 207, 211–217
perfect 87, 92–95
– *be* perfect 93–95, 229
– extended habitual progressive 87, 91, 93
– for simple past 130

periphrastic *do* 25, 81, 83–86, 91, 179, 183–184
phonetic respelling 188, 193–195, 199, 224
pidgin 79, 99, 120, 128, 189
plural (nouns) 74, 81, 126
– zero marking 120–122, 127, 175
– *see also* agreement; articles
possession 109–115, 201, 231
Powys 7–8, 50, 63, 83, 87, 108, 122–123, 129, 138–140, 144–147, 174, 216
prepositions 109, 112, 115, 117–120, 169, 231
– complex 116, 119–120
– compound forms *by here, by there, where to* 25, 117–118, 234
– phrases 175
– *see also* extension of *with*
prestige 26, 35, 56, 117, 213
– covert 27, 29, 64, 157, 198, 201
– overt 26–30, 185–186, 191, 196
progressive (form) 23, 71, 86, 89–93, 201, 212
– habitual extension 24, 29–30, 81–82, 86–87, 90–93, 179, 201, 229
– stative extension 86–90, 92
pronouns 73, 234
– exchange 122–123
– personal 122–123, 199
– possessive 76–77, 122–123, 183
– reflexive 123
– relative 103, 107, 123–124, 194, 199

quotative *go* 169–170

r-colouring 52–53, 57–59, 197
Radio Wales Corpus 24, 29–30, 39, 91, 101, 128, 165, 209
Radnorshire 122–123, 179–180, 215–216
relative clause 103, 106, 115
– *see also* pronouns
religion 10, 18, 174, 185, 189
Rhondda 4, 7–8, 23, 34, 36, 38, 40–41, 46, 52, 59, 68, 83, 86–87, 91, 97, 100, 106, 113, 117–118, 126, 134, 140, 142, 150–151, 154, 156, 166, 171, 179, 201, 207, 209, 211–212, 214–215, 233
right dislocation 29
– *see also* emphatic tags

salience 28–30, 72, 98, 103, 117–118, 134, 145, 148–149, 157–158, 165, 169, 172, 199, 201
– *see also* enregisterment
Scotland 5, 11, 18, 64, 146, 148, 176, 209
Scottish English 78, 86, 94, 186
second language, *see* L2
SED Spoken Corpus **42**, 85, 89, 94, 99, 110, 113, 121
semi-vowel realizations 58, 81, 200
standardization 71, 85, 113, 115, 117, 122, 166
– *see also* dialect levelling
stress 47–48, 50–52, 58–61, 65–69, 68, 82, 84–85, 215, 224
– *see also* emphasis
stylistic variation 31, 34, 36–37, 40, 46–47, 52, 55, 192, 194, 196, 207, 213
supralocalization, *see* dialect levelling
Survey of Anglo-Welsh Dialects (SAWD) 20, 30, 36, **39–40, 45–47**, 50, 54, 68, 73, 133–136, 143–145, 150, 174, 196, 198–199, 200–202, **205–207**, 212, 215–216
Survey of English Dialects (SED) 30, 39, 42, 50, 57, 65, 77–78, 80, 145–146, 196, 205, 207–209, 213
Swansea 2, 4, 6–8, 17, 19, 27, 32, 34, 36, 39–40, 46, 61, 142, 149, 178, 196, 200, 203, 205, 208, 210

tags, *see* emphatic tags; invariant question tags
Tonypandy Corpus 34, **38**, 83, 104, 117, 135, 137–140, 142, 144, 150–151, 153, 212, 219, 228, 233
topicalization 99
– *see also* focus fronting
translation 10, 120, 138, 174, 181–183, 185, 187, 194, 197, 219

urban dialects 21, 25, 27–28, 40–41, 46, 56, 46, 74, 131, 147, 200, 207, 211, 214
Urban Survey of Anglo-Welsh Dialects 26, 32–33, **40**, 102, 139

Valleys, the 4, 6, 17, 21, 24–25, 28–29, 31–33, 68–69, 87, 99, 102, 134, 141, 154, 178, 195, 198–199, 215
– *see also* Rhondda
verb morphology 128–129
vowel reduction 59, 68, 82

Welsh contact influence 30, 94, 130, 192, 194, 201
– discourse and phraseology 166–167, 174, 176
– historical 182–183, 191, 194
– lexis 33, 133, 136, 145, 148, 151–157
– morphosyntax 71–73, 76, 78, 82, 87, 89–91, 93, 95, 98, 100, 102–103, 105, 109, 111, 115, 118, 120, 179, 192, 212, 229, 233
– phonology 50–54, 56–60, 62–63, 65–68
– regional variation 20–21, 23–25, 178
– substrate 20, 23, 25, 37, 89–90, 97
– transfer 20, 23, 37, 80, 86, 89–90, 106–107, 116, 178
Welsh English representation in the media 177
– filmic texts 199–200, 226
– literary texts 193–194, 197–199, 224
– television texts 29, 69, 117, 148, 176, 202
– theatrical texts 186
– videogame texts 203
Welsh language
– dialects 3, 23, 60, 62, 65–66, 72, 136, 139–141, 143, 145, 168, 210, 213, 216
– morphosyntax 77, 80–81, 89–90, 94–96, 103, 107–110, 112, 115, 121–122, 130, 166
– phonology 50, 54, 58–60, 62–63, 65–67, 81, 184
– revitalization 12, 15, 26, 34
– *see also* Welsh contact influence
West Midlands 64, 122–123, 144, 146, 148, 156, 175, 197
– *see also* dialects of English English
word order 83, 95–107
– *see also* embedded inversion; focus fronting
Wrexham 3, 7–8, 40, 178, 207–208

zero past tense 29–30, 128

www.ingramcontent.com/pod-product-compliance
Lightning Source LLC
Chambersburg PA
CBHW031309150426
43191CB00005B/151